THE MEDIEVAL ROMANCE OF ALEXANDER

Also by Nigel Bryant

The High Book of the Grail:
A Translation of the thirteenth-century romance of Perlesvaus

Chrétien de Troyes, Perceval: The Story of the Grail

Merlin and the Grail

The Legend of the Grail

Perceforest

The True Chronicles of Jean le Bel

The History of William Marshal

THE MEDIEVAL ROMANCE OF ALEXANDER

JEHAN WAUQUELIN'S THE DEEDS AND CONQUESTS OF ALEXANDER THE GREAT

Translated by Nigel Bryant

D. S. BREWER

First published 2012
D. S. Brewer, Cambridge
Paperback edition 2019

ISBN 978 1 84384 332 0 hardback
ISBN 978 1 84384 520 1 paperback

D. S. Brewer is an imprint of Boydell & Brewer Ltd
PO Box 9, Woodbridge, Suffolk IP12 3DF, UK
and of Boydell & Brewer Inc.
668 Mt Hope Avenue, Rochester, NY 14620–2731, USA
website: www.boydellandbrewer.com

The publisher has no responsibility for the continued existence or
accuracy of URLs for external or third-party internet websites referred
to in this book, and does not guarantee that any content on such
websites is, or will remain, accurate or appropriate

A CIP catalogue record for this book is available
from the British Library

Set in Palatino by TheWordService.com

Contents

THE WAR AGAINST THE KING OF ARMENIA

FROM ATHENS TO TARSUS

THE SIEGE OF TYRE

THE RAID AT GAZA

EPHESUS

THE VOWS OF THE PEACOCK

MACEDON, ITALY, JERUSALEM AND EGYPT

THE WAR AGAINST DARIUS

BOOK TWO

ALEXANDER'S CONQUESTS IN THE WEST

THE WAR AGAINST PORUS OF INDIA

THE QUEEN OF THE AMAZONS

THE END OF THE WAR AGAINST PORUS

THE MARVELS OF INDIA

THE CONQUEST OF BABYLON

ALEXANDER'S DEATH

WAR BETWEEN ALEXANDER'S BARONS

THE AVENGING OF ALEXANDER

Introduction

As much as Arthur, as much as Charlemagne, the figure of Alexander the Great haunted the medieval imagination. His story indeed 'was translated more often in medieval Europe than any work except the Gospels'.[1] And this version by Jehan Wauquelin is arguably the single most important French Alexander text.

That may seem a surprising claim – as it may seem presumptuous to give the present book the generic title *The Medieval Romance of Alexander* – when Wauquelin's work is a late (indeed, almost the last) component of the vast corpus of medieval French literature on the great conqueror. But both the claim and the title are to an extent justified. Half a century ago, in his broad survey of 'the medieval Alexander', George Cary dismissively wrote that 'Wauquelin has little to add of his own [to the corpus] except prologues and occasional interjections... [and] the Paris fifteenth- and sixteenth-century press would invest no money in such a rebotch of the old tradition';[2] but it is precisely Wauquelin's respectful treatment of his sources – and the fact that he had the entire 'old tradition' available to him as he assembled his work in the middle of the fifteenth century – that makes his highly intelligent, finely paced and very readable version so valuable. It's true, as Cary says, that there was never a printed edition of Wauquelin's work, but the five surviving manuscripts, three of them of *de luxe* quality, attest to its (at least fleeting) success with a particular audience; and above all, it would be hard to imagine a more accessible, revealing and well-judged digest of the whole of the medieval French Alexandrian tradition.[3]

Wauquelin's Sources

Wauquelin, based at Mons in Hainault, was a well-established writer for the Burgundian court in the 1440s, formally engaged by Duke Philip the Good as a scribe and translator. His most notable works were translations of histories, such

---

[1]   Richard Stoneman, *Alexander the Great, A Life in Legend* (Yale, 2008), p.4.
[2]   George Cary, *The Medieval Alexander* (Cambridge, 1956), pp.34, 229.
[3]   After Wauquelin's, the only subsequent French Alexander text of note was to be Vasque de Lucène's (as yet unedited) *Les Faictz et Gestes d'Alexandre le Grant*, presented to Charles le Téméraire, duke of Burgundy, in 1468. But this, unlike Wauquelin's work, is not at all representative of the preceding French Alexandrian tradition: it rejects all tendency to mythologizing Alexander and omits his famous explorations of the sea and sky and other 'fabulous episodes'. Instead Vasque searched ancient Greek and Latin texts, especially Quintus Curtius (whose work he translated quite fully), in an effort to produce a more 'authentic' history and to 'avoid above all making Alexander a superman... It was vital that Charles could consider the Macedonians' exploits as being within his own scope.' H. Bellon-Méguelle, 'L'histoire à l'échelle de l'homme ['History on a Human Scale']: *Les Faicts et Gestes d'Alexandre le Grant* de Vasque de Lucène', in *L'historiographie médiévale d'Alexandre le Grand*, ed. C. Gaullier-Bougassas (Turnhout, 2011), pp.329-48.

as Jacques de Guise's *History of Hainault,* a *Chronicle of the Dukes of Brabant,* and Geoffrey of Monmouth's *History of the Kings of Britain,* so it's no surprise to see him chosen to deliver a history of Alexander. It was initially commissioned by Duke Philip's cousin Jehan de Bourgogne, governor of Picardy; that copy is lost, but the first of the superb surviving manuscripts was produced by Wauquelin's *atelier* at Mons for Philip the Good himself, presumably in 1447 as it is recorded as being paid for in April 1448.

The Burgundian dukes being great bibliophiles and literary patrons, Wauquelin had a rich ducal library on which to draw. It was indeed notably rich in Alexander texts, not just romances but didactic and historical works,[1] and, as he says himself at numerous points, he worked from more than one source: the verse *Roman d'Alexandre,* the Prose *Alexander* romance[2] and *La Venjance Alixandre.*

The first of these sources, the verse *Roman d'Alexandre,* is not really one source but several, being a composite text assembled and reworked by Alexandre de Paris in the late twelfth century from a number of existing poems. Already extensive in its first form, the work continued to grow to an immense length over the next two centuries as it accumulated further interpolations, and it is likely that Wauquelin had at his elbow a late and complete volume that would have included, most importantly, major interpolations such as the anonymous thirteenth-century poem *La Prise de Defur* ('The Taking of Defur') and, from the fourteenth century, Jacques de Longuyon's highly influential *Les Voeux du Paon* ('The Vows of the Peacock') and its sequel *Le Restor du Paon* ('The Peacock Restored') by Jean le Court.[3]

Wauquelin's second source, the Prose *Alexander* romance, had a huge readership in the Middle Ages. Dating from the mid-thirteenth century, it is an anonymous translation into French of the *Historia de Preliis* ('The History of [Alexander's] Battles'), which was in turn a translation into Latin, produced in the tenth century by Leo the Archpriest of Naples, of the Greek Alexander romance often referred to as the 'Pseudo-Callisthenes'.[4]

---

[1]   On the richness of the ducal library, see Chrystèle Blondeau, *Un Conquérant pour quatre ducs* (Paris, 2009), p.20 and tables on pp.287-323.

[2]   It seems, however, that in the case of the Prose *Alexander* he was working from the copy owned not by the duke but by another prominent Burgundian, Antoine de Croÿ: see Sandrine Hériché, *Alexandre le Bourguignon, Études du roman 'Les Faicts et les Conquestes d'Alexandre le Grand' de Jehan Wauquelin* (Geneva, 2008), pp.229-36. Hériché discusses Wauquelin's sources at length in this study.

[3]   At the same time, however, the ducal library contained more than one copy of *Les Voeux du Paon* in independent form.

[4]   Named after Callisthenes, the historian who accompanied Alexander for much of his great journey. His own work has not survived, but it was mined by the creators of more 'legendary' material which came to form the Greek *Alexander Romance.* In his outstanding study of the Alexander legend, Richard Stoneman (who has also translated *The Greek Alexander Romance* [Harmondsworth, 1991]) succinctly recounts how 'some time after his death, probably within a generation, a work of popular literature was produced which latched on to Alexander's dreams and longings and treated them as if they had actually happened. This was the [Greek] *Alexander Romance,* a work which went on being rewritten, expanded and modified throughout antiquity... It is remarkable that such a scrappy and unsatisfactory book... became so influential and inspired much greater works of lit-

The third source, *La Venjance Alixandre* ('The Avenging of Alexander'), is a poem of the 1180s by Jehan le Nevelon. Clearly dissatisfied by the existing ending of the verse *Roman d'Alexandre*, concluding abruptly as it does with Alexander's death by poison, le Nevelon composed a continuation and resolution which, to judge by the number of surviving manuscripts, appealed greatly to the medieval audience, as it did to Wauquelin.

Given the vast length of the source material at his disposal, it would be easy to see Wauquelin's relatively compact work as a mere compression, a convenient digest for his bibliophile patrons, and unworthy of serious consideration compared with the 'originals'. But the 'originals' themselves are for the most part composites, derivatives and reworked translations: the whole development of the Alexandrian tradition was one of accretion, incorporation and reshaping. Wauquelin can be seen therefore as completing the process, gathering together the unwieldy mass of material that had accumulated by the fifteenth century and editing it into a coherent and manageable shape and length.

And it would be very wrong to assume that he merely abbreviates and compresses. George Cary was quite wrong to say, as quoted above, that Wauquelin 'has little to add of his own'. While remaining faithful to the essence of his sources, Wauquelin is a very active and judicious redactor. He has an excellent sense of pace, of rhythm and proportion. When he judges a source to be verbose he will cut and compress; when, on the other hand, he finds it too terse, lacking in colour or missing the dramatic potential of a moment, he will expand and embellish. For his sources were, to say the least, varied – in style, scale and quality.

Perhaps the most obvious aspect of Wauquelin's editing is his treatment of battles, which he frequently condenses to a considerable degree. Many passages in his source texts may have appealed in the twelfth century when audiences had an appetite for the exhaustive squadron-by-squadron, man-by-man (and often literally blow-by-blow) accounts of battles that appeared in the *chansons de geste*; but Emmanuèle Baumgartner is hardly exaggerating when saying of the *Fuerre de Gadres* ('Raid at Gaza') section of the verse *Roman d'Alexandre*[1] that 'the interminable succession of repetitive skirmishes and the conventionally written *laisses* make it seem banal, in terms of both content and execution' and 'for us it seems a disaster area in the text'.[2] It is quite clear that Wauquelin shared this view and felt his fifteenth-century audience would do the same: times and tastes (and indeed styles of warfare) had moved on, and he describes battles with flair and drama and reports all key incidents to make sense of the narrative, but, to put it bluntly, he gets on with it. A typi-

---

erature, including… the French *Roman d'Alexandre*… Many of the legends emerge from a historical nugget, or from an ambition that Alexander expressed (to see the end of the earth, to be a philosopher, to live forever).' Stoneman, *op. cit.*, pp.2-3.

[1]   A twelfth-century poem by a writer known only as 'Eustache', *Li Fuerre de Gadres* ('The Raid at Gaza') was the basis of a major branch of Alexandre de Paris's *Roman d'Alexandre* compilation.

[2]   Baumgartner, "The Raid on Gaza in Alexandre de Paris's Romance" in *The Medieval French Alexander*, ed. Maddox & Sturm-Maddox (Albany, 2002), pp.29-30.

cal example is the moment during the raid at Gaza when the Greek foraging party is about to be overwhelmed by enemy numbers, and Alexander's lieutenant Emenidus calls upon his companions to decide who should forgo the imminent battle and ride to alert Alexander and summon reinforcements. In the verse *Roman d'Alexandre*, in the section based on *Li Fuerre de Gadres*, each companion declines in turn, in almost ritualistic fashion, in a passage running to many hundreds of lines. Wauquelin sees no virtue or necessity in this and, extracting the essential, writes instead:

> 'In God's name, sirs,' said Emenidus, 'decide who's to be our messenger.'
> And he called to Licanor, saying: 'Will you take the message, sir?'
>   But Licanor replied that he'd do no such thing: he would never have anyone accuse him of having left them in such danger. 'My shield,' he said, 'will be shattered, my lance in pieces and my sword stained with blood and brain before I ever leave this field!'
>   When Emenidus heard his refusal he asked Philotas, but he too said he wouldn't go; so he called upon Leones, then Perdicas, then Antigonus, then Antiocus and several more – I shan't name them all – but none of them would leave. He finally asked Ariscé de Valestre, who agreed to carry the message – but not until he'd tested himself against the enemy, for King Alexander would believe him more readily if he bore the marks of battle! [1]

Wauquelin's account of the combat that follows is by no means brief – it stretches to five chapters; but the chapters are short and, compared to the hundreds of lines of his source, it is a model of succinctness – and vivid, too.

In any case, brevity for brevity's sake is never Wauquelin's intention. On the contrary, he evidently found his source for Alexander's battles against Darius of Persia – the Prose *Alexander* romance translated from the *Historia de Preliis* – disappointingly curt and colourless, and here he regularly expands and embellishes with great economy but to great effect. For example, in the second of the battles between the Greeks and the Persians, Wauquelin read in the Prose *Alexander* that 'when the battle-lines met, such a great and mighty combat began that even the bravest heart must have felt fear, and the battle remained in the balance till noon: it was impossible to tell who was having the better of it'.[2] Presumably sensing that his readers would be less than thrilled, Wauquelin transforms this frankly lifeless prose into:

> Such a hewing, such a slaughter followed as would appal the bravest man, for both sides killed each other without the slightest pity. The piercing thrusts of lance and spear and the shattering blows of sword and axe struck down men-at-arms in mounds, and the others clambered over them, pounding them under their horses' hooves: once a man-at-arms was down he had no chance of rising again, and many died without even shedding blood. In

[1]   Below, p.63.
[2]   *Der Altfranzösische Prosa-Alexander-roman*, ed. Alfons Hilka (Halle, 1920), p.114.

this vast, hideous, trampling crush they were locked till noon, and it was impossible to tell which side was winning as they struck and slew each other without mercy.[1]

Similarly, the Prose *Alexander*'s account of the final battle against Darius leaves, it has to be said, quite a lot to be desired: 'The battle was so fierce and great that it can hardly be described. Although there were trumpets in hundreds and thousands, the cries of the combatants were greater than the din of the instruments; and they fought all day till nightfall. But then the Persians were defeated. When Darius saw his men defeated he left the field at once; but it was pitch dark by then, and they ran into the chariots they'd brought with them, and the men in the chariots, not recognising them, killed a good many. When Darius reached the river he found it was frozen and rode across; but a great number of them came and couldn't cross, and the Macedonians chased them down and slew them all.'[2] Wauquelin, evidently more than a little dissatisfied, devotes three dramatic chapters to the battle and transforms his source's blunt account of Darius's flight into:

> Bands of his men were fighting on in some parts of the field, where there
> were so many dead that the horses were up to their saddle-girths in blood;
> but as soon as darkness fell and Darius thought the river would have turned
> to ice he left the field and took to flight. But let me tell you, many were
> slain in the process, and this is why: the men who'd driven his chariots at
> the start of the battle had now regrouped and formed a great battalion to
> go and support their friends, so when the Persians turned and fled blindly
> through the dark they ran straight into the chariots, and the charioteers,
> imagining they were the enemy, slaughtered them. This disaster was the
> end for Darius. And the Greeks and Macedonians were hot on their heels,
> charging down with levelled lances and felling them in heaps and mounds.
> The baying fever of the chase was at such a pitch that it seemed the whole
> world would be consumed in slaughter: so many died on the frozen river that
> the blood flowed everywhere in torrents, the ice so slippery, half-melted by
> the steaming gore of the slain, that neither man nor horse could stay upright. [3]

It's not just in descriptions of combat, however, that Wauquelin adds or subtracts detail: he feels perfectly free – in relation to all his sources, both verse and prose – to contribute colour to images of places, dreams, feasting, artefacts, horses, weaponry. Indeed, whenever his imagination or his feelings are stirred he will expand or comment on a moment. A typical example is a passing reference to Fortune's wheel. As events conspire towards Alexander's poisoning, Wauquelin's source at that point, the Prose *Alexander*, introduces the idea that Fortune is at work: 'Fortune had seated King Alexander at the summit of the wheel, but

---

[1]   Below, p.160.
[2]   *Op. cit.*, ed. Hilka, pp.126-8.
[3]   Below, p.170.

wouldn't let him stay there long; instead, so that he would wretchedly fall as he had gloriously risen, it transpired one day that Alexander became angry with Jobas for no reason and hit him on the head with a stick.'[1] It is interesting to compare this with Wauquelin's more engaged, more emotional:

> But Alexander was forgetting the fickleness of Fortune. Having taken him
> to the very top of Her wheel, She, ever turning just as She pleases, chose
> not to keep him in his state of majesty; perverse and inconstant, never to be
> trusted, She was bent on dragging him to the depths just as She'd raised him
> to the heights. She somehow arranged it so that one day, so the histories say,
> Alexander, for no good reason, in a fit of temper struck Jobas on the head
> with a stick. [2]

Wauquelin is particularly good at amplifying passages in order to clarify characters' motivation and thinking, both emotional and practical. This applies not least to tactics. In describing Darius's preparations for his second battle with Alexander, the Prose *Alexander* tells how: 'When Darius went to secure the mountain pass that Alexander had already taken and passed through with all his army, he was amazed; he immediately summoned all the men-at-arms from the kingdom of Persia and the other realms which were subject to him. When they had all arrived, Darius went with his army to do battle with Alexander. But when Alexander knew of his approach he came to meet him with all his men. This was just as day was breaking.'[3] Wauquelin breathes life and spirit and introduces military thought into this, writing:

> Darius planned to take Mount Taurus so that he could block Alexander's
> passage, but was so slow in his preparations that Alexander and all his men
> reached the mountain before he'd made his move. When he realised this he
> was beside himself and didn't know what to do, and couldn't fathom how
> Alexander had managed to move so quickly – or had known he needed to.
> But his counsellors said:
> 'There's no reason to despair, sire: your power is still great. Summon all
> your men: let's bravely go to battle with these Greeks and clear them from
> our land.'
> So they wrote messages and letters and sent them everywhere they had
> a chance of raising troops, and soon assembled an army huge beyond
> imagining. Once they were all gathered Darius ordered them into squadrons
> and battalions. They proposed attacking Alexander early one morning and
> without warning, for they considered war to have been declared the moment
> he invaded.
> But Alexander was as sharp as ever: he was fully recovered from his illness
> and had spies everywhere and was immediately informed of Darius's plans.
> So he commanded all his lords to form their battalions and stand ready for

[1]   Hilka's edition, pp.248-9.
[2]   Below, p.273.
[3]   Hilka's edition, pp.113-4.

action, because he knew Darius was advancing and would be launching an attack as soon as he saw the chance. Alexander's orders were promptly carried out – and it was as well they were, for at the crack of dawn one morning Darius, advancing with his squadrons, fell upon Alexander's army expecting to take them by surprise. But he didn't: he found them ready and waiting – and bold and battle-hardened, too. [1]

Wauquelin is never happy simply to recount a series of events; he always wants to make plain the rationale behind decisions and manoeuvres, and to find a 'psychological reality' behind people's actions. When, for example, he needs to dovetail events in the 'Vows of the Peacock' section of the verse romance into an ongoing series of episodes based on the Prose *Alexander*, he does so by reference to a character's motivation: in an entirely original passage he emphasises that King Porus of India, after all the favours he has received from Alexander during the making of the vows, is reluctant to join Darius in battle against him. On receiving Darius's plea for support, Porus

> pondered a long while before replying. His mind was in turmoil: he thought firstly of the deaths of his father and all those dear to him [at the hands of the Greeks], which filled his heart with anguish and resentment; but secondly of the honours he'd received from Alexander, as recounted above in the story of the peacock; then thirdly that if he refused this request by Darius he'd take it as a mark of cowardice. In the end, however, he decided not to go, and to excuse himself on the grounds of sickness and ill health; but he would send him a number of troops – though not until he'd seen how matters progressed![2]

On occasion, too, Wauquelin interestingly makes a character's motivation more sophisticated. When a Persian knight plans to switch sides and join Alexander, the Prose *Alexander* suggests he does so simply because 'he thought Darius was striving in vain'[3] – i.e. was doomed to lose; but Wauquelin reworks his source in a notable way, writing that

> Darius did not impress the worthy men on whom his cause depended, the reason being that he surrounded himself with sycophants, schemers, two-faced rogues and men of little wit; the men of true worth despised him for this: they couldn't get to talk to him or counsel him for all these wretched fools. And so it was that one of the foremost knights of his company, appalled by his behaviour, decided to do what he could to scupper his plans.[4]

Wauquelin thus changes the knight's motivation from craven fear of imminent disaster to disdain for Darius's behaviour.

---

[1]   Below, p.160.
[2]   Below, pp.157–8.
[3]   Hilka's edition, p.124.
[4]   Below, p.166.

Advice to Princes

And indeed, Wauquelin's own voice comes to the fore most notably in relation to the behaviour of kings. As early as in the fifth of his short chapters, while following the *Roman d'Alexandre*'s description of the young Alexander, he expands a brief reference to the boy's judicious choice of advisers – 'servants of ill breeding never became his intimates; in all matters he followed the advice of noble men'[1] – into the following emphatic passage:

> Everyone, too, admired his mature discernment: he was only ever seen with the wisest and most worthy; he was never impressed by fools, snipers, frauds – he shunned them and despised them, and kept company only with honourable men, whose advice and guidance he heard with keen and polite attention.[2]

This is the first of numerous interpolations (or amplifications of his sources) in which Wauquelin sets up Alexander as a model for princely behaviour. While Darius listens to 'sycophants and schemers' and another enemy, Duke Melcis, 'has a retinue filled with liars and flatterers and pays heed to no one else'[3] and both are led to their downfall, Alexander's glorious triumphs, Wauquelin implies, are due in part to his well-judged choice of advisers.

And how well he cares for his men!

> When morning came he rose and dressed and then began to walk about the meadow to inspect his army, to see if all was in order and if his men were in need of anything, for such was his custom: no king or prince ever took such care of his men as Alexander, which is why he was so well loved and considered the most courteous prince of his time.[4]

Indeed 'he was utterly devoted to them and treated them with courtesy and love in every possible way';[5] he rewards them richly at every turn; when on a particularly arduous march he finds one of his knights 'all shrivelled up, through cold and age and sickness' he 'took him in his arms and carried him to his tent [and] laid him in his own bed, and took such good care of him that his body warmed up again and recovered strength and vigour';[6] he is even prepared to sacrifice himself for his flock by exposing himself to the terrors of the Perilous Valley in their place.[7]

And it's only right that he should love and respect his men, for he would have

---

[1]   *The Medieval French Roman d'Alexandre*, ed. Armstrong, Buffum et al., Vol. 2 (Princeton, 1937), Branch I, stanza 6.
[2]   Below, p.32.
[3]   Below, p 270.
[4]   Below, p.74.
[5]   Below, p.149.
[6]   Below, p.208.
[7]   Below, pp.214–6.

achieved little without them. Wauquelin is especially drawn to passages in his sources which encourage princes to reward those who serve them, and he copies almost verbatim the letter in the Prose *Alexander* in which Aristotle reminds Alexander that, although he should thank God for his triumphs,

> 'at the same time we give thanks to your men for their staunch determination to achieve what has never been seen before and will never be seen again. We pray you, be ever mindful of the blood they've shed in order to place you in your high and exalted position, and be sure to repay and reward their service and devotion: it will show the world that their service to you was effort well spent.'[1]

Yes, Alexander is guided by no less a figure than Aristotle: let us not forget that the great world-conqueror gained not only from his choice of advisers and the (well earned) devotion of his men, but also from having as his tutor 'a man of unparalleled wisdom: indeed, this tutor was the greatest philosopher the world has ever seen, celebrated by all scholars to this day. He was Aristotle, the master of philosophy.'[2] No wonder, then, that Alexander proves to be a prince who acts not only with military genius but with such all-round wisdom. In Wauquelin's version he behaves with almost unfailing self-possession – Wauquelin notably omits a passage in *Li Fuerre de Gadres* where Alexander gives way to rage and frustration when supplies are running short, and has him simply set about solving the problem.[3] Equally impressive is the meticulous preparation he makes for all his enterprises: typical of Wauquelin's interpolated comments is:

> Alexander, wishing to seek out and see all the wonders in the deserts and forests and waters of India, ordered his men to assemble copious supplies of food and water and to prepare their arms and gear meticulously. Any who found himself wanting was to come to him at once and he would be given whatever he lacked.[4]

He shows his wisdom also in the decency and mercy with which he treats the defeated – provided, of course, they have surrendered willingly.[5] He presents, indeed, a fine model of how to behave towards conquered peoples: with no desire to be seen as a plunderer he forbids 'any men-at-arms, on pain of death, to molest or injure any man, for all people without exception were to be left to enjoy their possessions in freedom and safety';[6] and after his epic victories in three bloody battles against King Darius, with shining magnanimity he tells the defeated Persians that

---

[1]   Below, p.267.
[2]   Below, p.32.
[3]   See below, p.62.
[4]   Below, p.204.
[5]   At the city of Damere, for example, its governor 'received him with the greatest honour and yielded to him his city and all he possessed, and Alexander rewarded his benevolence by granting it all back to him and treating him with the utmost respect... and left him to hold the city in peace as his vassal' (below, p.74).
[6]   Below, p.265.

'recognising that the service you formerly paid your lord King Darius can now be seen as service to us (even though at the time it was directed against us), we wish to reward you for the quality of that service. To that end we hereby decree and command that all of you Persians retain all revenue, possessions and rightful inheritances – chattels and estates alike – as were yours on the day we invaded the kingdom of Persia.'[1]

In another implicit piece of advice to princes, Wauquelin emphasises Alexander's disinclination to tax his people: King Clarvus of India is told that

'You've twice as many men as Alexander – and were it not for the harsh demands you've made you'd have seven times as many: you'd be strong enough to do battle with the whole world! But you know how you've inflicted ever greater taxes and maletolts[2] on your people, and they love you less for it; as they keep being exacted I've no doubt they'll betray you and turn their backs on you – many will, at least. That's not King Alexander's way: he respects his people and gives liberally: he cares only that he gains the honour from his conquests – his men can have the profit. And that's how a good ruler should behave if he wants to achieve high renown and prowess: you don't earn your people's love by robbing them and fleecing them, or by being harsh and oppressive, but by showing them courtesy and love. Would to God you'd been so inclined – you could have carried your banner over all the world!'[3]

Indeed, of all Alexander's virtues – and the lordly virtue on which medieval peoples depended when their lords were, after all, effectively the owners of *everything* – the greatest and most regularly stressed by Wauquelin is his generosity, his largesse.[4] This is in his genes: his mother Olympias, along with a multitude of other qualities, 'was wonderfully generous with her wealth: to all valiant men intent upon seeking deeds of arms and chivalry she would give unstintingly, providing them with the finest horses and chargers and armour and weapons and whatever else she imagined they might need'.[5] Alexander follows her example repeatedly and perfectly.

And his virtues, Wauquelin implies, are the keys to his success. This he makes plain in Alexander's first major battle against Nicolas, king of Armenia:

For a long while it was impossible to say who would win the honours, for King Nicolas was a big, strong man, a good foot taller than Alexander, and

---

[1]   Below, p.173.
[2]   A duty paid on wool.
[3]   Below, pp.102–3.
[4]   Indeed, the very existence of books like Wauquelin's depended on it! At the beginning of *Le Parfait du Paon*, the concluding continuation of the *Vows of the Peacock* poem, its author Jehan de la Mote says that Jacques de Longuyon had left *The Vows* unfinished because 'he'd no inclination to write more... But it's often shrewdly observed that many a good work in many a country is abandoned for want of money, for gifts are scanty.' (vv.6-11).
[5]   Below, p.30.

endowed with the greatest courage – had it not been for his avarice and covetousness and pride he'd have been one of the worthiest knights of his age, without a doubt; but King Alexander was generous, courteous, strong, brave and clever, incomparably more so than Nicolas.[1]

And so he wins. Virtues, Wauquelin says, decided the day, not physical might, and the first in the list of adjectives is 'generous'.[2]

The Conqueror: a Very Burgundian Hero

But in Wauquelin's case it may well be unwise to see the extolling of Alexander's virtues as being exhortations and *advice* to his princely patron. They could equally be seen as outright *praise* for a Burgundian duke who was already similarly endowed; for if generosity and all the other virtues were in Alexander's genes, might they not now be reincarnated in one who was, in Burgundian eyes, inheritor of the great conqueror's domains in the West?

Odd though that idea might seem to us, a watershed section of Wauquelin's work is the beginning of Book Two, in which the Burgundian dominions are unequivocally linked with Alexander. In passages derived ultimately from the fourteenth-century romance of *Perceforest* (a copy of which was itself produced in redacted form for Philip the Good in 1459), Wauquelin tells how the 'Forest Carbonniere' ('comprising a number of countries such as Picardy and Artois and especially Hainault, Flanders, Brabant, Liège') had been granted by Alexander to a maiden named Lyriope. This land (which was now an important part of the Burgundian dukes' territories) is gushingly described by Wauquelin as 'on the edge of Gaul…, a fair, fertile, prosperous land peopled by fierce and valiant knights, courageous, bold and strong, and adorned with many fine, rich, strong cities and towns and castles and abundant resources… a splendid, mighty domain'.[3] Once the land has been conquered for Lyriope by Alexander's knights, she arrives with her husband Taron to the most willing of welcomes, being

---

[1] Below, p.49. In contrast, King Clarvus of India's defeat, according to his own nephew, is down to his 'pride and miserly greed and rapacity', and 'the counsel of flatterers, which you always heeded more than the words of men of honour, has brought you now to your final day! Ah, lord, lord, you always loved robbers and murderers and mortally hated all valiant, worthy knights! Now your covetousness has brought you poor reward!' (below, pp.123–4).

[2] This notion, however, is by no means original to Wauquelin. In the epilogue to the verse *Roman d'Alexandre* he would have read: 'Princes and barons should take their example from Alexander: he was bold indeed, fiercer than a lion, and wise in speech and generous in giving gifts; he knew how to distinguish between right and wrong. That is why he conquered all the world…His largesse was greater than any other dared conceive.' (Branch IV, stanzas 73-4). In the prologue to *La Venjance Alixandre* Wauquelin would similarly have read: 'Never was a more bounteous man born of woman… If he had a dozen kingdoms to share out in a single day, one would be given to each of his twelve peers: never were such gifts bestowed by a single man. It was through his great largesse that he rose so high and was acknowledged lord of all lords upon Earth.' (vv.15-27).

[3] Below, p.182.

received with great joy, triumph and honour, all the cities, towns and castles
opening their gates in welcome as obedient subjects. All the lords and knights
and squires and ladies and damsels likewise accepted her as their lord with
all possible joy and honour, holding their lands and possessions as her
vassals, and acknowledging Count Taron as their king and lord and Lyriope
as their lady and their queen.

   Taron and Lyriope faced no hindrance or rebellion at all; they took peaceful,
joyous possession of the gift bestowed upon the virgin damsel Lyriope by the
noble and mighty King Alexander... Let that suffice for now: our purpose
was to show how Alexander was lord of the said lands and countries.[1]

There is not much doubt about the legitimacy of all this: the Burgundian dukes,
Wauquelin makes clear, have a noble inheritance indeed. And as Chrystèle
Blondeau has commented, the dukes of Burgundy 'were never sweet dream-
ers [interested in] nostalgically reviving chivalrous ideals... Rather, they had
an acute awareness of the power of texts and images upon opinion...[as they
sought to] legitimise their aspirations and demonstrate their power...; Alexander became a key figure in the propaganda campaign organised by Philip the
Good,... rooting his dynasty in the territories he controlled and associating it
with a pleiad of heroes..., a pantheon of spiritual or supposedly real ancestors,
...who had supposedly reigned over what would become the Burgundian state';
and the episodes describing Alexander's exploits in the West, writes Blondeau,
'were intended first and foremost to flatter the duke of Burgundy's pride and to
legitimise his expansionist endeavours by rooting them in Alexander's'.[2]

   For it should be emphasised that, according to this mythic history, the Burgundian 'inheritance' from Alexander had been originally acquired by conquest.
To us in the twenty-first century, of course, the figure of the conqueror, the
world-dominator, is hardly an appealing one: in our age of UN peace-keeping
forces and security council resolutions, we are deeply nervous about any in-
cursion by one nation upon another's territory; few would view the vast ambitions of Bonaparte or Hitler as admirable; and many fear aggressive expansion
of economies or religions. A history of Alexander written now might well present him with ambivalence and even as something of a monster – as he is indeed
seen in many Middle Eastern cultures.[3] But, as William Kibler has written, 'over
the centuries Alexander has been nearly everything for everybody. Each suc-
ceeding culture, as it gained identity and self-consciousness, projected on to the
legend of the great Macedonian its own aspirations, values and manners.'[4] A
fifteenth-century Burgundian view of the all-conquering king – and of conquest
itself – would have been quite different from our own. We are living in an era of

[1]   Below, p.184.
[2]   Blondeau, *op. cit.*, pp.12, 231, 247.
[3]   See, for example, Michael Wood's interesting experiences in his *In the Footsteps of Alexander
       the Great* (London, 1997), pp.105-8, 122.
[4]   William W. Kibler, "A paine a on bon arbre de malvaise raïs": counsel for kings in the *Ro-
       man d'Alexandre*", in Maddox & Sturm-Maddox (eds.), *op. cit.*, p.111.

clearly defined nations and boundaries; the Burgundian dukes, however, with their eyes ever on expanding their dominions, would have seen territory as little different from the frontierless expanses encountered by their hero Alexander. In their time, in the words of Richard Vaughan, 'Europe was by no means divided, as it was to be later, into mutually exclusive and independent polities... In the fifteenth century no ruler or state was completely independent... Every territory was riddled with enclaves of privilege and immunity... Power was everywhere scattered and diffuse. Spain did not exist; France was a sort of organisation; Germany merely a concept.'[1]

So the world, in medieval eyes, was an open field – the fighting class's playing field[2] – and conquest by a prince strong and daring enough was entirely valid, especially if people failed to resist: it's significant that when Alexander first enters Persia 'his scouts and foragers... started riding across the land pillaging and plundering and seizing towns and castles and forts as if the whole country belonged to them – as indeed it did, for they met with little resistance'.[3]

But it should be noted that, right from the outset, Alexander's conquests are presented as being prompted by nothing so unworthy as ambition or greed. His first campaign, against Nicolas of Armenia, is a response to Nicolas's aggression as the Armenian king sends an envoy to demand that Alexander's father Philip of Macedon, being

'...King Nicolas's inferior and subject, render him such tribute as befits his
noble, royal majesty; and do so without delay, and thank him for allowing
you to hold your land [of Macedon] in peace so long! If you refuse and make
any objection, you must understand he will come with such a mighty force
of Armenians and Turks that every tower, fort and stronghold in your land
will be battered to the ground, you and your people will be reduced to eternal
slavery, and your lordship will be annulled and given to a subject who'll pay
him the service that is his due.'

Philip is speechless with outrage, but with a self-possession that is typical of Wauquelin's presentation of the hero, Alexander

although he was no less enraged than his father... retained control; and like a
truly wise man he rose and... stood before the messenger and said:
    'You, who have just delivered King Nicolas of Armenia's bidding to my
father, will go and tell him from me that as long as I live my father will never
pay him tribute, for the land of Greece and its people have never owed any
– rather, they're accustomed to demand and receive it from their neighbours!
So I challenge him with fire and blood as my mortal enemy, and assure him

---

[1]   Richard Vaughan, *Valois Burgundy* (London, 1975), p.9.
[2]   What else, after all, was there for them to do? As Alexander says, 'there was nothing good
      about an idle life, and while certain things remained undone he should not be called a per-
      fect king: he meant to go on campaign and wage war once again' (below, p.176).
[3]   Below, p.54.

that, for his offensive arrogance – he's full of it! – and his slight to Greece's authority, I shall separate his head from his shoulders…'[1]

The great war against Darius of Persia is likewise presented not as a war of ambition and aggression by Alexander but as a war of revenge: he reminds his men before battle that they are fighting 'to avenge the shameful wrongs we've suffered at Persian hands'.[2] Darius is depicted as the one who is 'consumed by greed',[3] and as well as demanding tribute from Macedon he has robbed young Sanson Dailly, son of King Omer of Persia, of his inheritance; it is to redress that wrong that Sanson appeals to Alexander for help, and Alexander's great siege of Tyre takes place because the city is rightfully Sanson's.

But what about his invasion of India? Doesn't that show his lust for conquest? Not at all: Alexander, we are told, first goes to war with the Indian king Clarvus in response to an appeal for help from the Ephesians, who are being besieged by Clarvus because, aged though he is, he lusts after their beautiful young princess. The girl's uncle tells Alexander that

> 'the damsel, a good and bright and beautiful girl, would rather be burnt alive
> than accept him, not just because she knows he's old but because he's a foul
> man, the nonpareil of wickedness! Her name is Phesonnas. Of her two young
> brothers, my nephews, one is named Gadifer of Ephesus and the other Betis;
> they're both lords of the city of Ephesus through their mother… But now
> this Clarvus means to ruin them and drive them from their city: he's already
> besieging them there at Ephesus. So I beg you, lord king, help me bring aid
> to my niece and nephews against this Clarvus… Bring us peace and crush his
> pride.'[4]

It is, then, we are told, all Clarvus's fault – indeed, Alexander (no warmonger, he!) would rather have had Clarvus see sense and make peace, and tells the Indian envoys that he and his barons 'regret that Clarvus is unwilling to give way and is determined to do battle'.[5]

Clarvus's pride not only passes through the genes to his son Porus, who becomes king of India after him, but becomes even more intense, so that when Alexander later goes and invades India it is once again not out of lust for conquest but in response to Porus's outrageous arrogance as he shows no respect for the gods (and no gratitude for the generosity and courtesy earlier shown him by Alexander).

But in truth lust for conquest *is* lurking there; indeed, the following passage typifies perfectly what we today might see as an extraordinarily confused morality in the medieval attitude towards Alexander's conquests:

---

[1]   Below, p.40.
[2]   Below, p.154.
[3]   Below, p.42.
[4]   Below, p.75.
[5]   Below, p.112.

'Porus, king of India, bids the thief Alexander, who wins kingdoms, lands
and cities by robbery, not by chivalry, explain what a mortal man such as he
can do against a people whose nobility is acknowledged by the gods?... Let
me tell you: not only men but gods, too, bow before our empire! Don't you
know that Dionysus Bacchus, deemed the father of all the gods, came to India
to conquer her but returned in shame, unable to resist the Indians' might?[1]
And I know for a fact that before Xerxes was king of Persia the Macedonians
paid tribute to the kings of India – until they thought it was hardly worth
their while and wouldn't deign to take it! After all, noble men prefer the fine,
the great and grand rather than the paltry! So before your pride deludes you
into this foolish enterprise, we advise – no, we command you absolutely – to
go back to the land you came from and cease to set your outrageous sights
on places where you know you've no authority and no cause whatever to
claim it. Consider this very carefully, or your crazed ambition may lead you
to repent too late!'

When Alexander's knights heard the letter's contents they were so enraged
that they looked as if they were about to breathe fire and flame! Had it not
been for Alexander they would have killed the messengers on the spot out of
contempt for Porus and all who supported him. They thought how short his
memory was of the entertainment and honour he'd received from Alexander.
But Alexander, to pacify and cheer them, said:

'Oh, dear friends! Don't be upset at King Porus's haughty letter: remember
how Darius's pride and presumption drove him to write so offensively. I tell
you, all barbarians are the same!'...

[And Alexander wrote to Porus in reply:] 'Regarding your assertion that
we win kingdoms, lands and cities through robbery rather than chivalry,
we assure you we conquer and win them by chivalry in the open field. In
any case, even if we did acquire them in the manner you suggest there'd
be no reason to reproach us, for we challenge our enemies quite properly
and adequately, and you surely agree that a man who's received a formal
challenge has no right to pity if he loses.

'On another point: you say there's nothing worth having in the land of
Macedon while India abounds in riches; that's precisely why we, who have so
little in our lands, wish with all our hearts to do battle with you and conquer
your fine country, which we so badly need! You also say that men are bound
to prefer the splendid to the paltry: that's why we, such paltry, petty folk in
comparison to your greatness, wish to do battle with you to assume your
glorious state – not, however, that we wish the gods to bow to us as you say
they bow to you: no man should claim lordship over the one who made us.
So we wish you to know that we're coming to do battle with you – and we
won't be fighting a god, but a man stuffed full of vanity.' [2]

Alexander, then, *does* want the riches and the glory of conquered lands, but he
is taking them from 'barbarians' who are aggressive, ungrateful, haughty, and

---

[1]   A reference to a legend from at least the fourth century BCE, according to which Diony-
       sus's conquest of Asia ended at India.
[2]   Below, pp.187–8.

have no respect for the gods.[1] It's noticeable, too, that they are usually unworthy even in the eyes of their own people: when Clarvus of India is killed in battle 'a good many of his men were overjoyed, despite the calamitous danger they now faced, for they despised him for his boundless cruelty and oppression'.[2] Alexander by contrast is a paragon of noble qualities, loved by all his men, and his conquests are won 'by chivalry' after a 'proper and adequate challenge' – and 'a man who's received a formal challenge has no right to pity if he loses'.

And how indeed can those conquered by Alexander complain, when his victories, we are repeatedly told, are a sign of divine approval? When the Greeks accept Clarvus's challenge to battle, they say: 'May the glory and honour go to the one who is most in the right.'[3] This phrase, innocuous though it may seem, is highly significant, for it implicitly turns war into trial by combat; and from the very outset we are given no doubt whatever that Alexander's world domination is his divinely ordained destiny. His birth, we are told, is accompanied by wild disturbances in earth and sky and sea, and 'the meaning of these signs... is plain enough: reason suggests that everything trembled at his birth because everything was due to be his subject'.[4] Aristotle then interprets a dream that appears to the child Alexander as a sign that 'with his courage and his daring he will conquer most of the earth... And all others will count themselves fortunate to pay him tribute and serve him, and every man on earth will be his vassal.'[5] Later, Darius's mother Rodocton recognises that 'even if the whole world was ranged against Alexander they still would not defeat him, for he is destined by almighty God to bring the whole world under his lordship and dominion'.[6] She's not alone: the Romans quickly decide that 'it would be hopeless to do battle with him, for he was divinely destined to crush all opposition',[7] and they surrender to him without a fight. Willing surrender is implicitly the wise and proper way to behave. When the people of Tarsus outrageously refuse to yield, Alexander

> was enraged by their reply... and swore by his gods that he wouldn't stop till
> the city was at his mercy; he ordered all his men to prepare for an assault...
> The defenders' efforts were vain: the city was overwhelmed and taken and
> the king's banner was planted within; and Alexander commanded that all
> be slaughtered and the city's wealth be seized and each man in the army be
> given his rightful share. His orders were carried out: soon the entire city was

---

[1] Note that King Darius is almost as presumptuous as Porus, calling himself 'a rival or an equal to the sun, chosen to join the gods in heaven' (p.144), while Alexander, unlike his adversaries, remains a model of modesty in relation to the gods: he never forgets that he is "mortal and corruptible like you, created just the same, and the honour due to God should never be attributed to man" (p.175).

[2] Below, p.123.

[3] Below, p.112.

[4] Below, p.32.

[5] Below, p.35.

[6] Below, p.167.

[7] Below, p.138.

ablaze and its towers and gates were levelled to the ground, till not a single stone remained on another.[1]

The author shows no more pity than the conqueror (and his source, the verse *Roman d'Alexandre*, explicitly says that Alexander was *'avenged'* for the *'outrage'* of their resistance[2]). Unlike the men of Tarsus, the people of Syria by contrast *'judiciously* came to him and presented him with all their wealth along with the keys of their city', so that in response Alexander 'greeted them most kindly and approvingly and took them into his care and protection'.[3]

Perhaps the ultimate (and, to us today, possibly disturbing) statement of the belief that Alexander is the agent of divine will is his answer to a question posed by the ascetic Brahmans:

'Since he says he's mortal, for what possible reason does he march through the world doing all manner of harm?'

'That,' said Alexander in reply, 'is my destiny, ordained by Sovereign Providence, whom I obey as its minister. The sea is rough only when the wind blows upon it; I likewise stir only when Divine Providence drives me to act as you say: I'd be only too pleased to rest, if almighty God permitted it. And you'd surely agree that if everyone in the world was alike in nature and outlook, there'd be no way of recognising goodness and valour.'[4]

How the Burgundian duke must have enjoyed that passage! By implication it is the chivalrous prince's duty, if he feels himself so 'stirred', not to rest and recline in the luxury that his affluence makes possible, but to be the agent of Providence and prove his valour. It may lead to 'all manner of harm' – not least vast mounds of dead in battlefield and siege – but, after all, there is little honour to be won in peace, and Alexander, like any truly worthy prince, is 'burning with desire to win further honour',[5] and 'though peace appears good in itself, there is nothing sweeter in the world than peace after mighty war!... When storm clouds pass good weather will follow. I refer to the turmoil and strife and hostility and violence which have long raged between us – though our honour did not permit any less. We deeply regret the loss of so many noble men who were slain as a result – but enough! What's done is done!'[6] Any amount of collateral damage, apparently, can be overlooked when honour is at stake – especially when a prince, like Alexander, is working on behalf of power divine.

[1] Below, p.56.
[2] Branch I, stanzas 125, 126.
[3] Below, p.57.
[4] Below, p.210.
[5] Below, p.52. Note, too, that Alexander has the last word in the exchange of letters with the Brahman king, saying they are cursed in their confinement and restriction to their own land (below, p.212). Men, it is implied, need to 'venture abroad' and *expand*.
[6] Below, pp.154, 174.

The Sovereign God

But which divine power are we talking about? Surely we can't be talking about the Christian God in relation to Alexander the Great? He was, after all, a pagan, as acknowledged by Jacques de Longuyon in *The Vows of the Peacock* in his famous passage about the Nine Worthies[1] – the nine supreme exponents of chivalry, three of them Christian, three of them Jewish and three of them (including Alexander) pagan. Of course we might expect a fair amount of anachronism in a fifteenth-century history of Alexander – references to medieval instruments, for example (the organ, the psaltery),[2] or to medieval taxes (the maletolt)[3] – for after all, as Wauquelin says, his source doesn't even 'tell me at what time after the creation of the world these events took place';[4] and we might expect and overlook the near-total lack of geographical sense (the authors of medieval Alexander texts clearly hadn't the slightest idea where many of the places cited were); but surely they can't have got the *god* wrong?

Well, yes and no. The theological vagueness may in fact strike a modern reader as pretty staggering. In one and the same passage we read that '*God omnipotent, creator of all things*, has ordained that King Alexander should be lord and master of all the earth' and that Alexander is '*at the gods' bidding* master and conqueror of all the world'.[5] This apparent vagueness applies throughout: in true pagan fashion Alexander frequently swears 'by his gods',[6] he worships Mars in an elaborate rite,[7] he swears 'by the sky and earth and sun and moon and stars',[8] he intends at Tyre to 'worship the gods of that place',[9] and his tutor the great Aristotle assures him that 'Mars... wishes to make you lord of all the world... Rejoice... the gods are with you!'[10] Indeed, in one memorable episode one of the gods most certainly *is* with him: the Egyptian god Ammon appears to him 'in the shape of the god Mercury' and bids him 'assume my appearance and go to King Darius in person, and I'll help you see it through without a hitch!'[11] But on the other hand, Alexander is especially eager to meet Queen Candace 'because she believed in God omnipotent';[12] and when he arrives in her land and invites her to join him in offering a sacrifice to Ammon, she replies:

[1] See Appendix 3.
[2] Below, p.30.
[3] Below, pp.46, 103.
[4] Below, p.29.
[5] Below, pp.241–2.
[6] pp. 37, 54, 56, 57, 65.
[7] p.76.
[8] p.58.
[9] p.58.
[10] p.76.
[11] p.150.
[12] p.73.

'It does not behove us to make such a sacrifice, for we hold to a different faith to yours, believing as we do in God the Omnipotent. You may believe that you owe your victories over the Persians, the Indians and all the rest to your god Ammon, but we are certain that it was not Ammon who granted you those triumphs, for he has no such power; no, your debt is to God the Omnipotent, source and creator of all things, for without His sanction you would have achieved nothing.'[1]

Shortly afterwards, Candace's people, 'following their annual custom, gathered to make sacrifices to their god, who was God immortal',[2] and it's interesting that Wauquelin specifies this, because in his sources they worship either the pagan goddess Lucina or simply 'their god'.[3] It's as if Wauquelin is at least a little concerned to attempt some kind of 'conversion' in Alexander.[4] Alexander's willingness to be enlightened about divinity is seen most remarkably (and, it might be said, strangely) in his visit to Jerusalem. Here, as soon as he claps eyes on (in another striking anachronism) 'the bishop', Alexander

flung himself from his horse to the ground and worshipped Our Lord. Then all the Jews began to hail him, crying aloud:
'Long live King Alexander!'
When the Macedonians saw the deep respect King Alexander had shown to the bishop of the Jews and how he'd worshipped him, a great murmur arose amongst them all, until one of Alexander's princes... came to him and said:
'Most feared and mighty emperor, how is it that when all men honour and revere and worship you, you now worship in our presence the bishop of the Jewish people?'
To which Alexander replied: 'Truly, dear friend, understand I wasn't worshipping the bishop but the omnipotent God whose arms he bears and from whom he holds and exercises office. Let me tell you: when I was with my father and mother in the land of Macedon, I was lying in bed and turning over in my mind how I could gain dominion over Darius and the Persians and lead my armies to his land. I thought and thought and then I fell asleep; and the sovereign god of gods appeared to me dressed just as you see this bishop here, and He promised me that if I was willing to march into Asia without harming His people – and would worship His Law – I would journey in safety and win dominion over all. So my hope is that with His help I shall

---

[1]   Below, p.225.
[2]   Below, pp.226–7.
[3]   See footnote 1, below, p.227.
[4]   It should be noted, too, that Wauquelin rejects the tradition that Alexander had been fathered by Nectanebus or by the god Ammon (see Appendix 1). This notion was important to the historical Alexander – 'he used sometimes to dress up as Ammon, and it was possible to drive him into a fury by mocking his divine parentage' (Stoneman, *op. cit.*, p.8) – because it made him the legitimate pharaoh of Egypt; but it would not have sat well with a Christian audience for whom an equivalent claim by a present-day 'embodiment' of the conqueror would of course have appeared shockingly blasphemous. Alexander, in Wauquelin's and Burgundian eyes, had to be unquestionably the legitimate son and heir of Philip of Macedon and his queen.

vanquish King Darius and crush the might of the Persians and achieve all that
my heart desires. That's why, when I saw the bishop here in his vestments,
representing God better than any man I've ever seen, I went down on my
knees and worshipped him.'[1]

This apparent lightning conversion to Judaism is then soon followed by Alexander making a sacrifice to 'Our Lord',[2] and the deity who later helps him escape
from the Perilous Valley seems distinctly Judaeo-Christian: in thanksgiving

> Alexander made a sacrifice to God, who in His gracious mercy had freed
> him from his dismal plight; and as he made the sacrifice he gave his men to
> understand that no one with true faith in immortal God could ever come to a
> bad end.[3]

But lo and behold, these moments of apparent conversion are followed by his
sacrifice to Ammon which Queen Candace declines to join; and the inconsistency is even more striking when, later still, he has guiding encounters with
Sesostris and Serapis[4] and is given a potent healing herb by Ammon, who even
refers to him as 'Dear son'[5] as though Wauquelin has momentarily forgotten
having rejected the idea that Alexander was divinely fathered.

How can we account for such inconsistency? The answer perhaps lies in the
intriguing phrase 'the Sovereign God' which appears frequently in the Prose *Alexander* and is readily adopted by Wauquelin on many occasions. A reader might
feel there is a measure of uncertainty about what the phrase implies, as for Darius the 'sovereign god' is Jupiter;[6] but the audience is clearly meant to understand
it as referring to the Judaeo-Christian god, as the same being is called 'almighty
God', 'God omnipotent' and even 'Our Lord' with a fair degree of regularity.

The significant phrase 'Sovereign God' is used in far more purposeful fashion
in the romance of *Perceforest* which, although originally composed probably in
the 1340s, was reworked in the fifteenth century and produced in fine manuscripts for the Burgundian court at much the same time as Wauquelin's *Alexander*. Quite early in the romance, Alexander and his protégé King Perceforest
both encounter a 'Perilous Temple' where they are introduced to the idea of the

---

[1]   Below, p.142. This eyebrow-raising visit to Jerusalem derives ultimately from a passage in
        the Greek *Alexander* romance, on the 'transparent fictionality' of which see Stoneman, *op.
        cit.*, pp.49–51. It's important to note that Wauquelin expands upon his source considerably;
        the parallel passage in the verse *Roman d'Alexandre* is much shorter, telling simply how
        he 'would have destroyed the city [of Jerusalem] and laid waste the land, but the citizens
        humbled themselves before him… and brought before him the Law that God gave to
        Moses on Mount Sinaï…; Alexander honoured it and bowed and prayed to it.' (Branch II,
        stanza 111).

[2]   Below, p.142.
[3]   Below, p.217.
[4]   Below, pp.139, 235–6.
[5]   Below, p.150.
[6]   Below, p.157.

'Sovereign God', who proves to be unquestionably the God of Christianity, and are made to realise that

> 'the gods in whom you believe can do nothing but bad. However much people may think they've gained from them, their belief is wildly mistaken. They should renounce their misguided belief in all other gods, whose powers all derive from the Sovereign God.'

And Perceforest, at the feast he later establishes to the Sovereign God, appeals to his people to

> 'abandon all other gods and goddesses and put your faith in the Sovereign God; henceforth let all the others be merely examples to us: we may take note of the qualities we have found in them, and apply all the good precepts for which they have been renowned and for which they were considered gods. But gods they were not, for all the qualities they possessed were derived from the Sovereign God.'[1]

The anonymous author of *Perceforest*, then, does not say that the 'old gods' don't exist or have no power, but that their powers and qualities have been devolved: they are the vassals of a new 'Sovereign God'. The author's divine system is an exact reflection of the hierarchy in his contemporary world below: God is the king and Mars, Venus, Nature and the other deities are His vassals.

This admirably clear understanding of the phrase[2] is not matched by its use in Wauquelin's work. But there is every reason to suppose that Wauquelin, without stating it so cogently, shared the concept – as did his audience. After all, a measure of respect for pagans and their gods is necessary and only right and proper if you are claiming descent from them. For claim descent they did. 'Civilisation is a prize handed down through the centuries,' wrote Jean Seznec, 'and medieval man unreservedly and even with pride claimed the heritage of antiquity... The legend according to which the Franks were descended from the Trojan Francus was an invention of Merovingian scholars, but should not be dismissed as a mere fantasy of learned minds. It was taken seriously as genealogy, and became a veritable form of ethnic consciousness.'[3] The genealogy of King Arthur himself – shown to be a descendant of none other than Alexander – and 'ethnic conflict' between peoples descended from Greek and Trojan blood are indeed major elements in the romance of *Perceforest*. No wonder, then, that 'good pagans' such as Hector, Caesar and Alexander were the equals of the Christians among the 'Nine Worthies': chivalry transcended religions, and was derived from the pagan past. No wonder, either, that the Renaissance was to show such fondness

---

[1]   *Perceforest*, tr. N. Bryant (Woodbridge, 2011), pp.55, 424.
[2]   The *Perceforest* author may well have first encountered the term 'Sovereign God' in the Prose *Alexander*. He is very familiar with the Alexander romances and draws a number of characters and incidents from them.
[3]   Jean Seznec, *The Survival of the Pagan Gods* (London, 1940, reissued by Princeton University Press, 1995), pp.18-19.

for pagan motifs from the classical world: civilisation was derived from it, too.[1] This would certainly help to explain why Wauquelin felt able to give Alexander such a conceptually contorted line as: 'since the god Ammon by the grace of the Sovereign God has ordained that we triumph over the Persians, it is only right that we show mercy to the defeated and render thanks to all the gods'.[2]

At the same time, however, it was probably important for Wauquelin to show Alexander having *some* inclination towards monotheism and being on good terms with a clearly Christian god (every time he prays to 'Our Lord' his prayers are answered). After all, Wauquelin was writing for a duke who had an anxious eye on the aggressive expansion of the Islamic Ottoman Empire (an empire which coincided closely, of course, with that of Alexander's enemy Darius – Alexander's conquest of the East would have been an appealing theme[3]), and in Duke Philip the crusading flame still more than flickered. His famous 'Feast of the Pheasant' at Lille in February 1454 was to feature an elaborate interlude in which a figure representing Holy Church (played by the chronicler Olivier de la Marche) pleaded for aid against the Infidel, and Duke Philip (in a clear echo of the vows made to the peacock in the Alexander romance) was presented with a bejewelled live pheasant and asked to vow upon the bird to go on crusade; indeed, he vowed to confront the sultan Mehmed II, who had captured Constantinople the previous May, in single combat if he challenged him. For such a duke, the great conquering hero Alexander, crushing ruthless Eastern tyrants who practise a barbarous form of paganism (in the case of the Babylonians it even involves human sacrifice[4]), needed to be presented as thoroughly in touch with the *Sovereign* God.

But in any case, the vagueness of the theology and the lack of rigour in resolving inconsistencies are, it might be said, in themselves interesting. They evidently didn't matter; Wauquelin may well have felt his audience would be untroubled about exactly which deity was willing Alexander to dominate the world: a generalised divinity would be good enough for the myth of the Conqueror Fulfilling a Divine Will and Destiny, a myth which has of course continued to resurface and always appeals – as it did to the Burgundian dukes – to rulers and nations with imperial ambitions.

---

[1]   It is interesting to see that 'the three goddesses of destiny, the three sisters Cloto, Latesis and Antropos' are happily (and quite unnecessarily) included in B.N. MS fr.9342's illustration of Alexander's visit to the Trees of the Sun and the Moon: see the title page to Book Two.

[2]   Below, p.173.

[3]   Catherine Gaullier-Bougassas has suggested that, likewise, the attack upon the Macedonians by the Armenians and Turks under King Nicolas 'could not but have called to mind for men of the fifteenth century the Turkish threat to Constantinople which was soon to end in the capture of the Byzantine city'. C. Gaullier-Bougassas, "Alexandre héros païen ou héros pré-chrétien? Deux stratégies opposées de réécriture à la fin du Moyen Âge", in *Le Moyen Français 51-53* (2002-03), p.314.

[4]   See below, p.258.

Another Appealing Myth

It is not the only mythic element in Wauquelin's history of Alexander which would have appealed to his patrons. The final chapters deal with the avenging by Alexander's son of his father's treacherous murder,[1] and the central theme of these chapters is the absolute need for a single, strong leader. Beyond Alexander's crucial command and example in war (in battle after battle it is made plain that all would have been lost without him, the epitome of prowess), the closing section of Wauquelin's work dramatically shows that the moment Alexander is gone chaos reigns: his barons and former companions, consumed by greedy ambition, are not content with what he has bequeathed them and become embroiled against each other in a series of destructive bloodbaths until 'in less than fourteen years all King Alexander's barons were dead, killed in battles, wars and revolts'.[2]

This was very much a theme to chime with the time. Richard Vaughan, outstanding historian of Valois Burgundy, writes of 'the portentous and nearly ubiquitous increase in the authority of central governments that took place during the fifteenth century. The acquisition of more power by princes, the emergence of larger polities, the growing arbitrariness of governments; these changes, which took place at the expense of the nobles, of local autonomies, of local privilege, were often connected with the rise to power of a single remarkable, and usually powerful, ruler. These men were tyrants, dynasts, egoists.'[3] What a stirring example was presented to such men by Wauquelin's 'history of the good King Alexander'.

For 'the *history* of the good King Alexander' is the 'title' he gives his work in the final line, and a history it really is, rather than a romance. 'Romance' elements do infiltrate from time to time, especially in the section based on Jacques de Longuyon's 'Vows of the Peacock', in which knights begin to fight for individual honour inspired by love for their ladies and a great battle against Clarvus of India turns into something approaching a tournament, with ladies and maidens bestowing favours and watching entranced from walls and towers.[4] But this is not at all typical, and almost no attention whatever is paid to Alexander's love for Candace or Roxane (whereas in the romance of *Perceforest*, for example, a good deal is made of his love for the lady Sebile). And although Wauquelin incorporates, for instance, the famous stories of Alexander's exploration of the sea in a glass barrel and of the sky in a griffon-powered cage – adventures in

---

[1]   A narrative, incidentally, which may well have been sharply resonant for Duke Philip, who no doubt remembered all too well that his father John the Fearless had been treacherously butchered on the bridge at Montereau.

[2]   Below, p.296.

[3]   Vaughan, *op. cit.*, pp.3-5.

[4]   Below, pp.116, 122.

which he can be seen as a kind of Everyman figure yearning to probe the world's wonders, or perhaps, as Chrystèle Blondeau has suggested, 'displaying the insatiable curiosity of the conqueror'[1] – he does so quite briefly. Wauquelin is certainly interested in these fabulous elements of the legend, but much more so in Alexander as a 'political' model, and for the most part his work is a history: little concerned with any individuals but one, it tells the story of a great king of the past and presents him as an example for all time.

It is of course short of the factual accuracy we now deem essential and expect to find in a history, so that anyone hoping for a precisely traced itinerary or sequence of events will be dismayed to see, for example, Alexander dash home to Macedon between battles to visit his ailing mother, and reach India by way of Ethiopia. And did those feet in ancient time *really* walk upon England's and France's pastures as Wauquelin, *Perceforest* and Jacques de Guise's *History of Hainault* suggest?[2] We know of course that they didn't. Was he really poisoned in a monstrous act of treachery by people to whom he'd shown love and favour, and was he then dramatically avenged by his own son? Some modern historians may claim to know better, and have good reason to believe that Alexander succumbed to fever after indulging in drinking bouts of barely credible proportions.[3] But, as is shown by the mythic histories on which our major religions are based, people are more than willing to overlook the shakiness of a narrative if its mythic meaning suits them.

And suit the fifteenth-century Burgundian court the meaning of Wauquelin's *Alexander* certainly did, as it celebrated a myth of divinely endorsed conquest and dominion by a prince without whom his people could achieve nothing and without whose unifying presence all would be lost in conflict and confusion.

---

[1]   Blondeau, *op. cit.*, p.240.
[2]   Below, pp.179–84.
[3]   For particularly vivid accounts of Macedonian binge-drinking, see Michael Wood, *op. cit.*, pp.153-4, 206-8.

Further Reading

Editions of Wauquelin and his sources

Jehan Wauquelin, *Les Faicts et les Conquestes d'Alexandre le Grand,* ed. Sandrine Hériché, Geneva (Librairie Droz), 2000.

Alexandre de Paris, *Le Roman d'Alexandre* [the verse romance]: in *The Medieval French Roman d'Alexandre, Vol. 2,* ed. E. C. Armstrong, D. L. Buffum et al., Princeton, 1937.

The Prose Alexander romance: *Der altfranzösische Prosa-Alexanderroman,* ed. Alfons Hilka, Halle, 1920 [includes parallel text of the Latin *Historia de Preliis*].

Jacques de Longuyon, *Les Voeux du Paon,* ed. R. L. Graeme Ritchie in *The Buik of Alexander, Vols. 3 and 4,* Edinburgh, 1929.

Jean le Court, *Le Restor du Paon,* ed. R. J. Carey, Geneva, 1966.

La Prise de Defur, ed. L. P. G. Peckham, Princeton, 1935.

Jehan le Nevelon, *La Venjance Alixandre,* ed. E. Billings Ham, Princeton, 1931.

Studies

Blondeau, C., *Un conquérant pour quatre ducs,* Paris, 2009.

Cary, G., *The Medieval Alexander,* Cambridge, 1956.

Gaullier-Bougassas, C., *Les Romans d'Alexandre: Aux Frontières de l'Épique et du Romanesque,* Paris, 1998.

Gaullier-Bougassas, C., "Alexandre et les Brahmanes dans les *Romans d'Alexandre* français, du XIIe au XVe siècle", in *Le Moyen Age: Revue d'histoire et de philologie* 106 (2000), pp.467-93.

Gaullier-Bougassas, C., *La tentation de l'Orient dans le roman médiéval,* Paris, 2003.

Gaullier-Bougassas, C., "Alexandre héros païen ou héros pré-chrétien? Deux stratégies opposées de réécriture à la fin du Moyen Âge", in *Le Moyen Français 51-53* (2002-03), pp.305-26.

Harf-Lancner, L., Kappler, C., and Suard, F. (eds.), *Alexandre le Grand dans les littératures occidentales et proche-orientales: actes du colloque de Paris, 27-29 novembre 1997,* Nanterre, 1999.

Hériché, S., "Immersion et survivance dans *Les faicts et les conquestes d'Alexandre le Grand* de Jehan Wauquelin", in *Dans l'eau, sous l'eau: Le monde aquatique au Moyen Age* (eds. Danièle James-Raoul and Claude Thomasset), Paris, 2002, pp.339-55.

Hériché, S., *Alexandre le Bourguignon. Études du roman* Les Faicts et les Conquestes d'Alexandre le Grand *de Jehan Wauquelin,* Geneva, 2008.

Maddox, D. and Sturm-Maddox, S. (eds.), *The Medieval French Alexander,* Albany, 2002.

Stoneman, R., *Alexander the Great, A Life in Legend,* Yale, 2008.

BOOK ONE

Bibliothèque Nationale MS français 9342, folio 108

The glorious exploits, the deeds of arms, conquests and feats of courage performed by the valiant, mighty, noble men of ancient and former times are an inspiration. Recalling and recounting them rouses the hearts of their counterparts in the present day who yearn to scale the heights of prowess and fame; it inspires them to achieve ever greater experience, honour and perfection. The hearts of young knights and squires, especially, are sure to be stirred and filled with thoughts of glory and prowess when they hear such deeds recalled, and be ever fixed upon winning high renown.

And so it is that I, unworthy of such fame (poor and ignorant as I am), have undertaken, at the request – or more precisely the command! – of that most august, noble and mighty lord Sir John of Burgundy, count of Étampes and lord of Dourdan,[1] to set down in writing in our mother tongue the glorious deeds of arms, conquests and exploits of the noble King Alexander of Macedon.

I found the material in a book written all in verse. I don't know the name of the author, only that its title is the *History of Alexander*,[2] so if – God forbid! – I've strayed at all from the true story of that illustrious and mighty prince, or if any fault be found in my treatment of the subject, may it be judiciously, kindly and sympathetically corrected and amended. And if any part of this work be worthy of praise let the credit go to God, and any shortcoming be attributed to my negligence, which I hope will be treated with as much tolerance as censure! Also, since the said book doesn't tell me at what time after the creation of the world these events took place – at least, not with any certainty – I would ask that if anyone finds reliable evidence he add and append it to this present work, in the beginning, middle and end of which I crave and pray for the grace of the Holy Spirit to guide me.

---

1   'John of Burgundy' is Jehan de Clamecy (1415-91), count of Étampes from 1442-65, count of Nevers from 1464-91 and count of Eu from 1472-91. He was the cousin of Philip the Good, duke of Burgundy.

2   'Istore Alixandre'. This is the verse *Roman d'Alexandre*, an immense composite work from the late twelfth century attributed to Alexandre de Paris, who constructed it from a number of existing poems including, for example, *Li Fuerre de Gadres* ('The Raid at Gaza') by Eustache and *Alixandre en Orient* ('Alexander in the East') by Lambert le Tort, neither of which has survived in its original, independent form. Wauquelin, however, was certainly working from a late manuscript of the *Roman d'Alexandre* that incorporated work not originally included by Alexandre de Paris, notably the anonymous thirteenth-century poem *La Prise de Defur* ('The Capture of Defur') and Jacques de Longuyon's fourteenth-century *Les Voeux du Paon* ('The Vows of the Peacock'). And as will become clear, this massive verse compilation was not Wauquelin's only source: he is later to draw extensively on the Prose *Alexander* romance of the thirteenth century, and also on Jehan le Nevelon's twelfth-century *La Venjance Alixandre* ('The Avenging of Alexander').

CHAPTER II

Of the noble King Alexander's father and mother, and their positions and their characters.

Now, then: to explain who this most noble King Alexander was, so mighty and so valiant, and where he came from, these are the facts.

There was once a king in the land of Greece named Philip. He was king of Macedon, of all Alania,[1] of part of Greece and all of Slavonia. In his youth he was much feared and respected, and loved and esteemed by all his neighbours – save a few who envied him, such as King Nicolas, of whom we'll speak in due course, who so resented Philip of Macedon's qualities and renown that he was finally killed by the hand of King Alexander himself, the said Philip's son.

When he was ready to marry, this King Philip, so noble and so feared, with the guidance and approval of his barons took to wife a most noble lady, good, beautiful, worthy and wise, named Olympias. She was a princess, the daughter of the king of Armenia, who was one of the mightiest and wealthiest kings then reigning in all the world – and she was his only daughter. She was well raised indeed and had acquired all honourable qualities: according to my source, had all honour been lost or expunged from the world, it could have been rediscovered in her. This lady loved and respected all worthy men and, with the utmost discernment, would give to them generously when she saw the need. Of the joyful arts of the chase and the hunt, of training and flying the falcon and sparrowhawk, she was the mistress; of harps and all other instruments – the organ, the psaltery – she knew the notes and the songs and the words; of all elegance in dress and gracious adornment she was the sovereign lady; her judgement of when to speak and when to stay silent was perfect. And with all this, she was wonderfully generous with her wealth: to all valiant men intent upon seeking deeds of arms and chivalry she would give unstintingly, providing them with the finest horses and chargers and armour and weapons and whatever else she imagined they might need.

CHAPTER III

How certain malicious and envious men began to spread rumours about this worthy lady Olympias.

Olympias, then, wife of King Philip of Macedon and mother of the good King Alexander, was modest, gracious, courteous, generous in giving, beloved of all worthy hearts, ever constant in morals and conduct and seeking always to enhance her virtues. But certain false, wicked, envious detractors and scandalmongers began to slander, disparage, defame and denigrate this good lady (as

---

[1]   The medieval kingdom of Alania lay in the Caucasus, and the 15th-century audience, if they recognised the name, would probably have understood it to refer to a broad expanse of territory to the north and east of Macedon.

a good many still do today, and what a shame and a pity it is that they've been allowed to hold sway so long!). They whispered among themselves:

'Look how false and unfaithful that woman is! Her body wouldn't be satisfied by all the men in the world! What a cuckold she's making of our lord! He's well and truly deceived by her, that's certain!'

These rumours spread till they finally reached the ears of Alexander[1] himself – but more of that anon. For the moment let me tell you the grounds of their wicked slander. At that time there dwelt a man in the land of Macedon named Nectanebus: a man of devious ways indeed, full of arcane skills and knowledge, a master of astronomy celestial and terrestrial, and a perfect magician to boot, adept in all manner of sorcery and the arts of divination. On account of his divinations and his strange, outlandish, mysterious practices the noble lady Olympias had certain dealings with this man, for he told her of the future through his spells and conjurations: in particular he predicted the night she would conceive King Alexander, and when she would bear him, and that he would be a man of great valour. And indeed, at the end of her term, when she felt she was about to give birth, she summoned Nectanebus and he came to her at once and cast his spells. And he declared that the said Alexander would not live long and at the end of his days would be poisoned – but first would have mastery over most of the earth. 'And not only,' he said, 'will he be lord of the earth, but of the air and of the sea.'

And that's why those malcontents, with their false, treacherous, wicked tongues, claimed that this enchanter was Alexander's father.[2] A good few such two-faced slanderers are still around! God rid us of them!

CHAPTER IV

Of the wonders that attended the birth of the noble King Alexander.

Being a woman of fine constitution, this worthy and noble lady, the king of Armenia's daughter, wife and spouse of the noble King Philip of Macedon, had not been with him long before she was pregnant with a splendid son, named at his birth Alexander. She delivered him after the due and customary term of all women, but at the moment of his birth numerous signs were seen and heard in the heavens in every place across the whole wide world. According to my source, the skies changed to a multitude of colours and were filled with booming, pealing thunder, shocking and alarming many people. And not only was the sky disturbed: the earth, too, quaked in many places and large parts of the sea, indeed, turned red. What's more, animals shook with fear and dread – a

[1]   The text reads 'King Philip', but in view of later events (below, p.36), the following phrase – 'but more of that anon' – makes a reference to Alexander far more pertinent.
[2]   Wauquelin follows his source, the verse *Roman d'Alexandre*, in rejecting the tradition that Alexander's father was Nectanebus, a former king of Egypt, as clearly stated in the Prose *Alexander* romance – the anonymous thirteenth-century adaptation into French of the *Historia de Preliis* (Leo the Archpriest's tenth-century Latin translation of the Greek Alexander romance). For the Prose *Alexander*'s version of the story, see Appendix 1.

notable sign to be sure. But that's not all: beyond all this, and a mighty joy, at the very same hour as Alexander thirty princes' sons were born, most of them from Greece and the surrounding lands. In relating the deeds of the noble king the history will tell of these men, for they were the ones who helped him achieve his conquests and endured many hardships with him, suffering scorching heat in India and other lands and spending their whole lives in arms.

The meaning of the signs that accompanied the birth of the noble Alexander is plain enough: reason suggests that everything trembled at his birth because everything was due to be his subject, as will be clearly seen in the story that follows.

CHAPTER V

*Of Alexander's upbringing, and to whom he was entrusted
for his instruction in liberal and moral sciences.*

And thus it was that this child who proved to be so noble and valiant was born and came into the world, and you can well imagine that the people – in Macedon, that is – were overwhelmed with joy. But all their joy and happiness could not compare with his father's and his mother's: they more than anyone loved the child. And they rejoiced not only for their own son's birth but also for the births of the other noble children which, according to my source, saw mighty celebration throughout the land of Greece: the word among the worthy was that by these noble princes the realms of Greece and adjacent lands would come to be gloriously ruled and governed – and so they were indeed, as you'll hear in due course.

The upbringing of this newborn child, the subject of numerous divinations and predictions, was arranged as befitted his station. He was nursed and raised so well that, truly, he daily grew in beauty and understanding. At the age of one year, two and three, his ways and behaviour were already a dream to behold: he was so cheerful, charming, strong, brave and daring that no equal of his age could be found in all the world. He wasn't big in build, but he was so gracious and had such a way with words that everyone was amazed. And everyone, too, admired his mature discernment: he was only ever seen with the wisest and most worthy; he was never impressed by fools, snipers, frauds – he shunned them and despised them, and kept company only with honourable men, whose advice and guidance he heard with keen and polite attention.

And then, when he reached the age of five or six, he was given a tutor to educate him in all liberal and moral science. This tutor taught and instructed him as thoroughly as he saw fit, being a man of unparalleled wisdom: indeed, this tutor was the greatest philosopher the world has ever seen, celebrated by all scholars to this day. He was Aristotle, the master of philosophy. Anyone wishing to know what he taught Alexander should read a book called *De Secretis Secretorum*,[1] in

---

[1]   A vast literature in many languages surrounds Alexander's teacher Aristotle, and many different works are attributed to him with varying (and largely dubious) claims to authen-

which may be found fine, sublime learning for the edification of all worthy men – but we shall say nothing of it here, on account of its great length.

CHAPTER VI

*How at the age of ten Alexander dreamt a wondrous dream
while sleeping on his bed.*

One day when he reached the age of ten, so says my source, this child Alexander was lying asleep in bed when he was visited by a strange and mysterious vision. He dreamt he'd been given an egg to eat, an egg, it seemed, that no one else had wanted to touch or taste. As soon as he took hold of it he started to roll it across the floor, and he kept rolling it across the marble flags of the hall of his dream until the shell cracked; and the moment it broke there burst from the egg a huge and terrible dragon of monstrous and forbidding form. And then it seemed that, with astounding speed, this dragon's flight encompassed all the earth before it suddenly fell dead and was promptly buried in a tomb. The serpent's death so disturbed the sky that the whole world, it seemed, was engulfed in shadows which cast forth mighty storms and tempests. Amid the tumult Alexander woke, shocked and bewildered by his dream which had seemed to him completely real: his chamberlains had no mean trouble calming and appeasing him.

CHAPTER VII

*How King Philip of Macedon summoned several learned men
to interpret his son Alexander's vision.*

As I say, young Alexander was very unsettled by his dream, so much so that he went to his father as soon as he could and, very shaken, reported what he'd seen. When King Philip heard what his son had to say he was equally startled; he didn't know what to think, other than to send to the city of Athens at once, without delay, to seek out all the wisest scholars and soothsayers who could be found.

Only three came. The first was named in Greek Astatus, the second Saligor des Lieres and the third was Aristotle, who'd returned to Athens for no other reason than to fetch the other two. With these masters came a number of others, to escort them and to hear the recounting and discussion of young Alexander's dream. When all these learned men had arrived and assembled, they were ushered into a chamber where the king sat with his wife and their son Alexander. And there, in the presence of them all, King Philip explained why he'd sum-

ticity. Of these the most influential in the Middle Ages was one bearing the Latin title *De Secretis Secretorum*: it enjoyed a wide circulation from at least the tenth century until the seventeenth. Some of it is certainly Greek in origin and based on genuine Aristotelian doctrine, but much is clearly traceable to Islamic sources. In its structure *De Secretis Secretorum* takes the form of a lengthy letter from Aristotle to Alexander, supposedly sent to the king during his conquest of Persia.

moned them, whereupon they asked Alexander to relate his dream as accurately as he could. He described it in every detail, very clearly and carefully; and having heard his tale they began to discuss and reflect upon it from many different angles, until at last the aforenamed three arrived at a fairly similar conclusion, and each of them responded in his own way, as follows.

Chapter VIII

The interpretation of Alexander's dream given in Greek by Astatus.

Because he was the eldest Astatus was the first to speak, and he did so in Greek. He was a wise man indeed, a fine soothsayer well versed in magic and divination through fire. His mighty, brimming knowledge had earned him the name Astatus: he knew the paths of all the stars and planets in the skies.[1] And he said:

'Most esteemed lord, and all here present, as I understand and interpret it, I'd venture this explanation of young Alexander's dream. The egg represents a vainglorious pride which is doomed to be short-lived, for just as an egg cracks and breaks as soon as it hits the ground, so does pride when toppled from its height. As for the serpent that burst from the egg, you surely know that the serpent is a dangerous creature indeed, vicious and malign and always lurking, bent on destruction; and I understand the serpent to be some prince or lord who in his pride seeks to dominate all the world and to bring all – kings, dukes, counts, emperors – under his heel. He means to take by force their towers, their forts, their castles. But like a dragon's life, his reign will not last long: he will die young, his life cut short.'

King Philip was very shocked at hearing this: he began to wonder what it might mean, and feared he was going to lose his land or lordship to one of his enemies.

Chapter IX

The interpretation given by the second wise man, named Saligor de Lieres.

Once Astatus had delivered in Greek his explanation of the dream, Saligor de Lieres rose and said:

'Most esteemed lord, I put it to you that a dream has little weight: it is an idle thing that passes like a breeze. No one who sets much store by dreams is accounted wise or authoritative: we lapse into daydreams all the time! But one could, of course, draw some predictive meaning from the dream: an egg is a weak and fragile thing, easily broken; the serpent that came from it could be some creature or man or whatever who in his pride – the serpent is a proud

---

[1]   This line makes most sense if 'Astatus' (which appears as 'Astarus' in the verse *Roman d'Alexandre*) is taken to be a corruption of 'Astraeus', the god of the dusk in Greek mythology who was father of the four winds and, most significantly, of the five planets Mercury, Mars, Venus, Saturn and Jupiter.

beast, to be sure – means to wage war on the world or its people and force his neighbours into subjection; but you could say that the one symbolised by the serpent, being such a wild, unstable creature, will try to conquer lands and distant parts but will not live long at all, dying a rapid death in the true manner of the serpent or dragon.'

When King Philip heard this interpretation he was even more alarmed and shaken than before, for it corresponded so closely to the first.

CHAPTER X

How the wise philosopher Aristotle interpreted Alexander's dream.

These words of Saligor created a great stir among the lords and the learned men alike. Then master Aristotle spoke up, saying:

'Silence now, sirs, if you please, and I'll tell you what I take the dream to mean.'

They all fell silent then; and he said: 'Truly, my lord, in my view the egg of which he spoke is no trivial thing: it signifies this present world that we inhabit, and the yolk within, suspended in the middle, signifies the earth at the centre of the world, filled with people of their various stations. And the serpent that emerged from the egg is without doubt the valiant young Alexander himself who was visited by the dream: with his courage and his daring he will conquer most of the earth – provided, that is, he is given good guidance, as he shall be, God willing. And all others will count themselves fortunate to pay him tribute and serve him, and every man on earth will be his vassal. But as for his life and the length thereof, he will need to take care, for its course will be fraught with dangers.'

At this a joyous hubbub erupted in the hall, and no one, as you may imagine, felt more delight and joy than King Philip and his wife Queen Olympias. They began to pay Aristotle the highest honour, and presented him with all the gold and silver he could wish. And they bade him stay as Alexander's tutor, to give him whatever teaching and instruction he saw fit, and Alexander received him gladly.

So Aristotle began to teach him all manner of languages and sciences, though we won't discuss them here; and Alexander was so receptive and intelligent that Aristotle taught him readily whatever he pleased, for the youth treated him with all honour and respect.

CHAPTER XI

How Alexander killed the sorcerer Nectanebus,
who had slandered him and his mother.

Alexander, then, was instructed by his teacher Aristotle, and so effectively that all talk was of the young prince's learning and valour; people came from far and wide to see him on account of both his courage and his sound, wise judgement. Young squires above all counted themselves most honoured if they could enter his service, for he was so greatly endowed with courtesy as well as wisdom that no one could surpass him.

At the same time came Nectanebus, the sorcerer of whom we spoke before; he was highly commended at court, and strove hard to gain Alexander's affections. And indeed, Alexander listened to him avidly because of his intriguing ways and his magic arts: he made wonders appear before him – towers and castles and men-at-arms, and bridges and rivers – and sometimes he conjured visions of mighty, fearsome battles and, it seemed, civil strife. So Alexander was always pleased to see him.

But the populace, incorrigible then as they still are now, whispered that it was no wonder Alexander was well disposed towards Nectanebus: he was his father, and had used sorcery to sire him![1] These rumours reached the ears of Alexander, and he went and spoke of them to his mother. She was mortified, and told him the certain truth; and when Alexander realised his mother had been shamefully slandered he was so outraged that he didn't know what to do. But then he made up his mind, and I'll tell you what he did: one day, as Nectanebus arrived at court to see young Alexander and was making his way up a marble staircase, Alexander spotted him; he waited till he reached the top and then grabbed the surprised Nectanebus and flung him down the steps; he tumbled to the very bottom, scattering his brains on the marble as he fell. So Nectanebus was suddenly no more. But that didn't stop the rumours continuing as before; worse still, they were now saying Alexander had killed his father!

CHAPTER XII

Of the horse named Bucephalus, ridden by Alexander in many battles.

At the time of young Alexander's birth there was a queen of Egypt, a most wise and noble woman, who was eager to secure peace with her neighbours. Hearing that King Philip of Macedon had a newborn son by his wife Olympias, she decided to send him a gift of an extraordinary young colt, and dispatched an embassy to present it to him. Let me describe this horse: his crupper was fawn and his flanks were bay, and he had a head like an ox, huge eyes like a lion's and a tail like a peacock's; but he was superbly built: his body was all one could wish for in a horse. He had been given the name Bucephalus.[2] And truly, he was so fearsome that no one dared go near him, and when he was full-grown his size was such that he was kept shut up in a stone-walled pen[3] – and not without reason, for he would attack and devour men and women! That's why they locked him up, and when they caught any criminal they would put him to death by throwing him in this pen with the horse, who would crush

---

[1] See Appendix 1 for the story as it appears in the Prose *Alexander*.
[2] Its meaning in Greek is 'ox-head'.
[3] Literally 'in a wall of stone'. In the verse *Roman d'Alexandre* the horse is 'shut up in a tower, enclosed by walls' (Branch I stanza 19, from which Wauquelin has taken his description of Bucephalus); in the Prose *Alexander* he is kept 'in a big iron cage' (Hilka's edition, p.35).

and devour him instantly! There was no man brave enough to set foot inside those walls. And when the horse whinnied the sound was so terrible that all who heard it were filled with fear and dread.

Then one day young Alexander was out and about in the city with a crowd of young squires who all yearned to be knighted with him; and as they played and sported he heard the horse whinny and began to tremble. He went to his tutor Aristotle and asked him what it was he'd heard. But Aristotle wouldn't answer and changed the subject, knowing that Alexander's courage was such that as soon as he heard about the horse he'd want to go and see it, and he was very afraid it would lead to trouble. When Alexander saw his tutor reluctant to speak of it he didn't press the matter; but straight afterwards he asked one of his dukes, by the name of Festion, who told him all about it.

Chapter XIII
How Alexander mounted Bucephalus, the horse no one dared go near.

Seeing Aristotle unwilling to answer his questions, Alexander feigned indifference but left him as soon as he could, and went to the duke named Festion and implored him, by all the love he felt for him, to explain the noise he'd heard. Festion didn't dare withhold the truth, and when Alexander heard what he had to say he swore by all his gods that he'd go and see what this animal was like. He summoned most of the people around him, and when they assembled he placed his hand on his head and vowed to go and see the monstrous horse, and forbade anyone, on pain of death, to be so bold as to stop him.

He headed at once for the stone enclosure where the horse was kept and bade that it be unlocked. Then he opened the door. The moment he saw the horse he was filled with joy: he thought him astonishingly handsome; and likewise, when Bucephalus set eyes on Alexander he bowed before him in the most amazing manner, just as if Alexander were his master and he'd known him and been riding him since the beginning of time: the horse was as placid as a maid. And Alexander stroked his crupper and his mane; he let him do whatever he wished. Then Alexander called for a bridle; hardly anyone was brave enough to take it near the horse, but as soon as Alexander had it he placed it on Bucephalus himself. Once it was fitted he asked for a saddle, and they brought him one which he put straight on. Then he led the horse out of its pen. You'd have laughed to see the people fleeing in all directions! They were so terrified they didn't know which way to turn! But Alexander soon reassured them, as he mounted the horse and rode him wherever he wished and then dismounted when he chose, by which point the people's panic was stilled.

Chapter XIV
How Alexander was dubbed into the order of knighthood.

And so it was that Alexander tamed the horse Bucephalus, to the awe and amazement of everyone. It prompted a good many auguries and predictions, and his father and mother in particular thought it a wondrous deed and said their son was surely destined for great things – as will prove to be the case hereafter.

In the light of what had happened, the barons began to say that it would be good if Alexander were knighted now, for he'd grown sturdy, strong and brave, not to mention peerlessly wise. They discussed this with the king and queen, but because he was so very young – still only thirteen or fourteen – his father would not consent. But his mother the queen, always eager for her child's advancement, gain and honour, was delighted by the request of the barons and nobles of Macedon; she spoke to her husband and argued that he was growing old now and needed nothing so much as rest, and that it would be good to knight his son Alexander so that he'd be truly feared and respected.

'And you know,' she said, 'you've many enemies, and if your son were dubbed into the order of knighthood he could lead your men in battle – with the expert guidance of yourself and your men – and they'd be all the bolder and more committed to great deeds.'

The king could see the wisdom in his wife the queen's words, and gave orders for all due preparations to be made. Now, there were some four hundred young squires at the court who all longed to be knighted with Alexander, and when they heard that a day had been appointed for his dubbing they begged the king to let them be knighted with him, and he graciously agreed.

As you can well imagine, the preparations made throughout the land were glorious, magnificent. And when the day of the solemn ritual arrived the baths were prepared for the squires' cleansing as was then the custom. But the noble youth Alexander said he would bathe only in the salt sea; so they went down to the sea's edge, and there all those who wished to be knighted duly bathed.

CHAPTER XV
Of the rites performed and the garments and equipment bestowed upon Alexander.

And so the young Alexander bathed in the sea along with all the other squires. Then his mother called forward two packhorses laden with new raiment, all made of rich silk cloth, exquisite and most costly; and when it arrived Alexander's instant wish was that his companions should be dressed and equipped before him. This was done; and no expense was spared, either in gorgeous vair and miniver[1] or in the finest arms and horses. And Alexander bade that the poorest be the first to be supplied and served.

Once they'd all been clad they made ready to dress Alexander as befitted such a lord, and you may be sure he was superbly equipped and richly apparelled, both in garments and in armour. I can't describe his clothing, but I can tell you that he was given a magnificent hauberk, which the records say was forged on an isle called Dimer. Its ventail[2] was of pure gold and the woven links of its skirts

[1]   The French refers to *'beau vair'* and *'beau gris'*, squirrel furs of different colours.
[2]   The panel of the mailcoat that protected the lower face.

were finest silver; and truly, it was so strongly meshed and tempered that no lance or crossbow bolt could pierce or breach it, yet no man ever saw a coat of mail so good and light. The band that bound the crown of his helm was beyond all valuation; it bore twelve precious stones of wondrous might and power: they kept the helm as cool and fresh inside as out, no matter how hot the work it saw, no matter what punishment it took. The shield that hung from Alexander's neck was blood-red[1] scattered with crowns of gold; and his sword was of finest steel, superbly tempered, and the belt and straps were splendid, most handsomely wrought.

And then, once Alexander was clad and equipped, his father, to increase his honour, made him king, setting a magnificent crown upon his head, whereupon the joy of the assembled company intensified a hundredfold, as all began to cry at once:

'Long live the king of Macedon!'

And after all this his father gave him the accolade, dubbing him knight. Then Bucephalus was brought to him, richly saddled and caparisoned and behaving as demurely as a bride. King Alexander stepped in the golden stirrups and leapt into the saddle; and as soon as he was mounted all the other newly dubbed knights mounted likewise, and began to spur their horses forward to send them bounding and charging about the field: it was a wonder to behold. And lances were promptly brought to them, most of which were shattered in moments as they launched into jousts and furious combat to prove their worth against each other, and all who beheld them were amazed by the mighty blows exchanged. They spent the whole morning like this, right up till dinner.

CHAPTER XVI

How King Philip of Macedon and his son Alexander were challenged by Nicolas, king of Armenia and Turkey.

Alexander and his fellow new knights, having enjoyed this sport till dinner, went to take their seats at the tables. And twelve of his closest friends and companions, all of them high princes, took it upon themselves to serve at table that day out of the love and affection they felt for the young King Alexander: the first was Antigonus, the second Danselin, the third Ariscé, the fourth Ptholomer, the fifth Festion, the sixth Perdicas, the seventh Leones, the eighth Abilla, the ninth Caulus, the tenth Licanor, the eleventh Philotas and the twelfth Emenidus. And there's no need to ask if the fare was good, for as you surely know, those who can afford it are always well served!

It was in the middle of this splendid feast, which lacked nothing in the way of minstrelsy and acrobatics and all manner of entertainment befitting royal state, that a messenger by the name of Crebrus, herald of Nicolas, king of Armenia

---

[1]   '*sinople*'. Although in later heraldry this word came to mean green, 'sinople' was origi-nally a blood or brownish red, the word deriving from the red-ochre clay found in and around the Black Sea city of Sinope.

and Turkey, arrived and entered the court. He came before King Philip, and in the presence of his son the young Alexander and all the dukes and counts and barons he said this:

'Philip, king of Macedon, praise and ever greater honour be to the noble Nicolas, king of Armenia and Turkey! Through me, his envoy and herald, he commands you as his sovereign, recognising that you are his inferior and subject, to render him such tribute as befits his noble, royal majesty, and to do so without delay, and to thank him for allowing you to hold your land in peace so long! If you refuse and make any objection, you must understand he will come with such a mighty force of Armenians and Turks that every tower, fort and stronghold in your land will be battered to the ground, you and your people will be reduced to eternal slavery, and your lordship will be annulled and given to a subject who'll pay him the service that is his due. Consider and take counsel now and kindly give a prompt response.'

CHAPTER XVII

The reply given by the young King Alexander to King Nicolas's herald, on behalf and in the name of his father.

W hen the herald had finished this speech (or something very like it), you can well imagine the court's dismay. And if anyone was upset, King Philip, I can tell you, was outraged! According to my source he was so wildly incensed that he was incapable of speech: with glowering gaze fixed on the herald, he rolled his eyes and ground his teeth and shook his head – everyone who beheld him was stricken with fear and awe. But while King Philip was overcome with fury, his son the young King Alexander – although he was no less enraged than his father and his face was ablaze with loathing – retained control; and like a truly wise man he rose and in lordly fashion took Emenidus of Arcadia by the arm, and leaning on his shoulder he stood before the messenger and said:

'Listen! You, who've just delivered King Nicolas of Armenia's bidding to my father, will go and tell him from me that as long as I live my father will never pay him tribute, for the land of Greece and its people have never owed any – rather, they're accustomed to demand and receive it from their neighbours! So I challenge him with fire and blood as my mortal enemy, and assure him that, for his offensive arrogance – he's full of it! – and his slight to Greece's authority, I shall separate his head from his shoulders – if he's brave enough to meet me in battle! This I solemnly swear, and I shan't rest in town or city till my every word is accomplished.'

With that he gave the herald leave to go, and had him plied with sumptuous gifts as a sign of nobility, worth and power.[1]

---

[1]   A passage, almost certainly not written by Wauquelin, is inserted here in one of the surviving manuscripts. See Appendix 2: 'Aristotle's Advice to Alexander'.

CHAPTER XVIII

How King Alexander mustered his forces to march into the land of Armenia.

Once the herald had gone King Alexander began to ponder how to carry out his mission with greatest honour. He sought the advice of the wisest men at court and especially, once again, of the supremely wise philosopher, his teacher Aristotle, who gave him further guidance befitting such a king: he advised him to beware of taking into his trust or affections any slave or traitor or anyone coveting gold or silver, and to surround himself always with the worthiest, most valiant men. 'And never take their service for granted, but pay and reward them well and generously.' That was the way to achieve and accomplish his ambition.

King Alexander, having taken thorough counsel, and feeling strengthened and cheered by the words of his great teacher Aristotle, came to his father and declared his determination to achieve his goal. He asked for his aid in supplying him with a sum of money to pay for troops, both horse and foot; and King Philip, overjoyed to see such fine, noble, soaring courage in his son Alexander, opened his treasury at once. Then he sent letters and missives – some of them prayers and entreaties, others outright commands – to everyone he thought might offer support, calling upon them to come to his son's aid in the hope of winning glorious renown and booty, and promising they'd be paid as handsomely as they could wish. According to my source, in less than a week Alexander had assembled more than sixty thousand troops, both cavalry and infantry. Among them were a good many impoverished noblemen, poorly equipped, but Alexander greeted them with honour, and with such generous gifts that they were all astonished by his largesse, graciousness and bounty.

Then you'd have seen tents and pavilions and all manner of war-gear loaded on to carts and wagons, along with engines and artillery and a vast supply of lances, shields, javelins, swords and pikes.[1] And when everything was packed and laden, Alexander ordered his army to begin their march to the kingdom of Armenia: he was determined to get there, come what may.

On they journeyed till they came to a sea port. They crossed the sea without the slightest trouble, and once they reached the further shore they made camp – their tents and lodges and pavilions covering an immense swathe of land – so that they could rest and organise their troops into divisions and battle order, making sure they'd be ready if the enemy attacked: they didn't want to be caught unprepared or lacking courage and resolve.

---

[1]   'Pikes' is a somewhat rough translation of *'faussars'*: the 'faussart' was a shafted weapon with a blade like a sickle or billhook, derived from improvised weapons used by peasant levies.

CHAPTER XIX

How the king appointed twelve commanders of his army,
who were called the twelve peers.

The noble young King Alexander, now arrived in the land of his enemies,
arranged his divisions and battalions according to the advice and guidance
of his teacher Aristotle. And he appointed twelve commanders of the army, referred to as the twelve peers; they were the twelve named previously – that's to
say: Antigonus, Danselin, Ariscé, Ptholomer, Festion, Perdicas, Leones, Abilla,
Caulus, Licanor, Philotas and Emenidus. Foremost of them all was Emenidus,
duke of Arcadia, who became bearer of the royal gonfalon.[1]

With all duly ordered, King Alexander commanded every man to rally to his
banner, on pain of death; and he declared that no one should continue unless
he had the courage and the will to live or die with him. Then he gave orders for
the vanguard to advance towards the enemy, and that everyone, in his allotted
battalion, should march or ride in smart and serried ranks. So the army set off
at the king's command, and scouts and foragers started seeking out towns and
forts and castles.

As they advanced, the vanguard met a squire, a most handsome, pleasant
youth with sparkling eyes, fair hair and a bright and open face. They asked him
who he was and he replied that he was a poor squire in search of King Alexander, because he'd heard he needed soldiers and that he would re-equip poor
noblemen and restore their fortunes. 'So if you know where he is, sirs, please tell
me, for as you can see, I could do with help![2] And if I can be of assistance or serve
him in any way I'll do so gladly.'

So he was taken to Alexander; and as soon as his escort pointed to the king the
youth stepped up and bowed to him with great grace and maturity. And when
the king returned his greeting the squire said:

'Noble and most esteemed prince, may God enhance your majesty and honour! I pray you kindly hear me, poor though I am, and don't despise me for my
poverty and ill-clad state: poor though I am, I'm the son of King Omer, brother
of King Darius of Persia. The truth is that my uncle Darius, consumed by greed,
seized my father and threw him in prison where he died; and now he's robbed
me of my inheritance and driven me from my land, threatening to have me beheaded! For that reason – and because of your great renown and reputation –
I've come to your noble majesty to crave your aid and support; I wish to be your
servant and vassal, for I could serve no nobler or mightier lord under the canopy
of heaven! And so, most revered lord, I pray you take me into your service and I
shall serve you with perfect loyalty.'

King Alexander was moved to tears by the squire's words, as were all the

---

[1]   The royal banner.
[2]   In the verse *Roman d'Alexandre* he is described as 'barefoot, shoeless' and he tells Alexan-
        der "I haven't the money to buy myself dinner!" (Branch I, stanza 32).

princes present. He asked the youth his name, and he said: 'Sire, my name is Sanson Dailly.'

'Sanson,' said the king, 'I accept you into my service this day, as a member of my court.' Then he had him freshly armed and dressed in fine new clothes and splendidly equipped with everything befitting a king's son, and said: 'Dear friend, I swear upon my crown that I'll restore you to your land if I can, no matter what the cost.'

At this Sanson fell at his feet and kissed his leg, and paid him homage as his sovereign lord.

CHAPTER XX

How King Alexander sent Sanson, son of King Omer of Persia, to deliver a message and pronouncement to King Nicolas of Armenia.

Once Sanson, son of King Omer of Persia, had been restored to his proper state of dignity, he was clearly a noble youth indeed: he looked the part entirely, in his bearing and his every word. Alexander was delighted to see him so, and said:

'My army's much enhanced by the addition of a king's son! Praise be to all our gods!'

In reply then Sanson said: 'My lord, I must tell you in all truthfulness that when I left Persia, where many are intent on hounding me to my death, I passed through the great city of Caesarea. There I heard that King Nicolas of Armenia had lately taken it into his head to attack Greece and exact from the land the tribute he desired or put it all to the torch. To achieve this he was busily mustering all his forces: knights in countless numbers! I'm telling you this because I saw it with my own eyes: you need to take counsel and consider what to do.'

The king pondered Sanson's words for a moment, and then said: 'Sanson, dear friend and companion, you're to go back to Caesarea on my behalf, since you know the way better than anyone and also know Nicolas, who calls himself king of Armenia, and tell him he's no need to go to Greece to find its king, for he's already here in his land with a hundred thousand men-at-arms! And they'll either all die – and myself first of all – or they'll repay his demand by ensuring that after he's met them he won't feel like asking any king for tribute ever again! I want him to know from me – so this you'll tell him – that I mean to pay him tribute with my sword, and the receipt he leaves will be his head! And that's not all: you'll also tell him that if he's brave enough he can come and meet me in battle to defend himself and his land – that's all I want from him. And whoever wins will have his adversary's land and kingdom, for anyone who can't defend his land isn't worthy to be its lord.'

When Alexander had spoken thus, Sanson took his seal of commission and mounted and set out on his way as the king had bidden him. He rode on day by day until he came to Caesarea the Great, where he found King Nicolas in his palace surrounded by all his counsellors and the foremost barons of the land. As he stepped into his presence he bowed to him as his rank demanded; then he handed him the noble King Alexander's seal and said this:

Chapter XXI

How Sanson Dailly of Persia delivered his message to King Nicolas of Armenia.

'The noble King Alexander bids me repeat to you, Nicolas, who call yourself king of Armenia, the defiant threat of fire and blood he sent back with your herald, and to tell you that, since you've demanded tribute for his land, he's bringing it with an escort of a hundred thousand men! He's already in your land preparing to make payment; he won't leave till one of you is dead, and his only wish is to discharge the tribute by severing your head! So he challenges you to battle, either army to army or in single combat; the latter would be his preference, the condition being that the victor will hold his adversary's land in its entirety, freely, uncontested, as its sovereign lord.'

With that he fell silent. King Nicolas was hunched and glowering, wild with rage; then after a moment's pause he raised his head and, fixing a furious gaze upon the messenger, asked him his name and who he was.

He replied that his name was 'Sanson Dailly, son of King Omer of Persia and nephew of King Darius. But my uncle has robbed me of my inheritance and driven me from my land; so I made my way to the noble King Alexander who received me at his court with great grace and generosity and took me into his company; and he's done me the honour of promising to restore me to my land and to give me ten thousand men-at-arms to lead into battle under my banner! Truly, I believe he's the finest, most gracious, courteous, generous king who'll ever be born or who ever lived since Adam our first father left the earthly paradise. So I swear that if you meet in battle there's no doubt one of you will be killed or captured – unless you decide to flee in shame!'

At this King Nicolas shrieked with laughter, as if they were the words of an idiot; then he gave the following reply:

Chapter XXII

How King Nicolas tried to win over Sanson by persuasion or by threat, but failed.

'Sanson Dailly,' he said, 'it seems you hold this King Alexander in high esteem. Well, you can praise him all you like – we know all about him! Firstly, how his mother conceived him, and by whom;[1] secondly, how he's full of arrogance and presumption; and thirdly, stuffed with pride and vanity!

'But listen now: judging from what you say you're of my lineage and blood; it seems to me there's more reason for you, being a blood-relation, to give your faith, honour, service and aid to me than to one who's nothing to you – and

---

[1]   The insinuation being that he's the bastard son of Nectanebus.

who's a bastard born of poor blood![1] Think about it: cutting off your nose to spite your face is self-defeating and defiling! So I pray and entreat you, dear friend and kinsman as I consider you to be, avoid this grave mistake and leave that wretch, who before the month is out won't know where to put himself! He's going to find his adventure's a poisoned chalice – and I'm going to make him drink his fill! So join our side and lend us your support and aid. If you do, dear kinsman, I give you my word that a quarter of my kingdom will be wholly yours, and I'll make you my standard-bearer and chief counsellor. What's more, I promise to restore you to your land as free and sovereign lord, and to reconcile you with your uncle Darius, by force if he won't accept peace willingly.'

Sanson considered Nicolas's words; then he said: 'That's a generous offer indeed, sir. But I know you and my uncle well enough to be sure you wouldn't honour a single word! So I've no intention of breaking my commitment to my lord King Alexander; I shall serve him to the end: I know him to be a man who does what he says and fulfils his promises – he is fair, loyal and true, a man of unfailing integrity, justice and wisdom. So you're wasting your breath: I decline your offer absolutely.'

When King Nicolas heard this reply he was enraged beyond measure and said: 'Very well, then! I see I can't persuade you and you're set on being stubborn – so be it! But let me tell you, when you decide to repent there'll be no way back! And you'll realise your error soon enough! Yes: to show you the scale of your mistake and folly I bid you leave my presence forthwith and go back to that king of yours you rate so highly, and tell him from me that before ten days are out he'll have the battle he's after, army to army or man to man as he chooses. And let the upshot be as he proposed: either he or I shall be lord of his adversary's land!'

Chapter XXIII

How Sanson of Persia returned to Alexander with the news that battle would be joined.

With that Sanson mounted and thrust in his spurs, and rode back with all speed to the noble Alexander's army. He found his way to the king as soon as he could, and the moment Alexander saw him he ran to greet him with open arms and embraced him and kissed him, showing his great love and respect for the youth. After this hearty and courteous welcome he asked him how he'd fared, and Sanson replied:

'Esteemed lord, I delivered your message to King Nicolas as exactly as I could, just as you bade me. And the reply he gave – and you may be sure he meant it – was that in ten days at the most, unless you pay him tribute for your land, he'll give you a battle – army to army or man to man, whichever you choose – that will crush you so utterly that all who hear of it will be in awe. With his slippery

---

[1]   'Poor blood' because in Wauquelin's text Nectanebus is merely 'a sorcerer': there's no suggestion that he's the former king of Egypt as in the Prose *Alexander* (see Appendix 1).

tongue he tried to persuade me to change sides, but as I told him, I know his true nature; I'll never serve him as long as I live – rather, if it please you, my service and obedience I commit to you.'

When Alexander heard this message, and knew King Nicolas was set in his misguided ways and persisted in demanding tribute for the land of Greece, he issued orders for everyone to arm and prepare at once and for everything to be packed and loaded, for if his gods were willing he was going to set out at the crack of dawn next day. His command was duly carried out, 'and I'm not going to stop,' he said, 'till my enemy Nicolas and I are face to face; then he'll wish he was the other side of the Red Sea and that I'd never set foot in his land!'

Now I'll tell you about King Nicolas, who was deeply riled by Sanson's message, as I said. As soon as Sanson was gone he set his whole palace to work producing letters to all his knights and subjects, bidding them come fully armed and equipped – without a moment's delay, as soon as they read them – to the city of Caesarea. He wrote:

'Some Alexander of Allier[1] continues to defy me. Indeed he has now entered my land with a great band of thieves and murderers! I mean to make him pay for his haughty, insolent presumption, for this offensive outrage in daring to flout our might and royal majesty.' And he added: 'I will accept no excuses! Failure to answer this summons will cost you your head!'

And indeed, my source says he mustered more than two hundred thousand – some willingly, some by coercion, but all of them fearless, bold and strong. But the truth is that the majority harboured a mortal hatred of King Nicolas because of the taxes, levies and maletolts[2] he daily inflicted and piled upon them. All the same, he welcomed them with joy and honour, each according to his rank, and bade them pitch their tents and pavilions in a fine stretch of land beside a river called the Basir.

CHAPTER XXIV
How King Alexander and King Nicolas formed their battalions, and of the mighty battle that followed.

At first light next day the young King Alexander ordered his whole force to advance as he had said; and, in brief, he pressed on swiftly until he was so close to the enemy that the two armies could clearly see each other. Needless to say, he'd drawn up all his squadrons in fine order: as captain and commander of the first battalion he had appointed Emenidus; of the second, Perdicas; of the third, Caulus; of the fourth, Leones; of the fifth, Antigonus; of the sixth, Antiocus; of the seventh, Danselin; of the eighth, Ptholomer; of the ninth, Licanor; of

---

[1] This name first appears in the 12th-century *Fuerre de Gadres*, and Wauquelin would have found references to Alexander as *'le roi d'Alier'* at several points in the verse *Roman d'Alexandre*. Sandrine Hériché suggests in her edition of Wauquelin that *'Allier'* may have derived from 'Illyricum'.
[2] Usually understood as a duty paid on wool.

the tenth, Ariscé; of the eleventh, Philotas. He commanded the twelfth himself, but had one named Arides to oversee and lead them, because he wanted to ride from place to place so that he could better give steel and courage to all his men. He also wanted to begin the battle by striking the first blow, as indeed he did!

And just as Alexander had deployed and ordered his troops, so had King Nicolas: he, too, had formed twelve battalions, and they were vast and mighty – in his squadrons and divisions were fully twice the number of men-at-arms that could be seen in Alexander's.

Then, once all the battalions were in due order, they began to advance towards each other, step for step, amid such a clamour of clarions, trumpets and every imaginable instrument that it would have drowned out pealing thunder. And what an array you'd have seen of banners and pennons and lances, javelins, swords and pikes![1] All the knights were striving to keep their men-at-arms in line, but it wasn't long before a king, a man of mighty physique, bold and hungry to win praise and renown, broke from the ranks of Nicolas's battalion and rode out ahead of them all, straight towards the enemy line, inviting battle with some valiant man from Alexander's host. But Alexander wouldn't let anyone go but himself! He prepared to meet him, lowered his lance and visor, spurred his horse and charged, so fearsomely that he thrust his lance clean through his body and bore him dead to the ground; then he rode back to his cheering, awe-struck men.

Now all the battalions advanced and clashed, hand to hand. Bristling spears and lances pushed and thrust, knights and horses came crashing down, brains and blood gushed and spattered, and arms and heads and legs and necks were severed pitilessly: it seemed the sky was raining gore. Men were captured and rescued again with fearful effort and at terrible cost: the worthy, the brave and the valiant were killing each other in a slaughter piteous and terrible to behold. And in the midst of it all was Alexander, naked sword in hand, seeking out the greatest numbers and the thickest press, performing such feats that the truth would read like fiction! In the thick of it, too, was King Darius's nephew Sanson, striving with all his might to win honour and renown as he fought for Alexander, dealing such blows with his sword that no one could withstand him: every blow felled an enemy. And his feats of arms won him high honour indeed, for he killed one of Nicolas's dukes, the most powerful man in all his army.

The twelve commanders named above were fighting just as mightily; but if I were to describe their deeds in detail it might grow tiresome – they each performed a multitude! – so I'll say no more. But you should know that the Greeks and Macedonians fought so well that day that the Armenians and Turks were routed, and started fleeing in disarray towards the city of Caesarea.

[1]   See note 1 above, p.41.

CHAPTER XXV

How King Nicolas challenged Alexander to single combat,
in which he was to lose his head.

And so the routed Turks and Armenians fled towards Caesarea, and a hot
pursuit and chase began as you can well imagine: the Greeks went after
them with ferocious courage and sent them tumbling and trampling over each
other, especially the Armenians, who were crushed in narrow passes in their
desperate flight. There was rich and copious booty taken there, for many surrendered as prisoners. Among them was one of Nicolas's nephews who was
seized and killed – which was a great shame, as he would have yielded a massive ransom.

But I'll say no more about the captured – or the slain – for it would take an
eternity to record them all! I want to tell you about King Nicolas, who'd taken
refuge in his city as a shameful fugitive. Once he was back inside the walls he
assembled all his counsellors to discuss how to be rid of Alexander, who clearly
had no intention of leaving: he'd advanced right up to the city, and it seemed
he didn't mean to leave till he'd taken it by force or willingly. Opinions were
divided; one of his counsellors said:

'Our city is immensely strong, with high and mighty walls and towers and
ramparts, and garrisoned with fine men-at-arms who can deliver fierce and ef-
fective sorties against those Greeks if they decide to camp down and besiege us:
we can win more from them than they from us! So I say we let them stay there:
they can bore themselves to death!'

But another said: 'My lord, I say you should proclaim a general levy:[1] summon all men capable of carrying a club, on pain of death! And when your army's
mustered we'll do battle with Alexander again, and fight as men should when
they mean to defend their lands and possessions. Don't be dismayed if Fortune
was against us in the first encounter: She may well turn Her wheel again and
raise us up once more! We mustn't look so crestfallen that our enemies grow in
courage!'

These views and many more were expressed by Nicolas's men as they strove
to give him new heart. But after hearing them all he was overtaken by a spirit of
true prowess and courage, and said:

'My noble friends, I know you've all given me advice as you think best; but
I've come to my own decision now, and if I can I mean to see it through. I don't
want you to have to risk your lives; and since this Alexander is clearly endowed
with high prowess I shall offer him battle man to man, and whichever one of us
is victorious will take complete and undisputed possession of his enemy's land.
So it shall be: my mind is made up.'

He immediately prepared an envoy to take this message; and as soon as he

---

[1]   '*assembler tout votre arriere ban*'. The term '*arrière-ban*' usually implied a summoning of all
        able-bodied men.

understood the king's intention and the terms of battle, the envoy made his way to Alexander and delivered the message as precisely as he could. King Alexander, his spirits soaring, received it with pleasure; and in conclusion, the envoy went to work and carried pledges between both parties ensuring that the terms and proposed conditions would be observed.

CHAPTER XXVI

How Alexander slew King Nicolas on the field of battle
and gave his land to duke Ptholomer.

With terms and battleground agreed, it wasn't long before Nicolas emerged from his city. He was handsomely, strikingly armed and equipped, and came with a magnificent escort of all his foremost barons whom he chose to accompany him to the field of battle. As soon as he arrived there so did Alexander, who was no less richly armed and equipped than Nicolas. Then all the attendant barons from both sides made way and cleared the field at once, and the herald was at hand and declared that each man now should do his duty.

Then the two champions, filled with prowess and courage, drove in their spurs and charged at each other with all the force they could summon, each intent on destroying his foe; and in this first clash they exchanged such blows that their lances smashed to pieces. Then, valiant and worthy men that they were, they drew their swords and assailed each other with all their might, hewing and hammering on and on. For a long while it was impossible to say who would win the honours, for King Nicolas was a big, strong man, a good foot taller than Alexander, and endowed with the greatest courage – had it not been for his avarice and covetousness and pride he'd have been one of the worthiest knights of his age, without a doubt; but King Alexander was generous, courteous, strong, brave and clever, incomparably more so than Nicolas. On these two kings fought with might and main, buffeting and battering one another; but at the very end King Nicolas lost both sword and helm, and Alexander cast them aside and struck off his head, giving no thought at all to mercy or ransom. And so it was that King Nicolas of Armenia met his death.

His enemy slain, Alexander made his way back to his men, and bade them disarm him so that he could rest and have his wounds examined and treated – there's no doubt he had them in profusion.

Once he'd rested sufficiently he called for King Nicolas's guarantors to be brought before him, and asked if they intended to observe the proposed conditions. They made no objection whatever; rather, they ordered the city to open its gates to the noble Alexander, and it surrendered to him completely. But he had no wish to take the city for himself; instead he gave it to Ptholomer, for he'd promised it to him, and Ptholomer took possession of the city on behalf of Alexander and in due and proper fashion received the people's homage and oaths of fealty.

CHAPTER XXVII

How King Alexander laid siege to the city of Athens,
but did not take it, out of respect for Aristotle.

So, then, having conquered all the lands and cities of Armenia and Turkey and placed them in the hands of Ptholomer, and after seeing King Nicolas buried with all honour, Alexander set off with his whole army and headed for Athens, for he'd been told it was one of the noblest cities in the world, the most ancient and abundantly rich. And it paid no homage to any lord at all: its people were entirely self-governing;[1] Alexander resolved to make them his subjects if he could. At this point master Aristotle – Alexander's tutor – was in the city, being an Athenian by birth.

Alexander advanced with all his army till he came before the city, and as soon as they arrived he gave orders for tents and pavilions and lodges to be pitched. And he sent foraging parties right up to the gates to round up the herds and flocks and bring them back to camp; the people of Athens were aghast and shocked by this – such practice was something new to them. Then he sent a messenger to the city to call upon the citizens to surrender, and to make plain that if they refused he would never leave till the city was his, and if he had to take it by storm he would put them all to the sword.

When the governors and burgesses of the city heard this proclamation they were horrified, and went together to Aristotle to seek his advice and guidance. But Aristotle told them to leave it to him: he was confident he could resolve it to their satisfaction; and so saying, he dressed as quickly and as smartly and impressively as he could, mounted a handsomely harnessed mule and rode from the city and made his way to King Alexander's tent. The moment Alexander saw him he rose to greet him and bowed to him with the utmost respect as his former teacher; and then, with great care and delicacy, Aristotle began to address his lord.

The two were locked in discussion for the best part of four hours, and met for further talks for several days more. And finally, though with great reluctance, King Alexander granted his master Aristotle's request, because in the middle of their dealings he received a message from his mother telling of her distress that his father King Philip had unjustly cast her out by the advice of Jonas, seneschal of Greece, and planned to take another wife named Cleopatras, daughter of King Golias of Pincernie.[2] When Alexander heard this he was as angry as could be, and told Aristotle he would agree to leave the city of Athens in peace for the time being, for he meant to go to his father's marriage to his new bride and show his feelings in a way that would never be forgotten.

---

[1]   Literally 'they obeyed only themselves'.
[2]   A land to the north of the Black Sea.

CHAPTER XXVIII

How Alexander restored his mother to her rightful position with
his father King Philip, who had cast her out and rejected her,
intending to marry one named Cleopatras.

As soon, then, as Alexander heard his mother's message of distress he responded to his master Aristotle's plea; and he ordered a large body of
troops to make ready to march and set off as soon as he could. He made a swift
return to his Greek homeland and at last to his city, arriving at the height of his
father's marriage celebrations. And he caused quite a stir among the guests! He
had the seneschal of Greece seized and beheaded – right there in the middle of
the hall where the entertainment was in full swing! His father King Philip was
outraged and appalled, but for the time being there was nothing he could do, for
Alexander's mighty presence defied all protest. And it wasn't just the seneschal
he put to death, but everyone he found in any way responsible for his father's
action. Truly, King Philip was so wild with rage that he snatched up a knife and
rushed at his son, who was in the middle of the hall, sword in hand, mercilessly
executing all the traitors. But by some strange chance King Philip tripped and
fell, and for some while he was laid out on the floor, uttering not a word: they
thought he'd split his skull and died. His son Alexander came up and had him
hauled to his feet, but he was too dazed by his fall to support himself and had
to be carried to his bed. It wasn't long before he returned to his senses; then he
asked what had happened, and called for his son Alexander. He came at once,
and as soon as he saw his father he fell to his knees before him and begged forgiveness, but said:

'Dear father, what cause or reason, whose wicked words, can have prompted
you – and at your age! – to reject my beloved mother and cast her aside? I'd
say you've been ill advised indeed! I beg you to reconsider – and if you don't, I
swear by all the gods we worship that you won't like what I'll do! You should
be showing us how to behave! You should be our model, should be setting an
example, and here you are at the end of your days making yourself a laughing
stock! You've been woefully misguided!'

To this King Philip replied: 'I'll put a stop to this, dear son, I promise. I'll have
the lady Cleopatras escorted home to her land of Pincernie, and I'll take your
mother back. Let me entrust all this business to you: I want it done to your own
satisfaction.'

Alexander gave his father humble thanks; and then at once, without a moment's delay, he had the lady Cleopatras taken back to her land with great
dignity, and summoned his mother home where she was accepted back by
his father amid much joy and celebration. Then Alexander presented his father with King Nicolas's crown, which was so splendid, so magnificent, that it
would take a long time to describe so I'll say no more. I want to tell instead of
how King Darius sent his envoys to Alexander, and many other matters.

CHAPTER XXIX

Of Alexander's conduct and the envoys sent by Darius.

When all these affairs had been managed as you've heard, the noble King Alexander, his heart burning with desire to win further honour, had no wish to dismiss his troops; he retained them all, which he could well afford after winning so much booty in Armenia – and in any case he was so courteous and gracious that he was respected, loved and honoured by them all. So he pitched his tents and camped in their midst, and there he rested while he pondered how to bring King Darius to battle – and he found occasion very quickly, as you'll hear.

But first I want to tell you something of King Alexander's tent, for according to my source it was the noblest that ever was or ever will be. It was made in four panels, entirely of silk interwoven with fine gold, and had three golden pommels encrusted with carbuncles and other precious stones which shed such a dazzling light at night that it might have been the midday sun. And the four panels were embroidered with all manner of stories: of Hercules, for instance, and how he slew the dragon and planted the pillars that bore his name; and the history of Troy and Paris's abduction of Helen; how Jason won the Fleece, and how Troy and Thebes and Carthage were destroyed. It was blazoned, too, with images of the twelve months of the year and the signs of the zodiac, the planets and the stars and the shape of all the world, showing its division into three parts: that is, Asia, Europe and Africa. It was so utterly, wondrously rich that there was surely none to compare in all the earth: every last part was silver or silk – even the ropes were made of silk, and the pegs supporting the whole structure were finest silver. But I'll leave it at that and return to our main theme.

You've heard how Alexander had defeated King Nicolas and so won himself extraordinary renown. News of his victory had spread far and wide: it was the talk of the world, and many spoke of their astonishment that a man as young as Alexander could accomplish such a feat. Word at last reached the ears of Darius, king of Persia; and according to my source, when he heard the news he was so alarmed that he struggled to control himself, for it was also reported that his nephew Sanson was with Alexander and had performed feats of arms of unparalleled number, and even though Nicolas had been such a close relation, had helped to destroy him. But what distressed Darius most of all was that Alexander, without his leave, had given all Nicolas's land to a knight of his and would soon be making him its king. So King Darius of Persia now resolved to send envoys to the young King Alexander with presents on his behalf – the significance of which gifts they would explain.

CHAPTER XXX

Of the gifts sent by King Darius to Alexander by his envoys.

King Darius's first gift to Alexander was a cane, a reminder that he was still very young and should be disciplined like a child. Likewise a ball, a reference to his youth, his adolescence. He also sent a bridle, signifying that Alexander should beware of overleaping and should be reined in by obedience to him, who was his lord. Once these gifts were ready he dictated a letter setting down these explanations and entrusted it to his envoys with orders to deliver the message with all due diligence. He instructed them, too, to bid Alexander pay him homage, to make amends for the sin he'd committed in killing King Nicolas and to come and ask pardon for it; and they were to tell Alexander and his father that unless they paid him homage and tribute for their land he would wage such a fearsome, devastating war that it would be too late then to come and repent!

So the messengers departed and rode on day by day until they reached King Alexander, and delivered their message to King Philip and then to Alexander his son. Then they gave him the presents and the letter sent by Darius. When Alexander saw the gifts and read the letter he began to smile; then he said to the envoys:

'Truly, sirs, your king is right to send me these presents! And he's a clearer sense of what's in store for me than he's committed to this letter: the rod he's sent is a sign that I'll see him disciplined and obedient and will punish him for the childish, ignorant demands he's made, ignorant child that he is. The round ball signifies the round earth, over which I'll ride, rod in hand, to punish him and every other haughty rebel, and the reins signify that I shall have the whole world in my hands, my lordship controlling all. You're to tell him this from me! And as for the tribute he demands for my father's land and mine, tell him I refuse – rather, he'll be paying tribute to me for *his* land: either that, or one of us will be lying dead and bloody! Tell him that from this day forth, and for all time, I challenge him with fire and sword as my mortal enemy.'

Then he had the envoys served with wine and gave them leave, and they set off at once and made their way back to their king as swiftly as they could. They reported Alexander's response and message, and told him his interpretation of the gifts; and Darius was so incensed that he vowed to his gods that, if Fortune granted that he fell into his clutches, he would crush Alexander's pride.

CHAPTER XXXI

How Alexander set out with his army and defeated the Duke of the Rock,
and several other matters.

And so it was that Alexander matched King Darius's threat with a like threat of his own. And with every intention of carrying it out he ordered that everything needed on campaign was to be ready by the very next day. This was done; and when morning came Alexander took leave of his father King Philip and his mother Queen Olympias and set out with his whole army, which was of a strength amazing to record.

On he rode till he left his own land and began to cross into Persia. Then his scouts and foragers, as is always the custom of men at war, started riding across the land pillaging and plundering and seizing towns and castles and forts as if the whole country belonged to them – as indeed it did, for they met with little resistance.

But in the course of this scouting and foraging they came upon a great crag, the stronghold of a lord who called himself the Duke of the Rock. It so happened that by some chance or other this duke, himself out plundering with his band of brigands, ran into a party of Alexander's foragers. He attacked and battered and slaughtered them, but a few escaped and fled back to their army and found King Alexander. They told him of the duke's ferocity and the strength of his fortress on the rock, adding that it housed immeasurable wealth. When Alexander heard this he thought that, if he could capture it, it would enrich his army mightily! So he sent a messenger to this lord of the rock, bidding him surrender the place to King Alexander and become his vassal – 'and if he refuses, you're to challenge him in my name'.

The messenger set off at once; he followed the directions he'd been given to the rock and found the duke, and delivered his message as precisely as he could. But the duke was quite unmoved, and told the messenger that he knew little about this Alexander and had no intention of surrendering his base, and that Alexander would never set foot inside.

So the messenger departed and returned to the army and told the king what had happened, and how the lord of the rock had scant respect for him. Then Alexander swore by all his gods that he would never move from there till he'd vanquished him, and wouldn't leave this Duke of the Rock a single foot of land.

He ordered his men to pitch a great encampment of tents and lodges and pavilions, and to arm and form their companies ready to mount an assault upon the rock. But it was a mighty stronghold indeed: the crag was protected on one side by an arm of the sea and on the other by a great river, so fast-flowing that it would have swept away any boat or barge; and there was only one gateway, so that a hundred men-at-arms could easily defend it against the whole world. Alexander now bade his bravest, finest men prepare to launch an attack, and at the same time sent a body of archers and crossbowmen out to sea to engage from the seaward side of the rock, to rain missiles on the enemy while their comrades made a frontal assault.

Just as he commanded, so it was done: they began to attack and assail from both sides, so fiercely that the rock was swiftly conquered – but not without heavy losses: the king lost countless men and was wounded himself. But the rock was taken and so was the duke, and the king had him hanged from the crag's very tip: he wouldn't accept a ransom because he'd cost him so many brave men-at-arms, and also because the duke had pillaged and plundered all the surrounding country in amassing his incalculable wealth. The whole vast hoard Alexander now shared amongst his army, to each man according to his station.

C<small>HAPTER</small> XXXII

How King Alexander marched towards the city of Tarsus,
and several other remarkable events.

Having conquered the rock and put to death its keeper the duke and shared all the booty among his men, Alexander continued his onward march. The skies were cloudless and it was very hot, so hot indeed that it was a struggle to march or ride, and they followed the lines of the valleys and rivers.

Then one evening, after the king and his army had toiled hard all day, they were bathed in sweat and grey with the dust that had coated their faces and hands. So they made their way down to a river, fair and shining. But nothing was colder than its water! As soon as those young soldiers saw the beautiful clear water they stripped off their clothes – as did the young King Alexander, who was boiling hot – and leapt straight in; but some of them were so stricken by the icy cold that they died in an instant. The king himself was so frozen that he was thought to be dead, and word spread like wildfire among his men: indeed the army was close to breaking. But thanks to a fine doctor he recovered his health, though not before he'd suffered much.

Some suggest that in this troubled time King Darius sent a spy to make sure Alexander died, secretly promising his doctor a barrelful of gold! But the doctor was a worthy man and wouldn't think of it.[1]

So Alexander was restored to health and continued his advance, destroying and capturing cities and strongholds. Some surrendered willingly, and to these he did no harm but cherished, respected and protected them; but those he had to take by force he razed to the ground.

As they marched on they crossed a most perilous mountain; according to my source it altered the nature of those who crossed it: cowards turned brave but the brave became cowards, the sick became well but the well turned sick. Alexander crossed this fearful mountain with the utmost trouble and difficulty: at one point the twisting path was as narrow as could be, with a ravine below so deep that it seemed like a bottomless abyss. A number of horses and their riders lost their footing at this bend and were never found or seen again, all because some of the younger horses[2] were too impetuous.

Once the whole army had made its way across they found themselves in a

---

[1] The verse *Roman d'Alexandre* features a fairly lengthy episode in which a man sent by Darius to Alexander's camp, furtively disguised as a Greek, almost succeeds in corrupting the doctor. It sounds promising, but Wauquelin may well have thought it worthy only of passing mention because it ends rather undramatically with the doctor simply (and somewhat blandly) thinking better of it: '"If I murder such a man in return for gold...I should be tortured to death. The king chose me rather than anyone else to cure him: if I kill him, God might damn me." It was a wise decision by the doctor, not letting greed persuade him to commit such a terrible deed as to kill the man who was rousing the whole world; he worked hard instead to cure the king.' (Branch I stanzas 119-20).

[2] The text does read '*chevaux*'; it may seem more likely that '*chevalers*', their riders, were to blame, but the verse *Roman d'Alexandre* refers to the horses' natures as well as the men's

beautiful open plain. Here many good people came to surrender to the king and brought him everything they owned, but the king let them keep it all and took them into his love and protection.

Alexander stayed in this land for a number of days to rest and recuperate, and bade all his men do likewise. But as soon as they were fully recovered and back to their true selves he gave orders for the army to take to the road once more. He'd been told that not far away was a mighty city called Tarsus[1] in a land by the name of Arcaige,[2] and when he heard about this city he directed his vanguard straight towards it. He sent messengers ahead to discover first whether its people meant to resist him or whether they would yield, in which case he would show them mercy. But the city's defenders replied that they would never surrender, and that they had strength and power enough to withstand his attack.

CHAPTER XXXIII

*How King Alexander destroyed the city of Tarsus
and then rebuilt it after giving it to a harper.*

Alexander was enraged by this reply from Tarsus, and swore by his gods that he wouldn't stop till the city was at his mercy: he ordered all his men to prepare for an assault. You'd have seen his archers and crossbowmen loose a storm of bolts and arrows there, thicker than any blizzard – no one in the city dared show his head above the walls; then ladders were hauled forward, and men-at-arms started scrambling up while the defenders tried to hurl them down and flung boiling water and quicklime on them, the most fearful affliction imaginable. But for all that, the defenders' efforts were vain: the city was overwhelmed and taken and the king's banner was planted within; and Alexander commanded that all be slaughtered and the city's wealth be seized and each man in the army be given his rightful share. His orders were carried out: soon the entire city was ablaze and its towers and gates were levelled to the ground, till not a single stone remained on another.

One day shortly after, King Alexander was seated at dinner, very tired and weary from the trials he'd endured and assaults delivered, when a man presented himself at his table who played wondrously well on the harp, so well indeed that the king's delight at the music erased all thought of his labours. When he finished playing, the king, greatly soothed, asked him who he was and he replied:

'Ah, my lord, what can I tell you? Not four days ago I was a man of high

being changed by the mountain (Branch I stanza 121), so it may indeed make equal sense for the younger horses to have turned wildly brave and rash.
[1]   'Trache'.
[2]   This name is something of a mystery: it surely cannot be a variant spelling of '*Arcade*' – Arcadia – which would suggest even less geographical awareness than usual (and is very much connected with Alexander's companion Emenidus); but there is no obvious place-name in the region of Tarsus and the Taurus Mountains which seems to correspond, though there was a nearby city called Anchiale.

standing, wealthy and powerful, but you've brought me to such a lowly state that now I'm reduced to begging for my bread as you see!'

Then Alexander said: 'Well by my life I'll make you rich! I give you the city of Tarsus from this day forth, and by my will and command it shall be built and peopled anew!'

Masons and carpenters and all necessary craftsmen were commissioned at once to rebuild the city. The king saw it finished before he departed; he installed some of his men there to begin its repopulation, and appointed the harper its lord and master, just as he'd promised.

CHAPTER XXXIV

How King Alexander began to advance on Tyre, a city rightly belonging to Sanson, the prince aforementioned.

Once King Alexander had arranged all these affairs he set his army on the march once more. On he rode till he left behind the land of Arcaige and entered the land of Syria. It was rich, level, fertile, abundant; and its people judiciously came to him and presented him with all their wealth along with the keys of their city. The king greeted them most kindly and approvingly and took them into his care and protection; and he stayed there for several days to rest and take his ease, and to resupply and provision his troops and men-at-arms with everything they needed. The people of the land provided for them most willingly, making Alexander all the better disposed towards them.

As soon as he'd relaxed and rested enough Alexander commanded that tents and pavilions be packed again and all arms and gear be put in order, for he planned to march into the land of Persia and head for the city of Tyre. This city, by right of inheritance, should have belonged to Sanson Dailly, of whom we spoke earlier, but King Darius had driven him out and installed a captain there named Baillis, who was guarding the city with a great body of men-at-arms.

Alexander marched on till he entered the land, and sent a deputation to the captain and the people of the city to learn their intentions: whether they meant to resist him or surrender. It seems they had no wish at all to yield, and my source states that the city of Tyre was one of the strongest at that time in all the world: it stood beside a wide bay in the sea, and had been built long ago by a giant who had tyrannically brought all the surrounding lands into his power and built the city in that formidable place to give himself greater security. According to the history, it was built about seven hundred years after the Flood.

When Alexander heard that the people of Tyre were refusing to surrender he was furious, and swore by his gods that he would never leave till he'd conquered the city. And as he was preparing his squadrons and battalions Sanson Dailly came to him and said:

'Oh, my beloved lord! This land and city are rightfully mine: it was formerly my father's! I beg you, sire, let it be taken from King Darius, who has wronged me so much!'

Then Alexander repeated his vow that he would never leave till the city was in his hands.

CHAPTER XXXV

How King Alexander laid siege to the city of Tyre by land and sea.

The noble king pressed on till he came before Tyre and laid siege to the city, encircling it by land and sea. In the course of this siege there were numerous attacks and sorties by one side and the other; it would take a long time to recount them all, but to make full sense of our story it's important to tell you something of what happened.

So, then: the captain of the city knew Alexander wouldn't leave till he'd conquered Tyre, being a truly worthy man without a hint of cowardice and being accompanied, as he knew, by Sanson Dailly, the city's rightful heir. So as soon as he realised the king had them completely surrounded the captain summoned all his counsellors and the most powerful men of Tyre and told them of his plan: he would send Alexander a splendid crown of gold and precious stones, hoping he would accept it as tribute and move on and leave them in peace; and the crown would be an acknowledgement that he was a most potent king and worthy of being crowned above all others. The captain's plan was approved by all, and he gave orders for it to be duly carried out.

When Alexander received the crown he was thrilled and delighted: it was handsome and rich indeed; and he told the messenger he would spare the city and its people and all their goods and property, as long as they opened the gates to him and accepted the rightful heir, Sanson Dailly, as their lord and king. He wanted, too, to enter Tyre and see and explore the city and worship the gods of that place.

Baillis, the captain, was beside himself when he heard this, fearing that if the king and the Greeks entered the city they'd end up kicking him out! So he told the messengers he'd have none of it: if King Alexander wanted to worship their gods and would then agree to peace, he would have the gods carried to him outside the city! Alexander was frustrated and enraged by this reply, and swore by the sky and earth and sun and moon and stars that he wouldn't rest till he'd taken Tyre, either by force or willingly.

CHAPTER XXXVI

Of the first assault upon the city of Tyre.

As soon as Alexander realised the city wouldn't open its gates he gave orders to attack. All manner of soldiers began their assault: archers, crossbowmen and slingers exchanged a furious hail of arrows and missiles; and truly, if the Greeks attacked with courage and might, the men of Tyre fought back no less well.

This first assault lasted from early morning to the ninth hour,[1] and it didn't

---

[1]   The ninth canonical hour, about 3 p.m.

pass without heavy losses. But at the ninth hour a wild and fearsome storm arose at sea, so great that the attack had to be abandoned, for out in the bay the waves began to toss Alexander's ships around till it seemed they would surely founder – and indeed a good number were lost. And from the heart of this storm emerged something monstrous, filling them all with such terror that they thought it was the end of the world: out of the sea surged an immense and hideous serpent or dragon, its vast maw gaping wide enough to swallow the whole fleet, the whole army, the whole city; and this dreadful monster spewed out such gushes of searing flame that even the bravest men, defenders and besiegers alike, were sure they'd be consumed in fire if not in its gullet. And all the while terrible, deafening peals of thunder crashed about them, transfixing them with fear and dread. They were locked in the storm till almost nightfall, when it finally began to abate.

It so happened that on this same day there was a man in the city who set about forging darts of iron and steel to shoot and hurl upon the Greeks; they were so designed that the moment they hit a target they would burst into flame. But as this smith prepared to forge them, the iron began to bleed, spurting blood in great profusion. The people of the city were aghast: they didn't know what to make of the awesome wonders befalling them that day. One old man said it was a sign that the god Neptune was angry with the besieging army who were bent on destroying his city. This was reported to Alexander, but he took no notice; instead he said:

'Never worry if you don't win with your opening gambit. If he's willing to be patient and alert, the player with the better game rarely ends up mated!'

CHAPTER XXXVII

How King Alexander launched a second attack upon Tyre, but was unable to take the city this time.

And hearing the city's interpretation of the marvels, Alexander gave them a quite different gloss which he sent to them in writing:

'People of Tyre, you've suggested the god Neptune is angry. Indeed he is – because you're wrongfully withholding this city from its rightful king, for which you all must die! This is signified by the iron that bled when the smith tried to forge his darts: truly, your god doesn't wish such wicked people as you to remain here! So if you refuse to surrender, and Fortune grants that we take the city by force, you will all die.'

When the people of Tyre heard this their opinions were divided. Some wanted to surrender the city to Alexander, a view shared even by Baillis the captain; and I believe they'd have made their peace with the king had it not been for a prince who'd lately come to the city from King Darius: he changed their minds, putting forward one argument after another until they were all persuaded to make no concession but to wait for help from Darius. So they sent word to the Greeks that they could stay and die of boredom outside the city, but they wouldn't be coming in as long as they lived!

Seeing the rebels were bent on stubborn resistance, King Alexander devised a plan – according to my source it came to him by revelation. He had a huge number of trees felled in the nearby forests and massive logs dragged out to sea and bound together with great iron chains. They were then piled high with earth, cement and mortar till they looked like a proper island. On this he had mighty wooden towers erected, and manned them with archers and other troops who bombarded the city day and night with arrows, bolts, darts and stones from mangonels. The men of Tyre launched repeated sorties against them by barge and ship and engaged with courage and vigour, for there were great warriors in that city, which was well stocked and provisioned with food and everything needed for defence.

But it was clear that Alexander had no intention of leaving, and was mounting daily assaults; so the people of Tyre decided to send for help from Duke Betis, lord and king of the city of Gaza. They did so at once and speedily; and when Duke Betis received their message he vowed that, by the faith he owed his gods, he would come to their aid in a very short space and give this Alexander such a battle that it would be too late for him to repent! This was the message he sent back to the city, and the people were overjoyed, convinced that everything now was going their way.

Chapter XXXVIII

Of a defeat inflicted outside the city of Tyre.

King Darius, well informed by his spies that Alexander was besieging Tyre, had assembled a great body of men-at-arms and sent them to the city to guard and defend it. And one day their captains reckoned that between them and the men of Tyre they had a mighty force, and resolved to mount a sortie against Alexander because, they said, 'if Fortune granted that we beat him and could capture and kill him, we'd have accomplished the finest deed of arms ever performed by any knights!' According to the history, between them they numbered fully thirty thousand.

So these captains put their plan before the people of Tyre, promising that, if they were willing to join them in the sortie, they would fight with all their might to support their cause and free their city, and any booty that was won would be shared out equitably to all, of every degree. Everyone agreed, and the decision was made to mount the attack next day: word was spread throughout the city that every man was to be armed and ready to sally forth against the Greeks at morning.

But Alexander had spies in the city who promptly informed him of the plan; and as soon as he received the news he called all his men to arms and bade them be on guard and ready to meet the men of the city the moment they emerged.

The city was astir at the crack of dawn and all manner of troops started to sally through the gate on the landward side, splendidly arrayed and armed. But Alexander, knowing all about their plan, had readied ten thousand of his bravest men to surround them as soon as they were out of the gates. These ten thousand were lying in ambush, well hidden in a nearby valley: the men of the city were wholly unaware. So out came the men of Tyre, riding boldly forth, two by two, lances lowered, straight towards the king's army. The forces met with a mighty clash of thrusting lances and slashing, battering swords; the men of Tyre fought valiantly, killing the Greeks quite pitilessly, but the Greeks were no more merciful, sending heads, arms, brains and guts flying across the field. Knights and horses fell in colossal mounds; banners and pennons were fouled with blood and brain; it was appalling to the eye and to the mind. And while they were so embroiled, from behind them charged the men concealed by Alexander near the city. They inflicted dreadful damage, taking the men of Tyre completely by surprise: they didn't know which way to turn to save themselves, and many plunged in the sea and drowned. Only a few, with the utmost difficulty, fought their way back to the city; their leaders, captains and most of the city's garrison were slain.

It would be tiresome to describe it in every detail, so I'll leave it at that – except to add that Alexander, too, lost many fine knights, and that, according to the history, the aforementioned Sanson performed so many feats of arms that day that it seemed he owned the field, and he was much esteemed by the king and all his company. Emenidus, too, fought superbly, but was wounded – so badly that they thought he hadn't long to live.

The people of Tyre were distraught at their defeat, but Alexander's army were elated.

CHAPTER XXXIX

How Alexander built a castle outside one of the gates of Tyre.

Alexander, nonetheless, was as frustrated as could be: time was wasting away and still the city wasn't his. One day he was trying to relax beside a spring, gazing and musing upon the city of Tyre, when it struck him that there was no chance of winning the city unless he found a way of stopping the seaward gate: through it flowed a steady supply of fresh troops and provisions, causing him grave problems and delaying the achievement of his goal. What's more, the surrounding country was now stripped bare: there was no more food for his men to forage from the villages.

So Alexander commanded that every vessel that could be found along the shore was to be seized and brought before the city. This was duly done, and when all the craft had been collected he gave orders for a colossal platform, principally of wood, to be built and towed into the city's harbour. Then he ordered them to start building upon it with fine stone and good mortar; and as the weight grew ever greater, the platform sank into the water and sat firmly on the bed, and they kept building till at last on this foundation they'd constructed a mighty castle, superbly fortified with walls and towers and battlements. And when this castle was complete – though not without great cost and loss of men, for the men of Tyre delivered many a punishing blow to the workmen and their guards – Alexander stocked it with ample provisions and a fine garrison of men-at-arms, not to mention all manner of catapults, mangonels and springalds, which repeatedly bombarded the people of the city and inflicted heavy grief and damage.[1]

CHAPTER XXXX

How King Alexander sent some of his captains on a foraging mission to the city of Gaza.[2]

While this castle was being built before Tyre, Alexander realised his army's supplies were running out.[3] So he ordered Emenidus of Arcadia, Perdicas, Leones, Caulus, Licanor, Philotas and Sanson, along with seven hundred of the army's best-mounted and bravest men-at-arms, to go and forage for fresh supplies for their men and horses and to ward off the risk of starvation.

These captains set off as bidden, and kept riding till they entered the valley of Josaphat, which at that time was a populous and prosperous land, rich in all manner of crops and livestock. But the men of those parts have their thoughts always turned to war: they go permanently armed and armour-clad and are fiercely protective of all they own, fighting mercilessly, doing whatever is needed to defend themselves and their lands and possessions. Now, it so happened that the Greeks caught sight of rich quarry here: great herds of cattle, sheep and pigs; down they rode at once to round them up and drive them off. But at the very moment they were doing this there was a captain from those parts, by the name of Otheserie, leading a patrol to guard the land on behalf of the duke of Gaza. He spotted the Greeks driving the herds away and launched a bold and fierce attack. There was a mighty clash of swords and lances and many from both sides fell, for if the men of Gaza attacked with valour, the Greeks received them no less bravely – and with no more pity, for in the attack both Otheserie and a nephew of his were killed. When the rest saw their captains slain they took to flight, some taking refuge and hiding in the mountains while others fled to the city of Gaza, where they told Duke Betis what they'd suffered at the hands of the Greeks. Betis, who'd also received the plea for help from the captain of Tyre,[4] had already massed a vast army in his city: he was ready to attack the Greeks as soon as he knew where to find them.

---

[1]   The verse *Roman d'Alexandre* adds that the castle was also a successful blockade. 'The port was blocked; nothing could come or go; no barge or galley could reach the city.' (Branch II stanza 1).

[2]   'Gadres'.

[3]   While Wauquelin's Alexander remains impressively self-possessed, the verse *Roman d'Alexandre* stresses his frustration: 'Alexander was exasperated at being stuck there, for there were no provisions to be found round about, and in his rage he began to swear that any defender he could get his hands on would suffer!' (Branch II stanza 1, which is the beginning of the section based on *Li Fuerre de Gadres*).

[4]   i.e. above, p.60.

Chapter XXXXI

How Betis and the men of Gaza, Gadifer du Laris among them,
rode from their city and attacked the Greeks.

When Betis of Gaza heard how the Greeks had slaughtered his men he was enraged, and called for a trumpet to sound at once to rouse the city.

In Gaza there was a most valiant, worthy and courageous knight by the name of Gadifer du Laris, and the moment he knew Betis was preparing to attack his foes he armed and made ready and commanded his whole battalion to do likewise. As his warriors armed they rode out and thrust in their spurs and started galloping towards the foe in great squadrons, a hundred here and two hundred there, as if swept along by a storm. Then Emenidus, seeing the enemy surging towards them from all sides, assembled all his men-at-arms and bade them behave wisely, keeping close, tight order; and he said:

'Dear companions, we're in mortal danger; we must all play our part today and show how we love our king Alexander. If only he knew the peril we're in we'd have a better chance,[1] that's certain! Indeed, we must send him word of our urgent need, and swiftly; so in God's name, sirs, decide who's to be our messenger.' And he called to Licanor, saying: 'Will you take the message, sir?'

But Licanor replied that he'd do no such thing: he would never have anyone accuse him of having left them in such danger. 'My shield,' he said, 'will be shattered, my lance in pieces and my sword stained with blood and brain before I ever leave this field!'

When Emenidus heard his refusal he asked Philotas, but he too said he wouldn't go; so he called upon Leones, then Perdicas, then Antigonus, then Antiocus and several more – I shan't name them all – but none of them would leave. He finally asked Ariscé de Valestre, who agreed to carry the message – but not until he'd tested himself against the enemy, for King Alexander would believe him more readily if he bore the marks of battle!

Chapter XXXXII

How Betis slew Sanson Dailly, and of many more who were killed in the battle.

When Emenidus, leader of the Greeks, realised there was no other way of informing Alexander of their perilous plight, he felt both joy and grief: joy at seeing such courage in his men, but grief, too, fearing that through that very courage he would lose them. So he exhorted them to look after each other, and not to get drawn apart but to keep a tight formation.

---

[1]   Literally 'it would be much to our benefit'. I've interpreted this in military rather than material terms, but Wauquelin's source – the *Fuerre de Gadres* section of the verse *Roman d'Alexandre* – half-implies that they would gain in terms of reward as Emenidus tells his companions: "if Alexander knew what we'd had to deal with it would be worth a hundred thousand silver marks!" (Branch II stanza 8).

Then Duke Sanson, to whom the land rightfully belonged, came before Emenidus and begged to be allowed to joust against Betis if Fortune brought them together. Emenidus reluctantly granted his wish. And it so happened that, as the enemy battalions approached, Duke Betis rode forward challenging the Greeks to come and do battle, and Duke Sanson, burning to achieve his desire, levelled his lance and lowered his visor. He charged at Betis full tilt, and met him with such fearsome force that his lance flew into splinters as it shattered on his shield; but Betis didn't hold back: he thrust his lance through Sanson's shield and straight on through his body, striking him dead. It was a grievous blow for the Greeks: he was one of the most valiant of all their company. Emenidus was distraught, needless to say; but there was no time to lament or moan, for the Gazans were upon them in an instant, and both sides started battering each other so fearsomely that it was clear there was precious little love lost. The carnage and the slaughter then were too hideous to describe. A moment after Sanson's death Emenidus slew a Gazan named Salhadin; and if Emenidus fought valiantly, so did Leones, Perdicas and all the others. But the fact was that compared to the Gazans the Greeks were few: they numbered just six hundred men-at-arms, and though they were the flower of Alexander's knights, the Gazans had thirty thousand troops of one kind and another. Nonetheless the Greeks mounted a mighty stand against the men of Gaza: the feats of arms they performed that day, I swear, are beyond a man's imagining. They slew an unprecedented number of the foe, and truly, had it not been for Gadifer du Laris and his great company of valiant men I believe the Gazans would have had the worse of it. In that battle they lost Salhadin, a most powerful Turkish lord who was one of Betis's nephews; another of the slain was named Gallafre, son of the Beduin emir[1] and nephew of Gadifer du Laris; and an infinite number of others were killed.

But finally the tide of battle began to turn: the Greeks had lost so many men that they numbered only thirty knights. Then Emenidus came to Ariscé de Valestre and said that if they were going to send for help it was now or never. Ariscé saw he was right; he withdrew from the press and, wounded though he was, so badly that blood was streaming from every part of him, he thrust in his spurs and didn't stop spurring till he reached Alexander's camp.

CHAPTER XXXXIII

How Corneus found his uncle Emenidus locked in battle.

While this battle was at its height with both sides locked in combat, a nephew of Emenidus, Corneus by name, did him a mighty favour, arriving just in time to save his life. According to the history this Corneus was his sister's

---

[1]   The verse *Roman d'Alexandre* (in this episode derived from *Li Fuerre de Gadres*) recounts the whole battle in immense detail. It describes some of the combatants' lands as well as their horses, their arms and the blows they strike: at this point, as a typical example, it interrupts the flow to note that 'the people of [the emir's] land eat little bread; they drink camel's milk morning and evening' (Branch II stanza 30).

son, and – for what reason I'm not sure – had been a prisoner of King Darius for seven years but had somehow recently escaped. He'd heard his uncle had earned noble rank and high esteem at Alexander's court; and so, having a fine heart hungry for prowess and renown, he'd set out in search of his uncle in the hope that he could help him achieve his goal.

And this Corneus now arrived at the very time and place at which the Greeks were embroiled with the Gazans. The history tells that when he entered the fray he was so poorly armed that he was mocked by everyone; but he fought with such valour that before the battle was over he was one of the best armed and mounted in the whole company! And he finished by rescuing his uncle: seven Gazan knights had Emenidus on the ground, and had it not been for Corneus he would have been killed or captured. Corneus didn't know or recognise his uncle, and after the rescue, when Emenidus asked him who he was and he told him, Emenidus was astounded that Fortune had sent him a saviour nephew! And Corneus, likewise astonished to find that he'd done such a favour for an uncle, gave praise and thanks to his gods.

But now let's return to our main story and tell of Ariscé de Valestre, who'd ridden to seek Alexander's help for Emenidus of Arcadia and his company, who certainly needed it.

CHAPTER XXXXIV

How King Alexander came to the rescue with his whole army.

At the moment when Ariscé arrived at Alexander's camp, the king, Ptholomer, Danselin and all the other knights had just returned from launching a mighty assault on the city of Tyre, and a good many had suffered all manner of wounds. The king was outside his tent and had just taken off his helm to recover breath when Ariscé appeared, so covered in wounds and gashes that it was piteous to behold: according to the history you could have followed his path by the trail of his blood, and little wonder, for his body had been pierced clean through by two sword thrusts. He fell to his knees before the king and said:

'Dread lord, unless you take swift aid to your friends, most or all will be lost to you this day!'

As soon as the king heard what had happened he ordered every man to mount at once, and called for a fresh horse for Ariscé and bandages for his wounds. Then Ariscé mounted again to lead them to the battleground, a task he performed with such a will that his pains were quite forgotten.

They rode as fast as they could till they came to the field where their companions were embroiled. By the time Alexander came their strength was much reduced: of the seven hundred who'd begun the battle only thirty knights remained – though their valour, might and skill in arms made them seem innumerable! And at the very moment the king arrived the Gazans had captured four of the thirty and were in the process of tying them up; when Alexander heard this he was filled with rage, and swore by his gods that he'd rescue them or die in the attempt.

CHAPTER XLV

How Alexander routed the Gazans and rescued his men.

When Alexander saw the dire plight of his friends, and heard that Caulus, Aristé, Leones and Emenidus were captured, he called for the horns and trumpets to sound; then the Greeks set lances in rests and thrust in their spurs and charged upon the foe in such a raging storm that it sounded as if thunder from the heavens were falling on the Gazans. In this mighty onslaught countless fell, countless were slain, the Greeks savaging and tearing through their foes like a pack of wolves through a flock of sheep; so surprised were the prisoners' guards that they fled in panic in all directions, some this way, others that. On the Gazans' side the duke of Baloe, Callon by name, was slain by Alexander's own hand. He'd been well loved by the lord Betis, who for his part was performing wondrous feats of arms and holding his troops and companions together; and in this ferocious mêlée he dealt Alexander a two-handed axe-blow that bent him double over his saddle-bow. The king had charged so much to the fore in his burning desire to save his companions that he was surrounded by Gazans, and I believe he'd have been killed or captured had it not been for Ptholomer and Danselin, who were right behind him, keeping him ever in their sight; and the history tells that in rescuing Alexander they rescued also the four captive knights. Among them was Emenidus, so sorely wounded that his heart almost failed him.

How Gadifer and Betis fled from the battle, and of the death of Corneus.

Betis and Gadifer, seeing their men being slaughtered and the Greeks hewing and felling without mercy on all sides, pulled in their reins and turned tail. Gadifer was gravely wounded, pierced by a lance clean through the body; but though he now retreated, he sent his men ahead of him and stayed at the rear to protect them, as did Betis, who headed with his battalion toward the nearby crags.

As they took to flight, downcast and crestfallen, the first to realise was Corneus, Emenidus's nephew, who to prove his worth and place himself at the fore, yearning to achieve high prowess, plunged in his spurs to pursue the Gazans. He headed for Gadifer, at the rear of his battalion; he was close enough to hear him clearly, and Corneus cried out:

'Vassal! Vassal! Shame on you for fleeing! Turn and face me or I'll strike you as you run!'

Hearing these words Gadifer was ablaze with shame and wrath and rage; and though he was as sorely wounded as could be, he summoned up heart and turned on Corneus, set his lance in its rest and thrust in his spurs. He charged at Corneus, and Corneus at him, with such mighty force that their clash was like a peal of thunder. Corneus's lance flew into splinters, but Gadifer's didn't break: it went clean through Corneus's body and heart and bore him dead to the ground. He uttered not another word; but Gadifer, mocking, cried:

'Stay there, friend, and guard the passage and demand the toll! I've paid you mine today: enough to settle my dues with you forever!'

Emenidus had seen this joust and was distraught, for he loved Corneus dearly – and rightly so: his nephew had earlier saved his life.

CHAPTER XXXXVII
How Gadifer du Laris unhorsed Alexander, and Emenidus slew Gadifer.

The prisoners were rescued as you've heard, and their wounds were treated and bandaged and bound; then they armed once more and remounted, so eager to defeat the enemy, to achieve prowess and avenge their slain companions that neither wounds nor exhaustion were going to stop them. As soon as they were back in the saddle they set off in pursuit of the fleeing Gazans.

Emenidus, his heart afire, rode swiftly after Alexander who was a little ahead of him. It was now that they witnessed Corneus's misfortune. Alexander, seeing Gadifer strike him dead, was filled with admiration and said:

'Alas! There's a valiant man indeed! Would to the great god Mars he was on our side! I'd give him whatever he wanted, truly, and make him my companion in arms.' And so saying, he rode within earshot and cried: 'Turn back, sir knight! Turn and face me! Shame on a valiant man who flees when he's challenged to a deed of arms!'

Then Gadifer, hearing Alexander's cry, turned and charged straight back at him and delivered such a blow to his shield that he laid him flat out in the field, and would have led away his horse if Bucephalus had allowed himself to be taken. When Emenidus, who'd been following the king as I said, saw him struck down he was stunned and aghast, not knowing if he was alive or dead; but before Emenidus could reach him the king was already on his feet, stricken with shame – not at having been unhorsed but at having lain so long! Seeing this Emenidus dallied no more but went spurring after Gadifer. Now understand that Gadifer had felled not only Alexander and Corneus but so many more knights who'd tried to pursue him and his men that it would be lengthy and amazing to relate. He'd turned and faced them on all sides: wherever he'd seen companions attacked he'd charged that way and struck down foes with such ferocity that it was fearful to think a single body could do so much. But Emenidus now came at him crying:

'Ah, sir knight! Your strength has cost us dear today! I've come to take vengeance if I can! Turn and face me, turn! Or you'll die a shameful death!'

Then Gadifer, exhausted now – at least, he should have been! – but filled with rage, came charging back at Emenidus and struck him with his lance; but Emenidus returned the blow, thrusting his lance clean through his heart and striking him dead to the ground. It was a disaster for the Gazans; but Emenidus, too, had been sorely wounded yet again, for Gadifer's lance had gone right through his side: if the blow had been as well aimed as his, they would both have killed each other. Emenidus lost consciousness, and toppled and pitched to the ground.

CHAPTER XXXXVIII

How Alexander began to wage war against Duke Betis, and Emenidus was healed.

Alexander was now back in the saddle, his knights, swiftly following, having helped him remount Bucephalus. He rode up to find Emenidus stretched on the ground, and he drew rein beside his body, lamenting and grieving and wringing his hands and crying:

'Ah, noble knight! If you're dead, who will ever comfort us? If I lose you I don't think I'll ever feel joy again!'

So saying, the king dismounted, and Emenidus, who had heard these words, struggled to rise. Alexander helped him, and once he was up the king ordered his whole army to halt and make camp, and commanded that Emenidus be helped from his armour at once. This was done; and the surgeons came straight to examine his wounds, and said he wasn't in mortal danger: the blow he'd received was perilous indeed, but God willing, he would recover well. His wounds were treated and he was gently laid in a bed, as was Licanor likewise, who'd been gravely wounded and stricken unconscious that day: according to the history, in the course of the pursuit Betis had dealt him such a dreadful wound that his lung could be seen through his right side. The king bade that the two be given the best possible care, and hardly moved from their side as he did all he could to console and cheer them.

Meanwhile there was much grief in the company at the death of the noble Sanson Dailly, and for another worthy and mighty lord and baron named Pieron de Monfleur, and for Corneus and many others who'd died in the battle. And as soon as Emenidus had recovered speech he asked the king to have the slain barons buried with all honour, and Gadifer du Laris with them, saying he fully deserved it for the courage and prowess he'd shown in abundance. He was of high and noble lineage, too, and Emenidus said:

'You would be much reproached, my lord, if such a baron wasn't buried with due honour.'

And Alexander did as Emenidus requested.

A week now passed, and then ten days, and finally these valiant men began to recover health and strength; and before a fortnight was out, thanks to potions and the surgeons' skill, they were as fit and ready for battle as before, and Alexander and all their fellow knights rejoiced.

CHAPTER XXXXIX

How Danselin captured Count Midoual, one of the lords of Gaza.

Once these valiant warriors were healed and recovered, the king gave orders for all his men to strike camp and arm, for he meant to advance on the city of Gaza where he knew his enemies were gathered in great numbers. His command was carried out at once, and they rode on till the city's towers and ramparts came into view.

Their approach was seen by the men in the city, who promptly sounded the alarm; and the moment Betis – who was there inside the walls – heard that Alexander was coming he armed and bade all his troops do likewise. As soon as they were armed they marched out to the fields to meet their foes, and formed fine, well ordered battalions; then both sides loosed dense volleys of arrows and missiles at each other: there was clearly little love lost.

In one of the Gazan battalions was a lord named Midoual, a young knight eager to win esteem and praise. He rode forward from the lines and signalled a challenge for a prince or man of courage to joust with him in pursuit of honour. Danselin instantly saw this Midoual; he charged forward to meet him, and they clashed with such ferocity that their lances shattered; then they turned to face each other with their swords and dealt one another such mighty blows that they sent sparks flying from their helms. At last Danselin came right up to Midoual and seized him in both arms, and led him back, much against his will, and presented him to Alexander, who immediately gave orders that he be kept under closest guard.

Duke Betis, seeing his man seized and held captive, resolved to take immediate revenge. He rode from the ranks and picked out Ptholomer, who craved nothing else, and as they caught each other's eye they thrust in their spurs and charged at one another like thunder. They exchanged such blows that their lances smashed, and collided shield to shield with such violent force that they were both bent back over their saddles and could barely sit up straight again. But Ptholomer did so first, and he clutched his sword and charged at Betis and dealt him a blow that sent him crashing to the ground with his legs in the air. Then he grabbed his horse's reins and was about to demand that Betis surrender; but the Gazans had seen this and charged to the rescue, which started a mêlée, a clashing and shattering of swords and lances, too immense to relate. But in the end, through the bravery of Astaroth, a Persian duke,[1] Betis was remounted, not on his own horse but another. In this mêlée both Ariscé and Caulus were unhorsed, and had taken so many blows from mace and axe that they were thought to be dead.

So Duke Betis was rescued; and as soon as he found himself free again he decided to turn tail to his city, for the Greeks were all men of iron, their courage was boundless, and their king hated him so deeply for the death of Sanson Dailly and all the others who'd been killed by him that if he had him in his clutches he'd accept no other ransom but his death. He rode without stopping until he and as many of his battalion as could make it scrambled inside the gates. In the course of the pursuit there was many a skull smashed and many a knight felled; the Greeks were pressing so hard on their heels that they almost followed them into the city, and the portcullis was brought clattering down so fast that some

---

[1]   'duc de Presse'.

of the fugitives were locked outside: most of them were killed and the rest all seized and taken captive.

And so it was that the Greeks had the victory that day.

How the troops left by Alexander in the castle guarding the port of Tyre were put to death by the men of the city.

After this victory outside Gaza, Alexander gave orders for the Greeks to make camp. There he stayed for four days; and while he was encamped before Gaza, the men of Tyre, seeing that Alexander had left them, met to discuss how they could capture or destroy the castle he'd built in the harbour, which was blocking their access to the sea and preventing any ships or boats of any kind from reaching the city and bringing them food or aid. They decided to mount a sortie and attack the castle and, if they could, topple it into the sea.

They did just that. They ran and armed at once, and sailed out in the few craft they still had and launched such a fierce assault on the castle that the garrison couldn't escape drowning; for among the men of Tyre were a number of divers who plunged naked in the sea with picks and kept hacking away at the castle's masonry till it crumbled into the sea along with all the men inside – except a few who fought their way out and captured some enemy vessels and escaped certain death. The history says that all this happened in a single day. Then the men of Tyre, elated and rejoicing at their great success, made their way back inside the city.

CHAPTER LI

How King Alexander returned to Tyre and took the city by storm.

The handful of men who'd escaped from the castle headed out of the port and away from the city before coming back to shore; then they started riding and didn't stop till they reached Alexander's army outside Gaza and reported what had befallen his men and his fort. The king was enraged and vowed he wouldn't rest till he'd taken the city of Tyre and avenged his men's slaughter. He ordered his troops to strike camp at once and set off back to Tyre.

As he drew near the city and saw the destruction of his castle and the loss of its garrison he began to mourn and weep for them, crying:

'Ah, my dear friends! I left you here to die most piteously! Ah, Baillis, captain of Tyre, if I get my hands on you you'll pay for the deaths of these valiant men, I promise you!'

After much lamenting and bitter weeping he called for Licanor and Helie,[1] and bade them search every port along the coast and requisition every vessel they could find, either by force or willingly. This was duly done, and the his-

---

[1]   Another of his captains.

tory tells that these two lords carried out his order with such diligence that in less than a week they'd assembled a fleet of ships and barges and galleys that seemed to cover the whole sea; and they sailed them back filled with fine men-at-arms and blockaded the city walls so tightly that there was no way out at all. The men of Tyre were thoroughly alarmed, not knowing what to do, and Baillis their captain was horrified, realising it was a disaster: he could expect no help or relief from a living soul.

And so Alexander besieged the whole city by land and sea: it was so closely watched at every point that a cat couldn't have escaped.

Next morning he summoned his barons and said to them: 'My companions, dear sharers in prosperity and adversity, this city is very strong and well fortified: we'll never take it without engines; let's build catapults and mangonels[1] to batter and smash the walls and towers or it'll never be ours.'

So workmen were summoned from far and wide and all the engines were built. Then the Greeks began to pound the city, bombarding it on every side: it was awesome to behold; and Alexander led a pitiless assault – the history says he was the first to enter the city – and slew the captain Baillis with his own hand. He made his way in thanks to an ingenious engine he'd ordered to be made, which carried him on to the walls.[2]

And so the city of Tyre was taken as I've told you, and was now at Alexander's mercy. When the city's defenders realised all was lost they threw down their arms and wisely came to yield to Alexander, begging him to spare them; and he chose to accept their plea and showed them mercy.

CHAPTER LII
How King Alexander returned to besiege Gaza.

Having conquered and garrisoned Tyre, Alexander set out with his whole army and headed back towards Gaza. This was reported at once to Betis, who sent word to all parts where he thought he might find allies, aid and support, especially to Africa; and from there indeed came a mighty force of armed men.

On marched Alexander till he came before Gaza and laid siege to the city, surrounding it entirely: it wasn't long before his troops had the gates so well blockaded that not a single man could have found a way out. You may well imagine Betis's anguish, locked inside his walls, knowing the Greeks had him surrounded and seeing the smoke and flames as they fired all the nearby towns.

---

[1]   'perieres et coullars': both of these were stone-throwing devices with massive slings.
[2]   In Wauquelin's source, the verse Roman d'Alexandre, it's not exactly the engine itself that's ingenious but the way it's deployed: Alexander orders the building of "a wooden siege-tower ['un berfroi'] on boats, and at high tide the boats will carry it right up to the walls". He then bravely goes in it alone ("No one shall be in it but the Lord God and me!"), and 'in full view of everyone, fully armed, shield slung from neck, he leapt from its high top on to the city walls… The king leapt into the city: there was never such a man!' (Branch II stanzas 82, 84).

He was desperate to get Alexander out of his land. So he sent him a message declaring his willingness to pardon his past offences, both the killing of his men and the destruction of the numerous towns and strongholds that he'd taken; and he promised to send him, to confirm the peace, thirty-two packhorses laden with gold. But Alexander would have none of it: he told the messenger he'd no intention of leaving till the city of Gaza was his.

Now, Duke Betis had instructed the messenger that, if Alexander rejected his offer, he was to challenge Ptholomer on his behalf to a joust in honour of the ladies. He did so, and Ptholomer accepted the challenge with pleasure.

The messenger returned to the city and reported to his lord Betis all that had happened with Alexander, and that Ptholomer was ready to answer his request. When all the talking was done, the duke summoned every man in Gaza who could bear arms and commanded them to be armed and ready first thing next day, for he meant to go and drive away these Greeks who'd decided to pitch up as neighbours. His orders were duly carried out, and throughout the night he made every preparation and had the city securely watched and guarded to ensure that the Greeks, so sharp and cunning, didn't take them by surprise. Everything was done as he commanded.

CHAPTER LIII

Of the death of Duke Betis, and how the city of Gaza was taken.

When morning came Duke Betis armed along with all his knights. Once his troops were ready they marched from the city in vast companies and battalions. Ptholomer, well aware of their approach, was armed and ready for combat and had ordered all his men to arm likewise and, what's more, had sent word to Alexander the night before to expect battle with the enemy in the morning; so the Greeks were all prepared to receive and fight their foes.

Out came the Gazans in splendid array, archers and crossbowmen to the fore and men-at-arms behind; and as they drew near these bowmen split to either side to reveal the men-at-arms in the centre. Then they unleashed volleys at the Greeks, so great that they seemed like a mighty blizzard; but the Greeks covered themselves with their shields and advanced boldly on the enemy, though a good many were struck down and killed. And once the storm of arrows ceased the men-at-arms with levelled lances charged at one another, holding nothing back, and in the ferocious, shattering clash many fell, never to rise again.

In this battle there was a particular company of Africans on the Gazans' side who inflicted heavy losses on the Greeks; but Emenidus and his battalion surrounded them and not a single one escaped. These Africans had been led there by a lord named Medina, who rode a mare, so the history says, that was a better mount than any rouncey,[1] and Danselin won this mare from him by force of

---

[1]   The rouncey ('*roncin*') was a strong, well-bred horse, lacking the *cachet* of the true war-horse (the '*destrier*') and costing less, but often trained for battle and frequently referred to as a noble's mount in the *Alexander* romances (Alexander himself, after the death of

arms. In the course of this battle Alexander slew a great baron named Poinchon, much to the grief of the Gazans and of Betis most of all, for he loved him very dearly. And Betis, seeing the vast slaughter of his men, rode forward from the battle lines and challenged Ptholomer to joust; Ptholomer charged at once, and they exchanged such blows that their lances smashed to pieces and they sent each other flying from their saddles. From both sides men came galloping to assist their lords, and they met in such a fearsome clash that many were killed there, Greeks and Gazans alike. But after this Duke Betis, seeing his numbers ever falling, began to retreat towards the city; but the Greeks were hot on his heels and struck him from his horse and killed him before Alexander could get there. Indeed, according to the history, the Greeks were so swift in pursuit of their foes that they forced their way into the city behind them: the Gazans didn't have time to raise the drawbridge or drop the portcullis.

So the city was taken and surrendered to Alexander at once, and there he stayed till he had mastery and control of all the surrounding country.

We learn from the history that in those parts he conquered many cities in Calibe, Media and Turkey, such as the city of Pantapolus, outside whose walls was slain a king of India named Porus, brother of old King Clarvus of whom we'll tell hereafter, and the city of Defur, where Count Melcis was captured and killed with many others. And Alexander, so the history says, found wives in these lands for many of his barons and acquired a great number of allies; among these new companions was a valiant warrior by the name of Floridas.

It was in the course of these exploits that Alexander heard tell of a queen named Candace, a very wise and beautiful lady who was queen of Tradiaque,[1] and he was eager to see her because she believed in God Omnipotent; but his path for now was to take him elsewhere, though you'll hear of this lady later.

CHAPTER LIV

How after all these conquests the noble King Alexander met old Cassamus du Laris, brother of Gadifer who had been killed at Gaza.

After conquering the aforesaid lands and cities, Alexander set out for the kingdom of Tradiaque[2] in the hope of seeing the lady of his heart, Queen Candace.

As he was leaving the land of Chaldea and about to pass into Africa, he came upon a mighty city in a deep defile: it was called Damere, and its captain

Bucephalus, is described at one point as 'finely mounted on a handsome rouncey' – below, p.263). That a lord should have chosen to ride a mare might well have seemed remarkable to Wauquelin's audience: in the 14th-century romance *Perceforest*, which enjoyed considerable popularity at the Burgundian court, there is a lengthy passage revolving around the supposed disgrace of a knight being forced to ride a mare. See *Perceforest*, tr. Bryant (Woodbridge, 2011), pp.74-9.

[1] This name probably derives from Prasiaca, a land along the banks of the Ganges, though the geographical logic of the *Alexander* romances is, as ever, not to be examined too closely.

[2] Wauquelin abruptly changes the name of the land (here but nowhere else) to '*Tharse*' (the name that appears in *Li Fuerre de Gadres*).

and governor was a noble baron of the highest renown by the name of Fauvel. As soon as Alexander appeared, this Fauvel received him with the greatest honour and yielded to him his city and all he possessed, and Alexander rewarded his benevolence by granting it all back to him and treating him with the utmost respect.

The king stayed there just one day; early next morning he took his leave of Fauvel and left him to hold the city in peace as his vassal. He rode all that day without incident till evening, when he dismounted in a fair green meadow beside a beautiful river, broad and clear. There he ordered his army to make camp and rest for the night.

When morning came he rose and dressed and then began to walk about the meadow to inspect his army, to see if all was in order and if his men were in need of anything, for such was his custom: no king or prince ever took such care of his men as Alexander, which is why he was so well loved and considered the most courteous prince of his time.

And as he made his way up and down, inspecting his troops, he noticed a man of very great age: his beard was thick and his eyebrows long and he was dressed in black in the manner of Chaldeans at that time: they looked as hermits do now. When Alexander spotted this man he walked up to meet him; and he bowed to him and engaged him in conversation, and realised from the worthy man's speech that he was from Chaldea. So he asked him in Chaldean where he'd come from and where he was going, and the man replied that he'd come from quite close by and was heading for a temple of Mars which stood on a nearby mountain: he was going to sacrifice to the god on behalf of a brother who'd been killed outside Gaza.

'The king of the Greeks,' he said, 'sent seven hundred of his men to steal and plunder cattle there, and my brother was killed by one of the king's knights named Emenidus of Arcadia. His death was a grievous shame and pity, for he was a most valiant man and a fine warrior.'

CHAPTER LV

How Alexander made peace between Cassamus du Laris and Emenidus of Arcadia.

W hen Alexander heard the old man's words he replied: 'Good man, by the gods you worship and by the faith I owe my mother the fair Olympias, I'd gladly give up half the lands I've ever conquered to have your brother Gadifer alive and well as you would wish! I grieve for his death, as I do for the deaths of all the brave men on both sides who were slain in that battle. I'd rather have their company than all the land of Libya, or Colchis where the valiant Jason won the Golden Fleece.'

When the worthy man heard what Alexander said he realised he was the king himself, and his colour changed most fearsomely, turning black as coal and then blood-red: if he'd been able to, I believe he'd have avenged his brother on the spot. The king saw this but for a moment said nothing; then he smiled and said:

'Gadifer's death grieves me, yes, but so do the deaths on our side of Sanson

Dailly and Pieron, taken from us by Gadifer. But you seem to me a man of worth and wisdom, so let peace be made on your terms. And if I or my men can assist you in any way, I shall do so with all my power, against any man.'

At this the worthy man began to weep and was about to kneel and kiss the king's foot, but he wouldn't allow it. Through his tears the old man entrusted the making of peace to him, and the king thanked him deeply and asked him his name, and he told him he was Cassamus du Laris. Then the king summoned Emenidus of Arcadia and bade them make their peace with one another.

After their reconciliation Cassamus came to the king in confidence and said: 'Dear lord, you promised to assist me against all men; I'd be deeply grateful for your aid in an urgent matter. As I told you, I'm Gadifer's brother; he's left behind two fine young sons and a lovely daughter, and King Clarvus of India wants to have her for his wife, but he's much older even than I! The damsel, a good and bright and beautiful girl, would rather be burnt alive than accept him, not just because she knows he's old but because he's a foul man, the nonpareil of wickedness! Her name is Phesonnas. Of her two young brothers, my nephews, one is named Gadifer of Ephesus[1] and the other Betis; they're both lords of the city of Ephesus through their mother, who was a sister of Betis of Gaza. But now this Clarvus means to ruin them and drive them from their city: he's already besieging them there at Ephesus. So I beg you, lord king, help me bring aid to my niece and nephews against this Clarvus, whose brother Porus you slew before the city of Pantapolus.[2] Bring us peace and crush his pride.'

The king most courteously replied that he would do so willingly.

CHAPTER LVI

How Alexander promptly bade his army turn and march to the city of Ephesus.

When the talking was done Alexander had old Cassamus clad in fresh garments, and once he was fittingly dressed he looked a worthy knight indeed – as he undoubtedly was. Then the king gave orders for every man to decamp and follow his banner, and all his forces took to the road. Cassamus led the battalions, knowing all the tracks and passes better than anyone; and they rode all day till evening, when they pitched their tents and pavilions beside a wood just half a day's march from the city of Ephesus.

They stayed there till morning, when Alexander bade them strike camp and march on, which they did, Cassamus still at their head. He led them to a nearby temple of Mars and there they all halted, for the young king was moved to make a sacrifice to the god and ask for word of what would become of this new war he'd undertaken against old Clarvus of India.

---

[1] 'Epheson'.
[2] As mentioned above, p.73.

CHAPTER LVII

Of King Alexander's sacrifice to the god Mars.

When he arrived at the temple Alexander stripped naked and donned fresh clothes, all white. Then he took what he needed for his sacrifice and called upon some of his nobles to escort him to the temple door; there he bade them wait till he'd finished his business and received an answer from the god.

He entered the temple and stepped up to the altar. In his hand he held a vessel filled with milk and oil, and this he placed on the altar before the idol. Then he took off one of his white robes, the topmost, and spread it before the altar on a marble block set there for the purpose; he then stripped naked, and having done so, fastened four swords to the block's four horns;[1] then he processed around the altar three times, bowing and saying appropriate words each time he passed before it; then he took up his vessel filled with milk and oil and raised it high as an offering to the idol before pouring it over his naked flesh while praying to the god Mars for mercy. Then he came and lay upon the white robe he'd spread there, with his head towards the east, praying to the god Mars for an answer to the question he'd asked. Sleep came upon him, and he fell into a slumber; and as he slept the god Mars appeared to him, saying:

'Jupiter will rise above Saturn, and I shall help him raise his horns on high, to be seen and known by all the world.'

With that he vanished and Alexander awoke, the god's reply fixed fast in his mind. He donned his clothes again and returned to his knights who were waiting for him outside, and he told them of his vision and the god Mars's reply. Learned men were summoned at once to interpret the dream and the god's response; they came with eager speed, and among them was master Aristotle, whose verdict was as follows:

'My lord, I take the god Jupiter to be yourself, and Saturn I take to be Clarvus, king of India, whom you'll defeat and destroy and whose power and lordship you will crush. And you should mightily rejoice that the god Mars said "I shall help him", for – unless you yourself obstruct it – he wishes to make you lord of all the world and make every nation fear your might and sword. So rejoice! The gods are with you!'

When Alexander's barons heard this their jubilation was a picture to behold; and if anyone was happy it was Cassamus, who came straight to Alexander rejoicing as much as any man could, and asked his leave to ride to the city of Ephesus to tell his nephews and his niece the news of his joyous coming. The king gave permission, but bade him return swiftly with word of what was happening there.

---

[1]   Cf. *Exodus* 29, 12: 'And thou shalt take of the blood of the bullock, and put it upon the horns of the altar with thy finger…'

CHAPTER LVIII

How Cassamus brought the news to his nephews and fair Phesonnas
of the noble King Alexander's coming.

With the king's leave Cassamus du Laris mounted a palfrey and left the army and kept riding till he came to the Pharon, a mighty river that flowed before the city on the side from which he was approaching. There was no bridge and nowhere to ford the river, and so the citizens had ferrymen to carry people back and forth – as they still do – and a flight of steps led down to a boarding-place. Cassamus now arrived at the riverbank and found a ferryman waiting for passengers; he recognised Cassamus as soon as he saw him, and burst into tears of joy and said:

'Ah, sir! You are welcome indeed! You couldn't have come at a better time: we've so many troubles in the city now! First the death of the good Gadifer du Laris, your brother; and now old Clarvus means to put an end to your nephews – and what's more, means to abduct their sister, your good and worthy niece the damsel Phesonnas! If you doubt my words, look at the heights beyond the city: see the tents and pavilions of Clarvus of India – he's besieging us with twenty thousand men!'

'Peace now, dear friend,' said Cassamus. 'You'll soon hear better news. Ferry me across, and I'll go and hearten my nephews and niece and all the good men of the city.'

So the ferryman took him aboard and carried him over the water, and Cassamus rode through the city and up to the palace. His arrival was announced to the children at once, and they came and welcomed him with the utmost honour; and he cheered them exceedingly as he told them in the presence of all how Alexander was coming to their aid with thirty thousand men-at-arms and was less than three leagues away. 'So I pray you,' he said, 'make every vessel ready to ferry his army when he comes to cross the Pharon.'

These words sent joy running through the city as if God Himself had descended there! And Cassamus told them how Alexander had made peace with him for the death of his brother Gadifer: Emenidus was bringing a mighty force with Alexander to make amends to his nephews for killing their father by doing battle with Clarvus and the Indians.

CHAPTER LIX

How the men of the city of Ephesus launched an attack upon their foes.

As you may imagine, many words and stories were exchanged that night between uncle, nephews and niece. And there were many ladies and damsels of high lineage residing with the lady Phesonnas because of her fine reputation. Among them was a most beautiful, pleasant and gracious lady named Edea, and another no less worthy of praise named Ydoree and one named Heliot. These damsels were fair of speech indeed, in fact perfectly so, well versed especially in matters of love, whose powers and ways they well understood. And they weren't alone: equally so were the noble youths Gadifer and Betis and many other young squires and knights; old Cassamus, too, was gracious in speech and behaviour alike – his equal, indeed, would be hard to find – both in matters of love and of war.

And as they talked, the young knight Gadifer declared that next day, if it pleased the gods, he would go and give a wake-up call to the Indians, the Medes and the Persians who'd decided to make themselves their neighbours on account of his fair sister Phesonnas! Betis and the other young knights all promised to accompany him, and:

'Without a doubt,' said Cassamus, 'I shall be the first!'

'Ah, sir!' said Gadifer. 'You're old and stiff now, in need of rest! You couldn't cope with battle!'

Cassamus was so indignant that he could hardly be appeased.

All rose and armed at the crack of dawn; and when they were all armed the damsel Edea came to old Cassamus and took him by the hand and smiled and said:

'In faith, sir, I claim you for my sweetheart: to me you look better in arms than any man here! And to keep you mindful of me, I give you my ring.'

Cassamus set it on his finger, as filled with joy and gladness as could be. Then he took his leave of her with the tenderest of kisses.

All the troops of the city now made for the gate. Gadifer was at their head, mounted on a rouncey,[1] lance in hand, and so splendidly accoutred that he was a joy to behold. The gate was opened and forth they rode, and Gadifer, as soon as he was out, thrust in his spurs and shouted 'Corton!', his battle-cry, and went charging towards the Indians to wake them all; then he returned to his men – who numbered only four hundred and fifty – and ordered them to form their lines, ready to give and receive the expected fearsome blows.

CHAPTER LX

How Chaldeans and Rabians did battle with Indians, Persians and Medes.

The Indians and Persians, seeing the men of Ephesus – who called themselves Chaldeans and Rabians – sally from the city, sent swift word to King Clarvus, who immediately sounded the alarm. This Clarvus was king of India, and Porus, of whom we spoke earlier,[2] had been his brother. And Clarvus had four sons: one also named Porus, a strong man indeed and greatly feared who was to cause many a problem for Alexander, a second named Canaan, a third named Caneos and a fourth named Sallehedin. These four sons were with him there, as was his nephew the sultan of Baudres, who went by the name of Cassel the Baudrian; so too was another great lord named Marcien, king of Persia, and so many more that they numbered sixty thousand men-at-arms. But when the Ephesians

---

[1]   See note 1, above, p.72.
[2]   Above, p.73.

from Chaldea made this sortie the four sons weren't in Clarvus's camp: they'd gone hunting boar and deer in a nearby forest; so they knew nothing of what followed, which proved a perilous affair.

As soon as the Indians were armed they went to meet the Chaldeans; and it was a ferocious clash, you may be sure, with both sides eager to strike the foe. And strike they did: the blows and buffets they dealt each other, felling one another with their mighty axes, sounded like a thundering storm. The slaughter there was pitiless. And according to the history, young Gadifer performed amazing feats of arms, and struck and drove old Clarvus from his rouncey and would have taken him prisoner if he hadn't been bravely rescued by his men, in the course of which Gadifer, too, was unhorsed and would have been captured had it not been for his uncle Cassamus. In the battle that grew around the rescue countless men were killed in a merciless exchange of mighty blows of lances, swords and darts. And in this battle Cassamus slew a great lord of India and took his rouncey, nobly, richly harnessed, and bade a page-boy mount it and ride back to the city and present it on his behalf to the damsel Edea, who had given him her love that morning. This was duly done, much to the joy of all the damsels, especially the fair Edea, who gave the page a handsome gift for love of Cassamus. Then the boy returned to the battle, where he found Cassamus performing splendid feats; and he told him all that had happened and how his beloved lady had received him courteously.

Betis, too, performed most chivalrously in that day's fighting, achieving wondrous deeds of arms: by his hand was slain a mighty Indian lord named Agoris; and he won carts and wagons, too – I don't know how many – laden with wine and victuals, and drove them back inside the city.

CHAPTER LXI

A bitter exchange of words between Cassamus and Clarvus.

The men of the city were few in number compared with their besiegers, so they stayed close to their banners, with barriers[1] in front providing refuge. They attacked as if skirmishing: charging forward, then withdrawing behind the barriers. And now old Clarvus, his blood up, filled with fury, came riding towards the barriers, lance poised, inviting combat; seeing this, Cassamus rode out to meet him, thinking the challenge was his rather than any other man's because of his seniority. And when they were within earshot Cassamus cried:

'Lord king of India, what makes you so keen to have my niece, fair Phesonnas, when she doesn't want you? And what a waste it would be: all you need now is a soft bed! Sporting with women's beyond you! As long as I'm alive I swear you'll not have her or ever hold her in your arms! I suggest you go back the way you came before you find you've run out of time!'

'I hear you, Cassamus,' Clarvus replied, 'but you and your troops don't con-

---

[1]   '*Lices*': outlying palisades or barricades, beyond a castle's walls and gates, to slow and impede besieging forces.

vince me: in spite of you and them I'll have the girl by force or willingly. I know you've brought the bastard who calls himself King Alexander to come here to your aid – and that makes us all the happier: we'll have revenge upon him, if it please the gods, for the death of our dear brother Porus!'

'Ah!' cried Cassamus. 'You wicked, false braggart! How dare you speak so of the most valiant man in the world! I defy you! Defend yourself!'

And so saying, he thrust in his spurs and charged at Clarvus, and Clarvus at him, like thunder; and they delivered such blows to each other's shield that their lances flew into pieces. Then they drew their swords and began such a fearful hewing and battering that if they hadn't been pulled apart it would have gone badly for one or the other, as each strove to destroy his foe. In the fray that grew around them there were many felled and slain, for the sultan of Baudres charged with his whole battalion and drove the Ephesians back behind their barriers, as did Marcien, king of Persia, who was a valiant warrior indeed (and Clarvus's nephew, so the history says, though I don't know on which side).

While these forces were embroiled King Alexander had reached a high hill close to the river and could clearly see Clarvus's army and the fighting outside the city. The combatants caught sight of him likewise and were all the more inspired to fight well – the men of the city out of love for him and renewed hope of his support (which they were to have indeed), and their besiegers out of hatred, to show how little love or fear they felt for Alexander. So both sides strove all the harder to excel. In this combat Marcien of Persia was unhorsed by Gadifer but swiftly rescued and remounted. The ladies and damsels on the city walls had a full view of the contest, and it was the young knight Gadifer they praised most highly of all the combatants – and old Cassamus, too, for he took captive the sultan of Baudres, Cassel the Baudrian, after whose capture the Ephesians began to withdraw from the fight and rode back to their city, their spirits soaring, knowing they'd shown their worth and valour and rejoicing at the sultan's capture. On the other side the Baudrians were distraught to see their lord led a prisoner back to the city.

CHAPTER LXII

How old Cassamus had his captive the Baudrian fêted and honoured.

After the sultan of Baudres's capture no more attacks were mounted. The Indians returned to their tents and cooking-fires as crestfallen as could be, for they'd lost more than they'd gained, and all the more ashamed because the Ephesians were so few compared to them.

Meanwhile the Ephesians returned to the city in high spirits. When Cassamus reached the palace he had his prisoner disarmed and given fresh clothes as befitted his station; and once he was dressed he took him by the hand and said:

'Come, lord of Baudres, let's go and see the ladies. Be of good cheer, and don't fret at being our prisoner, for if it please the gods we'll give you pleasant entertainment!'

And with these words or the like he brought him to the chamber of the damsel Phesonnas, who rose at once to meet her uncle and greeted them both with all due honour and with her customary grace. And Gadifer and Betis promptly arrived, those valiant and noble youths, and began to pay the sultan all possible respect. After these words of welcome they sat down in pairs on silken carpets, holding each other by the hand: the lady Phesonnas held the Baudrian's, Betis held Ydoree's, Cassamus held Edea's, and so on in their pairs. And Phesonnas, seeking to raise the Baudrian's spirits, said:

'What's troubling you, sir? Cast all melancholy from your heart and turn your thoughts to true love! This chamber requires it! And if anything appeals to you, don't keep it hidden here: tell us something of your fancies and let's talk of the joys of love!'

Then Cassamus spoke up, saying: 'Sir Baudrian, shed all worry and heartache. There's no shame in being a prisoner: prowess and courage and your heart's noble striving have brought you to this pass! We'd struggle to find an opponent as fierce as you have been today: your strength made your sword an awesome weapon against us! Enjoy yourself with these damsels here, and if you're not yet in love, become so now! Here you can fall in love without fearing any wrongdoing or dishonour.'

'Ah, sir!' the Baudrian replied. 'Thanks for your great courtesy. My valour hardly compares with the prowess and mighty courage I saw in you today.'

They exchanged such words and pleasantries until it was time for the tables to be laid. Then they ate with great pleasure, and when the feasting and entertainment were done they all took to their beds. That they were well served is beyond question.

They apparently spent many days in sport and entertainment. And the history says that during his captivity the Baudrian made the damsel Edea his lady-love: all the while he was there, both day and night they spent their time exchanging love songs and sweet words. He was far more comfortable than his uncle Clarvus!

Chapter LXIII

How Clarvus's four sons were rebuked, and how they planned to lure the Ephesians out of their city.

Clarvus returned to camp as downcast as could be, and was joined there by the Baudrians, who wailed at him about the Ephesians having taken their lord captive in the battle. In the midst of all the talking and lamenting Clarvus's four sons returned from their hunt, and when they heard of the Baudrians' loss they were beside themselves: young Porus especially cursed himself for having missed the battle, and no less vexed were his three brothers Canaan, Caneos and Sallehedin. As soon as he saw them their father started berating them, too – Porus in particular, who took great offence and swept from his father's presence in a rage.

He went straight to Marcien the Persian and insisted they must devise a way to bring the men of the city to battle; so Marcien summoned Porus's brothers, and when they arrived he said to them:

'Lord Porus, and you, dear brothers and companions, we mustn't be upset about the Baudrian's capture: it was due to his great courage. But we must plan a way to rescue him. This is what I suggest: the men of the city always drive their herds to graze the pastures outside the Arborie gate, on the other side of that stream; so I propose we swim across on our horses – just thirty of us – and round up all their stock. As soon as the Ephesians get wind of it they'll ride out in a raging fury and we'll let them chase us; and the previous night we'll post four thousand of our finest men in the little wood or in the stream, so that if Fortune grants that Gadifer, Betis or Cassamus come out to rescue their herds I've no doubt we'll capture at least one of them and so recover the Baudrian. And we'll tell your father Clarvus to have his army ready, so that if anything goes wrong he can come to our aid.'

This scheme was approved by all, and they agreed to carry it out on the second day following – they'd spend the next day in reconnaissance and detailed planning.

But unbeknown to the Indians, a spy from the city had been present as they plotted, and he went straight to alert old Cassamus and his nephew Gadifer. He arrived just as they were about to go and cross the Pharon to meet King Alexander; they were delighted to be thus forewarned, and told the spy to say nothing to anyone till they returned.

CHAPTER LXIV

How peace was made between young Gadifer and Emenidus for the death of Gadifer's father.

Cassamus, apprised of the Indians' and Persians' plans, took his leave of the sultan of Baudres – joyously ensconced with the damsels in the chamber – and of the other lords and ladies; and taking his nephew Gadifer with him he set out to find the noble King Alexander whom he'd left on the other side of the great River Pharon.

They took the boat across the river and then mounted their horses and kept riding till they reached Alexander's camp, which wasn't far away; and as soon as they arrived they made their way to the royal tent where they found Alexander making merry with some of his lords. As soon as he saw him Cassamus bowed and paid him all due reverence, and the king, recognising him instantly, rose to greet him and took his hand by way of welcome. Then young Gadifer bowed to the king, who bade him rise and asked Cassamus who the youth was. He explained that he was the son of his brother Gadifer du Laris, who'd been killed by Emenidus outside Gaza. At this Alexander began to weep, and he kissed and embraced Gadifer, saying:

'My very dear friend, your father's death has upset me greatly, but it's done and can't be undone. But I'm ready to make amends now as you wish: tell me how I can be of service.'

Then Gadifer, seeing the king's great humility, began to weep so much that he was barely able to utter thanks. And Gadifer's arrival had been reported at once to Emenidus, who immediately summoned twelve companions and bade each hold a naked sword by the point upside-down before their breasts and to follow him, barefoot and bare-headed, to the royal pavilion. When he arrived he knelt before the king and saluted him; the king returned his greeting, wondering what Emenidus was about to do – though he had a good idea. Then Emenidus asked him which man was Gadifer, and the king said it was the young knight he was holding by the hand; and Emenidus said:

'Ah, gentle knight, I crave your mercy! You see before you the one who deprived you of a father! You may sentence him as you please: to death or life or imprisonment.'

When Gadifer saw his humble contrition he began to weep, and through his tears he said: 'Sir, your humility has purged all my bitterness and wrath! I forgive you all the wrongs you've done me: give me your friendship, I pray you, and I shall give you mine.'

'Most gratefully,' Emenidus replied, 'and for your kindness I give you, if it please you to accept it, the whole kingdom of Tiberias[1] that I won from King Aminargon; and I give you as your wife the sister of my nephew Pieron, whom your father slew outside Gaza: a most beautiful damsel, the lady of Medoine and part of India, who goes by the name of Lyndonie.[2] If you thus become my nephew, the love between us will be all the firmer.'

At these words Gadifer fell at his feet, thanking him for this great honour and favour, and Emenidus raised him and kissed him as a sign of love and peace. Hardly a man in the royal pavilion, you may be sure – neither the king nor anyone else – could help weeping at the sweet words exchanged by Emenidus and Gadifer.

CHAPTER LXV

How Cassamus and Gadifer returned to the city of Ephesus after this reconciliation.

After this peace had been made Cassamus began discussing a number of matters with the king, telling him all about the previous day's venture and how the sultan of Baudres had been taken and was now a captive in the city. And he told how Clarvus's four sons were planning an ambush by sending a party to round up their herds; and because the men in the city were few in number, he and Gadifer implored the king to send troops in support so that they could better resist the Indians. Alexander replied that all his men were at their disposal. They also spoke of fixing a day to meet Clarvus in open battle, and a party of knights

---

[1]   'Thabarie'.

[2]   The name appears here as 'l'Indoine', which could possibly be translated as 'the Indian', but the name of Gadifer's wife is later given as Lyndonie (below, p.133). She, along with Gadifer and Betis, is a major figure in *Perceforest* (which takes a number of characters and incidents from the Alexander romances, especially from *The Vows of the Peacock*), and there her name is transcribed as Lydore.

was sent to the Indian king and did their work well, securing his agreement to pitch army against army on the following Tuesday.

After lengthy conversation with the king Cassamus wished to take his leave, and Alexander summoned Ariscé, Perdicas, Caulus, Leones and Floridas and bade them take all their men to the city with Cassamus du Laris and give him all the help he needed. They did so as willingly as a fair youth kisses his sweetheart! They left the army with all their forces and crossed the river in boats and made their way into the city, where they were given the most glorious reception. Their arrival was reported at once to Betis and the damsels, who were revelling with the good Baudrian, and they all went hand in hand to give them a joyous welcome. Then they returned together to 'the Lady Venus's Chamber', the most luxurious, I believe, ever known to man; and as soon as they arrived they sat together on silken carpets and entertained each other with pleasantries and verse and song until it was time for the tables to be set, whereupon they rose and washed and took their seats. If I were to describe in detail the lavish service they enjoyed it would be tiresome, so I'll say no more, but you may well imagine that every honour was bestowed upon such a gathering of noble princes and princesses.

CHAPTER LXVI

How the lady Phesonnas and the sultan of Baudres played chess.

Once supper was done and the tables were cleared, in the interval before bedtime they entertained each other with playful talk as before. It was now that Cassamus called for a chessboard, and when it was brought to him he started to set up the pieces and bade his niece, the lady Phesonnas, play against the Baudrian. She said she would gladly do so if it pleased the sultan; he replied that he wasn't very good but would happily play, so they sat down together at the board. Then Phesonnas began to tease him, saying:

'To stop you getting upset, sir, you shall have an extra rook and knight – but I'll checkmate you in the corner with a pawn!'

Edea, already in love with the Baudrian, jealously interposed: 'Lady Phesonnas, if you put him off by teasing he's bound to lose!'

But the banter continued till the Baudrian didn't know what was going on; soon he was quite distracted and couldn't decide on a move. Then Phesonnas, taking his queen with a knight, said: 'Check!', and he had to move his king backwards; whereupon she said: 'Oh, sir! We can't trust much in your fighting powers if you're so quick to run away!' The Baudrian was too ashamed to think of a reply; he had no choice but to keep quiet and suffer the embarrassment. 'Ah, Sir Baudrian!' said Phesonnas. 'I see you're distracted by sweet thoughts of love! Come, come! Let's just enjoy the game! You'd better watch out: carry on like this and you'll be mated in the corner, if it please our goddess Venus – or out here in the middle, come to that!'

At this the whole hall erupted with laughter, and Phesonnas, realising the joke, flushed red and felt a little embarrassed. But she continued the game and was soon saying once more: 'Check, sir. Careful now: I'll have you mated next move unless you defend yourself better!'

Cassamus, propped on a cushion and hearing his niece's teasing words, roared with laughter; but not wanting the Baudrian to lose face he picked up his cushion and tossed it on the board, saying: 'You're both checkmated and I win! I've wiped out every piece – victory's mine!' And he called for wine which was brought in rich vessels of gold, and they all drank merrily.

After they'd drunk the party broke up and some took to their beds – notably the Baudrian in his chamber and the ladies in theirs.

CHAPTER LXVII

How that night Cassamus told Gadifer, Betis and the Greeks what his spy had reported the day before.

But while the sultan of Baudres and the ladies retired, Cassamus called together the other barons and told them how the Indians planned to come early next day and lead them into an ambush by rounding up their cattle.

'I've heard this,' he said, 'from a spy I sent to their camp. King Clarvus's four sons are coming, and so is Marcien the Persian. That's why your king has sent you here to help us – and next Tuesday, let me tell you, the noble Alexander and Clarvus, king of India, have sworn to meet in open battle. So we pray you, worthy Greeks, advise us what to do for the best.'

'Sir,' Ariscé replied, 'the best advice I can give is this: keep close watch for the ambush party from the city's walls and gates; and when morning comes and it's time for the herds to go out, we'll all be armed and ready – but we won't all ride out at once: a few of us will chase the enemy as far as their ambush, and when they then pursue us back the rest of us can charge out in a concerted attack. That's our best chance of surprising them. That's what I think, anyway: if anyone has a better idea, say so.'

But everyone concurred, and they all retired to their chambers to rest. But Cassamus first went to alert all the captains of the city, to make sure their men would be ready in the morning; and he gave orders for all the towers, walls, gates and barbicans to be well guarded, as the Indians were enraged about the Baudrian's capture and were bent on rescuing him by some cunning plan. 'So we must mount a closer guard than ever, both on account of the Baudrian and in readiness for Tuesday's battle.' Once he'd seen to all this Cassamus went and slept till morning, when he was the very first to rise and arm: his diligence in all matters was unequalled.

CHAPTER LXVIII

How Clarvus's four sons came to round up the city's herds.

As you've heard, Clarvus's four sons had resolved to go and steal the Ephesians' herds; and when the appointed morning came they went with Marcien the Persian to their father's tent to tell him of their plan.

'Sir,' said Marcien to old Clarvus, 'we're going to launch a raid on their herdsmen outside the Arborie Gate and steal their cattle. We know the Ephesians are men of spirit: they'll ride out against us, banners flying! So I suggest you mount an attack with all your battalions at the other gate, the Porte du Pret.'

'By my life!' said Clarvus. 'That's a mad idea! We'd have a thousand killed and wounded before we took the gate! There's nothing to be won that way: some wretched slave is as likely to kill a duke or a count as anyone else. In any case, we're due to do battle with the king of the Greeks next Tuesday! I don't want to risk losing my best troops: I'm not having anyone say he found me wanting! That false and cunning schemer wants dominion over every nation on the earth! But he's not going to lord it over me – not if I can help it: I'd rather be cut limb from limb.'

'As you wish, sir,' said Marcien; and without another word they left the tent and mounted, determined to do exactly as they'd planned. As soon as they were ready they set off, and rode to the little wood and prepared their ambush.

It was still so early that the sun hadn't risen; but the Ephesians, fully aware of their plan, were quite ready, and as soon as the sun shed its first rays on the city, Cassamus, well and richly armed, gave orders for the gates to be opened and the herds to be driven out. This was done; and the moment the cattle reached the pastures thirty raiders sprang forward, led by Porus, Clarvus's son, and Marcien with him, and rounded up the herd and started driving them off. At this the hue and cry went up from the herdsmen and the watchmen on the walls alike; and Floridas, armed and ready, having asked Cassamus and the others to let him lead the charge, was first to ride out, thrusting in his spurs, and his horse bore him swiftly over the fields. Porus, at the rear and keeping watch for the first to appear, saw him; and as soon as he did, without uttering a word or cry, he turned to confront him, lance levelled, and they dealt each other such fearsome blows that both were borne unconscious to the ground. Porus, a man of mighty heart, was first to rise and find his horse and remount; but he made no further attack on Floridas, who was still flat out: he vowed he'd never be accused of taking his enemy prisoner while prostrate.

CHAPTER LXIX

Of the fierce and bitter fight to rescue the herds outside Ephesus.

The unhorsed Floridas was still stretched out, completely unconscious. But his companions, who were right behind him and had seen his joust, rode up at once. They spoke to him as they hauled him to his feet, and he heard them and felt deep shame; but his horse was returned to him and he quickly remounted: even though he was still in a daze he was determined to be involved in the fight.

They set off swiftly after the foe, and Cassamus caught up with Marcien who'd no intention of being chased and turned to face him. They started battering at each other with their swords till sparks were flying, and their companions did likewise: if one attacked fiercely, his foe defended boldly, for the Indians, aggrieved at the capture of the Baudrian, were bent on taking prisoners so that they could win him back in exchange. Porus was performing many a feat of arms, jousting with anyone he met and dashing down horses and knights like a thunderbolt; and Floridas, seeing him and knowing he was the one who'd unhorsed him, charged at him again and struck him a two-handed blow with a mace that laid him flat over the front of his saddle. If he'd dealt him another he'd have killed him; but he couldn't, for Porus, seeing Floridas poised beside him, swung his gisarme[1] sideways and caught him on the shield, smashing off a huge chunk and forcing Floridas back. But Floridas didn't leave him – he delivered another blow that crushed his helm over his eyes. If their men hadn't intervened, one of them would never have left that place.

To watch his feats of arms the ladies and damsels were atop the towers of the palace – known as the Palace of Jupiter – along with their prisoner, the sultan of Baudres. They were there in time to witness the combat between Floridas and Porus, and as they discussed it the sultan told them that the knight from his side was young Porus, son of Clarvus, king of India; they praised him highly for his great courage, saying that if he lived long he'd be one of the most valiant in the world.

At that very moment the men hidden in the little wood charged out – it was very close to the combat – and began a mighty fray, for they were all men of great spirit and didn't want to be left out of things, and feared death no more than the cattle! But as they sprung their ambush, a huge body of men-at-arms sallied from the city, too, fresh and well rested, and fell upon the enemy like thunder from the sky. Soon you'd have seen riderless horses careering around, and many a knight with guts trailing, brains spilling, and severed hands and severed feet scattered across the field – it was horrific: there were piles of brain and pools of blood spread everywhere. The brave were busily slaughtering the craven: it was a savage and terrible wonder. Amid the carnageAriscé de Valestre and Porus's brother Caneos were raining blows on one another, and would have killed each other if they hadn't been rescued by their men; and Canaan, brother of Caneos, would have taken Ariscé captive if Gadifer hadn't realised and charged in with his whole battalion. Gadifer and Canaan were locked in combat then; but to describe their fight would be a long affair – as would a description of the other, for all four fought unsparingly.

Into the fearsome fray rode the Baudrians, desperate to claim a prisoner to exchange for their captured lord; and they drove into the Greeks so fiercely that they forced them back, whether they liked it or not, more than twice the length of a bowshot.[2] There was a hammering clash of swords and axes that would have drowned the sound of thunder, truly; and the history tells that the air was dark with the steaming breath of men and mounts and the smoking blood of dead and wounded.

---

[1] A pole weapon similar to a halberd, combining a hook with a point or axe-blade.
[2] Literally 'more than four arpents'; the *arpent* was a unit of length roughly equivalent, in medieval France, to 70 metres.

Chapter LXX

How Gadifer's brother Betis was captured by the Indians, and Porus by the Greeks.

Marcien of Persia, seeing Clarvus's sons in reckless danger and the Ephesians sending a steady stream of fresh reinforcements, realised they were likely to lose more than they gained; and knowing Clarvus was in no hurry to send help he feared imminent calamity and sounded the retreat. Porus, his blood boiling in the heat of battle, was enraged at the sound, convinced he had the strength to take the city; but he had no choice but to retreat or he'd have been left alone with all his foes. But their withdrawal was conducted in such good order that it was a pleasure to behold, the most valiant forming a rearguard – Porus among them, his eyes fixed on the Ephesians' next move.

Gadifer's brother Betis, who had yet to do anything of note, saw the Indians retreating and decided to pursue them; and so he did, spurring so hard that he'd soon left his men far behind. Porus saw him coming and could see he was seeking a joust, so he lowered his lance and charged with all the speed his horse could summon. Betis, craving nothing more, rode to meet him likewise, and so swift was their charge that the blows they exchanged were too much for their lances, stout though they were, and they flew into splinters. On they galloped past each other at such a rate that Betis careered into the midst of the Indians where he was seized and taken prisoner, and Porus plunged into the Greeks likewise and he, too, was captured. But it wasn't without cost to both sides, for these two knights were brave and valiant indeed: first Betis, bursting with confidence, drew his sword and started scattering the Indians in incredible fashion, killing them with every blow, beating and battering them to the ground, until Marcien finally seized him with the help of his men. And if Betis was performing valiantly so was Porus, in an amazing display of arms: the history says he dealt such mighty blows with a two-handed axe that he was felling everyone; even when they took his horse he set himself with his back to an ancient wall and was surrounded by a mass of Greeks bombarding him with darts and missiles, but they could find no way to get near him. There was a fearful yelling from men and women alike, and Cassamus headed towards the din and saw the knight fighting to the limit of endurance. He ordered all his men back and said:

'Sir knight, surrender to me now: there's no point fighting on. Unless you yield you'll die, I fear; it's better to make an honourable surrender than carry on and suffer worse. Come quietly now with us and see the ladies and damsels in the palace, and enjoy the company of Cassel, the sultan of Baudres.'

But at Cassamus's words Porus swelled with defiant rage and cried: 'Truly, sir knight, you must take me for a child if you think I'll yield just because you tell me to! I'll never surrender as long as I live and have the strength to raise my arm! And you'll not have me in your power except by force!'

Cassamus, worthy man that he was, saw that Porus yearned to win honour and a name for prowess. He dismounted and told everyone to step back: he would handle this. Then he drew his sword, set his shield before him and advanced upon the knight and attacked him at close quarters. Porus mounted a fierce and bold defence, and as they fought Cassamus cried:

'Surrender, friend! Don't get yourself hurt or maimed – or, if chance will have it so, killed!

But Porus gave no sign of having heard; he fought on with might and main, and they dealt each other blows that made sparks flash from blades and helms. Betis's brother Gadifer – who knew nothing of his brother's capture – was there, watching his uncle's combat with the knight. He thought it a joy and a pleasure to behold, and said:

'This is the best fight we've seen all day! It's fine entertainment – let them carry on!'

Cassamus heard this and began to laugh inside his helm, saying to himself: 'It's all right for you, dear nephew: you're not feeling the blows!'

After many such words and clashes and buffets, which would take too long to relate, Porus was knocked to the ground, and the Greeks seized him and took away his sword and other weapons so that all he had left to fight with were his fists, which weren't much use to him: he had no choice but to surrender.

CHAPTER LXXI

How Porus was received with honour in the ladies' chamber.

Just as I've described to you – or very like – Porus was taken and held captive by his foes. A prisoner now, but with only helmet, sword and spurs removed, they mounted him on a rouncey. Cassamus remounted likewise, and as he looked about he couldn't see his nephew Betis and began to ask after him; but the only person to reply was Porus who said:

'Truly, sir, he jousted with me just now: it was the joust that brought me to my present plight! I haven't seen him since; he may well be in the same boat as me – it's more likely than not that he's been taken captive, too. It's all the better if we're both prisoners: perhaps it'll lead to peace if there's the will for it; war between you and us is a dangerous business, that's for sure!'

So saying, they passed through the city gate and from there to the palace. The damsels, hearing they'd arrived, came down to meet them and welcomed them with all honour. Then Porus was disarmed and given a rich gown that became him well, for he was a handsome figure in every way: the ladies especially couldn't take their eyes off him and were full of praise, whispering that he showed every sign of being a worthy warrior indeed! Lady Phesonnas took him by the hand and seated him beside her on a silken carpet and said:

'Sir! You've dealt us many a blow with your prowess today: your valour has done us much harm! But we're sorry, too, that you've suffered so much at the hands of our people: they put you in great danger. But your high prowess saved you – praise be to God and my lady the goddess Venus!'

'Ah, lady!' he replied. 'Your words are most courteous and I thank you a thousand times; but had it not been for this worthy old gentleman I think they'd have killed me.'

'God help me, niece,' said Cassamus, 'if I hadn't been rescued he'd have throttled me with his bare hands!'

There was laughter on all sides at this. Then a page entered the chamber
bringing the news that Betis had been caught and taken prisoner to the Indian
camp. They were very upset, but the capture of Porus was a comfort. Then the
sultan of Baudres arrived: he'd just come from worshipping at the Temple of
Diana. He gave Porus a most joyful greeting, though he'd have preferred it to be
in a happier circumstance – but when Fortune's against you, you have to make
the best of it: despair's no help at all. Phesonnas rose to meet him and seated him
on the carpet beside Porus, saying:

'Ah, my lords, would to the gods that all our allies were as valiant as you, our
enemies! We'd fare better in our war against our foes!'

'Truly, lady,' Porus replied, 'I've no wish to be your enemy. And if you
think of Clarvus as a foe, he's not: he's a friend, desiring nothing so much
as your good and gracious self. And very old though he may be, no lady or
damsel should disparage him: he's descended from the noble Trojan blood of
the valiant King Priam himself! And I assure you I'm not saying this because
he's my father!'

The lady Phesonnas felt a little ashamed at this; she realised from Porus's
words that she alone had caused the war, by refusing to take Clarvus as her husband because of his old age. So she changed the subject, and they started talking
of other matters to turn their minds from present woes.

CHAPTER LXXII

How Betis was honoured in the Indian camp, and other matters.

Having captured Duke Betis, the Indians, Persians and Baudrians turned
back with their prize and kept riding till they reached their camp. There
they disarmed Betis and dressed him in a splendid gown before leading him to
King Clarvus's pavilion.

Clarvus was as distressed as could be that his son Porus had been taken
and led captive to the city, all the more so because he didn't know if he'd been
wounded. Now his three other sons and Marcien of Persia arrived with their
prisoner. The moment he saw them, before giving any word of greeting, Clarvus
asked after Porus; but all they could tell him was that he'd been captured, and in
his place they'd taken Betis who said he was Gadifer's brother.

'So don't distress yourself, sire,' they said, 'for if it please the gods we'll exchange this captive for your son and the Baudrian. And grieving achieves nothing. "If you're frightened of leaves," the saying goes, "stay out of the wood!"
– and the same applies to war. If we lose this time, we'll win another.'

So said the Indians to comfort their king. And as they were talking a page-boy
entered Clarvus's tent and bowed and said: 'My dear lord, your son Porus has
been taken prisoner. But he was captured in most honourable fashion, fighting
beside a ruined stone wall: before they took him he killed more than a hundred
of their men, truly, but he was forced to the ground as he fought and his helmet

and sword were seized from him. But however roughly he was treated he has no wound – except on the chin from a sling-stone thrown by some base rogue: but it's nothing, just a scratch. So be of good cheer, for in his capture he earned only high honour.'

'You'd better be telling the truth, boy!' Clarvus said. 'If not you'll feel my distress!'

'Indeed, my lord, no!' the boy replied. 'It's the certain truth!'

'In faith, sir,' said Marcien, 'he may be right. Perhaps your son was embroiled with one who recognised his prowess and courage and so helped him: no worthy man, as you know, should ever fail another.'

'Well, so be it,' Clarvus replied. 'Let's hope it's as you say. I'd rather he was captured with honour than fled in shame.'

'Well said, sir,' said Marcien. 'Have no fears on his account. Now, we need to make a five or six day truce between ourselves and the Ephesians – and the Greeks, too: if we can secure a favourable peace with them by forging a good alliance it would be for the best. Too much warfare does no one any good.'

'By my life!' Clarvus replied. 'As long as my soul's in my body I'll not make peace with Alexander! He killed my brother! Either I'll die, or the deaths of so many valiant men – kings, dukes, counts and barons – who've died or been slain at his hand or in his cause will be avenged with his dead body! But I'll be happy to have a fortnight's truce if they'll agree – or at least until we've exchanged or ransomed our prisoners. And a break in hostilities will let people go about their business as they please.'

After this discussion they sat down to eat, and Betis was seated with all due honour, being treated merely as a prisoner under oath. Indeed, throughout his captivity Marcien and Canaan offered him excellent company, and they went and sported together wherever he chose.

And if Betis's captivity was pleasant enough, Porus's was even more so, spent as it was in the company of the ladies where he found consolation in talk of love – a subject very dear to their hearts and to which their quarters were so conducive.

CHAPTER LXXIII

Here follow the vows of the peacock and the fulfilling thereof;
firstly how and by whom the bird was killed.

According to the history it was in the month of May – though it doesn't say in which year after the Creation – that Porus, as you've heard, was captured outside the city of Ephesus and found himself a prisoner of the ladies upon his word as a gentleman. I've an idea he'd have been happy to stay there! Among the ladies of the palace he found himself surrounded by all the love and courtly refinement he could have wished, both in entertainments and diversions and in talk of love and its effects; and truly, he was as enamoured of the lady Phesonnas as could be.

One day during his captivity, Porus was wandering through the palace in search of entertainment when he met a boy with a catapult[1] aiming pellets at birds. He asked if he could borrow it for a moment, and the boy gladly handed it to him along with a pellet. Porus loaded the catapult ready for a shot at a bird, and as he looked round for a target Cassamus, who was watching him, saw a peacock on the roof of Venus's Chamber proudly displaying, fanning his tail; and he called to Porus, saying:

'Look, Lord Porus, up on the roof! There's a fine target! Take a shot – show us your marksmanship!'

'Ah, my lord, that wouldn't be right! I can't start killing the palace birds, especially on the ladies' pleasure-house!'

'Oh, shoot away!' said Cassamus. 'There are plenty here – more than we need!'

So Porus, egged on by old Cassamus, raised his catapult, took aim and loosed a shot that went clean through the peacock's head and sent its eyes and brains flying, and the bird fell dead to the ground. The ladies and damsels who'd been watching came running up, and lady Phesonnas ran forward and seized Porus by the hand and, laughing, said:

'You're under arrest, sir! You've done me wrong!'

'Ah, lady!' said Porus. 'I crave your mercy, and surrender as your prisoner from this day forth!'

'Very well!' she replied. 'I ask nothing more, and will hold you to your word!'

The way the Greeks and Indians celebrated the peacock's death was a pleasure to behold and hear: they knew how to party! The bird was gathered up and carried to the kitchen to be suitably prepared.

Dinner time was fast approaching, and when the time came and the tables and the cloths were laid, the lords and barons took their places with the maidens and the two captives to feast and entertain them. All indulged in jest and laughter, loving thoughts and glances, freely following the promptings of their hearts. And the lady Phesonnas said to the handsome Porus:

'Ah, sir! The death of my peacock is on your head!'

'Truly, lady,' he replied, 'if I've done wrong the guilt is mine and forgiveness yours! I'd say it makes me all the more your subject – and if the gods grant that this war ends and I come through it alive I shall be your faithful friend for evermore.'

To this the lady answered: 'Sir, God forbid that it be otherwise: I dearly wish you'd never been our enemy.'

At that the peacock was carried with great honour to the table, one of its bearers being a maiden of the court named Heliot; and when it was placed upon the table Cassamus said:

'Come now, gentlemen! We must give this bird new life – with vows! At this table I see some of the most valiant knights in the world, and the most gracious of ladies and damsels; so if you all agree, I'd have justice be done to the noble peacock in a joyful, spirited manner that will bring our company pleasure and delight.'

---

[1]   Literally 'a little bow'.

Knights and squires, ladies and damsels all concurred, and the maiden Heliot was asked to present the peacock to each person as she chose and to receive their respective vows. She raised the bird aloft and came before Cassamus and said:

Chapter LXXIV
The first vow, made by Cassamus du Laris.

'Sir, you have been involved in so many deeds of arms, in which your high prowess has been recognised by so many worthy men that word of it has spread through every land and country; and since, too, you are senior in knighthood in all the present company, I invite and summon you by the power that you and the others have vested in me to make such a vow to the peacock as may be to your honour and the company's delight.'

Then Cassamus replied: 'I've no wish to refuse; so I pledge and vow to the god Mars and to the peacock here before us that, if the battle agreed and promised by the noble King Alexander on the one hand and King Clarvus of India on the other comes indeed to be joined, and we prove to be so dominant that I see Clarvus beleaguered and hard-pressed, I shall go and aid him with all my might and either help him to recover or die in the attempt; and if he lacks either horse or weapons I shall make sure he regains them. And all this shall be done for love of his son Porus whom I see here present, whose valour has led him to be our captive.'

And Porus responded, saying: 'Sir, I shall be sorry if it comes to that, but may the gods repay your courtesy with many blessings – and such courtesy will indeed have its reward, for fine deeds and fine words will never perish.'

With that the lady Heliot took the peacock and placed it before Ariscé, who was seated next to Cassamus, and said:

Chapter LXXV
The second vow, made by Ariscé de Valestre.

'Good sir, you are a knight of the Greek company and have been victorious in so many wars and combats that your renown shines far and wide. Swear a vow to the noble peacock as it please you, according to the company's decree.'

'Ah!' said Ariscé to the lady. 'You may say what you please, but I would to the god Mars I was worthy of your words – I fear I fall a good deal short! Be that as it may; I vow and swear to the peacock here that, if the battle pledged by the Indians and the Greeks takes place, I shall fight with all my strength in support of the men of Ephesus. And everything I do shall be for love of the ladies – especially for the sake and benefit of the lady Phesonnas. Nor shall I leave the battle till the Indians are forced to make peace with you – unless the king of Macedon, my sovereign lord, insists.'

'Thanks indeed, sir!' said the maiden lady Phesonnas. 'It's clear you're determined to repay a hundredfold the favour we've shown you!'

The second vow thus made, the damsel Heliot took the peacock and placed it before Perdicas, who was seated beside the lady Phesonnas, and said:

Chapter LXXVI

The third vow, made by the valiant Perdicas.

'Come now, good lord Perdicas! You are so worthy and valiant that your deeds are inscribed in the annals of prowess and chivalry! Now it's your turn; you must make such a vow to the peacock as shall be to your honour: you are more than able.'

'I've no wish to refuse, lady,' he said. 'I am your knight, ready and prepared to serve you in praise of love and chivalry. So I vow and swear – and may it be pleasing to the god Mars – that if the noble king of Macedon meets King Clarvus in battle on the agreed day, I shall fight in the battle dismounted, in support of the foot soldiers, and am happy to live or die there as the gods ordain. And I shall not leave the fight until the battle has run its course and one side or the other is victorious.'

'Ah, thanks indeed, sir!' said Cassamus. 'The love you have for us is plain to see – as are the prowess and the valour you possess: there's not a grain of cowardice in you!'

And according to the history this Perdicas was a handsome knight indeed, tall and strong, of strapping build, young and courageous, about thirty or thirty-two years old.

When he had made his vow the lady Heliot took the peacock once again and carried it before lady Phesonnas, seated right next to Perdicas. She was a most beautiful, elegant, gracious lady – she seemed to be made, says the history, as an endless feast for the eye! – and Heliot addressed her thus:

Chapter LXXVII

The fourth vow, made by the fair lady Phesonnas.

'Lady, you know all the mysteries of true and perfect love, and are renowned as the most gracious of all ladies and damsels in the world. Make such a vow to the peacock as you may keep to your honour and to the enhancement of your gracious name.'

'Damsel,' said Phesonnas, 'I shall make a vow that I trust will be pleasing to the king of Macedon: I pledge and vow to the peacock, by the faith I owe my lady Venus to whom this house of ours is dedicated, that as long as I live I shall have no husband or lover save with the approval and agreement of my lord King Alexander of Macedon, who for my sake has been willing to cross the Pharon[1]

---

[1]　The text reads *'la mer du Pharaon'*, which might be translated as 'the Egyptian Sea', but for the sake of consistency I take this to be the previously mentioned river Pharon. The inconsistency is caused by Wauquelin now drawing upon a new source, *Les Voeux du Paon* ('The Vows of the Peacock'), Jacques de Longuyon's poem of c.1310 (probably as interpolated in a late manuscript of the verse *Roman d'Alexandre*), which re-interprets the place-name.

to confront our foes. And if anyone doubts my word he doesn't know me, whatever favour or behaviour I may have shown in the past.'

'Truly,' said Cassamus, 'you have made a most fair and pleasing vow, and I thank you for it.'

And Cassamus's admiration of the lady's vow was shared by all. Then Heliot took the peacock once more and set it before Porus, who was deep in thought – so lost in thought indeed, the history says, that he seemed oblivious to anything said to him. The damsel addressed him thus:

CHAPTER LXXVIII

The fifth vow, made by Porus, son of King Clarvus of India.

'Sir, you're a skilled deliverer of mighty blows with axe and sword – leave your musing now and tune your thoughts to ours![1] Pay the peacock his due as others have done: you're more than capable!'

'Ah, lady,' said Porus, 'I'm in no position to make a vow: I'm a slave, a poor prisoner – I can do nothing.'

'Truly, sir,' some of the lords replied, 'make whatever vow you wish: you'll be set free before the day of the great battle.'

'Yes indeed, sir,' said the lady Phesonnas, 'and make it a bold one: we're eager to see your worth and prowess!'

Porus smiled and blushed as he looked at her: his heart was stricken with a shaft of loving desire for the beautiful Phesonnas. He resolved to make a vow that would make everyone talk, and paused a while to consider this. So Heliot called upon him again, saying:

'Sir! Sir! Rouse yourself and pay our peacock his due!'

'Very well! Since the company – and you above all, dear lady! – so wish, I pledge and promise and vow to the peacock that, if the armies meet on Tuesday as planned, I shall perform in such a way as to be vanquisher and master of every enemy battalion and rout them all, if the gods choose by their gracious favour to preserve me from death and injury. And I vow furthermore that, though the fame of Emenidus's might and prowess has spread through many lands, anyone who cares to witness it will see me capture his horse! This vow I shall fulfil or die in the attempt!'

One of the knights present, named Leones, replied: 'Truly, lord Porus, that's quite a challenge you've set yourself! I promise you, if you can bring it to fruition I'll give you eighteen times the horse's weight in gold!'

Leones's view was shared by all the others: they declared it the most audacious vow they'd ever heard!

After this vow the lady Heliot carried her peacock before the fair Edea, who was seated at Porus's side, and said:

---

[1]   Literally 'your hurdy-gurdy's out of tune'!

CHAPTER LXXIX

The sixth vow, made by the fair lady Edea.

'After my lady Phesonnas you, lady, are the paragon of beauty and goodness. By the faith you owe the high and wondrous god of love, you must make a vow to our peacock, and let it be to your honour, for in the presence of the whole company I am ready to receive it.'

'I am only too willing, truly,' said Edea, 'and I pledge and vow to the present company, and to the peacock, that I shall have this bird recreated in the finest gold I can acquire, and it shall be set upon a pillar, of fine gold likewise; I shall commission a design from the most skilled of craftsmen. This I shall do as a memorial to the vows made here and to this illustrious company. And all who see it will call it the Peacock Restored.'[1]

'Oh, lady!' said Porus. 'Thanks indeed! What a noble vow, truly! It is born of a good and sincere heart.'

Everyone shared Porus's admiration. With this vow made, Heliot came bearing the peacock to Cassel, the sultan of Baudres, and said:

CHAPTER LXXX

The seventh vow, which was great and remarkable, made by Cassel the Baudrian.

'Sir knight, sultan of the Baudrians, accomplished in performing and withstanding feats of arms, I summon you to pay our peacock his due.'

'I'll keep it short, fair lady, truly,' he replied. 'I pledge and vow upon my faith and loyalty that, if the battle goes ahead as I trust it will, whoever wishes will see me rob King Alexander of his sword – in the midst of all his men! Help him all you like – I'll achieve my goal!'

There was uproar at this, with people saying: 'Listen to him – the man's deranged!' And a knight named Caulus strode forward to make a vow before the peacock had been brought to him; he was so enraged by the Baudrian's words that he didn't wait to be bidden, but declared:

CHAPTER LXXXI

The eighth vow, made by Caulus.

'Sir knight, you show little respect for the noble Alexander's might and valour – and even less for ours, boasting that you'll take his sword in our presence! How ill repaid he'd be for his favours to us! I promise by the faith I owe the god Mars that if I meet you in the battle – and God forbid I fail – I'll have your helmet unless it's stuck on with cement and the head comes with it! You'll

---

[1]   '*le restor du paon*', which became the title of a sequel to 'The Vows of the Peacock', written by Jean le Court c.1330 and interpolated into a number of late manuscripts of the verse *Roman d'Alexandre*. See below, p.134.

have to cut off my arms to stop me! If you accomplish your vow and bring me the sword, I'll give you a hundred thousand silver marks – so you stand to profit if your plan works out!'

To this Cassel the Baudrian answered courteously, saying: 'Good sir knight, anger and offence have no place here: the vows are made to any and all – let them be taken as they will. Say what you like but don't let my folly upset you! Talking's easy – achieving's what counts.'

'Sirs,' said Cassamus, 'no more quarrelling – let's leave this now. Anyone who achieves his goal will have done well. Carry on, damsel, and complete your business.'

So the maiden Heliot took the peacock and came before Ydoree and bade her make her vow, saying:

Chapter LXXXII
The ninth vow, made by the fair Ydoree.

'Dear damsel, pay our peacock his due, as the company requests.'
'Indeed I shall,' lady Ydoree replied. 'First of all, it's true I have a faithful sweetheart who's given his love to me, and I've given him mine for I'm sure he's free of all base thoughts – and he's handsome, young, full of courage and prowess, without a hint of cowardice. And so I pledge and vow to him – and I shall keep my word – that I shall love him faithfully always, with a sincere and guileless heart; this vow I make to the peacock in the presence of you all.'

You may well imagine the joy with which her words were greeted, for they were delivered with the utmost happiness. And old Cassamus replied to her, saying:

'Well, damsel, since true love has you in its thrall I wouldn't dare disapprove of your vow: I can only applaud it heartily!'

With this vow made, the damsel Heliot came before Leones, a wise and temperate knight and a marshal of the Greek king's army, and said:

Chapter LXXXIII
The tenth vow, made by Leones, marshal of the noble king of Greece's army.

'Dear friend, you have won the highest renown with many great feats of prowess, and they say your valour shone before the city of Gaza. I and all the company pray and entreat you to pay our peacock his due.'

'Fair damsel,' Leones replied, 'I am ready to do so. I pledge and vow to the peacock that, as soon as our feasting's over, I shall go to King Clarvus of India's tent, fully armed, and challenge his son Canaan to joust. For the rest, come what may: that's what I've resolved to do.'

'Truly,' everyone said, 'that's a most noble vow, and will surely be speedily achieved for it comes from an honest heart.'

'Proceed, Heliot, dear damsel,' said Cassamus.

'As you wish,' she said, and came before Floridas, who was brooding and angry about the Baudrian's vow that he would rob King Alexander of his sword. 'Sir,' she said to him, 'tell us your thoughts and pay the peacock his due.'

CHAPTER LXXXIV

The eleventh vow, made by the valiant Floridas de Vallestre.

'To be honest,' said Floridas, 'I don't know what to say: I've heard amazing vows made here – especially by the vassal sitting there, boasting that he's going to rob the Greek king of his sword in the midst of all his men! He respects us little – and fears us even less! I'd say our king will have ill bestowed the fine gifts he's lavished on us if we sit there and let his sword be taken – damn him if he lets us keep a single scrap of land: he should destroy us all as craven traitors!'

'Truly, sir,' said the Baudrian, 'there's no need for rage and indignation: I meant no offence! I don't know what came over me – but I can't help it now: my mad vow's made! And if I manage to achieve it, I'll win all the more honour! Let's take everything in good heart, that's what I say. Speak as you please, regardless of rank of prince or king – we're all on an equal footing here, so feel free.'

'That's well said, sir,' Floridas replied. 'So I pledge and vow to the peacock and to everyone present that, if you do as you say, before you've carried the sword thirty yards[1] from the king I'll have you at Death's door[2] and take you back to him a captive – or cut in half, even if you're made of steel! If I don't, I pray the king will have me hanged before I ever return to my noble city of Defur! So have a think about that: you might like to ask someone for advice!'

The Baudrian laughed and answered: 'Truly, sir knight, you've given me as good as I gave! Bless the man who sired you! Your king's wise to have you as a friend: you're worth your weight in gold to him.[3] Forgive me your resentment now: let's both do the best we can.'

'Fine words indeed,' said Cassamus, 'for there'll be many a mighty sword-blow struck to sort the wheat from the chaff,[4] and to make for glorious stories when we're all long gone! Let's carry on – it's your turn now, dear nephew Gadifer, to make a vow. Heliot, fair damsel, receive the vow from this man.'

So the maiden came before Gadifer and summoned him to make his vow, and he replied:

CHAPTER LXXXV

The twelfth vow, made by the worthy Gadifer of Ephesus.

'By all the gods in heaven, uncle, I don't know what to say! I'm overwhelmed, speechless! These Indian knights have made such lofty, extravagant vows

---

[1]   'half an arpent': see note 2, above, p.87.
[2]   Literally 'confessed and given absolution'.
[3]   Literally 'he couldn't provide himself with a better treasure'.
[4]   Literally 'by which the good may be distinguished from the bad'.

that all others will seem lame! First we have Porus boasting that he'll defeat all comers – and truly, I think he's capable: he has the courage and physique to do it! – and that he'll capture Emenidus's horse. And then we have the Baudrian claiming he'll rob the king of his sword in the midst of all his men! And Caulus vowing to have the Baudrian's helm unless it's fixed on with cement and the head comes with it! These are men of steel, I'd say! I don't know what to think. But I want to make a vow, so this is what I pledge and swear – and I want everyone to know it: I vow that if the battle takes place as proposed and planned, then when it's at its height I shall make for King Clarvus's standard, axe in hand, and not leave till I've cut the pole in half and brought the flag to the ground in view of everyone, or die in the attempt!'

'Truly, sir,' said Porus, 'it would be a calamity for us if you achieved your goal – it would mean we were defeated!'

'Oh, sir!' said Heliot, bearer of the peacock. 'That's an amazing vow you've made – and quite a challenge you've set yourself!'

'Dear damsel,' Gadifer replied, 'it's completely mad but I couldn't help it! It's a rash, wild boast to match the others! But it's there to be achieved, and if it pleased the gods that I could pull it off I think I'd be credited with fortune and prowess indeed. I hope with all my heart it happens!'

'Well now, sir,' said the damsel, 'we must share out the peacock for us all to enjoy. Who should do the honours?'

At this Gadifer rose and took the peacock from the damsel; and while a great band of minstrels struck up on a vast array of instruments – it was a delight to hear, as it was a joy to behold that lordly company – Gadifer, accompanied by the maidens Heliot and Ydoree, stepped up to Ariscé de Valestre and presented him with the peacock and called upon him, as the most gracious member of the company, to share out the bird as appropriate. Ariscé was quite reluctant, but everyone agreed that he was more deserving than any; so he divided the peacock with great finesse and sent it round the table to the knights and ladies, and they began to feast with all possible joy and pleasure.

Chapter LXXXVI
How Leones set out to accomplish his vow against Clarvus's son.

When dinner was over and the cloths had been cleared the minstrels set about their business. But Leones called for his arms and was soon armed to perfection, and he came into the hall and asked leave to go and fulfil his vow. He left the knights and ladies then, and went to his horse and sprang into the saddle, and took his stout and sturdy lance and set off, all alone, towards the Indians' camp.

While he was on his way, King Alexander was beside the river Pharon with Emenidus, Danselin and Ptholomer, and they clearly saw him riding towards the Indian tents. While they stood watching, wondering what was going on, a boy arrived, sent from the city by old Cassamus du Laris; he told them all about the vows and explained that the knight they'd spotted riding to King Clarvus's camp was Leones who'd vowed to go and joust with Canaan, Clarvus's eldest son. When Alexander heard the boy's report he wondered what on earth had prompted them to make all those vows, and he and his companions began to discuss it with much amusement.

Meanwhile Leones had reached Clarvus's camp, and as soon as he rode up he told the first boy he saw: 'Go, friend, to the king's pavilion and tell Canaan, his eldest son, that a foreign knight has come to challenge him to joust: for taking my message I'll give you my gown when I dismount.'

The boy heard this and went straight to Clarvus's tent and found Canaan and told him: 'Great honour and joy are come to you today! There's a fully armed knight outside our camp, sir – one of King Alexander's, I think; his name is Leones, and he's challenging you to joust! So you must arm now, if it please you, and meet him like a valiant knight!'

'Upon my honour,' Canaan replied, 'you'll not see me refuse!'

And he called for his arms at once and they were brought to him; and while he was arming he sent the boy back to the knight with word that his challenge would be met without delay.

CHAPTER LXXXVII

How the vow was accomplished.

With his father's blessing Canaan was now clad and equipped for combat, and he set himself in his saddle, took up his lance and, fully armed, rode to the jousting-place where a great crowd had gathered to watch the contest. At the king's command a herald bade them all stand clear and called for each man to do his duty. And thereupon Leones and Canaan, raring to go, lowered their lances and charged at each other full tilt; they exchanged such blows that their strong, sharp lances smashed to pieces, and they crossed so fiercely and so close that they almost dashed each other to the ground. The herald was sent to ask if Leones wished to charge again; he answered that he did indeed: for that very reason he'd brought several lances with him, and he took one and Canaan took another. Then they launched into a second charge. As before they sent their lances flying into shards, and this time they met with such force that their saddle-straps sundered and they were both sent hurtling to the ground where they lay prostrate for a good while. King Clarvus declared that he'd ridden in many a fine battle but had never seen a better joust.

'Nor I, truly!' said Marcien. 'Such bold resolve should always be admired in a knight: that Greek is a valiant man indeed, dear uncle. Let's go and speak to him and help him to his feet, and send him back with honour to his city. It would be a great courtesy on your part to honour him – and only proper. If it please you, I'll go with him to seek a truce so that we can discuss an exchange of prisoners.'

'Agreed, dear nephew, upon my honour,' Clarvus replied. 'We'll do exactly as you say.'

Then they came to Leones, still prostrate, and spoke to him most courteously, asking him his name and why he'd come. He told them everything, all about the vows that had been made, and then asked them to return his horse. Clarvus replied that he was welcome to have it back, but if he liked he would give him a palfrey for an easier ride, and Leones thanked him and said he would gladly accept, for he'd been badly injured in the fall. Betis was there and recognised him at once and greeted him most joyfully; and it was agreed by Clarvus, the captive Betis and the whole army that Marcien the Persian would go to the city with Leones to discuss an exchange of prisoners. This was duly done, as you'll now hear.

Chapter LXXXVIII

Of the agreement made for the return of prisoners.

And so it was that Leones fulfilled his vow and set off back to the city escorted by Marcien the Persian. As soon as his return was known it was reported to the ladies of the palace and they came with all speed, reaching him before he was even at the gate. The moment he saw them he dismounted and threw down his shield, and came to meet them with glowing salutations, as they greeted him. Then he introduced the knight who'd come with him, and as they spoke they made their way into the palace, with everyone thronging about them as you may imagine.

They entered the glorious Chamber of Venus, where Porus and the sultan of Baudres were playing chess. As soon as they saw the company they rose and came to greet them and welcomed them with all the joy they could muster. Then Marcien said to Porus:

'My word, dear cousin! As prisons go you've landed on your feet! I'd say you're the prisoner of Love!'

'Perhaps,' said Porus. 'I really don't know.'

While they were talking Cassamus and Gadifer and the Greek knights Caulus, Ariscé, Perdicas and Floridas entered the chamber, and they came and gave Leones a most joyful and respectful welcome and asked him about his vow. He told them all that had happened, and then spoke of the courtesy Clarvus had shown him in giving him a palfrey, and how Marcien who'd come there with him had shown him all possible honour. 'So I pray you, sirs, treat him with all the courtesy you can, for truly, he deserves both honour and friendship.'

'By my life,' said Cassamus, 'we shall be both friends and servants to him; and if he needs us, then, our honour permitting, we shall lend him our aid. We bid him welcome!'

To this Marcien replied: 'My lords, I pray it will not displease you that I come here with this valiant knight who has graciously granted me safe conduct. His protection gives me confidence to relay the message entrusted to me by the noble King Clarvus. As it stands you have two prisoners here, Clarvus's son Porus and the sultan of Baudres and Media, while for our part we're holding captive that most valiant and judicious knight Betis – there's no need for me to say more about his good character: you know him better than we. My lord King Clarvus would gladly see a truce and suspension of hostilities by both sides until Monday, and to have his two captive liegemen returned either in exchange for your prisoner or for money as you prefer.'

'Truly, sir,' replied Cassamus, 'you have spoken well; I shall consult my companions for a moment and bring you a swift response.'

Then Cassamus drew aside with his knights, and after they'd discussed the matter Cassamus returned and sat down on the silken carpets, bidding the rest do likewise; then he said: 'You, sir knight, have clearly stated the case: my nephew Betis is your prisoner and Porus and the Baudrian are ours, and you and your king would gladly see an exchange arranged, and would first like to agree a truce until the day you said. My response is this: I agree to a truce until sunset on Monday, and I will grant your request to exchange my nephew Betis for Clarvus's son Porus and the Baudrian, on condition that if battle is joined on Tuesday as your king desires, then after the battle – no matter who wins – one of the two will return to captivity as a prisoner of my fair niece Phesonnas and the lady Edea. If I come to regret it, it can't be helped: courtesy demands it of me! So if it please you, we'll meet again tomorrow and deliver the prisoners and make our preparations for battle – or for peace.'

'I thank you, Lord Cassamus,' said Marcien, 'for your great courtesy. God grant that we deserve it – and would to God we were all united in peace!'

Chapter LXXXIX
How Marcien returned to camp to tell King Clarvus of the Greeks' response.

After these various words had been exchanged Marcien graciously took his leave of the knights and ladies, and returned to his horse and mounted and set off. He didn't stop riding till he reached his uncle Clarvus's pavilion; he dismounted and entered the tent and hailed his uncle and the attendant company, and began to report everything the lords at Ephesus had said. He spoke of their great courtesy – especially that shown by old Cassamus. 'Never in my life,' he said, 'have I met a more courteous man.' Then he told how, if they wished, the Greeks were willing to meet next day and negotiate a peace.

Clarvus replied that he would gladly have a truce but had no intention of discussing peace. 'Since you say you've found them so courteous I want you to take back their man, either tonight or first thing in the morning, and they can complete the deal as they see fit. But I assure you there'll never be peace between me and that false, low bastard who calls himself king of Macedon. Far from it! If the gods grant that I meet him in battle, I'll exact such revenge for the good lords and knights who've been killed by him or on his account that it'll be talked of for evermore! Heed my words! I promise you, I wish he was at my mercy now: I'd have him cut into a thousand pieces – even if it meant I died straight after! Yes! For I'd die happily if I knew that such a thieving rogue, bent on robbing other men of their honour, had died a hideous death!'

'Ah, dear uncle!' said Marcien. 'Those are senseless words that spring from an angry heart! You'll have your revenge, if it please the gods, without all that! And your honour will be undiminished. You've twice as many men as they'll have, even when they join their forces – and were it not for the harsh demands you've made you'd have seven times as many: you'd be strong enough to do battle with the whole world! But you know you've inflicted ever greater taxes and maletolts[1] on your people, and they love you less for it; as they keep being exacted I've no doubt they'll betray you and turn their backs on you – many will, at least. That's not King Alexander's way: he respects his people and gives liberally: he cares only that he gains the honour from his conquests – his men can have the profit. And that's how a good ruler should behave if he wants to achieve high renown and prowess: you don't earn your people's love by robbing them and fleecing them, or by being harsh and oppressive, but by showing them courtesy and love. Would to God you'd been so inclined – you could have carried your banner over all the world! But enough of that – there's no point keeping on. I'll go and see our prisoner and do as you've commanded.'

With that they parted till dawn next day. Then Marcien rose early and came to the king's main pavilion, where Betis was lodged. He greeted him with all due respect and said:

'Come, good sir, you're free to go! And when it please you we'll take you back to your city.'

'Truly, sir,' Betis replied, 'there's nothing I'd like more!'

Chapter XC
How the prisoners were exchanged.

Palfreys were made ready at once, and they mounted and set off towards the city. Meanwhile a truce till Monday evening was announced throughout the Indian camp, as it was in Ephesus.

Clarvus's other three sons rode with Betis, too, to keep him company and to show him respect – and also to have a sight of the ladies and damsels of whom they'd heard so much!

They came now to the city; and the moment they entered, word of their arrival spread everywhere – not least in the palace where, as you may imagine, the ladies and damsels as well as the lords came eagerly to meet them. Betis, needless to say, was given a glorious welcome, and up the steps to the palace they went, hand in hand. To describe all the celebrations – between brother and brother and lady and lover – would take too long: we'll leave it to the reader's imagination. We'll tell instead of the captives' release.

The history says that when they reached the palace they sat in a circle on silken carpets in the middle of the hall as though in their places for a dance: lords and ladies side by side alternately, in delightful fashion, each lord holding his lady most graciously by the hand. Then Marcien, sent there on King Clarvus's behalf and charged with pronouncing his intentions as discussed the previous day, spoke thus:

---

[1]   See note 2, above, p.46.

'Lord Cassamus,' he said, 'you've shown us such great courtesy that you've entirely won us over! Would to God we could make peace and be fully reconciled! But it's not possible: firstly, because King Alexander is great, proud and mighty and doesn't believe there's any man, however powerful, who shouldn't be his vassal; and secondly, on our side, my uncle King Clarvus of India is fierce, proud and resentful, and would rather die than pay homage for his land to a lesser man – and he considers himself, in power and strength, as well endowed as Alexander. For both these reasons no agreement can be struck between them: to put it simply, King Clarvus will not countenance a treaty or talk of peace – he's vowed that either he or Alexander will be stopping here; it's as simple as that! So there's nothing more to be said. But here, sir, is your nephew Betis, whose valour led him to be taken prisoner: I've brought him back safe and sound just as he was when he was captured, with his arms and his horse and all his other belongings, and on King Clarvus's behalf I return him to you a free man. So if it please you, good sir, return our companions to us as you promised – though, unless I'm much mistaken, their imprisonment here has been little hardship!'

To this Cassamus replied: 'I shall, sir knight, on the condition proposed: that is, that when the battle is over, no matter who wins, one of the two will return to be our prisoner. But for the moment I release them, for truly, I wouldn't want their valour and prowess to go unseen because they're in captivity – and I wouldn't want them to have an excuse for not fulfilling their vows! You can take them back whenever they wish, and we grant you safe conduct: you may come and go as you please.'

'A thousand thanks, sir!' said Marcien. 'From your prisoners' manner I'd say they'll return here with pleasure! They seem to be enjoying your company! And with good reason: it's a delightful place, truly – I do believe they'd as happily dwell here as in Paradise.'

'That's very kind, sir!' said Cassamus. 'If it falls at all short, may God amend it! But truly, I'm sorry we must be at war: peace between us would surely be better. But since Clarvus is adamant there's nothing I can do, though I fear he may come to regret it too late – and soon.'

And with that leave was taken by both parties.

CHAPTER XCI

How the prisoners took their leave of the ladies of the palace.

Then Porus took the lady Phesonnas by the hand as he asked her leave to depart; and she, smiling, softly replied:

'Ah, sir, go and may God go with you. But – though your imprisonment here is hardly onerous! – you're still under my jurisdiction for having killed my peacock, as you know.'

'Ah!' Porus replied. 'My only comfort, hope and sweet obsession, I surrender to you entirely and consider myself your poor knight and prisoner! I've no wish ever to leave your gracious service! No, if it please you, I wish to live and die your servant, and though filial love demands that I leave your sweet sight, I promise, upon my faith and honour, that my heart remains your captive, to do with as you wish and please.'

'Indeed, sir knight,' said the lady Phesonnas, 'I shall hold you to that – I am satisfied!'

These and other words passed between them, but I'll leave them now as there were many! Similar words were exchanged by the sultan of Baudres ('the Baudrian', that is) and the lady Edea, whom he loved faithfully and completely; and as they parted he promised her that if, in the great battle in which he expected to be fighting very soon, he found himself confronting any of those dear to her, he would defend them and protect them for her sake, come what may. The lady Edea thanked him deeply for this; and from that time forth the bonds of love between them were so fast that they were never to be parted until death.

And so it was with Marcien, too, who was holding the damsel Heliot in his arms. He loved her as deeply as could be – and according to the history had done so for a long while. I'll tell you how it came about: the fact is that when Clarvus had first sent his embassy to ask Cassamus du Laris for the hand of the lady Phesonnas, the lord Marcien of Persia had been one of the ambassadors, and during their stay at Ephesus he had made the damsel Heliot his beloved – and, the history says, had promised to take her for his wife and to make her queen of Persia and Media.

There's no doubt that there were many difficult and impassioned exchanges in the course of those leave-takings, for it was hard to part when they knew they were heading into mortal danger – and moreover would be fighting those ladies' and damsels' own blood, their very brothers and kinsmen, which made the parting all the harder and more painful.

But at last the palfreys were ready, and all the knights who had to leave mounted and rode from the city. Cassamus, Betis and Gadifer and some of the Greeks escorted them a fair way until they'd left the city well behind; then they returned to Ephesus, leaving the others to ride on to the Indian camp and to Clarvus's pavilion. You may well imagine the welcome they received, especially Porus, who was much loved by everyone for his strength, nobility and abundant prowess.

Chapter XCII

How Clarvus received his son and the sultan of Baudres; and of the day of the great battle.

King Clarvus of India, you may be sure, was overjoyed to see his son Porus safe and sound, for he loved him above all others; he rejoiced likewise to see the Baudrian, loving him, too, as he should. And the moment he saw Porus he jokingly said to him:

'Well, Sir Laggard, your conduct plainly shows you're a worthless rogue! From what I hear you've not been properly imprisoned day or night – I rather wish you had been! The same goes for you, Sir Sultan of Baudres!'

'Oh, dear and honoured father,' Porus replied, 'that's most unfair! And I'd rather you changed the subject, for by my life, I'd swap four times your wealth in land and treasure for the experience of visiting that mansion in Ephesus: I promise you I've seen a being there who fills me with constant thoughts of courtly love,[1] which I hope will inspire me to greater deeds.'[2]

His father had no idea he was referring to the fair Phesonnas – he imagined he was speaking of another – and he smiled and said: 'You find empty-headed idlers far and wide, dreaming of what will never be! But enough of this: tell me about the Greeks and what they're planning. Are they brave enough to meet us in battle? What does haughty old Cassamus say? In his overweening pride he denied me his niece's hand – a refusal I hope he'll come to regret!'

'Most honoured lord,' said Porus then, 'I can assure you of this: on Tuesday you'll see the Ephesians march and ride forth with banners flying, armed with weapons or with clubs, advancing upon you and all your forces. From what I hear they'll have twenty thousand fighting men – not counting Alexander of Allier's[3] army: he's coming to support them with ten thousand troops, and they're not to be taken lightly – they're all knights and troops of quality: every one of the Greeks, I promise you, has the courage and strength to deal with any foe, bar none. They're going to cross the Pharon on Friday, ready to confront and crush you if they can.'

'Oh!' cried Clarvus. 'Will I finally see him face to face, the overweening bastard who's guilty of the slaughter of so many valiant men? I tell you, if I can get my hands on him I'll give him what he deserves!'

'Ah, dearest lord!' said Marcien. 'Stop such talk, I pray you! No prince should listen to others' grievances, for these days you'll find no one daring to admit he uttered them; so a wise and prudent man pays no heed to rumoured offences. And I tell you, by the faith I owe all our gods, I'd give half of all my land to have you resemble Alexander: he's always ready to be bountiful – the moment he wins anything he gives it away – and that's what earns a man a reputation for prowess, which Alexander has most certainly.'

'Truly, dear nephew,' said Clarvus, 'I'll soon be cured of my bile – I hope to be completely purged after our great battle.'

'I tell you, uncle,' Marcien replied, 'I fear that'll too late.'

'Enough of that,' said Clarvus. 'Tell me, are these the young knights who made such noble vows to the ladies?'

'They are indeed!' said Marcien. 'What do you make of that?'

'It's all to the good, by God it is,' Clarvus replied. 'They wouldn't have dared make such vows unless they were valiant-hearted. I love them the more for it, as will all worthy men who hear the tale. But what about *us*? How will *we* perform, and what deeds will *we* achieve? We haven't seen the fair ladies and damsels who've inspired the mighty exploits which no man would have dared undertake without the joyous thoughts of the ladies firing his heart!'

---

1   'fine amour'.
2   Literally 'which I hope will make me of greater worth'.
3   See note 1, above, p.46.

'Quite right, dear uncle,' said Marcien, 'and you know what needs to be done – you need no one's advice in such matters! Let's stop this talking now, and make full and thorough plans for Tuesday's battle.' Then Marcien proposed the following:

CHAPTER XCIII

How King Clarvus of India formed his battalions to do battle with the Ephesians, Greeks and Macedonians.

'As you know, uncle, we've brought a mighty army far from our own countries, to a foreign land where we find enemies on every side. So it's essential that our plans and preparation be beyond reproach, for the foes we face are clever and artful, especially Alexander, the most accomplished king who ever walked the earth: he's wise and bold and valiant, astute in mind and powerful in body – and most fortunate in battle! So you need to order your men, form your squadrons and battalions and decide who'll be in the front line and who in the second.'

'Well said indeed, dear nephew,' Clarvus replied. 'Let's get started! We've a hundred thousand men in our company, as you know, enough to make six great and mighty battalions. And now we have my dear son Porus here, whose soaring courage has persuaded him to vow that he'll rout every enemy division in an instant! I'll entrust the first battalion or squadron to him, with fifteen thousand strong, brave, sturdy, mighty men!'

Porus sprang to his feet and said: 'Upon my honour, sir, you won't find me refuse, but I pray you, don't mock me for having made that vow – the place where we were imprisoned demanded it! If it's outrageously daring, well, I'll win all the more honour if it's accomplished!'

Then Clarvus decreed that Canaan would command the second battalion with fifteen thousand men, Caneos the third and Sallhedin the fourth; Marcien was commissioned to take the fifth and the Baudrian the sixth; and Clarvus himself and his nephew Marcien would ride from squadron to squadron to hearten and exhort the troops, and would fight with might and main wherever they saw the greatest need. With this decided, Clarvus summoned all his sons and all the kings, princes, dukes, counts and emirs who were to fight alongside them and under their command, and called upon them to be mindful of their honour and to fight with valour and might so that there'd be no stain upon their names after their deaths. He told them:

'Dear brothers and companions, we've only one death to die! In the certain knowledge of this, let's conduct ourselves in such a way that our children will be esteemed and honoured. Think of valiant men of former times like Priam and his sons, who behaved with such courage that their valour and feats of prowess will be remembered till the world's end. These Greeks are arrogant, haughty men – as they've always been! I tell you, they'll come fired up, expecting to shock us with their daring – we need to be prepared for it, and if they attack boldly, respond in kind! Meet them with heart and spirit, on the heads of your lances!

Don't hold back! Let's have our gleaming, shining sword-blades crimson with their blood! And I promise you, all the booty that comes with victory will be yours: I'll see you so well rewarded that you'll all say: "That's enough!"'

Such were King Clarvus of India's stirring words to all his men; for truly, according to the history, had it not been for his boundless greed and covetousness he'd have been one of the finest warriors of the age.

After his exhortations he bade Marcien see his standard raised next morning in a prominent place so that all injured and wounded men could take refuge there. 'And since,' he said, 'Gadifer of Ephesus has vowed to strike it down and cut it to pieces, I want twenty strong, brave, well-armed knights posted as its guard, so that if Gadifer reaches it he'll have no cause to crow! By the faith I owe all my gods, I don't know how he dared make such an outrageous vow! Did anyone ever hear the like?'

'Ah, uncle!' said Marcien. 'It was the love of the ladies that did it, truly! You surely know that love and ladies can inspire a desire that at times drives men to say and do things leading sometimes to glory and sometimes to their downfall – look no further than these vows made in the ladies' chamber!'

They spent the whole day in such talk and debate – it carried on, indeed, until the day came when the armies were to meet.

Now it's time to return to Alexander.

Chapter XCIV

How King Alexander and his whole army crossed the River Pharon.

Early next morning King Marcien of Persia, already awake, gathered a band of his knights together and went to seek out a good position for Clarvus's banner. After reconnoitring the whole battleground they chose what they thought was the best place and planted it there, in plain view not only of the men in Ephesus but also of the Greeks in Alexander's host on the other side of the river. They reported it at once to Alexander, who didn't take long to see it was a sign that the Indians had no desire for peace but wanted battle. He ordered his men to prepare to cross the river as best they could. A message had already come from Cassamus telling him all that had happened, including the vows, and how Clarvus was threatening him and had no intention of making peace or reaching an agreement. So Alexander responded accordingly.

He took with him only his fighting men, leaving a large number of lesser folk behind to guard the camp. And when they were fully armed and ready they came down to the river's edge where boats and vessels were standing by, and made their way across. But not without great difficulty: according to the history they had to lash ropes around their horses and lower them into the boats and likewise haul them up on the other side, because the rocks and crags made the riverbanks so high. But machines were devised for this very purpose, with stone steps alongside leading down to the boarding-place; and Alexander, regardless of the difficulty, succeeded in making the crossing with ten thousand troops.

There's no need to ask if he had a glorious welcome in the city – from the knights and lords and princes especially, but also from the ladies – you may be sure he did! The history says they all came down to greet him with all possible honour: such a joyous, reverent welcome had never been seen or heard. The lady Phesonnas was there, sublimely dressed and adorned, and with perfect decorum she came, a vision of utter loveliness, to greet the king. As soon as she reached him she went down on one knee, and the king, with equal decorum, immediately stepped forward and took her by the hand and raised her up and kissed her and embraced her, saying:

'I have come, fair damsel, to serve you and accomplish your desire.'

'Ah, my lord!' she said. 'You are welcome indeed! May God ever enhance your goodness, peace and honour, and grant you the will to rid us of our enemies, as we are sure you can. Hear my plea, sir: the king of India has long waged war on us, seizing our towns and burning and sacking our cities and castles, so that little is left to us now beyond these walls! So I pray you, sir, by your gracious will, bring us remedy and redress, and we shall forever be at your service and command.'

To these words Alexander replied: 'Truly, lady, we deeply regret not having known of your plight much sooner: we'd have addressed it long ago. But have no fear: by the will of the gods and with the aid of our good friends and companions we hope to make your enemy pay so dearly that it'll be remembered for evermore!'

Cassamus likewise welcomed and fêted the king and all the other lords and princes: no one knew which way to look, as honours were showered and celebrations erupted on every side! Amid this jubilation they all went together to the palace – and what a noble palace it was: I've read of none more splendid or more gloriously adorned than this was to receive King Alexander. The history says it looked as if the whole world's wealth was gathered there, in silken drapes and cloth of gold, in ornaments of gold and silver and precious stones: carbuncles and rubies there were, and sapphires, diamonds, topaz, agates, pearls and other jewels, in numbers beyond all belief, decorating the walls and pillars and ceilings with richness and magnificence as wondrous as anyone could wish or ever possibly describe. It was called the Palace of Jupiter.

Chapter XCV

How the Indian lords came to see the noble King Alexander in the Palace of Jupiter, and other matters.

The palace was spread with carpets strewn with rushes and all manner of flowers; and there the noble King Alexander sat with lords and ladies in circles about him. They began to talk of many things, including the vows that had been made just two days before in the Chamber of Venus. The king said he'd be very glad to see the man who'd vowed to rob him of his fine, sharp sword, and also the one who was to capture Emenidus's horse, 'for truly,' he said, 'they're worthy and valiant men indeed – or hope to be!' And he kept looking at Gadifer, who'd vowed to cut down King Clarvus's banner, and said to himself: 'Daring words, for sure, and praiseworthy indeed, and no doubt they'll lead to great honour.'

The king being deep in thought, Cassamus approached and asked him: 'What's troubling you, my lord? Be of good cheer!'

'I promise you,' the king replied, 'all my thoughts are positive! The style and conduct of your household delight me more than all the charms I've ever seen. But I was reflecting on those vows, and thinking how much I'd like to see the Indians who made vows with such panache!'

'You'll see them tomorrow, sire,' said Cassamus, 'before the ninth hour;[1] they've asked permission to come here then, and we've agreed a truce till Monday evening.'

The king replied that he'd receive them gladly.

Then the conversation continued till supper time came, when the tables and cloths were laid and a trumpet sounded for the washing of hands; then they went to take their seats, and supped with great pleasure and in the highest spirits. After supper they spoke of other things till bedtime, when they retired and slept till morning.

Then the king rose and his lords with him; the ladies and damsels came to join them, and they all made ready to go and worship at a temple outside the city walls called the Temple of Diana. While they were there and in the midst of their devotions, the Indians arrived on their way to see their sweethearts. At their head was the sultan of Baudres, with Marcien king of Persia and King Clarvus's son, Porus. Seeing the great throng of people they stopped outside the temple and asked what was happening; and when they were told that King Alexander was inside at worship they decided to wait there till he'd finished – though what really made them wait was hearing that the ladies of the palace were with him! Once their prayers and devotions were done the king and the knights and ladies and damsels left the temple; and as soon as they stepped outside the ladies saw the three princes waiting for them, fine figures indeed, most elegantly dressed, and they greeted them with all honour and courtesy. The king hadn't seen them before and didn't know who they were; but they struck him by their bearing as men of high degree and he said to Cassamus:

'Truly, sir, I don't know those knights: tell me who they are.'

'Indeed, my lord, they're the ones you were talking about last night: those you said you'd be glad to meet.'

He identified all three; and when Alexander knew which was Porus and which the Baudrian and Marcien he walked towards them, and the Baudrian, at their head, hailed the king in the Greek tongue. The king returned his greeting and then greeted the other two likewise and took them by the hands, bidding them a joyful and most courteous welcome. Then he fixed an amused eye on the Baudrian and said:

'Well, sir, may God grant that I see your joy and honour doubled in both love

[1]   i.e. the ninth canonical hour, about 3 p.m.

and war; and that, no matter who I meet, I'm man enough to defend my body –
not to mention my sword!'

At this the Baudrian blushed, a little embarrassed; but he responded cheer-
fully enough, saying: 'No offence was intended, sir! Sometimes the ladies make
vows and pledges obligatory! And if need be we must lay our bodies on the line
if we're to enhance and advance our reputations.'

'In that case,' said Alexander, 'it's clear that love and the ladies are going to
make me pay for the pleasures we sometimes seek from them!'

As they talked they made their way back to the palace, and when they arrived it was time for dinner: the tables were laid and dinner was ready and the
trumpet sounded for the washing of hands. Then the king took the Baudrian and
Porus by the hand and led them to the table saying:

'Don't argue, sirs: you're to sit with me and be served exactly as I am, for
would to God we were friends as I would have us be – even if it meant giving
you all the land I've conquered in my life!'

With that they sat at table together and were served with all due grace and
plenty. And when they'd eaten and drunk their fill they rose and went hand in
hand to the Chamber of Venus, that gorgeous, opulent chamber draped in richly
embroidered velvet. There they conversed of many things, but especially of love
and its wondrous powers. Each made his own contribution to the subject – but
their tales might seem quite fanciful, so we'll leave it at that.

Chapter XCVI

How the Indian lords returned to their camp.

But only the Indian lords and a few others were engaged in this merry talk
in the Chamber of Venus; Alexander and his loyal companions had climbed
a lofty tower to discuss how to arrange their battalions, and to observe the
strength of the Indian army. They saw that it was vast and mighty indeed; but
King Alexander said:

'Dear friends and companions, don't be dismayed: victory doesn't always de-
pend on numbers! Sometimes the more men there are, the greater the confusion!
It's better to have a few well ordered and organised than a vast mass working
without rhyme or reason. And we've met the Indians before, elsewhere, when
old Porus of India was killed outside Pantapolus:[1] they're wretched fighters,
poorly armed, with little skill in war; it doesn't take long to send them packing.
I'm sorry Clarvus wants it this way: I'd rather have peace with him than many
others – not because I'm afraid of him, but because of his great, deep chivalry
and his trusty and valiant allies, who seem to me most worthy men.'

Such were the words that passed between Alexander and the Greeks. And
when they'd made plans to their satisfaction they came down from the tower to
the Chamber of Venus, where they found the Indians at play with the ladies –

---

[1] As mentioned above, p.73.

some at chess, some at dice[1] – laughing and joking with each other. The king had heard about the lady Phesonnas's witty quip,[2] and so he asked her, since she was playing her beloved Porus, if he'd be mated in the corner or somewhere more exposed! The lady was a little embarrassed – but all she did was laugh! In any event, they rose to welcome the king and his lords and then sat down again. Emenidus had been instructed to relay the view of the king and his council, and he said:

'Dear sirs, you see before you our lord the king and all his barons; they wish you to know how much they regret that Clarvus is unwilling to give way and is determined to do battle. That being so, the king's mind is clear: on Tuesday next he and all his company will be fully armed and ready; and then it'll be down to doing one's duty, and may the glory and honour go to the one who is most in the right. If it please you, my dear lords of India, you will tell your king to consider this.'

'Truly, sir,' said Marcien, 'his mind has been long made up. But I hope you don't object to our visiting you: your courtesy drew us here! If it please God we shall be firm friends hereafter.'

'Indeed, sir,' Alexander said, 'we're happy for you to come and go exactly as you please. Come whenever you wish – we're only too pleased to see you.'

After these words and many more the Indians took their leave of the king and the ladies. Porus had special words for Phesonnas, for he'd already made her his lady love: the history says they'd exchanged promises to marry after the battle if he came through it alive. But if his father had known this he'd have been enraged, that's certain: as you've heard, it was his own desire for Phesonnas that had brought him there!

The palfreys were now ready, and the three knights and their accompanying servants mounted and headed back to rejoin the Indian army. Gadifer, Betis, Cassamus, Perdicas, Floridas and Caulus mounted, too, and escorted them out of the city and most of the way to their camp. Then the Indians made their way to their tents where they found Clarvus in cheerful conversation with the king of Pincernie.[3] All the lords present rose and greeted them with honour and respect, and King Clarvus took his son Porus by the hand and seated him at his side; then he bade all the others sit, for he was eager to hear their news.

CHAPTER XCVII

How Porus told his father all about the Greeks, and Marcien rebuked Clarvus for his response.

'Dear sirs,' he said, 'you've been to the city and seen the Greeks and Macedonians and Ephesians making merry. Tell me about that rogue King Alexander, who lives solely by robbing others: what's he like and what's his mood?'

'Oh, truly, sir,' Porus replied, 'I'm hard pressed to tell you of their ways and manners: such are their nobility and splendour that I'd struggle to describe them

---

1   'tables': the generic name for a group of dice games similar to backgammon.
2   i.e. above, p.84.
3   See above, p.50 and footnote 2.

– and you wouldn't believe me if I did! But I assure you, King Alexander's a handsome man indeed, strong and brave and imposing. And very little daunts him: never in my life have I seen a man of such unshakeable confidence. But truly, their army is much smaller than I'd expected: I reckoned they'd no more than thirty thousand troops all told – though I have to say I've never seen finer men or better armed or more accomplished fighters.'

'He's plainly an arrogant fool, then,' said Clarvus, 'if he wants to take on a force as great and powerful as ours! It's all pure greed and pride, and it'll be his downfall! I hope this battle will see them avenged – all who've been wickedly, wrongly dispossessed and driven from their kingdoms by that ruthless tyrant! The whole world, I'm convinced of it, abhors him for his cruelty!'

No one would reply to this except Marcien, who spoke out, saying: 'Well all I'll say, dear uncle, is I wish you were like him and cut from the same cloth! I beg you change your ways and leave him to live his life, for truly he's a fine man indeed, noble, gentle and gracious of speech, generous and kind in bestowing gifts – unlike you!'

Clarvus was overcome with shame at his nephew's words and made no reply, knowing as he did that they were true. But then he found his tongue again and said in apparent good humour: 'Hark at him! It seems I've done something to upset my nephew – or someone else, maybe. If anyone has a grievance against me, speak up – feel free – never mind your rank! I'll amend it to your total satis-faction. From now on I want all wrongs redressed and all rights respected.'

At this a good number spoke up, saying: 'Thanks indeed, sire! And God save Marcien for procuring us this favour! Truly, he's a man of great goodness and honesty!'

Their talk now turned to other matters, as Clarvus commanded that everyone prepare his arms without fail, meticulously, so that all would be ready on Tues-day – for there was nothing for it now but to fix their minds on doing their duty. It was announced throughout the army that next day, Monday, everyone was to make ready – and any who were unwilling to defend their person and their honour and live or die beside their king should leave without more ado: but no one did, fearing that even worse would befall them, which would indeed have been the case. Then a company was selected to guard Clarvus's banner, so that if Gadifer of Ephesus came there to fulfil his vow they could deal with him.

Now, while all this was going on, Alexander's men were crossing the deep river: it was two full days before they were all across. And while they waited for their men the king and his barons were in the city, busily talking and planning – and ribbing each other, too: the king asked Emenidus if he'd met his horse's future owner, to which Emenidus replied:

'And have you seen how strong he is, sire, your sword-bearer-to-be?'

When the Greeks, Macedonians and Chaldeans had all crossed the river, Al-exander, who knew exactly how to operate, went up and down the city to all the houses where his troops had lodged. There he welcomed them and made a fuss of them as a mother would her children, giving them lavish attention – and gen-erous promises, too: and what he promised he always delivered, which was such a fierce incentive to his men that when it came to fighting, each one was worth three! That was King Alexander's way, and he carried on till the Monday. The following day, the Tuesday, the armies that had pledged to do battle were due to appear in the field – and so they did, as you're about to hear.

CHAPTER XCVIII

How the history says Alexander ordered his battalions.

Now then: on the Monday morning the noble King Alexander rose and dressed in a magnificent purple mantle and came to the palace's great hall. His princes and lords were already there in fine and mighty array, and as soon as they saw their king they greeted him with all respect and reverence and he saluted them likewise. Then they all sat down, each according to his degree, as if in formal council; and the king, in the most splendid seat of all as was his due, spoke first, saying:

'My dear friends and companions in prosperity and adversity, I thank you deeply for your fine and honourable service. I'm very mindful that you've served me well and faithfully, and have often put your lives at stake to enhance my name and honour – but that honour isn't mine alone but yours to share. And now we face a greater test than any before – and the size of the test is matched by the prize! Those Indians are laden with all manner of riches! But listen: if you're going to do battle against large numbers you need to think first about winning honour and only then about booty. Anyone who fights with his mind only on the money can be distracted by greed and lose not just honour but everything else. This is the situation: we've heard our enemies have formed six huge battalions, and by all accounts Porus is to command the first – the same Porus who's vowed that he'll vanquish us all! Cassel the Baudrian has the second, and he's made a vow, too, as you know! Caneos has the third, and so on and so forth. As for Clarvus, he'll be sitting prettily at the rear with forty-five thousand men each side of him, and it seems he's going to be setting up his battalions like a shield: we need to think about that. So Cassamus, accomplished veteran of many a fine battle, what would you advise?'

'My lord,' Cassamus replied, 'there are others more experienced than I, but I'll give you my opinion. It's this: while the day's still ahead of us – the truce ends at nightfall – I suggest we all go out to the battlefield and form our battle line, or the enemy might advance so close to the city that we wouldn't be able to deploy as we would wish. And in ordering our battalions I'd ask that we men of the city form the first, because this war began on our account. That's what I've been thinking.'

Alexander answered, saying: 'Truly, Cassamus, that's well said. We should indeed head for the field now. But as for all of you Ephesians going and leaving your city defenceless, that cannot be. It could prove disastrous: Clarvus is very shrewd, and if he got wind of it he could dispatch a body of men-at-arms – he has more than enough! – to take the city with ease for there'd be none but women left here, and you know they wouldn't have the strength to defend it. We must proceed with care.'

Then Emenidus said: 'Sire, you say Porus is to lead their first battalion. He's bragged he's going to unhorse me, so I'd say command of our first battalion should fall to me and no other!'

The king agreed at once and granted his request, but appointed Philotas, a most valiant lord, to accompany him. Then he committed two thousand brave, strong, battle-hardened men-at-arms to this first squadron, and as soon as they were called to arms they were sent out of the city to take up their position on the field. While they marched forth the other battalions were formed. Danselin and Ptholomer were appointed captains of the second squadron, which likewise had two thousand troops, and they set out at once to follow the others to the field. Le-ones and Licanor took command of the third battalion with two thousand men-at-arms; Festion and Antiocus took the fourth and Cassamus and Ariscé the fifth.

CHAPTER XCIX

And likewise how he ordered the sixth.

As commander of the sixth battalion King Alexander wanted to appoint Per-dicas. He'd vowed to fight dismounted with the foot soldiers, but Alexan-der said:

'Sir Perdicas, you'll have to forget that and fight on horseback, as chief and captain of the sixth battalion.'

Perdicas was upset by this, and replied: 'Esteemed lord, I shall always obey you to the utmost; but by the gods in heaven I've made a vow and will do all in my power to keep it – even if I knew it would cost me every limb! I shall fight on foot when the squadrons meet, armed with my own arms – my lance in my hand and my sword in my belt – and I shan't mount unless I win a horse for myself by force of arms: if another man wins one and offers it to me I'll not take it.'

Betis of Ephesus, overhearing this, came up to Perdicas and the king and said: 'Esteemed lord, I wish to keep Perdicas company; I likewise will have no mount in the battle unless I win it by force myself. Come what may, that's my decision and I'll not change it.'

The king said he would agree to this, since it was their firm desire. And no sooner had he said so than one hundred and fifty knights, all newly dubbed, declared they'd have no horse unless they'd won it with their own swords, and would live or die with Duke Betis and Perdicas, fighting at their side on the battlefield on foot. Alexander was amazed by this, for at that time it wasn't the custom for knights to fight dismounted – but it struck him that they might de-fend themselves with more resolve and courage on foot than on horseback. As soon as these knights were ready they marched from the city like the rest. Mean-while Alexander formed his sixth battalion, which he entrusted, to their utmost joy, to Caulus and Floridas.

Now all the battalions were in order, and they camped out in the field in swiftly pitched tents and pavilions. Alexander rode out, too, to spend the night there with them. He organised a watch, since the truce ended at sundown, and all that night he went tirelessly from troop to troop and squadron to squadron to cheer and exhort and hearten his men, pouring out words of warmth and affection, filling them with such courage that they felt the day was too long in coming and night was getting in the way! Alexander took Gadifer with him, showing him all the respect due to a man rich in wealth and friends and prowess; and Gadifer, who'd vowed to cut down Clarvus's banner and chop up the pole, couldn't wait for the day to come.

Alexander's own banner was now raised in full view of his Indian foes, and it so alarmed them that they all rushed to arm without delay. The history says they would have attacked Alexander that very night had they not been stopped by Marcien of Persia, who insisted that the day of battle had been fixed for the morrow. All the same every rank was fully armed, ready to fight if the need arose.

On both sides, then, there were many knights magnificently armed on superbly caparisoned horses, as each man strove to display his might and wealth. And between the two armies were the heralds[1] with trumpets and clarions; they went about their business with such gusto that you'd have struggled to hear God's thunder, and they carried on all night long. And prominent amidst all the ranks were Perdicas and Betis and their men – knights and squires who, although on foot, made a wondrous show: splendidly armed, with lances in hands, shields slung from necks, and many clutching mighty axes, massive, strong and sharp as well-honed razors. Everyone who beheld these dismounted men-at-arms was in awe at the sight, for they'd formed in companies, each with its own emblem worn by its members for recognition in the mêlée; and they were ranged in such densely serried ranks that they looked strong enough to crush the Indian host.

Meanwhile in Ephesus a well-ordered guard had been set on the walls to defend the city, men-at-arms and archers, too, and they were watching the battle-lines take shape; and Phesonnas and the other ladies were atop the palace towers, from where they could see and identify the combatants. The combatants could see them likewise, and the sight filled some with courage and daring, suffering as they were the sweet pains of love.

The Indians, too, were in awesome array and ready for battle, ranged and deployed in squadrons with banners billowing. They'd drawn up as if to form a great shield, on a good level stretch of ground like a parched meadow. The two armies weren't far apart and had a clear sight of one another, which made them all the more determined to make a bold and brave display; and thus they stayed all night till morning.

Chapter C
Of the great battle, and how Porus fulfilled his vow to capture Emenidus's horse.

When morning came the sun streamed down on every side: it was a beautiful day, neither too hot nor too cold, as if God was sending them perfect

---

[1]   *'menestreux'*.

weather. And to the sound of clarions and trumpets the two armies began their advance towards each other, step for step, in tightly serried ranks.

Emenidus of Arcadia, in first Greek squadron with his finely clad and armed Arcadians, was riding out in front, a great, stout lance in his hand. His mind was fixed on Porus, who'd bragged in his vow that he'd capture his mount, and now he was twice the range of a bow ahead of his battalion to seek him out – and Porus, too, was riding ahead of his, for that was the custom in those days, the history says. And now Porus saw Emenidus in front of his squadron and Emenidus saw him – they recognised each other by their devices; and without another word or sign they thrust in their spurs and charged with drawn swords and started raining blows on one another, hewing and hacking pieces from shields and armour with all their might. Their troops plunged in to join the fray with such a violent clash that many must have died in this first charge. And in the heaving crowd of men and horses were Porus, striving to fulfil his vow, and Emenidus, striving to prevent it; and as their furious fight raged on Porus, sword poised, suddenly spurred his horse Bauchant forward, and Emenidus likewise spurred his horse Ferrant, and they both plunged into the press with such force that they were sent flying to the ground. So heavy was their fall that their men thought they were dead, but such was Porus's hunger to win Emenidus's horse that he leapt up in an instant and seized its reins and mounted despite all attempts to stop him. Emenidus couldn't get there before Porus was in the saddle, and realising Porus had his horse he started yelling:

'Vassal! Vassal! You're not taking him! Come back here – I defy you!'

Porus heard him and cried: 'Truly, sir, I'll never fight you on foot! But since I have your horse I'll give you mine – we'll swap! So mount if you like, and let chance decide the outcome.'

Emenidus took Porus's horse and mounted, and as soon as he was in the saddle he came at Porus once again, determined to win his horse back if he could; but it was in vain, for Porus resisted with might and main – and both their squadrons were fighting just as fiercely. At this point, so the history says, Emenidus, overcome with shame, flung down his sword, seized Porus and started wrestling; but he was wasting his time: if help hadn't arrived Porus would have hurled him to the ground. But Philotas entered the fray, and gave the Indians such a battering that Porus left Emenidus and went to the rescue of his men who were being slaughtered by Philotas on all sides. So Emenidus was left distraught and raging at Porus's capture of his horse – though the one he'd swapped was its equal, if not better.

With these two battalions locked in mighty combat, Perdicas and Betis advanced with their men on foot clutching spears and darts, all needle-sharp, and they struck the Indians like a bolt of thunder, hurling such a hail of missiles at them that they sent their mounted enemies toppling dead. Marcien of Persia saw this and launched a charge to break them, attacking them with his whole battalion, thinking they could crush these men on foot. In this charge he struck Perdicas full on the shield and brought him to the ground; but Perdicas was up again in a flash and laid about Marcien with such might that he sent him crashing down amid the trampling hooves, and truly, if Marcien's men, the Persians, hadn't been as courageous as they were, their lord would never have left that place! But they managed to pull him free and put him back on a horse, in spite of the Ephesians.

CHAPTER CI

More details from the history.

Now each army's second battalion advanced, the Greeks led by Danselin and Ptholomer and the Indians by Caneos, Clarvus's son. As the squadrons closed their captains clashed with their lances, and Ptholomer wounded Caneos in the side; but the wound wasn't fatal: Caneos didn't leave the fight but gripped his sword in both hands and started wielding it so mightily that each blow felled a man-at-arms. Seeing this, Danselin spurred towards him and struck him to the ground; but he was rescued in an instant, for he had so many men that it was fifteen thousand against two thousand, so the history says, though the Greeks kept formation and fought with such resolve that for every Greek who died twelve Indians fell.

Into this furnace of killing, hewing, thrusting and felling the other squadrons came, the third first of all, plunging into the mêlée. Licanor and Leones, their battle-hardened captains, had been through this many times; but Clarvus's son Canaan, leading the Indians, was unseated, causing such panic among his men that the majority turned and started to fall back, and Canaan was beside himself with shame. But he proved what a tough, bold knight he was as he battled on alone for a good while, and the history says he escaped by the strength of his sword-arm and fought his way back into a squadron where Cassel the Baudrian was displaying admirable prowess.

It was now that the fourth battalions met in a clash of unbelievable ferocity: an appalling number of knights were felled and soldiers slain, and Festion and Antiocus were severely hurt though they had no open wounds. And Sallehedin was driven to the ground where he lay for some time amid the horses' hooves, but he was finally remounted with the help of his men.

Now all the battalions on both sides were battering each other; and all the while Cassamus was ploughing through the ranks in search of Clarvus alone. At last he found him; and the history says they met in a joust that brought both of them to the ground, but Cassamus was the more agile and leapt up and remounted before Clarvus was back on his feet. His men tried to rescue him, but they were so hard pressed by the Greeks, especially by the dismounted men-at-arms, that they couldn't get him back on his horse, and he was left on foot in the middle of the field for a long while, fighting mightily and performing so many deeds of arms, considering his age, that no more could have been asked of him. Word that he'd lost his mount spread like wildfire, and when Marcien of Persia and the king of Pincernie heard the news they raced to his aid. But they couldn't rescue him, for Perdicas and Betis, performing wondrous feats of arms, had him locked in a combat in which they looked sure to kill him or capture him alive.

But then Cassamus, returning and seeing their fight, decided it was time to accomplish his vow, and he rode forward and cried:

'Ah, sirs! Stop now, I pray you, and surrender him to me!' At this they drew back and left him to Cassamus, who said: 'Lord Clarvus, in fulfilment of my vow I return your horse to you. You're bent on doing us great harm and we mean to treat you in kind: so get back to your men now, for I promise you, if I meet you again today it'll be the death of you! That I swear before all our gods, so prepare to defend yourself if you dare!'

At that Clarvus, already back in the saddle, spurred his horse away and rejoined his men who were fighting with might and main against the battalion led by Ariscé. No man could have fought better than Ariscé himself, and in this fearsome mêlée he killed the king of Pincernie. Marcien of Persia was beside himself with anguish at the loss, and seeing Clarvus close at hand he rode to him and cried:

'Ah, dear uncle! Your folly will destroy us all this day! Thanks to you most of your fine knights are going to die here! Behold the king of Pincernie, lying dead beneath the horses' hooves – and so many are already slain with him that I couldn't count even half of them! These Greeks are men of iron: every one of them is worth a thousand of ours!'

Then Clarvus, hearing his nephew's words, clutched his sword and thrust in his spurs and rode among his squadrons, exhorting his troops to fight bravely; and from time to time he would charge at the foe to fire and encourage his men.

CHAPTER CII

How the sultan of Baudres accomplished his vow
but was captured by Floridas in doing so.

In the thick of these mighty mêlées, where many men lay dead or maimed, was the sultan of Baudres, performing awesome feats of arms. He kept looking for a chance to accomplish his vow to capture King Alexander's sword. Alexander was mindful of it, too, and had his eye out for the sultan – there was no one he was more eager to fight – and he finally caught sight of him. At the same moment he saw Caulus nearby, Caulus who'd vowed to take the sultan's helm if he robbed the king of his sword. So he called to him:

'Caulus, do you see that knight's device? He's the one who's meant to take my sword! Let it be as the gods ordain: I'm going after him!'

He was doing this in part to test Caulus. And no sooner had he uttered these words than he lowered his lance and summoned the Baudrian to defend himself; and the Baudrian, realising who it was and wanting nothing more, charged at him full tilt. They met in a clash that shattered their lances; then they clutched their swords and came at each other and dealt such blows that sparks flashed from their blades and helms. Any adornment on their armour was sent flying across the field, for if the Baudrian's attack was mighty Alexander's defence was just as fierce. All the same, the history says that the Baudrian launched himself at the king and seized his arm and grabbed his sword by the guard; they wrestled with each other till they were boiling and bathed in sweat, and the Baudrian kept hitting the king with a sharp steel buckle on his wrist, causing him much pain, till finally he wrenched the sword from his hands. As soon as he had it he raced away from the king as fast as he could and disappeared among his men, who were locked in ferocious combat with the Greeks, neither side holding anything back or taking any prisoners but killing each other pitilessly. And in the midst of the tumult Caulus, who'd spotted the Baudrian and slain a huge number of his men, battered and cut his way through to face him. They started exchanging fearful blows to the helm; then Caulus seized hold of the sultan and tore the helmet from his head, and with only his mail hood left beneath the Baudrian was overcome with shame. But it didn't put an end to his part in the battle: on he fought with all his might.

You can well imagine the trampling and the chaos, the carnage and the slaughter of this great battle; indeed, the history says there were so many killed and wounded that the blood flowed like water in a time of deluge, of torrential rain.

At the heart of the storm was Floridas, who'd vowed to deliver the sultan of Baudres as a captive to the king of Macedon. He'd been watching the Baudrian's exploits and seen him accomplish his vow by robbing Alexander of his sword, and then seen Caulus valiantly win his helm so that he was protected only by his shield and chainmail hood; he decided it was time to venture forward and fulfil his own vow. So he thrust in his spurs and his horse leapt into the Baudrian throng; and Floridas, felling horses and riders and sending them crashing, cut his way through to the sultan, who didn't refuse the challenge but began to fight back with the utmost valour. They exchanged blows that made them buckle face-down over their saddle-bows; Floridas strove with all his might to get close enough to seize the sultan in his arms, but the Baudrian, realising this, drove him back with ferocious blows. They were both tested to the limit, for they were equally battle-hardened knights. But Floridas proved to be even stronger than the sultan, for when he saw there was nothing else for it he threw down his sword and in a blaze of courage hurled himself at him, flinging his arms round his neck; he hauled and pulled as the Baudrian fought back, and they wrestled with each other till their heaving breath was like belching smoke from a furnace: no man could describe the scale of their efforts. But finally Floridas had him in such a grip that he crushed his armour and almost stopped the heart in his chest; it sapped the Baudrian's strength so much that Floridas hauled him from his horse and spurred away, dragging the Baudrian, almost bereft of pulse and breath, back to Alexander; and in this state he presented him to the king, who received him as his prisoner. Then the sword was prised from his grip: it was still fast in his fist, his hand so swollen from his struggle with Floridas that it could barely open. They also took from him a massive steel mace with huge spikes that was hanging at his side: the Baudrian had evidently been bent on massacring most of the Greeks!

How Gadifer of Ephesus accomplished his vow, and other matters.

You can well imagine how Alexander rejoiced at the Baudrian's capture – and with good reason, for his enemies were greatly weakened and diminished by his loss: he wouldn't have returned him for all his weight in gold, I'd say! He had him kept under close guard and taken to his tent.

Then he gave orders for all his forces to be rallied together, so that all his squadrons joined as one. But truly, those men-at-arms who were fighting on foot were doing immeasurably more damage to the Indians than the cavalry, and Porus was almost mad with rage. All day he kept trying to scatter them if he could, but in vain, for they kept tight formation and, whenever they saw an attempt to break them, they planted their lances before them like a line of stakes. And among them were a good number of strong but lightly armoured men, big lads armed with massive metal clubs, who made a pulp of countless knights and mounts. The horses had never experienced this and recoiled in terror, bringing themselves and their riders down in a heap with broken necks and legs and arms: no one could even half describe the carnage wrought by these men on foot. From the mayhem many had to be carried to Clarvus's banner to be strapped up and bandaged and put back together, and around the banner was such a groaning and wailing that no one knew who to attend to first.

But all the strong and courageous men were still fighting, striving to defend their lives and their honour, locked in mortal battle against Alexander and his troops. And there was Gadifer, seeking a way to accomplish his vow; he kept pressing on till he'd gone right through the Indian lines – I don't know how: perhaps they didn't recognise him or thought he was on their side and heading for some reason toward the banner. When he reached it there was such a howling throng there, as you've heard, that no one knew which way to turn, so he drew his sword at once and cried:

'To the death! To the death! You rabble, you're all going to die!'

In startled panic they scattered in all directions, and he cut and struck them down, killing and maiming till hardly a single man remained: all were fled and gone except the thirty posted by Clarvus to guard the banner. It had been set up high on the back of a cart as if it were a little castle, but these thirty were beside themselves with terror and offered scant resistance: Gadifer slaughtered sixteen on the spot and soon had driven the rest away. Then he hacked and hewed through the pole to bring the banner crashing to the ground. He jumped down from the cart and returned to his horse and remounted without delay and fought his way back to his men.

You can imagine the alarm in the Indian host when they saw the banner fall; they were dismayed indeed, and some began to slip away from the battle and take to flight. But those were the cowards; the brave were undaunted and summoned up more courage and started fighting even more fiercely than before. The history says that on one side they drove the Greeks right back to the moats below the walls of Ephesus; Alexander, on another flank, saw this and led his whole force against them, mowing down so many in a ravaging charge that he forced the Indians to retreat. In this mêlée one of Clarvus's sons, Sallhedin, was killed; Porus was so distraught when he heard the news that he started felling knights and horses like a man gone wild, performing supernatural feats of arms.

But if he fought well, so did Alexander and his men such as Ptholomer, Emenidus and the rest. According to the history Emenidus had only one thing on his mind: to win back his horse taken by Porus. Feeling the utmost shame at the loss, he kept attacking Porus; but he did little to unsettle him, and however hard he tried to grab him his efforts were wasted: Porus knew how to fend him off. All the same, Emenidus delivered some mighty blows that made him bow face-down over his saddle and wounded him in the head, though not severely. And as they fought on, Emenidus seized him in his arms and hauled him to the ground, finally winning back his horse in the face of Porus and all his supporters. Porus lay on the ground so long that they thought he was dead; but he wasn't: he clambered to his feet and realised he'd lost his prize. But his original mount was now riderless, so he grabbed the bridle and remounted with all speed, though he felt the utmost shame. But for his part Emenidus was jubilant, fired and inspired anew to kill and confound his enemies; and from that point on, Porus began to fear and dread him.

Chapter CIV
How Clarvus's three other sons were killed, and other matters.

On the walls and gates of Ephesus were the townsfolk and the citizens, all armed, posted there by Alexander to guard the city so that, if Fortune turned against them in the battle, they could withdraw and take safe refuge there. These townsmen were watching the slaughter and carnage below their walls and reacted in different ways: many were almost too appalled to look, but others' hearts were so inspired that they'd have rushed straight out to join the fray if they'd been allowed. Atop the palace towers, too, the ladies and damsels such as Phesonnas, Edea, Ydoree and Heliot and many more were watching and fretting as their sweethearts performed deeds of arms that filled them with both joy and dread: they rejoiced at the great renown they were winning with their mighty blows and charges, but constantly dreaded that some terrible misfortune would strike. It would be a job to record everything they said!

But let me tell you, some of those in the battle were so fired with desire to win the ladies' favour that they took many a fearful risk – Porus was a prime example, but he wasn't alone. You've heard how Porus lost the horse he'd won from the duke of Arcadia, the duke having bravely won it back; now Porus, sorely conscious of the shame, headed for his two brothers, Caneos and Canaan, and joined their squadrons, who at that point were in the thick of battle, and fought first for a long while under Caneos's banner. Alexander, observing this, led such a fearsome charge at Caneos that he smashed his squadron apart, and after a mighty slaughter of horses, knights and infantry alike, Alexander dealt

Caneos such a blow with a gisarme[1] that he split his head right down to his teeth and sent him crashing among the trampling hooves. His men were so aghast that they started to scatter in all directions, but Porus rallied and kept together as many as he could and went to join Canaan's squadron who were still in good shape. But truly, no one could describe the howling and wailing when the Indians realised Caneos was dead; and Canaan was so distraught when he heard of his brother's death that he swore he'd rather die than live and leave his two brothers unavenged. He began to cry:

'Forward, forward, friends! If you love me, follow me!'

And with that he thrust in his spurs and charged into the thickest mass of the Greeks, a double-headed axe in hand, and battered and struck down knights and horses like a devastating storm: every man he met he felled, as if they were there just for him to destroy. But the good King Alexander solved the problem: he sent his head flying from his shoulders. Thus all three of Clarvus's sons had been killed by Alexander's hand. And though we've lavished praise upon the prowess of other lords on both sides, there was none to match the strength and prowess and daring of Alexander, whose self-belief could never be surpassed.

Chapter CV

Of the death of Clarvus, slain by Cassamus, and how Porus again won Ferrant, Emenidus's mount.

The father was told at once of the death of his three sons; and the history says that when Clarvus heard the news his rage was such that he took an axe in both hands and clove the messenger's head to the teeth as if he'd gone wild and lost his mind. He demanded to know who'd killed his sons, but no one dared reply; so he thrust in his spurs and headed for the enemy. He rode straight to where Cassamus was fighting with might and main, and Cassamus saw him instantly and charged towards him. They started hewing and battering each other till they sent sparks leaping from their helms; and their combat finally ended with Cassamus killing Clarvus, whereupon the Indians around them began abandoning the battle in huge numbers. But the history says that a good many of his men were overjoyed, despite the calamitous danger they now faced, for they despised him for his boundless cruelty and oppression.

His death was reported to Porus, his other son, who was distressed beyond measure; but he didn't fly, no, he rallied his men and kept them in good order. Marcien was likewise told of Clarvus's death, and was so overcome with grief that he looked as if he'd die, and cried:

'Ah, uncle! My uncle Clarvus! You were so brave and daring! You undertook and won so many tough and fearsome battles! But your pride and miserly greed and rapacity, and the counsel of flatterers which you always heeded more than the words of men of honour, have brought you now to your final day! Ah, lord,

---

[1]   See note 1, above, p.87.

lord, you always loved robbers and murderers and mortally hated all valiant, worthy knights! Now your covetousness has brought you poor reward!'

Such was Marcien's lament for his uncle; and as he lamented he could see the Greeks creating vast mounds of shattered shields and battered helms on every side: everywhere he looked was a scene of horrific carnage. But undaunted, like the brave and valiant knight he was, he rallied and summoned back his men and charged once more into the fray, and in this new attack and onslaught incomparable numbers were felled and left dead upon the ground; indeed, in many places the bodies lay in such deep piles that those still upright could barely stand. And the history says that the sky was bright and clear that day, but over the site of the slaughter it was black with the smoking sweat and blood that reeked from the bodies of knights and horses, so dark that those still fighting struggled to see each other. The valiant men-at-arms who'd been fighting on foot were near exhaustion – and could no longer move about the field for the multitude of corpses – so they mounted now, all winning strong and powerful horses from their foes.

Porus, who was riding back and forth, this way and that, was watching out for Emenidus and saw him wreaking havoc among his men; he decided to attack him again and see if he could win his horse a second time. Afire with passionate rage, and determined to fulfil his vow to rout the Greeks, he charged into the mêlée where Emenidus reigned supreme; he struck out to right and left, making even the bravest fall back and give way, and ended by unseating Emenidus and taking his horse for a second time, mounting at once and swiftly. This was an amazing feat, bearing in mind that the histories deem Emenidus the most valiant knight of his time. But Fortune did Porus this service and he is credited with this honour, achieved through his deep love for the lady Phesonnas, who was atop the palace tower with her eye ever upon him, making him all the more inspired to attack and assail his foes.

CHAPTER CVI

How Porus unhorsed King Alexander and many other lords of his army.

After winning the duke of Arcadia's fine horse Ferrant for a second time, Porus was so elated that all the pain and woe he'd suffered that day were forgotten: he seemed as blithe and fresh as he'd been when he began that morning – though it was now well past noon. With a dash and a flourish he rode among his men, exhorting them to show their mettle, and rallying a good body of troops he charged at the squadron led by Alexander. In the course of his charge he met Floridas, newly mounted, involved in a mighty contest with the Persians. Blazing with desire to crush the Greeks, giving no thought to life or death, Porus aimed a blow at Floridas's head which would have split it to the teeth had Floridas not flung his shield up to meet it: as it was, the shield was smashed clean through and the blow fell on his left arm, slicing off the armour and cutting into the flesh; blood came gushing forth, and the force of the blow sent him crashing to the ground with his legs in the air and almost killed him, but he was instantly rescued by his men. Alexander had witnessed this and could see the mêlée gathering around the rescue of Floridas, and was mightily impressed by Porus's strength. And as he watched, Porus came charging at him crying:

'To the death! To the death!'

The king charged full tilt to meet him and they started a fearsome sword-fight; one blow aimed by Porus severed the head of Alexander's mount and brought down horse and king in a heap. For a long moment the king lay there with no one knowing how he was; but then, with his strong and fervent spirit, he leapt up, sword in hand, and crying 'Macedon, to the rescue!' he started fighting on foot like a common soldier, gutting horses and knights alike and performing wondrous deeds of arms. But the Indians had seen Porus fell the king, and their belief that he was dead gave them such fresh heart that it seemed the day would surely be theirs. Porus, intent on fulfilling his mad vow, had left Alexander, for the mêlée around his rescue made further fight with him impossible; he turned his attention elsewhere and was working wonders, felling knights and horses and robbing foes of their helms, swords, heads, arms and legs. Anyone who beheld it would have thought it utterly supernatural: all around him he was strewing the ground with dead horses and men until it was almost covered; no one he encountered could survive.[1]

But if he was performing miracles, Emenidus surpassed him: Porus may twice have robbed him of his mount, but in both cases he'd unhorsed him in a kind of ambush whereas Emenidus, as you'll shortly hear, outfought him in single combat. And whatever we may say about Porus, he dreaded meeting Emenidus, for wherever the duke of Arcadia went he thinned the enemy lines and made them flee, and the Indians were stricken with terror whenever they saw him near.

CHAPTER CVII

How Porus killed Cassamus but was captured by Emenidus.

Seeing their king Alexander fall, Betis and Perdicas, Ptholomer and Danselin and a host of other brave knights rode swiftly to the rescue. In the fight that followed Porus was very close to being captured – and would have been had he not been saved by his cousin Marcien of Persia; also, all the Greeks' attention was on remounting their king and asking how he was, so they partly forgot about Porus, who promptly unhorsed Licanor and would have killed him but for Gadifer, who saw them clash and mounted such a fierce defence that Porus withdrew for a little to rest and gather breath – and Marcien of Persia, very afraid he'd lose him, insisted that he should.

By now Alexander was back in the saddle, and there's no need to ask if the Greeks were cheered by the sight! Now they launched themselves against the Indians, whom Marcien was keeping in excellent shape and heart. Then Porus, a little refreshed, thought of the deaths of his father and brothers and:

---

[1]   It is at this point in *Les Voeux du Paon* ('The Vows of the Peacock') that Jacques de Lon-guyon digressed into his famous passage about the Nine Worthies. See Appendix 3.

'Oh!' he cried. 'Are such grievous blows to go unpunished? No indeed! I'll avenge them or die!'

And as he said this he remembered the vow he'd made before the lady Phesonnas, that he would defeat the enemy battalions; so he charged once more into the Greeks, beating and striking down all in his path and driving right through their lines. When he found himself on the other side he turned and spotted Cassamus: he was resting beside a young bush after toiling and fighting mightily all day. Porus rode towards him crying 'To the death!'; and the moment he saw him Cassamus drew the sword that hung at his side and came vigorously to meet him, his heart ablaze, and they started exchanging blows that sent sparks flying from blades and armour. Shield and buckler, surcoat, tunic they cut to pieces, littering the ground; even the rings and rivets of their mail were smashed apart and helms and armour plates stove in. Porus, ashamed at the old man's long resistance, in a seething rage delivered a double-handed sword-blow to his head that clove it to the teeth, and as he pulled the blade free Cassamus dropped to the ground, stone dead.

No sooner had he slain him than Porus charged back into the turmoil of the battling squadrons, who seemed to be intent on fighting till there was no man left to kill. There he encountered Ptholomer, and sent him crashing down so hard that he almost broke his neck; then he felled Duke Betis together with his horse. Truly, his charge was such that the Greeks began to retreat somewhat, and in that part of the battle the only cry was 'Porus! Porus!', for it seemed he would crush and cleave and fell them all! If you could picture how the Greeks assailed him then with axes, lances, swords, gisarmes and espadons[1] you'd be amazed; so intense was the mayhem of the fray and pursuit that even the strongest could barely cope. The ground was so awash with blood that in some parts it was up to their saddle-girths, and the air was dense with the steaming sweat of their straining bodies; and all around were the screams of men on the ground amid the trampling hooves pleading for 'Help! Help!', and trumpets blasting out so loud that they could be heard two leagues away.

Now Emenidus, hearing the commotion surrounding Porus, and enraged by the indignity he'd twice suffered at his hands, rode to seek him out and found him fighting with might and main just as you've heard. Burning with fury and resentment, he forced his way right up to him and starting raining blows; Porus would have made his escape if he could, but no: Emenidus was right upon him and he had to defend himself; and Emenidus, armed with a fine, strong spear, delivered such a fearsome thrust that he felled both knight and horse together, breaking Porus's leg in mid-bone. Emenidus stepped down and came to him, still prostrate and unable to stand, and cried:

'Yield to me, lord Porus, or I'll make you pay for the deaths of the valiant knights you've slain today!'

So saying, he raised his sword and struck Porus on the head with the flat of

---

[1]   The espadon was a heavy, long, double-handed sword.

the blade, for he could see very well that he was wounded; and Porus, realising he was helpless, said:

'Ah, sir knight, full of prowess! I yield and pray you spare my life! And help me stand, for I'm sorely hurt.'

So saying, he surrendered his sword to Emenidus, who accepted it and had Porus helped to his feet; but he couldn't stand, and had to be carried to Alexander's tent for treatment to his broken leg.

But truly, though Porus's vow to defeat all the Greeks was mad indeed, he shouldn't be charged with dishonour for his failure, for when he made the vow he pledged to achieve it 'if God preserved him from death or injury'.[1]

CHAPTER CVIII

How Marcien of Persia's battle ended with capture at the hands of Floridas.

And so, as you've heard, the brave knight Porus was taken prisoner. With the loss of him the Indians were quite undone; now their only remaining leader was the valiant Marcien, fighting on with might and main, rallying his men and firing them with passion. But when he heard what had befallen Porus he was utterly downcast: he realised defeat was imminent, and could see only a handful of Indian knights left fighting.

'Alas!' he cried. 'Fortune, how you've turned your wheel against us! Ah, my dear friend Porus, now you've been taken and held by your foes, who can do as they please with you! Your father's tyranny is to blame, I swear, for I haven't seen his men fight today as they would have done if they'd truly loved him.'

Bewailing his misfortune, Marcien rallied together the few men-at-arms and others still fighting here and there about the field. He commended their valour, telling them they'd fought with courage and might, and then said:

'Forward, friends! Let's live and die as brothers side by side, and let our descendants never be abused for their fathers' or kinsmen's cowardice! It's better to die in honour than live in shame, and truly, I'd sooner die than live without avenging our flesh and blood lying dead and slain here on this field! All who love me and love honour, follow me!'

So saying, he made straight for Alexander, who was still embroiled against a band of valiant knights; and all his men followed him in a mighty charge that swept and plunged into the Greeks with such force that they sent them staggering and reeling back at least half the length of a bowshot.[2] And it wasn't without heavy loss of men-at-arms: more than a thousand on both sides fell in this onslaught, with countless numbers killed. According to the history, if it hadn't been for Floridas King Alexander would have been in trouble; but Floridas, returning from a short rest, came and dealt Marcien a blow that brought down him and his horse together. Marcien was taken prisoner then and stripped of his sword and

[1]   To be precise, the text reads at this point 'wound or injury', but I've repeated the phrase used by Porus when he made the vow, above, p.95.

[2]   *'bien un arpent'*: see footnote 2, above, p.87.

armour; he gave his word of honour, accepting his captivity, and was sent to join Porus and the Baudrian, fellow prisoners in the Greek camp.

Now all ranks among the Indians, Medes and Persians started throwing down their arms and turned their backs and fled, every man for himself. They dived and hid in bushes and hedges, ravines and ditches, wherever they thought they might be safe; but the Greeks were on their heels, cutting and striking them down as they ran. Spurs were more use than weapons to the fugitives; and indeed, none of them attempted to resist but surrendered when they could flee no further, begging for mercy. The tumult and the wailing were so great, and the chase conducted with such fearful zeal, that everyone was awestruck.

Once Marcien had been captured the Indians made no attempt to do anything but flee, and abandoned everything to the Greeks – pavilions and tents both great and small and their whole vast train of chariots, carts and wagons: the hoard of booty was beyond all counting, for they'd come with all the wealth they possessed. But Alexander took no part in the chase: once he saw the Indians were broken beyond recovery he calmly headed back to his pavilion to wait for his knights, now immersed in rampant plunder.

CHAPTER CIX

How Porus was presented to Alexander with the other captives, and what the king said to him.

On reaching his tent with a band of his lords, Alexander was helped from his armour at once and his injuries and wounds were tended; then he was nobly dressed in a fine mantle of deep red[1] befitting his royal status. Then the barons arrived to present their prisoners to him. Among them was Porus, in such bad shape that he genuinely couldn't stand. The king surveyed the captives one by one and then bade them be seated, since Porus could stand only with support. Alexander sat and considered them a second time before saying:

'Truly, lords of India, your prowess has cost me dear this day! But by the grace of God and with the help of our dear friends and companions, we've managed to defeat you and now you're at our mercy. But by the faith I owe the noble god Mars, believe me when I say I mean to show you such courtesy that you'll all say "It's a deal!"[2]

'You, lord Porus, first of all: with your courage and mighty strength you've checked and repulsed our forces many times today – indeed your daring almost cost me grave dishonour! But by the grace of God, Duke Emenidus of Arcadia has saved me that and has placed you in my power, to do with you as I will: to put you to death or imprison you or spare you, as I please. But by the gods I've served and honoured, you'll suffer no harm or ill at my hands – not this time. Rather, out of respect for your abundant courage, which has earned you renown surpassing all knights in the world, you shall be free to go whenever you wish,

---

[1]   'pourpre'.
[2]   Literally 'It's enough'.

exempt from any ransom, and I shall guarantee you safe conduct back to your lands exactly as you please.

'You may make war on me anew, it's up to you; but you need to realise that if you do, and I meet you again in battle or joust, all the gold in the world won't stop me taking your life, no matter what. But if you'd rather not leave, and prefer to stay with us as our companion, I'll see you have all the wealth and honour you could wish, and promise I'll give you all the land you desire till you say "Enough! Enough!" – provided you agree to hold it as my vassal.

'What's more, I'll give you a wife I believe you'll accept most gladly! I know you've set your heart on the lady Phesonnas, for whom the vows were made – vows which almost cost me dear: I know my horse was beheaded for her sake, which landed me with the common soldiery, fighting on foot for quite a while! But I gladly forgive you that, out of respect for your courage and valour, and ask you to consider taking the lady Phesonnas in marriage: I'll give you her hand if you wish and if you'll forgive her brothers all resentment and ill-will, for you'll find they can lend you aid and support against any threat or enemy. Moreover, if it please you to accept, I promise you my help and support in any eventuality, on condition that you acknowledge me as your liege lord for all the lands in your possession.

'And you, lord of Baudres, I make you the same offer I've made to Porus: I excuse you your ransom and you may go if you wish, or stay with us as a cherished companion. And if you choose the latter, I know you've had your eye on the fair Edea! So if you wish to take her as your wife, I give you her hand on the same conditions proposed to Porus.

'Likewise to you, lord of Persia, I give the fair maiden Heliot, on the aforesaid conditions. Reflect upon this and make your decisions.'

Chapter CX
Porus's reply to Alexander.

When Porus heard the king's noble, gracious offer to excuse him and his companions ransom, he was astonished. But he reflected a long while before he replied, his thoughts being these: first, pride and shame and hurt whispered in his ear that it ill became him to forget so soon the deaths of his father and those close to him, especially since Alexander was giving him leave and freedom to attempt revenge if he chose; he told himself it would be better to go back to his lands and enlist and rally his men to avenge the wrongs inflicted, rather than to reach such swift accord. But then he considered how this King Alexander was so valiant, so strong and so loved by his men that it would be hard indeed to defeat him, 'for Fortune,' he said to himself, 'keeps him at the very top of Her wheel!' What's more, the true and total love he felt for the lady Phesonnas loosed five shafts into his heart: her beauty, her modesty, her bearing, her grace and her courtesy; and these five shafts lanced and purged the aforesaid pride and shame and hurt. With this sweet thought he gave a deep sigh and said:

'Noble emperor, most exalted lord who conquers conquerors, humbles and tames the proud and makes the poor rich and mighty, I realise I'm your prisoner and entirely at your mercy to do with as you will; but now I see that through your fine, noble compassion and outstanding valour you're willing to excuse me both ransom and imprisonment, and have given me the choice to be your friend or foe. It seems to me I'd be forever deemed a fool if I opted for the worse! So my reply, dread lord, is this: my father and three brothers were killed and put to death in this day's merciless and awful battle, along with many of my friends and kinsmen, and I myself have been sorely hurt and wounded – and, worse still, captured and am now held prisoner; but since you have so graciously deigned to accept me as your knight, I shall be your friend and liegeman, and beg my two cousins here to act wisely and follow my example.'

Hearing Porus's words, Marcien and the Baudrian replied in turn that they were entirely willing to do as the king and Porus pleased. At this King Alexander smiled and said:

'Praise be to all our gods! I've gained more today than ever before in my life, winning the love and company of three such valiant men! For your kind response, dear lords and friends, I hold you to be from this time forth my companions in adversity and prosperity, sharers in all future conquests and deeds of prowess undertaken by us and our followers, and I appoint you members of our close and privy council.'

Just then Gadifer and his brother Betis arrived at the king's pavilion with fully five hundred knights, all returning from the pursuit. And what an awesome sight they were: their bucklers, shields and armour were battered and smashed, and they were covered in blood and brain – they looked like butchers who'd been slaughtering cows and calves or sheep, smothered beyond all recognition. As soon as they reached the pavilion Gadifer and Betis dismounted with nine or ten of the greatest lords and stepped inside, still armed as they were apart from their helms, and hailed the king and his company. The king was overjoyed to see them back and returned their greeting most graciously. He asked them where they'd been, and they told him they'd come from the pursuit, which had gone well for them and badly for their foes.

'Hugely so!' they said. 'Thanks to you, we've crushed all opposition! But the reason we took so long is partly that we didn't know where you were: we were worried you'd been caught up in the pursuit, and spent a good while searching the fields and woods and heaths until a boy told us you'd returned to camp. That's why we've been gone so long.'

'Truly, sirs,' said Alexander, 'you're welcome indeed! I came back once I saw our foes were powerless: I thought there was nothing more for me to do and so returned here to my pavilion as you see.'

With that he rose and took them by the hands and seated them beside him; then he said:

Chapter CXI
How peace was made between the Ephesians and the Indians.

'Gadifer, and you, Betis, valiant knights, my dear and perfect friends and companions, kindly hear my proposal and request. As you know, a while ago now I sent a band of my knights to forage outside the city of Gaza and round up cattle; and when your uncle Duke Betis and your father Gadifer du Laris made a sortie against them, they killed a most worthy knight of mine named Sanson Dailly, nephew of King Darius of Persia, and a good many more such as Salibor and Pieron. But then during a counter-attack your father was killed, which was a grievous loss; indeed, I was as sorry as I've ever been for any event, for I'd been hoping he might yet become a true friend and companion. But now you may feel fully compensated for this loss and affliction – for here before you is the valiant knight Porus, son of King Clarvus of India: with the aid of his men he has caused you much harm and grief and woe, but now he is your prisoner, and his father has been slain in this day's battle. But I pray you forgive him your ill-will and make peace with him: if you do so in the way that I've conceived, it will be much to your advantage, benefit and honour.'

Then Gadifer, elder of the brothers, replied: 'Most dear and dread lord, you are well aware of the shame and hurt the Indians have forced us to endure; but despite it all I sense your honour, valour and wisdom to be so great that you would never wish to see injustice done. So for my part I bow to your judgement; let it be as you wish, and I pray that my brother here will graciously agree to peace.'

Betis replied that he had no objection whatever and would never contradict the king whose valour and discretion he trusted.

'Thanks indeed, sirs!' said Alexander. 'Then help Porus to his feet now: he's sitting there on that couch. But be as gentle as you can – he's sorely injured. We'll all go together to the city, and once we're gathered at the Palace of Jupiter I'll conclude a peace, if it please the gods, to the satisfaction of all parties.'

Porus was assisted as the king had bidden and taken to the city; and everyone began to strike camp – the king first of all and the other lords – and set off towards Ephesus where they were greeted so triumphantly that to describe the pomp and celebration would take forever, so we'll leave it at that!

But Gadifer and Betis didn't go so soon: first they supervised the burying of the dead; most were buried on the field, but they had the great lords such as Clarvus and his three sons, and also their uncle Cassamus and a good many more, carried to a nearby temple called the Temple of Diana, so that they could be given burial with full honours and funeral rites according to their custom.

Of the marriages that confirmed the peace, and other matters.

When King Alexander returned and dismounted at the palace – where, as you may imagine, he was given a glorious reception by the ladies and maidens – he wanted to sit straight down to supper, for it was already very late, and the horn was sounded for the washing of hands and everything laid ready. Then the king took his place with the ladies and maidens and many great lords at his side.

While they supped Gadifer and Betis entered the hall and came before the king and gave him due greeting; he greeted them in return and invited them to be seated, and they all ate and drank with the greatest joy and pleasure. When they'd finished they rose and the tables were cleared. Then the king took Gadifer and Betis aside with the lady Phesonnas. He asked them where they'd been and they explained. When Phesonnas heard of her uncle Cassamus's death she was obviously distressed; the king felt the deepest sympathy and gave her all the comfort that he could. They spoke of many matters before they parted and took to their beds to rest till morning.

When morning came and they were ready they all went to the Temple of Diana with great pomp and in fine array for the funerals of the princes and great lords who'd been killed the previous day as you've heard. There the grief of Phesonnas and many other ladies and maidens flooded forth anew, as they wept most piteously for their dead sweethearts, lords or kinsmen. But the good King Alexander spoke so many words of loving consolation that they all felt greatly comforted. Many men, too, nobles and non-nobles alike, were lamenting and bewailing the loss of their lords and vassals, and the grieving continued till the burials had been completed according to pagan custom. When all was done they returned to the city.

After dinner King Alexander called together a number of his barons and in particular Gadifer and Betis, and asked them to take good care of their prisoners, 'for,' he said, 'I shan't leave till Porus has recovered.' Indeed he summoned the surgeon to ask how Porus was; he replied that he would soon be healed, and Alexander was clearly cheered by the news.

So time passed and the king remained at Ephesus, waiting for Porus's healing and recovery to be complete. When he was better, the king called most of his barons together in the hall of the palace, to lay before them his proposed terms of peace as he'd conceived them in his heart. When they'd all arrived and gathered and taken their places, each according to his degree, the king commanded Gadifer to let him see the prisoners, and all three were led before him: Porus, that is, and Cassel the Baudrian and Marcien of Persia. They were seated with all honour as befitted their rank, and the king began thus:

'My dear lords and friends and companions, Gadifer and you, Betis, and you, Porus and you, Cassel and you, Marcien: you know there has been discord between you for a long while, leading to a deeply bitter war and the deaths of many valiant men, which is a grievous pity. But I intervened on behalf of one party, and the upshot is – praise the gods – that you've placed matters entirely in my hands: I want you to confirm that before all here present.'

They declared the king's words to be true, and gave their oaths to abide faithfully by whatever he decided about the terms of peace; and so, with confirmation given, he continued by saying:

'Firstly, to secure the peace between you, Indians and Ephesians, I wish these three prisoners to be released without demand of any ransom, on condition that, once all has been arranged, they recognise us as their sovereign lord and acknowledge that they hold their lands and possessions as our vassals. Secondly, if they approve and so desire, I wish Porus to vow to take Phesonnas for his wife, the Baudrian the damsel Edea, Marcien the damsel Heliot, and Betis the damsel Ydoree. This I propose so that there may be a greater love and stronger alliance between you; for it seems to me that with the forging of these bonds no one will be able to do you harm – if you're willing to agree.'

Then the king gave them lavish and countless gifts, which I'll pass over for the sake of brevity. Thus accord was reached, for no one on either side raised any objection but thanked the king most fulsomely for arranging matters so.

CHAPTER CXIII

Of the marriages and the recreation of the peacock, which the damsel Edea commissioned to be fashioned from pure gold; and sundry other matters.

At the same time that these princes wed, the union was celebrated of Gadifer of Ephesus to the damsel Lyndonie, Emenidus's niece; and at their marriage, with Alexander's approval, Emenidus gave Gadifer lordship of Tiberias.[1]

There's no need to take time describing the ceremonies and festivities that followed – they lasted more than three weeks! Anyone can picture for himself the pomp and glorious celebrations, with no expense spared, that accompanied the marriage of such noble lords. But I must tell you this: in the course of all the joyous feasting, the lady Edea, now wedded to the Baudrian as you've heard, commissioned the making of a magnificent peacock of pure gold and silver, covered in every conceivable kind of enamel decoration, and had it set in a special place atop an imposing silver pillar. Then she had letters inscribed around the pillar to record the reason for its making.

In similar fashion the young lady Heliot, wife to Marcien the Persian and considered the brightest of women in every way, ordered the forging of a splendid eagle of gold; and one day, while all were immersed in revelry, she had it carried into the hall where she presented it to Alexander as the most valiant king in all the world, declaring in an eloquent speech that no man alive could compare with him in courage and in prowess. But Alexander called upon everyone to say who in his opinion had fought best in the battle: he wanted the eagle to be awarded to that man, 'for,' he said, 'I have not deserved this; it shouldn't come to me.'

---

[1]   As he promised earlier: see above, p.83.

After much dispute and argument this way and that, it was decided that if Cassamus had still been alive it should rightfully have been his, for he had performed better than anyone.[1] The reason given was this: that when a man has vanquished his foe it is an act of great nobility to let him go free again – and not only that, but to provide him with a fresh horse and equipment – as Cassamus had done for King Clarvus of India, despite the grave misfortune that might follow. When the noble King Alexander heard this he commanded that the eagle be given to the young knight Betis to take with all reverence to his uncle Cassamus's tomb. The king's bidding was done, you may be sure, accompanied by all manner of rites and celebrations too lengthy to record. But I should tell you that, according to the history, Cassamus's tomb was made of pure white marble, erected and adorned in grandest style, with a detailed inscription so that all who wished and were able to read could learn the circumstances of his death. And on the tomb, atop a tall white marble pillar, the eagle of gold was proudly placed as a memorial of the outstanding and boundless valour displayed by Cassamus in his life.

When all these matters had been arranged, the lords all gathered to make an offering as a mark of respect to the peacock recreated in gold. And from what I understand from the history, the offering took the form of elaborate words, in rhyme or otherwise, the finest that each person could compose.

But Alexander's thoughts were now fixed on King Darius; and at last, very mindful of Darius's past and recent messages of defiance, as mentioned above, Alexander called together all his barons and instructed them that everything was to be packed and loaded, all arms and gear repaired and put in order: he meant serious business. Then he took his leave of King Porus of India[2] who acknowledged him as his lord, and likewise of all the others, bidding them remain firm friends. And he also told them that if any lord, no matter who, threatened them with trouble they were to let him know, for he would bring aid immediately and without fail. With that he departed and set out on his way.

CHAPTER CXIV

The death of King Philip of Macedon, as recorded by Vincent, an historian who proposed a theory about Alexander's parentage.

But here we'll leave Alexander for a little and tell of the death of his presumed father King Philip of Macedon, as recorded by the historian Vincent

---

[1]   This chapter ultimately derives from Jean le Court's continuation of *Les Voeux du Paon* entitled *Le Restor du Paon*. In this poem, Alexander finds it so hard to decide who should receive the prize that he calls upon the eleven vow-makers to write down their vows on slips of paper; he will then draw lots and '"Let us pray to God who reigns supreme over nature, and to the good god Mercury, that the right lot may be drawn..." The king stepped forward and drew a slip, and when he read it he was dumbfounded...[because despite the fact that the twelfth vow-maker, Cassamus, was dead and could not therefore have written a slip] "I find here the name of Cassamus du Laris!... Mercury and Jove, Mars the god of battles and Jupiter and Venus, whom he always served with all his heart, are performing miracles for him!"' (*Le Restor du Paon*, ed. Carey, vv. 2422-44).

[2]   Porus having now succeeded his father, the dead King Clarvus.

le Jacopin[1] (who, in his treatment of the story of Nectanebus, suggested that Nectanebus was Alexander's true father).[2] His version of events is this:

Not long after the noble King Alexander left his father Philip of Macedon and his mother the lady Olympias, there was a king in Bithynia named Pausanias, a most valiant warrior, bold and daring and wise and shrewd in all his deeds, who, according to Vincent's history, was afire with love for the lady Olympias, considered at the time to be the most beautiful queen in the world. Her husband King Philip for his part was an avaricious hoarder of wealth, hated by many of his neighbours as he burdened them with repeated levies and taxes, fleecing them and bleeding them dry. King Pausanias of Bithynia was well aware of this; and when he learned that Alexander, as you heard earlier, had been sent to distant lands and had taken all the young knights of Macedon with him, so that now there was no one left in the kingdom but old, decrepit, battle-weary men, he thought the time was ripe to make his move.

So he assembled all his country's forces and swooped down on the land of Macedon and arrived outside the city where King Philip and Olympias were residing. He laid close siege to the city, encircling it completely. Philip was shocked by Pausanias's presumption, and amazed that he, his subject and regular payer of tribute, should have launched this attack so suddenly and without any word of challenge. But after brief reflection his pride had the better of him and took hold of his heart, and he sent word through the city summoning all men to prepare and arm at once, for he meant to take the field against this wicked King Pausanias. His bidding was done, and he marched from the city with all the men he could muster and launched a furious attack upon his enemies. But their numbers were so few that they were swiftly overwhelmed, and King Philip received a mortal blow; they fled back to the city, every man for himself, leaving their king dying on the field. The history says that Pausanias's men pursued the fugitives through the gates and took control of the city, and Queen Olympias, realising all was lost, fled to a tower on one side of the town and took refuge there as best she could with a small band of followers, blockading it against Pausanias while she waited for help from her son, if he should ever hear of the disaster. And in fact she'd sent word to him some time before, warning him of her suspicions that Pausanias was conspiring against her husband.

---

[1]   Vincent of Beauvais, the Dominican monk who in the thirteenth century wrote the encyclopaedic *Speculum Maius* including a complete history of the world. Wauquelin evidently believed Vincent to be the author of the Latin text translated in the Prose *Alexander* (perhaps misled by a reference to Vincent in the prologue to one redaction). The Prose *Alexander* was in fact anonymously translated into French in the thirteenth century not from a work by Vincent but from the *Historia de Preliis*, Leo the Archpriest's tenth-century Latin translation of the Greek Alexander romance, the 'Pseudo-Callisthenes' (see Introduction, p.2, footnote 4). The *Historia* is certainly the ultimate source for this passage which, along with much of what follows, is based on the Prose *Alexander*: see Hilka's edition, beginning at p.46.
[2]   For the passage in the Prose *Alexander* suggesting that Nectanebus was Alexander's father, see Appendix 1.

CHAPTER CXV

How, according to Vincent's history, King Alexander took revenge upon Pausanias
for his father's death.

As Alexander was making his way through numerous lands and regions, his mother's messengers arrived with her plea that he return as soon as he could, for she greatly feared King Pausanias and his mobilising of troops: she was convinced he was planning to move against his father Philip, knowing as she did that Pausanias was in love with her. So Alexander turned his army about at once and marched back with all speed to the land of Macedon.

The history says he arrived outside his father's city on the very day of the aforesaid battle, but not from the side where the battle was fought but from another – the side where the tower stood in which his mother had taken refuge. And according to the history, when his mother saw him coming with his mighty host she thought at first that it was some other prince marching to support Pausanias and was beside herself with fear; but like the strong-willed lady she was she hid her alarm and exhorted her knights to do their duty and mount a stout defence. In doing so she climbed to the top of the tower. From there she could see her son advancing swiftly and now quite near; she recognised him by his banners and devices, and began to cry aloud to her knights to rejoice, for help was close at hand:

'Here is my beloved Alexander, who'll save us from our enemies!'

Alexander, who'd already learned from the fugitives what was going on, had now ridden right up to the tower so that his mother could call down to him, and she cried at the top of her voice:

'Ah, dear son! Show your prowess now! Show why you've earned your god-given praise and renown for victory in all you undertake! Take revenge for your father and me upon this wicked King Pausanias of Bithynia: he has slain your father on the field and driven me to this tower where I'm attacked and besieged by his rabble!'

While she was calling to her son, the cry went up around the city that King Alexander had come; and when Pausanias heard this, like the shrewd and able commander he was he decided to sally forth against Alexander at once, without delay, and to attack him before his men were rested and fully assembled: that way, he thought, he had the best chance of routing them. So he had the trumpets sound to call his men-at-arms to order, and burst from the city just where Alexander was calling to his mother. Alexander saw him instantly, and rode full tilt to meet him. The history says their charge was so fierce that the very earth trembled, and they struck each other with such force that their lances smashed to pieces. They turned back to do battle with their swords, exchanging awesome blows that sent sparks and flames leaping from the blades, such was their strength and passion. On they hewed and hammered till Pausanias smashed Alexander's shield to the ground; Alexander was so incensed by this, so fired with rage, that he delivered a blow that sent Pausanias's head flying across the field. At this his troops began to break and flee, and Alexander's men launched an assault so overwhelming that, according to the history, hardly a single man escaped: all were slain or perished in the flight.

Chapter CXVI

How Alexander had his father buried, and then set off once more to march with his army against King Darius.

Having killed Pausanias and routed all his forces, Alexander rode out to the field where his father had lost his battle that day and found him close to death, stretched out on the ground amid the vast sea of corpses. Alexander spoke to his father with the utmost reverence and tenderness, and told him how he'd taken revenge upon his enemies, not imagining his father was as near to death as he was. Hearing his son's voice, Philip opened his eyes and saw him there and heaved himself up a little and said:

'Ah, my dear son Alexander! May the gods increase and multiply your prowess and your valour! I feel my death is imminent, truly, but I can accept it happily now that I see you in good health and spirits and know you've taken revenge upon my foes. I pray you, be to your mother as a son...' But with those words he died.

Alexander lamented bitterly then, as you may well imagine. Then he had his father's body carried back to the city and buried with all honour. After all the rites had been performed he withdrew to the palace to be beside his mother – for how many days I don't know – and comforted her and spoke of many matters.

Then he assembled all his barons once more and raised a number of issues, including the notion that men should fight all their lives to protect their freedom.

'For freedom,' he said, 'is the noblest thing Nature has bestowed upon man, and when he's lost it he should strive with all his might to win it back. Some of our neighbours,' he said, 'prompted by greed and by our predecessors' weakness, have robbed us of our liberties and diminished our honour. Our prime duty now must be to seek to win them back; so I, your king and lord by rightful lineage, the kingship having newly passed to me as you know, pray that all of you will help me recover this kingdom's honour, as I am committed to do but cannot without your aid and guidance – for as you know, a head is helpless without limbs as are limbs without a head! Since I'm willing to offer my person and all my strength and resources to this task, it seems to me that you cannot and should not refuse. So I pray you prepare your arms and everything necessary for campaign, for I mean to march against my foes.'

At this point the history says that some of the elderly knights tried to excuse themselves from going to war; but Alexander argued that their knowledge and experience made them just as valuable as the young, whereupon they all bowed to his will.

Then all ranks began to make their preparations, assisted by the good King Alexander; if he found any lacking proper means he gave them unstinting help, making all his resources available to them.

When everything was ready and loaded on carts and wagons – tents, trunks, siege gear, mattocks, forks, spades, wedges, bill-hooks, stakes, iron bars and iron chains, lances, axes, gisarmes, lanterns and so many other things that I'd struggle to list them all – he gave the order to march, took his leave of his mother and set out from Macedon. The history says he was about twenty years old at this time.

On he marched with his whole army till he made camp near a temple. It was known thereabouts as the Temple of Apollo, for it housed an idol by that name which sometimes gave the local people answers to their questions. That's why Alexander had camped nearby: he wanted to question the idol about the outcome of his enterprise.

CHAPTER CXVII

How the god Apollo answered, and Alexander came to Italy,
and of the response of a god named Serapis.

And so, having camped beside the temple with his army, Alexander entered with all humility and made the required offering. Then he posed the relevant questions to the idol; but according to the history, the idol's only response was:

'Ah, Hercules!'

When Alexander realised no other words were to be forthcoming, he said: 'Oh, Apollo! If you're going to call me "Hercules" your powers have clearly waned!'[1] And he strode straight from the temple and gave orders for the whole army to march on.

And on he advanced, conquering cities and fortresses all the way, until he reached the sea. Then in a fleet of ships and galleys and barges he crossed with all his forces and landed in the country of Italy. The history says that when the Romans learned of his coming they assembled all their people to discuss how to respond. They decided it would be hopeless to do battle with him, for he was divinely destined to crush all opposition, so they sent a party of their most eminent men, laden with magnificent gifts, to welcome him and honour him as their king. They gave him such a fine reception and showed him such humility that he took them into his favour. And the history says they presented him with six thousand gold bezants,[2] a thousand horses and palfreys and a hundred birds of prey.

After all this, with the whole of Italy conquered and obedient to him, Alexander put to sea once more and sailed on till he came to Africa and brought all the Africans under his dominion.

Then he set off yet again and sailed to an island known at that time as Farondine, seeking a reply from an idol named the god Ammon – a god of whom, ac-

---

[1]   According to the legendary genealogy of the Macedonian kings, Heracles (Hercules) was their ancestor. Alexander's dismissive reaction may imply that he intended to surpass his forebear's achievements.

[2]   The bezant was a coin originally minted at Byzantium.

cording to Vincent le Jacopin[1] in his book, Nectanebus had once claimed Alexander was the son.[2] To the temple came Alexander and he made his offering there; but the history does not suggest he received any answer from that god, and he left the temple and returned to sea with his whole army.

He was carried by the wind to make landfall in the kingdom of Egypt, at a place then known as Tofotirin.[3] This kingdom had twelve great rivers, each flowing directly into the sea, and (so says the history) fifteen strong and mighty cities, all of which he brought under his lordship and dominion. In this kingdom, too, there stood a temple called the Temple of the god Serapis. Its doors were locked and barred so that no man could enter, but Alexander made his offerings as best he could, imploring the god Serapis to answer the question his heart yearned to ask; and the history says that the god Serapis appeared to him that night in a dream and spoke thus:

'Alexander, can you take the weight of this mountain on your shoulders?'

And Alexander dreamed that he replied by saying: 'You know the answer well enough, Lord!'

Then Serapis said: 'You can no more change your destiny than carry or move this mountain.'

Alexander began to press the god then, saying: 'I pray you, Serapis, tell me how I shall die.'

'It is better for a man,' Serapis replied, 'not to know the hour of his death: he lives then with more confidence and less care – a man who fears death misses out on life's joys. But since you've asked me, let me tell you this: don't become preoccupied by death; the fact is that at some point you'll drink poison and be gripped by a sickness from which, after many a torturing agony, you'll die.'

At this Alexander awoke, disturbed by the reply he'd heard; and he rose and dressed and returned to his knights. He told them part of what he'd dreamt, which they all interpreted in different ways.

CHAPTER CXVIII

How the city of Alexandria was founded, from which the land of Alexandria took its name; and of the capture of Escalone.

After hearing these responses from the god, Alexander gave instructions for all kinds of craftsmen to be mustered and for a noble, mighty city to be built there to commemorate his dream. His commands were duly carried out. But as the workmen started building the foundations – especially along the banks of a river that flowed there – a vast multitude of birds appeared and plunged into the water and caught and carried off unprecedented quantities of fish. Alexander was disturbed by this: he was convinced it was an omen – a bad one, he feared. So he called together all the learned men of the land to discover its significance;

---

[1]   See footnote 1, above, p.135.
[2]   See Appendix 1.
[3]   This name is probably based on Taposiris Magna, a major city near Alexandria.

but they told him he should boldly carry on and complete what he'd begun, for it was a sign that the city would come to give sustenance to a great many people. Alexander was overjoyed, so much so, the history says, that he had the bones of the prophet Jeremiah brought from another part of Egypt and set in a place of honour upon the city's walls. And he prayed to almighty God that the prophet's virtues would keep the city free of all serpents – and so it was: never again were crocodiles or any other reptiles seen there as they had been before.

When the city was completed and amply peopled and garrisoned, Alexander decreed that from that time forth it should be named Alexandria after him, and so it is still called to this day.

He ordered his army now to march on towards Escalone, another Egyptian city; and when its people heard of his approach they were aghast, and decided to submit entirely to his will, which they did: they came out to meet him in the utmost humility, placing themselves completely at his mercy. He received them with all good will, and entered the city in pomp and honour. And once all the lords of the land had sworn their allegiance he left there and went to every city and castle and took them into his power.

Now, by all accounts this land of Egypt had been paying tribute to King Darius of Persia; and when reports of these new events came flooding to him, he was deeply troubled in his heart.

CHAPTER CXIX
How Alexander found a statue of Nectanebus, referred to in his book by the aforesaid Vincent.

As Alexander was riding through the land of Egypt he came upon a black stone statue, carved in the likeness of a king. Seeing this statue, he asked some local people what it was and why it was there.

'Truly, dread emperor,' replied one, 'there was once – not so very long ago – a king in this land by the name of Nectanebus, skilled in all magic arts and a master of astronomy, celestial and terrestrial. A Persian king named Artaxerxes[1] defied him and went to war with him, and Nectanebus, without any of his knights knowing what had become of him, fled and was never seen again; the lords of the realm sent search parties out to many lands, but when they realised he was nowhere to be found they submitted to the Persians and condemned us to paying them tribute. As a memorial to our vanished king it was decided that this statue should be built, because without a doubt, since his reign the land of Egypt has never been as well governed as it was in his time.'

When Alexander heard this story he shook his head, remembering how Nectanebus had come to his father's court disguised as a scholar, and how some had claimed he was his father and he'd killed him.[2] So he climbed down from his horse and kissed the statue and said:

[1]   *'Arxasés'.*
[2]   Above, p.36.

'If you were my father, God knows.'

And as he made the kiss he saw the letters inscribed on the plinth which read: 'This is the statue of Nectanebus, king of the Egyptians.'

Alexander now left Egypt and came to the land of Syria, which took its name from a city named in some accounts as Tyre. Now, we've already told of the destruction of that city, and it might seem as if we were repeating ourselves, which we're very loath to do;[1] but as I understand it, when Tyre was destroyed, and Alexander had left and gone to support Cassamus du Laris against King Clarvus of India as described above, King Darius, who held sway over all the bordering lands of Egypt, Syria and Jerusalem, had the city rebuilt and newly provisioned and garrisoned with a mighty force of men-at-arms, because it was the greatest of all the surrounding cities and finely situated beside the sea, and all the tributes and taxes raised in those parts were collected there. So when Alexander arrived in Syria he headed first for Tyre and laid siege to the city from every side; and such were his strength and prowess that he captured it and destroyed it utterly, along with two other cities built nearby by Darius to supply aid to Tyre if the need arose.

And while Alexander was overseeing the city's destruction, he sent messengers to the bishop of Jerusalem, requesting him to make provisions available to his troops at a good price; as for the tribute the bishop paid to Darius, they asked him to send it to Alexander: if he wouldn't do so willingly, Alexander would take it by force.

Chapter CXX

How Alexander went to Jerusalem and, according to the history, worshipped Almighty God in the person of the bishop.

Having seen to the destruction of the aforesaid cities, Alexander ordered his army onward to Jerusalem. Word of this soon reached the bishop and the people of the city; they were terrified, for they feared him very greatly. The bishop summoned all the people urgently, and bade them by God Omnipotent commit themselves to prayer and fasting for three days; this they did, scattering ashes on their heads and begging Our Lord for guidance in the face of this imminent danger. And on the third day the bishop made a sacrament to Our Lord with the utmost solemnity and devotion; and the history says that on the following night Our Lord appeared to the bishop – whose name was Jadus – and told him what he should do. Jadus reported his vision to the people, which was this:

---

[1] Wauquelin has indeed already told of Alexander's conquest of Tyre – above, pp.58–62, 70–1 – in a passage taken from the verse *Roman d'Alexandre*. Having then based his work on material derived mainly from *Les Voeux du Paon* ('The Vows of the Peacock') – a poem written c.1310 by Jacques de Longuyon and interpolated into several of the later manuscripts of the verse *Alexandre* – he has now started following another source, the Prose *Alexander* romance (the thirteenth-century French translation of the *Historia de Preliis*). This has involved taking Alexander home to Macedon and then to Italy, Africa and Egypt; now it brings him back to Tyre, so Wauquelin realises he has a narrative problem to solve.

they were to adorn their city as richly as they could, and then don white robes and go out to meet Alexander at a place called Scopalus.

So when they heard of Alexander's approach they prepared according to the bishop's bidding and marched out of the city to the aforesaid place. The priests, dressed in their richest vestments, went ahead of the common people, and at the very front of them all was the bishop in glorious attire, clad in a magnificent stole and bearing a mitre upon his head, sumptuously embroidered and adorned with precious stones. From the place where they stopped there was a clear view of the city of Jerusalem; and Alexander, riding towards this spot and seeing the vast multitude of people all dressed in white and the priests in their vestments and in particular the bishop bearing on his mitre the high names of Our Lord, immediately ordered his army to halt and to go no further. He rode on towards the crowd alone. And as he approached the bishop he flung himself from his horse to the ground and worshipped Our Lord. Then all the Jews began to hail him, crying aloud:

'Long live King Alexander!'

CHAPTER CXXI

How Alexander entered the city of Jerusalem and was received with great reverence there.

When the Macedonians, Greeks and others saw the deep respect King Alexander had shown to the bishop of the Jews and how he'd worshipped him, a great murmur arose amongst them all, until one of Alexander's princes, Emenidus of Arcadia, came to him and said:

'Most feared and mighty emperor, how is it that when all men honour and revere and worship you, you now worship in our presence the bishop of the Jewish people?'

To which Alexander replied: 'Truly, dear friend, understand I wasn't worshipping the bishop but the omnipotent God whose arms he bears and from whom he holds and exercises office. Let me tell you: when I was with my father and mother in the land of Macedon, I was lying in bed and turning over in my mind how I could gain dominion over Darius and the Persians and lead my armies to his land. I thought and thought and then I fell asleep; and the sovereign god of gods appeared to me dressed just as you see this bishop here, and He promised me that if I was willing to march into Asia without harming His people – and would worship His Law – I would journey in safety and win dominion over all. So my hope is that with His help I shall vanquish King Darius and crush the might of the Persians and achieve all that my heart desires. That's why, when I saw the bishop here in his vestments, representing God better than any man I've ever seen, I went down on my knees and worshipped him.'

So saying, Alexander entered Jerusalem with the priests and carried on to the temple, where he made a sacrifice to Our Lord as instructed by the priests and according to the strictures of God's Law, the Law given by God to Moses on Mount Sinaï. The sacrifices made, the priests brought the books of the Law to

Alexander, notably the book of the prophet Daniel, which made reference to the coming of a king who through his prowess would win dominion over the might of the Persians. Alexander, taking this as a prophecy about himself, was elated, overjoyed. The prophetic words were these:[1]

'*Ego Daniel vidi Danielis*: in a vision I, Daniel, saw myself atop the Gate of Ulai;[2] I raised my eyes, and on the edge of the marsh I saw a ram with long horns, one of them longer than the other; and I saw this ram brandish his horns first towards the west and then the north and then the south, and in no land could any beast withstand him or defend itself against his horns. But out of the west I saw a goat approach, his hooves appearing not to touch the ground; and this goat had a horn of fearsome sharpness set between his eyes, and he attacked the ram with such fierce might that he broke both his horns and drove him to the ground where he trampled and crushed him with his hooves till he couldn't stand again. And thereupon the goat grew to a wondrous size.'

This prophecy was explained by the archangel Gabriel, who spoke to the prophet Daniel,[3] saying: 'The ram you see with the two horns is the king of Media and Persia, and the goat is the king of Greece; the great horn between his eyes signifies that he is the first king of the Greek kingdom, now growing and expanding.'

The archangel's words led the Jews to say that the two-horned ram was Darius, for he was king of Media and Persia, and the goat with the horn between his eyes was Alexander, for he was the first king of Greece. Alexander now thought this could be true, and was elated; and he had the bishop and the priests showered with fine and lavish gifts, saying they could ask him for anything they wished and he would grant it gladly. So the bishop of the Jews asked that the Jews be allowed to observe their Law, and to live for seven years without paying tribute – not only those dwelling there in Jerusalem but also those at Babylon and in Media. Alexander agreed to this most graciously, and willingly declared it binding.

CHAPTER CXXII

How according to the history Alexander ordered his army onward to the land of King Darius.

Afﬅer staying awhile in Jerusalem Alexander mobilised his army and departed, making his way to the other cities of the land which all surrendered to him without the slightest resistance. And because of their friendly reception he graciously took them into his favour: from some, it might be said, he took a little and to others he gave as he saw fit.

It was at this point that some men who'd escaped from the city of Tyre[4] took ref-

---

[1]   See Daniel 8, vv.2-8.
[2]   '*Ulay*': Daniel (8, v.2) refers to the River Ulai.
[3]   See Daniel 8, vv.20-21.
[4]   The text reads '*Sur*', which is the name as it appears in Wauquelin's source at this point, the Prose *Alexander*. The linguistic confusion is evident in Wauquelin's earlier reference to

uge at the court of King Darius, and told him how the great conqueror Alexander was advancing towards him and bringing every region in his path under his dominion: all were powerless to resist him. Darius was deeply angered by this news: he'd imagined that, since he'd earlier written to Alexander telling him to desist from such action, he'd been behaving accordingly. Having heard nothing of him for some time (the reason being that Alexander had had numerous distractions, as you've heard in the course of this story), Darius had assumed that Alexander had beaten a retreat. So he decided to send him new letters to find out what his intentions were; and this he did: he dictated letters immediately and gave them to his messengers along with a number of gifts, with strict orders not to stop until they'd delivered them to Alexander on his behalf and discovered exactly what kind of man he was, this King Alexander who was earning such a mighty reputation.

The messengers set out and made their way to Alexander and presented him with the letters from their king. He promptly summoned all his lords and knights to hear the letters' contents, and had them read aloud in their presence. They read as follows, or very like:

'From Darius, king of earthly kings, a rival or an equal to the sun, chosen to join the gods in heaven, to my servant Alexander, greetings. We understand that the vainglory residing in your heart has driven you to advance upon us, accompanied by a bunch of wretched rogues, to provoke our enmity and to test yourself against the vast multitude of Medes and Persians. We cannot think what has possessed you to do this. Do you understand how futile it is? Truly, even if you had mustered all the forces in the world you could not resist, let alone vanquish, the Persian and Median hordes! They are as many as the stars in the sky, as the sand-grains on the margins of the sea! So repent of your wild folly, of this crazed mission you've undertaken! We command you to go back and take comfort at your mother's breast! Find other games to play, not this presumptuous escapade! People might think you were short of gold, and coveted the treasures stored in our land of Persia, which outshine the brilliance of the sun! Abandon this folly forthwith and quell your pride; if not, you will see our goodwill towards you turn to rage, and we will send our knights to treat you not as King Philip of Macedon's son but as a Prince of Thieves, with orders to oversee your bloody execution.'

CHAPTER CXXIII

How according to the history some of Alexander's knights
wanted to kill King Darius's messengers.

When they heard the letter's contents Alexander's knights were so incensed that some of them snatched up daggers and were about to kill King Darius's messengers. They'd have cut them down in seconds had it not been for the valiant Alexander, who sprang forward saying:

'the land of *Syria*…[having taken] its name from a city named in some accounts as *Tyre*'
(above, p.141).

'Oh, my dear friends and companions! Don't be upset about this letter, I pray you! Don't you know that the dog that barks the loudest is the least strong in the fight?[1] Consider this in a positive light and let's rejoice! Didn't you hear the letter say this land of Persia holds a hoard of treasure that dazzles like the sun? So take courage now and think with joy of the glory and honour of conquering such a land! I promise you, beyond a doubt, nothing will stop us winning everything we desire!'

Then the knights seized hold of the messengers, but Alexander spoke out again, saying: 'My good, dear friends and companions, Darius has sent these men here with his letters because he didn't know how strong and great we were; so we need to send them back so that they can stress to him our glory and magnificence! Leave them be, I pray you, and honour them – not out of respect for *his* worth, but for ours!'

At this they let them go, and the king commanded that they be provided with their every need. Indeed the history says he had them dine with him in his chamber; and as they dined, they told Alexander that if he would send them with an escort of a thousand men-at-arms they would deliver up their king, for in their eyes Alexander was filled with such nobility and prowess that he was worthy of even more than the kingdom of Media and Persia! But King Alexander would not subscribe to this treachery; rather he told them:

'Eat and drink, sirs. I'll not have a single knight of mine besmirched by such treason.'

And when they'd eaten and drunk their fill he had them escorted to their lodgings in style, with orders that they be provided with whatever they required.

CHAPTER CXXIV

How Alexander sent letters back to King Darius by Darius's own messengers.

Next morning the king dictated his letters and delivered them to Darius's envoys – they'd already come to the palace to take their leave – and gave them some very distinguished gifts. They took most gracious leave of Alexander and his knights, and set off and made their way back to Persia, where they found their king and presented him with the letters they'd received from Alexander, the substance of which was as follows:

'To the high and mighty emperor Darius, king on earth and peer of the sun shining with the Persian gods, from Alexander, commander of the Greeks, son of King Philip of Macedon and that wisest of ladies Olympias, greetings.

'It seems to us, and is assuredly the case, that it is a shame and disgrace for a high and mighty emperor like you to send such a missive as you have done, and to be in such a constant state of fear and suspicion, when you claim to be the equal of the sun, sitting on your wondrous throne, shining like a god over the Medes and Persians, and to be so troubled by me when you consider me such a

---

[1]   Literally 'a barking dog hasn't the strength to defend itself'.

lowly soul. How demeaning for one who likens himself to the immortal gods, to go to war against me, a mortal – and with trepidation, too! But I'm delighted by it all, I assure you, and I'll tell you why: if you, so high and mighty, do battle with me, mere mortal that I am, then everything is in my favour; for if you succeed in defeating me it won't earn you any credit – not when you're the god you claim to be, for the gods by their very nature do as they please, and men have never been known to contain them! In any case, you'll only have beaten, as you put it, a wretched rogue! But if I can vanquish you – as I shall if it please the omnipotent God – I'll earn outstanding praise, for I'll have beaten a most valiant, feared and mighty emperor! The very thought of it fills me with resolve to press on with the mission I've begun, especially since you've told us that your land abounds in gold and all manner of riches, which we need if we're to drag ourselves out of the wretched poverty you say has been our lot in life!

'And judging by those tokens you sent me[1] I'm clearly going to achieve my goals: first the ball, being round, I take to be the earth's sphere which shall be in my possession and pay me tribute – as you have done already with the gifts you sent; then the rod[2] with bending head I take to be a sign that all the princes of the earth will bow before me; and the whip[3] suggests the punishment I'll mete on all who rebel against me and refuse to obey and pay me tribute for their lands as courteously as you have done – for which I thank you heartily: I consider myself well paid by your gifts and letters, as I think I've now explained!'

CHAPTER CXXV

How Alexander defeated Copimus and Anthiocus, two of Darius's greatest captains.

Hearing Alexander's letter, Darius was most unsettled by his wit, and after a moment's thought he asked the messengers what Alexander was like, especially in terms of physique. But when they told him his build was small he began to mock him roundly, and decided to send word at once to two mighty lords on the borders of his empire bidding them muster sufficient forces to take Alexander alive and bring him to him like a wayward child. The letter he sent was worded thus:

'Darius, king of Persia, wishes his lieutenants Copimus and Anthiocus health and happiness. We have heard that Alexander of Macedon, Philip's son, has risen to such heights of presumptuous folly that he has marched into our land of Asia accompanied by a wretched band of scoundrels and has already started pillaging. So we bid you, as staunch supporters and defenders of our empire, bring him to me. I shall chastise him like a child, and dress him in such authority as I

---

[1]   i.e. above, p.53.

[2]   The word used earlier is *'verge'* (cane, rod); here the word is *'croche'* (crook, stick with crooked head).

[3]   The third of the gifts was originally (in a passage based on a different source) a bridle rather than a whip: above, p.53.

choose and send him back to the bosom of his mother, Olympias of Macedon; for he has no business waging war with me – he should behave like the child he is and go and play with other infants.'

At this very point, the history says, King Alexander met these same lords Copimus and Anthiocus in a great battle; he lost a fair number of valiant men, but the two lords lost immeasurably more as they were bloodily routed. It was on the very day of their defeat that they received the letter from Darius, and they were filled with shame when they heard what it said. But they returned word to Darius, telling him of their dire misfortune and begging him not to delay but to muster his forces as soon as he could, for Alexander was already advancing rapidly and had made camp beside a river known at that time as the Granicus.[1] Their letter read:

'To Darius, mighty king of Persia, from Copimus and Anthiocus, health and happiness. Your Noble Highness should know that the Alexander whom your letter calls a child has destroyed this whole province. He has a very great army; we did battle with him and killed a good number of his knights, but to little effect, for we lost twice as many and were forced to flee the battle to save our lives – which we did only with the utmost difficulty. You wrote to us as supporters and defenders of your empire, and as such we need to request your help: we beg you to summon and gather all your forces, for truly, Alexander's knights are no children! And if they are valiant, he is even more so! What's more, he can dress himself in whatever authority he likes, for he has already plundered such riches from your land that his whole army is piled high with booty. He is encamped along the Granicus river, and gives every sign of having no other goal in mind than your subjugation. You need to take advice and counsel.'

CHAPTER CXXVI

How according to the history King Darius sent his messengers back to Alexander.

When Darius received his lieutenants' letter he was very shocked and even more enraged. What alarmed him most was the news that Alexander was advancing by the day – according to the letter he was already in the land of Persia and had reached the Granicus river. He decided to send another message to Alexander and to present him with a new and different gift. He dictated his letter hurriedly, and as soon as it was written he gave it to his messengers along with a sack full of delicious white poppy seed.[2]

The messengers set out and made their way to Alexander's camp, and gave him both the letter and the sack of seed. Alexander called for the letter to be opened and read. They contained, I believe, the following (or very like):

'From Darius, king of Persia, to our servant Alexander. You will be pleased to learn that the name of Darius is praised throughout the world: the gods them-

---

[1] Wauquelin consistently transcribes the name as 'Gangis', not recognising the 'Grenike' and 'Grenique' that appear in his source at this point, the Prose *Alexander*.

[2] 'oliette'.

selves extol it! So we are amazed that you dare to cross rivers, sea, blazing sun and mountains to confront us! We would have thought it was enough for you to hold the kingdom of Macedon without our approval, a kingdom rightfully subject to us and owing us annual tribute. But like a fool you have taken it upon yourself to raise a band of companions and roam around fighting our people and destroying our cities, forts and castles. We suggest you repent of your wicked and self-glorifying deeds – your vanity is clear from your response to our last missive. To give you an idea of the scale of our might I've sent you this sack of poppy seeds: it's a symbol of our power, for you could no more count those seeds than count the number of men we'll lead against you unless you go straight home, wipe what you've done from your mind and never again conceive such extravagant folly.'

Then Alexander, having heard the letter, took a glove-full of the seed and began to eat; and as he ate he said: 'I can see the people of Persia are numerous; but they're as soft and yielding as this seed – they'll be easily crushed!'

CHAPTER CXXVII

How Alexander sent Darius some pepper, and received a letter asking him to go and see his mother.

While Alexander was talking to Darius's messengers and pondering what to send him in return, messengers arrived from his mother with word that she was very ill and implored him most passionately to go to her. He was exceedingly upset, rightly fearing it would mean his army had to withdraw. So he called his barons together at once, to discuss how to deal with this; but they told him not to worry, but to go and leave them there in Darius's land, and if it pleased the gods they would handle things so well that they would earn his gratitude when he returned! To conclude their discussions Ptholomer and Danselin, two valiant captains, were appointed the army's Constables, and Emenidus, so brave and fine, was appointed Marshal along with Perdicas, to be overall commanders of the knights and captains and men-at-arms.

Once all had been arranged Alexander dictated his letter to Darius and entrusted it to the messengers along with a sack full of pepper to be presented to their king. And when the messengers had gone he took four of his barons – Antiocus, Philotas, Licanor and Permenon – and four thousand men-at-arms and set out for Macedon to visit his mother.

Meanwhile Darius's messengers came before their lord and presented him with the letter and the pepper sent by Alexander. Darius had the letter opened and read out at once, and this is what it said:

'From Alexander, son of King Philip of Macedon and Queen Olympias, to Darius, king of Persia, greetings. We have received certain messages which will delay our current enterprise. You must not imagine that it is fear of you and your soaring pride that causes us to leave our army here – for they will stay, to carry on our work. The reason is that we have received word that our mother has fallen ill. We are telling you this so that you do not suppose we are responding to your bidding to return to her gentle breast! We simply wish to see and comfort her, and will soon be back to resume the war in which we are engaged. And since you sent us that meaningful gift of poppy seeds, I have sent you pepper, to show that your seed-like multitude will be outdone by ours!'

CHAPTER CXXVIII

How Darius summoned all his forces
and Alexander returned from seeing his mother.

When Darius heard Alexander's letter and realised he'd no intention of re-treating but had left his finest knights to look after his army, he dictated letters at once summoning numerous great lords of his realm to join him with-out delay or demur, for he meant to do battle with this King Alexander, who'd brought a band of pillagers and thieves to his land with such outrageous daring that they were already encamped along the Granicus river. Darius was planning thus to crush Alexander's forces before he could return from visiting his mother.

But Alexander, sharp and astute and with spies placed everywhere, managed to visit her and rejoin his army – his presence having helped her recover from her sickness – before Darius could achieve any part of his plan. His men of course rejoiced to see him back – and with good reason, for he was utterly devoted to them and treated them with courtesy and love in every possible way.

He now summoned his twelve peers[1] and all the knights of his Council, and when they were assembled he addressed them thus:

'My dear friends, companions in prosperity and adversity, you know that for some time now King Darius has been sending messengers to tell us his mind; but we've returned no word of our intentions except by those same messengers, which is hardly the worthy and honourable way. I think it would be good to send him our own now, to tell him to yield lordship of the land of Media and Persia to us, freely and entirely, or to come and defend it against us in open battle, army against army; he mustn't, at least, be able to claim we didn't give fair warning.'

The lords discussed this and all agreed wholeheartedly, and asked him to choose whichever one of them he wished to be the messenger: whoever was chosen would go most willingly. And Alexander answered, saying:

'Many thanks, sirs – I'll think about that tonight.'

With that they departed, each to his own lodging, and Alexander gave orders for the posting of a very strong watch.

CHAPTER CXXIX

How the god Ammon appeared to Alexander in his sleep.

That very night, as Alexander lay in bed turning the business over in his mind, he fell asleep; and as he slept he saw in a vision the god Ammon – once

---

[1]   See above, p.42.

claimed by Nectanebus to be Alexander's father[1] – in the shape of the god Mercury, clad in royal attire in the manner of the kings of Macedon at that time; and he addressed him thus:

'My dear son Alexander, I am ever ready to alert you in times of need: that's why I gave you the impulse to send your own messenger to Darius. And now I'm advising you not to let anyone take the message but yourself. And I'll tell you how to do it: I want you to assume my appearance and go to him in person, and I'll help you see it through without a hitch! It's exceedingly dangerous, but don't let that worry you! And it'll give you a better idea of your enemy's plans and numbers, and so speed you on your path to crushing him!'

Alexander was delighted by the dream; and as soon as he was awake he related it to some of his captains, and told them that, since the gods had promised him aid and bidden him take the message himself, he alone would go. They all encouraged him to do so.

So straight after dinner he summoned the valiant Emenidus of Arcadia, one of the bravest men in all the army, and told him to prepare a palfrey and lead it out of camp and down to the River Tigris and to await him there. Emenidus did exactly as bidden. Now, according to the history, the Tigris river is such that at nightfall it becomes frozen solid, so much so that it can bear the weight of horses, carts and wagons as well as any bridge, but when morning comes the ice melts in the sun's heat and turns to a clear and rushing torrent that no man would dare attempt to cross if he wanted to avoid an instant death, for anything venturing into the water is swept away and swallowed in a moment. And at its narrowest point this river is a league across, and a good deal wider elsewhere.

Chapter CXXX
How Alexander spoke to Darius in the shape of the god Ammon and then rejoined his army.

With the coming of evening, Alexander slipped away from camp as quietly as he could and made his way to his knight and dear friend Emenidus. Then he mounted the palfrey and kept riding till he came to the aforesaid river, where he told Emenidus to stay and wait for him. Emenidus was most reluctant: he would much rather have gone with him to be at hand if the need arose; but Alexander insisted otherwise: no one would go with him but the god who'd promised aid.

So the king set off leaving Emenidus behind. The river was frozen, and Alexander rode straight across with ease. Once he reached the further bank he waited for day to break; then as soon as it was light he rode on, and about terce[2] he reached the city where Darius was based, though he wasn't there just then – he'd gone into the mountains to gather the forces with which he planned to vanquish Alexander.

---

[1]   See Appendix 1.
[2]   The third canonical hour, about 9 a.m.

Into the city Alexander rode; but the history says that he arrived in such array that the citizens thought he was a god descended from the skies. They asked him who he was, however, and he replied that he was a messenger from King Alexander. And while he was talking to the Persians, King Darius returned to the city with a vast multitude of troops, and elephants carrying little wooden castles on their backs manned by forty men-at-arms: all these he'd mustered to confront King Alexander. And Darius, chancing to arrive back at this point and casting his eyes this way and that, saw Alexander talking to his people and instantly took him to be a god – Jupiter to be precise, descended from the heavens. He dismounted at once and greeted him with the utmost honour and reverence and asked him to say who he was indeed; to which Alexander replied straightway, saying:

'Alexander, King Philip's son, sends me to say that you appear to be beset by fear, not daring to meet your enemy in open battle; if you won't propose a day for battle you should submit to his prowess.'

Darius said: 'I'd say you were Alexander himself, speaking so boldly! You don't sound like a messenger to me, but like a king! But let me tell you, your words don't trouble me in the least. And since King Alexander treated my messengers to fine food and drink, I bid you come and eat with me at supper.'

And so saying, he reached out and took him by the right hand and led him into the palace.

CHAPTER CXXXI

*How Alexander supped with King Darius and then returned to Emenidus
who was waiting for him by the River Tigris.*

As Alexander entered the palace he began to observe the splendour surrounding this King Darius, who had paid him the high honour of leading him in at his right hand. Soon it was supper time, and the tables were set and Darius took his seat and bade Alexander sit directly before him. Every conceivable dish was served in vast abundance. They began to eat, and as he ate Alexander said to himself:

'What a sight this is; and truly, this kingdom will be mine.'

Now, at that table were seated a number of Darius's princes, and they started talking about King Alexander – disparagingly, mocking him for his short stature, knowing nothing of his valour or his prowess or the courage housed in his little frame.

As they ate the butler served wine to the princes in vessels of gold, and set one before his lord and one before Alexander. Alexander took the vessel and drank, and as soon as he'd drunk he slipped the gorgeous bejewelled cup inside his shirt. The butler saw this and served him with another; Alexander did the same again, and so too with a third. There was much murmuring around the table, until one who was seated at Darius's side whispered about it in his ear – though Darius had already spotted it himself, and was moved to ask:

'What ever are you doing, friend, hiding those golden vessels at your breast?'

'Truly, sir, it's the custom in the household of our noble lord King Alexander that those invited to sup with him can keep their drinking vessels if they wish; but judging by all the muttering you don't share the same custom here, so I'll return them to the butler.'

Hearing this, many knights seated at the table, and others standing in attendance, too, declared it a fine and noble custom! And as they talked some were gazing at Alexander, marvelling at his behaviour and his speech, not to mention his unimaginably wondrous dress. Among them was a man named Amepolis; he was one of Darius's foremost knights and had seen Alexander before, for he was one of the messengers previously sent by Darius to demand tribute from Macedon. That's why, as he gazed at him, he said:

'From this man's voice and looks I'd say he was King Alexander himself: I'm sure of it!'

He said this loud enough for Darius, Alexander and everyone at the table to hear and understand; which is why, without saying a word, Alexander rose from the table and left the chamber. As he did so he met a servant holding a torch; he snatched it from him and went to his horse and mounted as fast as he could, and then thrust in his spurs and with torch in hand kept galloping all the way to the river. It was already frozen solid, and over he rode and found his companion waiting for him; but before he had quite crossed the river his mount collapsed dead beneath him: it was a great shock for Alexander, but he managed to make his way to safety.

CHAPTER CXXXII

How King Darius proposed marrying his eldest daughter to Alexander.

You mustn't imagine that Alexander wasn't followed when he left Darius's table: according to the history, as soon as the knight Amepolis said he was King Alexander and they saw him make his escape when he heard these words, they leapt up and rushed to arms and began their pursuit. But it was too dark to see where they were going – indeed they tumbled over each other in their haste – and realising it was wasted effort they turned back.

Darius, who'd stayed sitting at the table, began to reflect admiringly on what Alexander had done. Now, there was a golden statue at one end of the table, erected in honour of the former king of Persia, Darius's father; and as Darius's eye chanced to light upon it he saw it topple to the floor without anyone having touched it. He was bitterly distressed by this and began to weep, saying it was a sign that the kingdom of Persia was on the wane: it seemed Alexander had already won a large part of it; what's more, his every move was so cleverly conceived that no one could find a way to resist him.

So Darius urgently summoned his full council and all his greatest princes, and next morning when they were assembled Darius came before them and addressed them thus:

'Dear friends, guardians and defenders of Persia's honour, I have called you here to seek your guidance. You know the king of Macedon has invaded our land and already pillaged, robbed and looted far and wide, destroying cities,

forts and castles and vanquishing many of our knights and winning their obedience. This same Alexander should be our liege man and hold his land as our vassal! He refuses to do so! But that's not all: he wants to be lord over me and you! It
was ever thus: the wise striving to correct the fool and the fool a constant trouble
and vexation! So I mean to take measures to protect our kingdom now, to ensure
above all that you suffer no loss and shed no blood. Listen: I've been considering
the daring and the cunning of this King Alexander – you witnessed it yourselves
– as he came in person to observe our ways and state and then escaped us. So if
you're in agreement, to avoid still greater disaster, I'll gladly give my beautiful
daughter to be his wife on condition that there be peace between us. And with
her hand I'll give him half my kingdom to hold in full lordship throughout his
life, along with all the marches, lands and territories he's already won from us.'

Darius's barons all agreed to this, declaring it a wise proposal, though they
were ready and willing to do battle with Alexander whenever and however often he might wish.

CHAPTER CXXXIII

How King Darius sent an embassy to Alexander to sue for peace.

Darius, hearing his knights were as eager for peace as for war, organised an
impressive company to go as an embassy to Alexander and inform him of
his council's decision; and before setting out, each member of the party took an
olive branch as a sign of peace.

They rode straight to Alexander's camp: he'd already crossed the Tigris with
his whole army as he continued to advance upon his foe. When the Greeks realised they were Persians they received them with great respect, and escorted
them in stately fashion into the king's illustrious presence. Alexander, seeing
this grand embassy approach, rose and gave them lavish greeting; and after this
splendid welcome one of the party spoke up, saying:

'Noble emperor, glory and honour be to you and victory to King Darius, who
has sent us here to express his gracious and most generous intentions. You are
well aware that, without any provocation from our king towards you or your
people, you have come here to attack him. And you know full well that your
father, your grandfather and all your forebears have paid him tribute for the
land of Macedon without protest or resistance; yet you instead have burnt his
cities, forts and castles, slaughtered his men and robbed and pillaged most of his
realm! But Darius our king, conscious of your courage and prowess and seeing
your desire to live in freedom and independence, and wishing also to avoid all
harm to you and your people and his own, bids us propose on his behalf that,
if you have no objection, there shall be firm and lasting peace between you and
him on the following terms: firstly, he offers you the hand in marriage of his eldest daughter, if you wish to take her, and with her half of the Persian kingdom;
secondly, he declares you rightful lord, free of any obligation, of all the cities,
lands, forts and castles you have already won from him. Kindly tell us your
response to this proposal.'

Then Alexander answered: 'Sirs, tell your king I don't want his daughter, and as for his land, inform him that I shall never share it with anyone: I shall have it all or no part of it – and I trust in God that I shan't fail to have the whole! So go back to your king forthwith and tell him to come tomorrow, if he's brave enough, and defend his right against me, for if it please God he'll find me and my men all ready to receive him.'

And the history says that the messengers departed without more ado and returned to their king, and told him how Alexander had no interest in his daughter or in sharing his kingdom with anyone. King Darius was beside himself, and gave orders for every last man to be armed and ready next morning, for he was going to test himself against this Alexander.

CHAPTER CXXXIV

How Alexander exhorted and heartened his men for battle against King Darius.

As soon as Darius's embassy had gone, Alexander summoned all the lords of his host to gather on a fine open plain. He mounted a scaffold so that all could hear him clearly and then began thus, saying:

'My dear lords and companions, you know that your united, common will to avenge the wrongs you've suffered at the hands of the Persians has brought us to engage in this present war, in which we've already endured much toil and hardship – more, I think, than any men could bear were it not for their great desire and hope to have peace thereafter through victory. So, then, having suffered so much – and with all possible patience – in the hope of ultimate peace and rest, you've come to the lands where these Persians who have wronged you dwell, and your desire now must surely be to stick to the task to the utmost, until our shame is expunged and your honour enhanced – and you're properly rewarded for your labours!

'Now, it appears you could achieve all this with the immediate peace offered by your enemy; but if your nobility and honour are to shine we must seize the moment joyously and do battle with all courage, for though peace appears good in itself, there is nothing sweeter in the world than peace after mighty war! So let us fight now with a will as we contemplate the sweet peace to come, remembering too our noble blood and the shameful wrongs we've suffered at Persian hands. Behave in tomorrow's battle, I pray you, with true valour to safeguard our honour, as I trust you will wholeheartedly. And don't be daunted by the size of the Persian host: not even the biggest swarm of gnats, you know, is a match for a band of horseflies! And I trust in almighty God that, with the great courage I've always seen in you, which increases by the day, you'll conduct yourselves with such strength and discipline that the honour will be yours!'

When Alexander came to the end of his address they all began to hail him, crying: 'Long live King Alexander, who surpasses every man alive in wisdom, prowess and largesse!'

With that they all made their way to their tents to rest and sleep till morning, when each man made ready, arming and equipping himself as finely as he could, as you're about to hear.

CHAPTER CXXXV

Of the first battle fought by Alexander and King Darius.

You've already heard how Darius had gathered his forces to confront King Alexander; the history tells us at this point that he had more than forty thousand cavalry, all brave and strong and accomplished and well armed, and two hundred thousand infantry. With these he formed six immense battalions, two of horse and four of foot (they called these companies phalanxes: in France we call them squadrons). Then he sent word to Alexander bidding him come and do battle, since he wouldn't agree to peace; but by the time the messenger arrived Alexander had already deployed his men likewise in these squadrons called phalanxes. According to the history, Alexander could call upon some four thousand five hundred mounted men-at-arms and thirty thousand foot.

In front of his battalions King Darius had positioned elephants with castles ingeniously strapped to their backs, and in these castles were men-at-arms wielding strange curved weapons of steel, sharp as any scythes. These elephants were placed at the front so that as soon as they were goaded from behind they could charge Alexander's squadrons and smash everything in their path. But when Alexander, so clever and astute, saw this animal battalion coming he ordered his squadrons to open wide, and the elephants charged straight through, unswerving; and as they passed, the Greeks felled so many with a rain of arrows (loosed from machines of theirs, akin to springalds) that almost every single beast was slaughtered, along with the men-at-arms upon their backs. After this first victorious round Alexander reformed his battle lines at once.

Darius, burning with desire to destroy Alexander, had marched his troops into the field and deployed them as he'd ordered, with the elephants at the front as you've heard. When he gave the signal to advance there was such a blast of all manner of horns and trumpets that you wouldn't have heard God's thunder, and the elephants were goaded into the charge that ended as we've described. Darius was distraught to see his elephants have no effect, but it didn't stop him ordering his troops to the attack. The two armies advanced upon each other in a wicked hail of arrows, darts and slingshots that brought down many a man-at-arms, and as they closed, both sides spurred their horses forward and launched into an earth-shaking charge. The numbers felled and slain then were uncountable. And once they'd clashed they gripped their swords and started battering each other with a noise like smiths pounding on their anvils; knights and horses were falling and tumbling in piles and mounds; rallying cries and wails of agony rang. And in the midst of it all was Alexander, performing so many feats of arms that no one could ask for more, and cheering and inspiring his men to such a pitch that they forced the Persian cavalry back into their own infantry. This wasn't achieved without heavy losses, but the history says they were so afire with desire to rout their foe that they risked death without restraint. With the

Persians piled back into their infantry there was utter carnage, as both sides levelled lances and drove at one another in a fury; they fell in heaps, but the Persians lost immeasurably more than the Greeks.

The history says they were locked in this ferocious turmoil till well past noon.[1] Then the Persians started to break completely, seeing most of their captains slain. The history names some of them, such as the king of Valage, Ballot by name, and another king named Percael, both valiant warriors by whom the Persians had set much store; also Nabon of Mont Gibier, Luciien, Pinados, Leon, Godinas, Lipas, Passien and Orlas and many more I'll pass over. All of these men had been commanders of squadrons, so that when the Persians saw they'd lost their leaders they began to turn tail. King Darius himself fled from the field, for his bodyguards had been slaughtered.

C<small>HAPTER</small> CXXXVI

How Alexander proceeded after this first battle.

And so, as you've heard, the Persians were routed and King Darius was driven from the field. But the history says that Alexander forbade any pursuit of the fugitives: he gave orders instead to pitch camp there on the battlefield as a sign of victory. This was done; and then he commanded that all those killed in the battle were to be buried – of the Persians, forty thousand infantry and cavalry had been slain, and of the Greeks, one hundred and twenty mounted men-at-arms and one hundred and ten on foot[2] – and the nobles were to be carried to a nearby castle where there stood a temple to Jupiter, for he wanted to honour them as highly after their deaths as before. He had the Medes and Persians buried just as well as the Greeks, and when the Persian and Median lords and King Darius himself heard this they deemed it a sign of great nobility.

Then Alexander sent letters to those he'd left acting for him in the lands he'd conquered – in Syria, that is, and Cappadocia and Arabia and many other parts – bidding them send him various things he needed as soon as the letters were received. According to the history he asked for a thousand leopard skins and a thousand asses' pelts and a thousand leather garments and many other things which I'll pass over for the sake of brevity. But above all he bade them make sacrifices to almighty God for the fine victory he'd won against Darius, which was duly done. And all his lords and captains sent him everything he'd asked for; the goods were taken to Antioch, carried by camels as far as the Euphrates river and from there by boats to Alexander's camp. At this point the history says that out at sea, close to his army, Alexander had one hundred and eighty great ships laden with supplies and men-at-arms, and this fleet had such control of the sea that no enemies along the coast dared to move a muscle.

The day after the battle, Alexander oversaw the burial of all the high lords

---

[1]   Literally 'till the ninth hour' – i.e. about three in the afternoon.
[2]   The same remarkable disparity appears in the Prose *Alexander* (Hilka's edition, p.106).

who had fallen, and ordered great sacrifices to God; he was present throughout in person to show them full respect.

Then he called his barons together to discuss the next move, for he was sure Darius wouldn't be letting matters rest. It was agreed that he should send spies, as he always did, to discover Darius's position and his plans, and this was duly done. But we'll leave that now and tell what Darius did next: how he sought aid from King Porus of India.

CHAPTER CXXXVII

How Darius sent letters to King Porus of India requesting help.

King Darius, having fled the battle and taken refuge in one of his cities, as distracted and tormented as could be, assembled all his counsellors to discuss what he should do. They advised him to send for help from Porus, king of India, but he replied:

'That would be a waste of time, in faith! You know yourselves: Alexander by all accounts married him to the lady Phesonnas, and has released him from imprisonment on his word of honour.'[1] (As you heard when we told of the war at Ephesus.)

But one of them said: 'Have no fear, mighty emperor: in his heart Porus has no love for Alexander, whatever impression he may give, for his father and his brothers died at his hands!'

When Darius heard this he dictated the following letter: 'To the excellent and mighty prince Porus, king of India, from his well-wisher King Darius of Persia, honour and joy! We send you word that one Alexander, who claims to be the son of our subject Philip of Macedon, has invaded our land of Persia with a great mob of rogues and has already robbed and pillaged and destroyed extensively, and killed a good number of our knights and worthy men. It seems he thinks nothing of shedding human blood, as you know yourself from the deaths of your father, brothers and dearest friends. So we pray and implore you, our special friend, kinsman and true companion in arms, to assist us with your presence and your company and all the forces you can raise, so that in battle together we can show this Alexander that a war inspired by pride can never come to a good end, and that he's started something he'll find hard to finish! May the sovereign god Jupiter grant you ever greater honour and triumph and send you health and happiness.'

The letter written, messengers were made ready and ordered to ride with all speed to India to find King Porus and deliver it to him on Darius's behalf. This they did; but when Porus received and read the letter he pondered a long while before replying. His mind was in turmoil: he thought firstly of the deaths of his father and all those dear to him, which filled his heart with anguish and resentment; but secondly of the honours he'd received from Alexander, as recounted

---

[1] Literally 'holds him prisoner at his will' – i.e. Porus is free only on the understanding that he owes his liberty to a generous captor and should in all honour not act against him.

above in the story of the peacock; then thirdly that if he refused this request by Darius he'd take it as a mark of cowardice. In the end, however, he decided not to go, and to excuse himself on the grounds of sickness and ill health; but he would send him a number of troops – though not until he'd seen how matters progressed! So he sent him the following message:

CHAPTER CXXXVIII

How King Porus of India dictated the following letter.

'To the most exalted, mighty and redoubtable prince Darius, king of Persia, from Porus, king of India, health and happiness. We have received your gracious letter informing us of the outrage you have suffered at the hands of King Alexander, which we take as an affront against ourselves. We therefore wish you to know how eager we would be to respond to your request for help, were it not for the infirmity that currently afflicts us and prevents us assisting you in person; but if it please the gods we shall send you a brigade of men-at-arms to provide more than ample support. God enhance your honour and reputation and send you all possible joy.'

The letter written, Porus entrusted it to the messengers and bade them return to their king and deliver it on his behalf. They did as commanded, and when Darius received and read the letter he was elated and told his companions, whose joy was just as great. Then he mustered all the troops he could and headed for a mountain called Mount Taurus,[1] for he'd heard Alexander meant to march that way, through a very narrow pass, and Darius thought that if he could arrive in time he could easily destroy Alexander's army.

But Alexander had spies everywhere and was informed of this at once; he set off for the mountain with all speed, accompanied only by his cavalry, and rode thirty-four leagues in a single day, the rest of his army following smartly as commanded. He reached the pass and made his way through unopposed.

From there he came to a city named Tarsus.[2] Now, through this city flowed a river colder than any in the world: it was called the Cydnus;[3] and it so happened that when Alexander arrived there he was very hot and weary from riding and fancied bathing in the river, for it looked so beautiful and clear. So he stripped off his clothes and dived straight in. But the moment he hit the water he was stricken by the icy cold and paralysed from head to foot. Somehow he struggled out and was carried to his tent in such a state that he could barely speak; and he could neither stand nor move – it seemed he was surely on the brink of death. All manner of doctors were summoned to him, but no surgeon in all the army could say what was wrong. The lamenting of the Greeks was piteous to behold and

---

[1]   'Torpor'. In Wauquelin's source at this point, the Prose *Alexander*, it is referred to as '*le mont de Tor*'.
[2]   'Trace' ('*Tarsse*' in the Prose *Alexander*).
[3]   'Edmon'.

hear; they were beside themselves with fear that their king would die, though Alexander did what he could to reassure them.

It was now that a young doctor was called from the land of Europe; his name was Philip, and he was a most accomplished scholar, unrivalled in all the seven arts.[1] And according to one account, King Darius had offered him his daughter and half his realm in return for poisoning Alexander, but he had refused to consider it, much to the fury of a knight named Parmenon – despite the fact that this Parmenon was one of Alexander's knights and had received many favours from him: he'd made him governor of all Armenia.[2]

CHAPTER CXXXIX

How Parmenon was beheaded in King Alexander's presence.

This young doctor now came before the king, and as soon as he saw his symptoms he said he understood the cause and declared that he would cure him without fail. The king told him to see to it as soon as he could, and he assured him that he would.

Now Parmenon, governor of Armenia, had heard of the arrival of this doctor Philip and, enraged (as we've just explained) at his refusal to poison him as Darius had bidden, resolved to have him put to death by Alexander himself. So he wrote a letter to Alexander telling him to beware at all costs of the doctor Philip, for he knew for certain he'd done a deal with Darius to poison him. The letter arrived when Alexander was on the very point of taking Philip's cure: Philip was right before him, proffering the medicine. The king read the letter just as he was about to take it, and stared at the doctor, deeply shocked. But he kept proffering the potion, and Alexander took it from him, so he was holding the potion in one hand and the letter in the other. His face was so troubled that the doctor realised he doubted him, and he went down on his knees and said:

'Mighty, dread emperor, have no fear of this potion: drink it with confidence, in God's name!'

Then the king, who held the doctor in the deepest affection, drank every drop. And when he'd drunk he handed the letter to Philip who read its contents straight off; and realising Parmenon's wicked plan he cried:

'Ah, great emperor! I'm guilty of none of this! Investigate, and you'll find the reverse is true!'

---

[1] The seven branches of knowledge known as the liberal arts (because they trained the *liber*, the 'free man', rather than serving an economic purpose) which were taught in the medieval schools: grammar, rhetoric and dialectic (the 'trivium'), and arithmetic, geometry, astronomy and music (the 'quadrivium').

[2] Wauquelin has subtly altered the details of his source in order to incriminate Darius. In the Prose *Alexander* 'there was a great lord in Armenia named Parmenon who hated this doctor because he had refused to poison Alexander, and when he saw that the doctor had won Alexander's trust he feared the king would kill him, so he sent him a letter saying "…King Darius of Persia has promised to give your doctor his daughter and a share in his kingdom if he succeeds in poisoning you, and Philip has promised to poison you with a potion with which he will promise to cure you…"' (Hilka's edition, pp.111-2).

No sooner had Alexander drunk the potion than he was cured, and he said to the doctor: 'Philip, you can clearly see how high you stand in my affections: I drank your potion before I gave you Parmenon's letter.'

And Philip replied: 'I pray you, sire, summon the man who sent it; I tell you truly, he asked me on King Darius's behalf to kill you with poison, and he hates me so much for refusing that he's tried to have me killed!'

Alexander sent for Parmenon at once. And as soon as he came before the king and was accused of the deed he admitted it; so the king, right there and then, had his head sent flying from his shoulders.

CHAPTER CXL

Of the second battle between Alexander and King Darius.

You earlier heard how Darius planned to take Mount Taurus so that he could block Alexander's passage, but was so slow in his preparations that Alexander and all his men reached the mountain before he'd made his move. When he realised this he was beside himself and didn't know what to do, and couldn't fathom how Alexander had managed to move so quickly – or had known he needed to. But his counsellors said:

'There's no reason to despair, sire: your power is still great. Summon all your men: let's bravely go to battle with these Greeks and clear them from our land.'

So they wrote messages and letters and sent them everywhere they had a chance of raising troops, and soon assembled an army huge beyond imagining. Once they were all gathered Darius ordered them into squadrons and battalions. They proposed attacking Alexander early one morning and without warning, for they considered war to have been declared the moment he invaded.

But Alexander was as sharp as ever: he was fully recovered from his illness and had spies everywhere, as you've heard, and he was immediately informed of Darius's plans. So he commanded all his lords to form their battalions and stand ready for action, because he knew Darius was advancing and would be launching an attack as soon as he saw the chance. Alexander's orders were promptly carried out – and it was as well they were, for at the crack of dawn one morning Darius, advancing with his squadrons, fell upon Alexander's army expecting to take them by surprise. But he didn't: he found them ready and waiting – and bold and battle-hardened, too. Such a hewing, such a slaughter followed as would appal the bravest man, for both sides killed each other without the slightest pity. The piercing thrusts of lance and spear and the shattering blows of sword and axe struck down men-at-arms in mounds, and the others clambered over them, pounding them under their horses' hooves: once a man-at-arms was down he had no chance of rising again, and many died without even shedding blood. In this vast, hideous, trampling crush they were locked till noon, and it was impossible to tell which side was winning as they struck and slew each other without mercy.

Chapter CXLI

How Alexander was almost killed in this battle.

It was now, around noon, that a strong, bold and accomplished knight of Darius's company, who'd been performing an unsurpassable number of deeds of arms, withdrew from the fray, took off his armour and donned the arms of a Macedonian. His arms thus changed, he returned to the battle and found his way through to Alexander's battalion and finally to the king's very side. Then when he saw the right moment he raised his sword to deliver a mortal blow, and struck Alexander with such force that the blade cut clean through his helm and mail hood and into his head. So grave was the wound that blood poured forth in torrents and the king buckled over; and, without a doubt, if the knight had been able to deal a second blow he would have killed him. But the Macedonians had seen what had happened and seized the Persian instantly. They were shocked and baffled, for he looked like one of their own, and they would have killed him on the spot had it not been for the king, who turned and saw him in Macedonian arms and cried out to them to bring him to him. They did so; and when Alexander was able to speak he said:

'Most valiant knight, what possessed you, a man of our blood, to attack me now?'

And the knight replied: 'Great emperor, don't imagine I'm from Macedon just because I'm armed like you! I assure you I'm from Persia! King Darius promised me his daughter's hand and provinces worthy of royalty if I succeeded in killing you. So I donned Macedonian armour the better to achieve my goal.'

Then Alexander cried aloud for all to hear: 'On, sirs, on! Let this give you all the heart you need: our enemies are powerless against us unless they resort to trickery! Let this man go, so he can bear witness to our valour!'

They did so, but most reluctantly: they would have dearly liked to kill him.

Chapter CXLII

How Alexander defeated King Darius and the Persians a second time.

Once he'd gone, the Greeks, filled with new heart and courage, launched a fresh attack upon the Persians, with such ferocity that vast slaughter was inevitable, and they drove and thrust relentlessly and forced the Persians back. And in the thick of it all was the noble Alexander, lance in hand: despite his wound he was riding along the battle-lines, brandishing his lance and cheering on his men.

But for his part Darius, king of Persia, was distraught as he saw his troops fall back. Ablaze with rage he grabbed a spear and yelled to his men to follow him, and plunged into the very thickest of the press. He found himself confronting the battalion led by Emenidus of Arcadia, who charged and met him with such fearsome might that he smashed his lance clean through his shield: had Darius's armour been less strong it would have gone straight through his body, too, for the impact sent him tumbling under the horses' hooves where he was trampled and wounded grievously before he was rescued. Through the efforts of his men, fighting with all their might, he was picked up and remounted; but he was in such a state that he hardly knew where he was, and withdrew from the battle as best he could to rest and recover breath. Sitting there watching his men-at-arms being slain on every side he was beside himself with anguish. And he realised that Alexander's battalions were now so close as they pushed on, scything down his men, that they were almost upon him; he thrust in his spurs without another word and took to flight so secretly that hardly any of his knights were aware.

But many now fled with him, and soon his whole army broke completely: almost all were rounded up and slaughtered like sheep. The history says that in this battle the Persians lost thirty thousand foot and ten thousand cavalry along with forty thousand prisoners – not just men but women, too: Darius's mother, wife, two sisters and two daughters were captured there.

But for all that, don't imagine that Alexander's victory was won without great cost and pain, for according to the history, in this second battle he lost seven thousand mounted men-at-arms and seven thousand infantry.

CHAPTER CXLIII

How Darius bewailed his defeat, and the Persian cities surrendered to Alexander.

Having defeated Darius a second time as you've heard, Alexander ordered Ptholomer and Danselin to go with ten thousand men and take possession of the land; all those cities and castles which surrendered willingly they were to treat with courtesy and spare all harm. They did as bidden, and soon you would have seen the nobles and governors of the cities, castles and strongholds come with keys in their hands to yield unreservedly to Ptholomer in the name of the noble Alexander, and Ptholomer received them with kindness as instructed. To some he restored their offices and dignities; others he relieved of their positions and gave them more important posts as he saw fit; and however he chose to proceed he treated them so well that he was everywhere respected and held in high regard, and the glowing reports of his noble conduct brought many to him who would never have come had he acted otherwise.

Meanwhile Darius, who'd fled the battle as you've heard, kept running all the way to a city of his called Persepolis, which I believe was the capital of the Persian kingdom. As soon as he arrived he ran up to the palace and threw himself full-length on the floor, face down, and began to weep so copiously that the floor was flooded with his tears, and lamented so bitterly that no man who heard him could have failed to be moved.

'Alas!' he wailed. 'Wretch that I am, most wretched man alive! What a trial and curse and cruel disaster heaven's wrath has inflicted on the Persian people, when Darius, once the lord and master of every city and fortress, of so many strong and noble castles and mighty, brave and powerful men, is brought to the ground and humbled! What's more he's a fugitive now, forced to flee by the ruthless strength and courage of foes who compared to his great might are paltry

fleas! Oh, alas! Why does Death not take me now? Why does She leave me to suffer all this misery and torment?'

With such words of lamentation, or very like, King Darius bewailed his lot.
And he had more than one good reason to lament: firstly, the defeat he'd now
twice suffered at Alexander's hands; secondly, the knowledge that his mother,
his wife, his two sisters and his daughters were Alexander's prisoners, and he
didn't know what he would do with them (though in fact he treated them so well
that he should be forever loved, admired and honoured for it); and thirdly, he
was so gravely wounded through the body that he was streaming blood.

Chapter CXLIV

How King Darius sent a new letter to Alexander.

Darius was surrounded by knights and squires who'd fled the battle and followed him. Hearing his anguished lament they were filled with pity; they
helped him to his feet and began to console him with all possible kindness, and
bandaged his wounds and helped him regain his composure. Once he'd recovered a little he pondered his next move long and hard. Then he called for one of
his secretaries to come at once, and dictated a quite amazing letter. He bade that
it be taken straight to Alexander, which was duly done.

When the letter reached King Alexander it was publicly opened and read in
the presence of all his knights. The contents were as follows, or very like:

'From Darius, king of Persia, to my servant Alexander greetings and wishes of
joy and friendship. We would ask you to remember, mighty though you may be,
that you were born into this world as a man, and that it is a man's finest quality to
show modesty and moderation as he achieves his mighty deeds, and not to wax
proud after the victories which Nature or Fortune bestows upon him, for no man
driven by pride will ever come to a good end. Let me give you as an example my
ancestor the good King Xerxes,[1] who won so many victories and achieved so many
feats of prowess in his life, but pride then took him to a height that guaranteed a
mighty fall. And Mellanda,[2] too: so powerful and so rich in gold and silver – the
same kind of wealth you've seen us display! – and convinced he'd prosper endlessly, but he finished his life a beggar and died in abject poverty.

'So consider: just because sovereign Providence has granted you this victory
over me, don't let pride or arrogance take hold; be all the humbler and more
inclined to acts of mercy. We pray and entreat you, trusting as we do in your
wisdom and noble breeding and extraction, to avoid the aforesaid pitfalls and
kindly restore to us my mother, wife, sisters and two daughters; in return I shall
give you all the riches amassed by my ancestors in the lands of Asia, Susa[3] and

---

[1]   'Erciens'. The name is given as 'Herciés' in the Prose *Alexander*, a transliteration of 'Xersen'
      in the *Historia de Preliis*.
[2]   The *Historia de Preliis* refers to Xerxes having been 'in Hellas' ('*in Ellada*'), which led its
      French translator, followed by Wauquelin, to refer mistakenly to a second king, '*Mellanda*'.
[3]   One of the capitals of the Persian empire.

Mactra,[1] and make you lord of the Medes and Persians for the rest of your days. May the sovereign god keep you and grant you victory.'

CHAPTER CXLV

How Darius sent letters to King Porus of India.

When this letter had been read and heard there was joy and celebration among Alexander's knights, eager as they were for an end to the war. And one of them, Perdicas by name, said to the king:

'Sovereign emperor, most mighty and most feared, you surely won't refuse Darius's offer? Please send him back his wife and mother, his sisters and daughters.'

Hearing this, Alexander shook his head and called the messengers before him and said: 'I'm amazed, sirs, that your lord King Darius dared imagine he'd win me over with gifts, and thought he'd get his mother and wife and sisters and daughters back with money and reward! No! No! Go and tell him that, as long as he lives, he'll never buy me off with cash or presents!'

So saying, he presented them with an array of magnificent gifts before bidding them return to Darius. And so they did, not stopping till they reached their king and told him all about Alexander and his response. Darius, astonished and dismayed, turned his thoughts to how he might confront Alexander in battle once more.

It suddenly struck him that Porus had not yet sent him the help he'd earlier promised, and he decided to write to him again and inform him of his position and press him for support. So he dictated the following, or very like:

'To Porus, king of India, wishes of health and joy from the king of Persia. Just as we previously sought your aid and support against King Alexander and his forces who are bent on ravaging and laying waste our land, so once again we have to report that we have done battle with him, trying our strength army to army. But the will of the gods has been against us. Twice we have been driven from the field in confusion – and little wonder, for the courage, prowess and valour of Alexander surpass any on record: I don't believe any man who ever lived can compare with him for strength, endurance and resolve in all high deeds. That was all too clear when we made him a generous offer in exchange for our mother, wife, sisters and daughters and he replied that, since we couldn't defeat him in battle, we wouldn't win him over with gifts or payment! And now, because we'd sooner die on the battlefield than witness the desolation of our land and people, and know it is a finer thing to die in honour than to live in shame, we have decided to attack and fight this Alexander once again.

'But because of the grievous losses we have suffered of men and knights, we feel we can do so only with the support of friends. We consider you to be

---

[1]   *'Matran'.*

such a one, and pray you most affectionately, remembering the bonds of kinship between us, to extend a merciful hand towards us in our hour of urgent need and rescue us from this perilous plight. And since it would be unjust that you and your people should aid us without reward, I promise without fail to give each one of your men, in return for your efforts, five pounds of fine gold and all the food and drink and everything else you need. And wherever you choose to lodge I shall send you eighty girls for your entertainment. And I promise you, you shall have Alexander's horse Bucephalus along with all his gear and armour, and all other booty shall be equally shared between your men and ours, half and half. But don't delay, I pray you: as soon as you've read this letter come to us in force befitting your high majesty. And may all the gods grant you honour, joy and victory!'

Chapter CXLVI

How Porus wrote excusing himself from coming in person to help King Darius.

Having read King Darius's letter Porus pondered a while. Then he summoned ten thousand of the bravest men-at-arms in all his kingdom, and commanded them to go to Darius's aid and to fight as well as if he'd been with them. Then he dictated a letter to Darius saying:

'To the most excellent, mighty and redoubtable emperor Darius, king of Persia, greetings. King Porus of India prays the gods will send you strength and force against all your foes. But wise men should always draw on their own resources, especially when the cares of the world strike thick and fast! Anyone can swim in the sea when it's calm and inviting – a man proves his true worth if he copes with it when it's storm-tossed, churning! I say this, my lord king, in relation to yourself: hitherto you have always governed yourself, your land and your people in exemplary fashion; but now that Fortune has turned a little against you, you have lost your nerve to such a degree that you want your army and mine to combine – forces which together the whole world could not resist – simply to do battle with your foe. We would suggest, lord king, that you show your customary wisdom and courage, for a truly worthy, valiant heart earns rightful admiration when it's just as staunch in bad times as in good. It would bring deep dishonour on us both, I think, if we joined our two great armies to confront such a small force as your foe!

'In view of this, we pray you most affectionately to excuse us for not joining you in person. Don't imagine it's through fear or trepidation – or because I want an easy life! No, it's for the sake of your honour and mine. Nor would I have you think I've forgotten you, which is why I'm sending ten thousand cavalry, such able men that I believe they'd overcome your enemies on their own! We've instructed them to undertake this mission – and to take payment from you – as men-at-arms committed to your cause and to all matters concerning honour. May honour indeed be granted you by the sovereign god,[1] along with total victory.'

---

[1]   In the Prose *Alexander* this is 'our sovereign god Jupiter'.

CHAPTER CXLVII

How Darius gathered his forces again to confront Alexander a third time.

The letter written, it was taken back to Darius by his own messengers accompanied by the aforesaid ten thousand troops. Together these messengers and men-at-arms made their way to Darius, who was delighted by the letter and even more so by the men-at-arms, though he would have preferred King Porus to have come in person.

Once they'd arrived Darius summoned forces from everywhere he thought might lend support: first to come was Castarot, king of Ethiopia, who arrived with ten thousand men and a brother of his named Corunbios, king of a realm called Perregart; and so many other dukes, counts and knights then came that Darius had soon amassed twelve hundred thousand men, all experienced, strong and ready for action.

But despite their numbers, no sooner had they gathered than everything started to go wrong. Darius did not impress the worthy men on whom his cause depended, the reason being that he surrounded himself with sycophants, schemers, two-faced rogues and men of little wit; the men of true worth despised him for this: they couldn't get to talk to him or counsel him for all these wretched fools.

And so it was that one of the foremost knights of his company, appalled by his behaviour, decided to do what he could to scupper his plans.[1] So he left Darius's entourage in secret and made his way to Alexander's camp. He talked his way into his presence and gave a detailed report of his king's preparations so that Alexander could plan accordingly. He also told him how Darius had sought aid from King Porus of India, and how Porus had declined to come but, to appease him and stay on good terms, had sent him ten thousand troops.

When Alexander heard this he was shocked by Porus's actions; and with a shake of his head he said: 'Sometimes it's not a good idea to wake a sleeping cat.'

Darius's mother was shocked to see this knight with Alexander; but she asked after her son, and when the knight told her that Darius meant to do battle yet again she was aghast, and decided to send him word that he should do no such thing, convinced as she was that he'd be powerless to resist Alexander, let alone

---

[1]   Here Wauquelin reworks his source in a notable way. The phrase he uses is '*s'il pooit, Daire se travilloit en vaing*' (literally 'if he could [he'd see to it that] Darius's efforts would be in vain'), whereas the Prose *Alexander* says bluntly that '*uns siens chevaliers a qui il sambloit que Daires se traveilloit en vain, se parti de Dayre et vint en l'ost Alixandre*' – i.e. the knight changed sides simply because 'he thought Darius was striving in vain' – in other words, was doomed to lose. Wauquelin changes the knight's motivation from craven fear of imminent disaster to disdain for Darius's behaviour. Indeed the previous paragraph, warning against surrounding oneself with sycophants and schemers, is Wauquelin's invention – though he was doubtless prompted to write it by reading the passage in the verse *Roman d'Alexandre* (Branch III stanzas 8-10) in which Darius is abandoned by his people: 'Darius summoned all his barons from all his lands, but few came because he was so hated on account of the wicked servants he promoted above them' (Branch III vv.231-3).

defeat him, and that the more he tried the more he'd lose. So she immediately dictated a letter along the following lines:

'To her dear son Darius, king of Persia, from his mother Rodocton wishes of health, joy and honour. We hear you have once again assembled countless forces to attack and engage King Alexander. You'll achieve little or nothing! We earnestly beg you understand that even if the whole world was ranged against him they still would not defeat him, for he is destined by almighty God to bring the whole world under his lordship and dominion, governed as he is by a true and valiant heart. We appeal to your great wisdom, and beg you restrain yourself and abandon this enterprise: if you insist on pursuing it, you will jeopardise the mercy he has shown us – a mercy so great that, unless your pride prevents it, we will secure a fine and gracious peace between you, to your honour and glory. May moderation – and the gods – guide you to a wise decision.'

CHAPTER CXLVIII
How Alexander prepared for a third battle against King Darius.

His mother's message disturbed Darius greatly; but then he told himself he'd rather die on the battlefield, defending his land and his honour, than evade the situation as she suggested and bring shame upon himself and his people. So he ordered all his forces to set off and advance towards the Tigris, each man under his respective banner, ready to cross the river as soon as the moment came.

On the other side Alexander was readying all the forces that he could, well aware that Darius had amassed numbers beyond counting. That's why, when his squadrons and battalions were drawn up to his satisfaction, he bade every man drag a branch behind him and raise a load of dust, to make the enemy imagine there were more of them than there were. This was duly done, and when the Persians saw them advancing in a mighty dust-cloud they were aghast and didn't know what to do.

On rode Alexander with his whole army, and made camp just a thousand paces from the city where Darius was based: only the River Tigris separated the two armies. There he stopped, knowing Darius to be so strong that it would be foolish to cross the river before he'd seen what the enemy meant to do.

Darius meanwhile had fifteen thousand chariots packed with archers, crossbowmen, slingers and other weaponry, and between them eighty thousand well armed infantry, their intention being to smash and break through Alexander's lines. And when midnight drew near and the river began to ebb and drop in level as it always did, Darius issued a general order to prepare to make the crossing. The chariots, as planned, were the first to cross; but as they did so, at deepest midnight, Alexander caught them unawares, launching such a swift attack that they had no time to deploy and were forced to flee this way and that as best they could. The Greeks set fire to the chariots, consuming them in flame, and the pursuit that followed was so intense that you would have struggled to hear God's thunder. In attacking these, the first of Darius's forces, Alexander wiped out the majority, the rest not daring to cross the river when they saw the Greeks slaughtering their fellows. Now indeed they were forced to cross elsewhere, not where they'd planned; and let me tell you, before day broke and Darius's forces were all across, countless numbers from both sides had been killed.

CHAPTER CXLIX

How Alexander defeated King Darius a third time.

As day broke Alexander realised, to his surprise, that Darius's whole army had crossed the river. He quickly deployed his men in fine array, with a great body of infantry forming a dense hedge of lances; they were interspersed with slingers and archers, the archers loosing clouds of arrows from their little Turkish bows and the slingers hurling fearsome volleys: every missile felled a man-at-arms and horse together, killing vast numbers before the battalions clashed, sending them tumbling one upon another in colossal mounds.

Seeing this chaos, King Darius launched ten thousand élite cavalry, the finest in all his army, bidding them charge and smash this squadron of Alexander's who were wreaking so much havoc. They charged indeed; but let me tell you, those infantry gave them such a reception with their hedge of lances that of the ten thousand hardly a single man escaped, for the men-at-arms closest to the infantry swept in and slaughtered them like calves or sheep. The massacre and carnage were so great that no man could describe the half of it. Indeed the history says that, for all the blaring horns and clarions, the yells of men were louder still as all screamed out their battle-cries and whatever they thought would give them courage. And when the archers and slingers had exhausted all their stones and arrows they drew great leaden clubs from their belts; then they opened their lines like double-doors, and through the gap charged the Greek and Macedonian cavalry, magnificently armed and mounted, lances levelled, with Alexander at their very head like the worthy, bold and valiant man he was; and spurring all the way they smashed into the Persians all together. But the Persians met them gallantly; and truly, as this battle joined the thunder of the charging hooves and the shattering smash of weaponry made the very earth seem to shake. With spears and lances, strong and stout, they thrust at one another in a clash too appalling for any man to behold or contemplate: believe me, there were many skewered and disembowelled, many felled and stricken down, and many butchered, crippled, maimed; and severed limbs, shattered heads and scattered brains could be seen in monstrous, hideous mounds.

And in the midst of all this was the noble Alexander, mounted on Bucephalus, lance in hand, performing countless feats of arms as he felled and toppled knights and horses as if it was all quite effortless. Danselin was in the thick of it, too, and Ptholomer, Perdicas, Caulus, Ariscé – not to mention Emenidus, who was dealing out punishment to the Persians in indescribable fashion. Truly, they were worthy men indeed, assured and battle-hardened. The foot soldiers, too, armed with clubs as you've heard, were battering foes quite pitilessly, offering no quarter, showing no mercy.

King Darius, fighting furiously himself, was urging his men to greater efforts and summoning them to drive on; and this they did, and mightily, often
forcing the Greeks and Macedonians back. And their numbers were so great
that no matter how many the Greeks slew it seemed to make little difference.
And according to the history, they were locked in this deadly mêlée until
nightfall.

Chapter CL

More about this battle.

The ten thousand Indians sent by Porus to aid Darius, as you've heard, remembered their king's injunction to fight as well in his absence as they
would have done had he been there; and seeing the bloody execution wrought
by the Greeks and Macedonians they decided it was time to show their mettle.
Ablaze with wild rage they charged into Alexander's battalion, bent upon taking him dead or alive. But what a reception they met from head of lance and
edge of sword, as Alexander, seeing the danger, raised his battle-cry and called
on his companions to prove their worth. The moment they heard his voice they
launched themselves at the Indians with such ferocity that every single one, I
believe, they killed or felled. King Darius was shocked, aghast, appalled by this
disaster, and lamented their loss most piteously, crying:

'Ah, Porus, dear cousin, when you hear of this dire misfortune you'll be distraught – and with good reason!'

And with Darius already in deepest anguish, one of his knights came to him
and said: 'Sovereign emperor, everything is turning against you! Your Constable
the king of Ethiopia and his brother are slain, and the Greeks and Macedonians
seem to grow in strength and courage by the hour! What will you do now?'

At this King Darius went wild: he seized a lance and screamed his battle-cry
like a man possessed, and spurred towards the foe in such a fury that he sent
nine or ten knights crashing to the ground before his charge was done. But as
he did so he was met with a hail of darts and spears and lances that drove him
from his saddle and sent him tumbling to the earth, with more than a dozen
wounds right through his body. But such was his desire for vengeance that he
was oblivious to hurt or pain: that was clear as he leapt to his feet in an instant,
drew sword from scabbard and, yelling his battle-cry, hewed and smote at the
Greeks and Macedonians with such might that all who saw him declared him
a valiant man indeed. Alexander praised him highly in his heart as he saw
him hold his foes at bay in a ring around him, like a wild boar amid a pack
of hounds. But, pelted by Greek and Macedonian darts and spears, he would
surely have been captured had it not been for a band of his bravest knights
who came charging to the rescue; and in the battle to save him, knights and
men-at-arms beyond all counting were struck down and killed. By this time
night was setting in; it was incredible that they could still fight on, having
battled all day without sustenance; but so hungry were they for victory that
they gave no thought to food or drink.

Chapter CLI
How Darius fled the battle, utterly crushed.

By the time Darius was remounted and back among his men he was in such a
state that he could barely carry on and didn't know what to do: there was no
way of retreating yet as the river had not yet frozen. Bands of his men were fighting on in some parts of the field, where there were so many dead that the horses
were up to their saddle-girths in blood; but as soon as darkness fell and Darius
thought the river would have turned to ice he left the field and took to flight. But
let me tell you, many were slain in the process, and this is why: the men who'd
driven his chariots at the start of the battle had now regrouped and formed a
great battalion to go and support their friends, so when the Persians turned and
fled blindly through the dark they ran straight into the chariots, and the chari-
oteers, imagining they were the enemy, slaughtered them. This disaster was
the end for Darius. And the Greeks and Macedonians were hot on their heels,
charging down with levelled lances and felling them in heaps and mounds. The
baying fever of the chase was at such a pitch that it seemed the whole world
would be consumed in slaughter: so many died on the frozen river that the blood
flowed everywhere in torrents, the ice so slippery, half-melted by the steaming
gore of the slain, that neither man nor horse could stay upright.

But somehow Darius and a handful of his men managed to get across; and he
didn't stop at the city he'd left the day before – he kept running till he reached
the furthest corner of his realm, a land called Persepolis,[1] where he stayed to
see what Alexander would do next: it was an expansive region with many fine,
strong and mighty cities; at the border of this land King Darius halted.

Chapter CLII
How according to the history Alexander pursued Darius to the land of Persepolis.

Utterly crushed in this battle by the Greeks and Macedonians, the Medes and
Persians had lost all hope and self-belief, and they who for so long had held
lordship and dominion over Alexander now submitted to his will and mercy.
Then Alexander shared the spoils among his men, so fairly that they were all
well satisfied.

At this point the history tells us that in the three battles fought between Darius and Alexander, the numbers killed, cavalry and infantry combined, totalled
fifteen times one hundred thousand, with a further million[2] slain in Alexander's

---

[1]   'Persinpolios'.
[2]   Literally 'ten hundred thousand'. The numbers are forbidding, but Wauquelin has in fact
moderated the overwhelming death-toll (surely the result of a scribal error?) given in
his source: the two figures suggested by the Prose *Alexander* (at least, in the manuscript
edited by Hilka) are 'fifteen times ten hundred thousand' and 'twenty hundred thousand'
(Hilka's edition, p.128).

assaults in the same campaign upon those strongholds, cities and castles that he took by storm.

A few days after this third victory, once Alexander had rested, he crossed the River Tigris with all his forces and came upon a most prosperous land adorned with rich cities and palaces, which all surrendered to him and placed themselves at his mercy. There King Alexander took lodging as he chose, and he stayed there all that winter; in which time the Greeks seized and pillaged the fine palaces and even put them to the torch: Alexander was furious and forced them to stop.

In this land was a beautiful field, broad and long, filled with rich tombs and sepulchres; according to the history it was the burial-ground of the Persian kings and greatest lords: hence the number of opulent tombs. One tomb in particular, the resting-place of a king, was made of amethyst, as clear as crystal, in fact more so, for through the stone the body – fully preserved, even the hair – could be seen lying upon its bier. Elsewhere in this same field stood a mighty tower of marble housing a vast number of prisoners; some had had their feet cut off, others their hands or ears: some were mutilated more than others, each according to his deserts as judged by those who'd imprisoned them there. And when these men heard the voices of the throng of strangers they all began to cry 'Alexander! Alexander!', knowing as they did that he was in that land; and the Macedonians, hearing their cries, set them free and brought them before him. Alexander was so moved by the sight that he had to hold back tears, and bade that each of the prisoners be given a thousand silver drachmae (the equivalent of ten *livres*), and that all their possessions be restored to them.

Then, as soon as spring came, Alexander ordered his men to decamp and take to the field once more, and headed towards the land where he'd heard Darius had taken refuge. On he marched with his whole army and entered the land of Persepolis, where the Greeks set about seizing and plundering villages and strongholds and putting all to the torch as if they were bent on total destruction, and they met with hardly any resistance.

CHAPTER CLIII

How King Darius was killed by two of his closest kinsmen.

Darius, hearing of Alexander's approach and realising he wouldn't stop till he'd stripped him of his whole inheritance, left the city where he'd taken refuge and headed deeper into the land to raise troops to do battle with Alexander yet again. To assist him in his mission he took two of his closest kinsmen, both full cousins on his mother's side, one named Bisso and the other Barsanes. And what happened was this: as they were riding towards another city, these two, who were false, wicked, treacherous men, plotted together to seize their cousin Darius and deliver him to Alexander, and so bring an end to the war and earn themselves rich profit and reward. And the plan they conceived they carried out: they suddenly whipped out their swords and grabbed their king, shouting that if he made a move 'You're a dead man!', and bound him tightly with ropes – they even clapped him in irons. Darius, finding himself suddenly assailed by these two wild villains, began to cry most piteously:

'Oh! Dear friends and companions, close in blood, my cousins! Do you mean to put an end to me so basely? Alas! You'll be reproached for it eternally! Ah! Do you imagine you'll be honoured for it by the Greeks and Macedonians? Do you think you'll earn more from them than from me? No indeed! Oh, my dearest friends, leave me with my trials – I've enough without you adding more! Abandon this wicked plan of yours, for which my gracious heart forgives you; for truly, if you kill me thus, Alexander will consider you murderers and make you pay for my death – kings and emperors rightly avenge any emperor killed by treachery, especially by his own liegemen, as you know you are to me.'

But at these words the two murderers went mad and plunged their swords clean through his body, and he fell to the ground as if dead. Thinking he was dead indeed, they left him there and fled.

It wasn't long before someone – I don't know who – took the news to Alexander, who wasn't far away. He was filled with grief; and he took six hundred knights and rode swiftly to the place and arrived in time to find Darius stretched out in the open field, now very close to death. As soon as Darius saw Alexander he recognised him by his arms and accoutrements; he greeted him as respectfully as he could and begged him there and then to avenge his murder. And Alexander, weeping bitterly, with great tears welling from his eyes in pity that such a valiant and mighty lord should have been so basely slain, said:

'Oh most sovereign lord, I pray you let me help you rise: be a king once more, as you once were king of your great empire! Take strength and heart: from this day forth I shall be your loyal friend and companion!'

'Ah, most worthy emperor,' Darius replied, 'may the almighty god grant you the blessings you wish me. There is no way back for me: I feel my death is near. But truly, I shall die more happily in your presence than otherwise, for in you I see all the honour, prowess and valour there could ever be in a man, and I commend to you my mother, my wife, my sisters and my daughters.'

With that Alexander bade that he be carried to a nearby castle – he himself acted as a bearer; but before they reached there, Darius died in their arms. No one, I think, who saw Alexander then and the anguish he displayed could have failed to be filled with pity.

Chapter CLIV
How Alexander proclaimed peace throughout Darius's realms.

When Alexander saw that Darius was dead, he had him buried with all possible honour, as was only right. Once this was done he sent his captains with great bodies of men-at-arms to take control of the towns and cities, all of which yielded to Alexander without demur. And as soon as he'd installed his bailiffs and provosts and officers so that all was well in hand, he dictated letters proclaiming peace and sent them to every part of Persia, Media and Mactra,[1] the essence of which was as follows:

'From Alexander, commander of the Greeks, son of King Philip of Macedon and Queen Olympias, to all Persians greetings and goodwill. You might well rejoice at the great victory God has granted us – through His bounty, not through our deserts – were it not that it has cost so many lives. Nonetheless, since the god Ammon by the grace of the sovereign God has ordained that we triumph over the Persians, it is only right that we show mercy to the defeated and render thanks to all the gods.

'To this end we request and entreat you to pray that God may grant us the wisdom and ability to govern you to the honour and benefit of the common weal. And since peace and concord more than anything in the world contribute to the prosperity of all, we, committed in our office to the aforesaid goal, do desire, command and decree by our lifelong authority that true peace and concord be preserved in perpetuity in the kingdom of Persia, and that every man must swear an oath to his commander in due time and place, and every commander must swear an oath to those below him, to uphold the peace absolutely, any infringement of which is to be punished by death. The better to ensure the observance of our edict, we wish the aforesaid oaths to be renewed every seven years.

'We further command and decree that all merchants be free to conduct their business throughout the realm of Persia with their persons and their goods, whatever they may be, in confidence and safety. And because we wish no one to be so bold as to flout our authority and commit fraud or trade dishonestly, we decree that anyone accused of such offence, and proven guilty under oath, shall repay the damages in full and then a quarter more, and moreover suffer capital punishment.

'Furthermore, just as each man should be punished according to the gravity of his crime, so each man should be paid and rewarded as befits his service; and we, desiring to fulfil all matters pertaining to our office, and recognising that the service you formerly paid your lord King Darius can now be seen as service to us (even though at the time it was directed against us), wish to reward you for the quality of that service. To that end we hereby decree and command that all of you Persians retain all revenue, possessions and rightful inheritances – chattels and estates alike – as were yours on the day we invaded the kingdom of Persia to begin the conquest we have now completed; all, that is, except your weapons and your armour, which we wish you to place in the hands of our castellans, bailiffs and provosts. Honour and joy be granted you and all who obey our command.'

This decree was displayed in all the customary places.

---

[1] 'Matran', as above, p.164.

CHAPTER CLV

How Alexander cleverly caught Darius's two murderers and had them hanged.

After issuing this proclamation, the good King Alexander thought once more of the dismal killing of King Darius. He summoned most of his council and a number of others to his palace to discuss the well-being and the interests of the kingdom as a whole, and among other matters raised when they assembled he said:

'Sirs, I very much regret that I haven't yet repaid you all for your fine services to me; I say this knowing that among you are men who took revenge for me upon King Darius, and so brought relief to us all and an end to the grievous war between us. I'd dearly love to know who those men were, for by the faith I owe my mother Olympias, if they were to make themselves known to us, I would elevate them above all other Persians!'

Word of this spread throughout the kingdom and reached the ears of Bisso and Barsanes; and not realising what he meant by 'elevation' they came and presented themselves to Alexander, expecting to receive a rich reward. But as soon as Alexander saw them and heard from their own lips that they were Darius's murderers, he had them hanged from a lofty gibbet. Thus was his promise exactly fulfilled: they were elevated to such a height that all Persians looked up at them from far and wide. And the way Alexander had exacted justice earned him the Persians' love indeed, for they loathed those two men for their gross treachery.

CHAPTER CLVI

How Alexander married King Darius's eldest daughter, named Roxane.

Alexander, wishing to win still deeper love from the Persians and the Medes, decided to marry Darius's eldest daughter, as indeed, according to our history, Darius had requested when he died; Vincent's history[1] says her name was Roxane. So he summoned all the great lords of the land and of his own company to the magnificent palace where he'd taken residence; and when they were all assembled he called for Darius's mother, sisters and daughters (his wife, the history says, had lately died) to present themselves before his imperial majesty. When these ladies came into his presence they were received with all possible honour; then Alexander addressed the whole assembly, saying:

'Dear friends and companions, when storm clouds pass good weather will follow. I refer to the turmoil and strife and hostility and violence which have long raged between us – though our honour did not permit any less. We deeply regret the loss of so many noble men who were slain as a result – but enough! What's done is done! And now it has pleased the sovereign god that I should be

---

[1]   See note 1, above, p.135.

your ruler, and I mean to fulfil that office to the benefit and honour of you all. And because we wish to establish firm bonds of brotherly alliance between us, I ask you all, Persians and Medes and ladies and damsels, and especially you, my lady Roxane, to grant your loving approval that I answer the request your father made me at his death: that I should take you as my wife and spouse, and you should take me as your lord and husband. Let me know your true feelings and response.'

At this, Roxane fell on her knees before Alexander and replied: 'Praised be all the gods that my dread lord should choose to seat me on his throne when I was his subject, at his mercy!'

Then all the Persians started crying with one voice: 'Long live King Alexander! Honour and victory be granted him – and our entire obedience and free and willing service!'

Were I to describe all they said and did you'd be amazed: they wept for joy, and showered all possible honour and praise on Alexander and all his men.

Then preparations began for the marriage, in a style befitting their station. And Alexander, whose heart was ever steadfast in nobility, honour and courtesy, sent a letter to his mother telling of all his victories and conquests and also of his marriage, and asking her most graciously to celebrate the wedding in her city, so that all the people of Macedon would know what he'd achieved; and this she did.

Chapter CLVII

How the Persians worshipped Alexander as a god,
for which he severely rebuked them.

On the day of the marriage, when the ceremony was over and complete, the great lords of Persia and a countless throng of people came before Alexander as he sat upon his throne with his bride, to whom he had decreed all honour and reverence should be shown. That was why, indeed, these Persians had all come; but I tell you, the moment they arrived they went down on their knees and started worshipping the king and queen in the very manner in which they worshipped their gods, uttering words which implied in fact that they took Alexander to be a god and his wife to be a goddess. Alexander was most disturbed by this and rebuked them very strongly, saying (to put it in the words of the Psalm): *Non nobis, domine, non nobis*, etc.[1]

'Ah, good people!' he said. 'Such reverence is not due to us or fitting – we are mortal and corruptible like you, created just the same, and the honour due to God should never be attributed to man. From this day forth I forbid you to behave like this again, for both you and I might incur God's wrath – you by your actions and I by allowing them!'

---

[1]   Psalm 115 (in the King James Version) begins: '*Non nobis, non nobis, Domine, sed nomini tuo da gloriam*' ('Not to us, not to us, Lord, but to your name give glory').

The Persians were thoroughly taken aback, and couldn't stop talking about the goodness, worth and wisdom of this Alexander.

Realising he'd won the love of them all, Alexander decided the time was ripe to take revenge upon King Porus of India, who'd so offended him by sending troops to fight as mercenaries against him: how quickly, he felt, Porus had forgotten the great kindness he'd shown him, as you heard recounted when we told of the vows of the peacock.[1] And now, being so well loved by the Persians, whose lands moreover bordered India, he felt he'd achieve his goal better with their help than with anyone else's – though the Greeks and Macedonians remained his closest companions in all endeavours.

Thus resolved, when spring came he called all the Persians together and declared that there was nothing good about an idle life, and that while certain things remained undone he should not be called a perfect king: he meant to go on campaign and wage war once again. And since he'd be leaving the country and didn't want it to be left without a governor, he asked them to choose one of their own, whoever they thought would care for the kingdom best. They chose one named Auricus, a knight now advanced in years, formerly an uncle of King Darius and an honourable man in all his deeds. Alexander entrusted the land's government to him, and then set out with his whole army.

Here ends Alexander's conquest of Darius and the kingdoms of the Medes and Persians, who for so long had held sway over many other realms and domains.

[1]   See especially Chapter CIX.

BOOK TWO

Bibliothèque Nationale MS français 9342, folio 164

CHAPTER I

Here follow various digressions about Alexander, relating to parts of the West such as France, England, Scotland and other lands thereabouts.

At the behest of my aforesaid esteemed lord[1] I have undertaken to record in our mother tongue the deeds and conquests of that mighty and feared emperor Alexander. Now, it is universally recognised that his prowess won him lordship and kingship over all the earth, both East and West, and so it follows that he was lord of the whole of France and all neighbouring lands. But in none of the sources I've consulted in compiling this work of mine – such as Vincent le Jacopin[2] or Guillaume,[3] both of whom wrote records of Alexander's deeds – have I found how or in what manner he came to subjugate this region. And since France or its neighbouring countries are the native lands of my esteemed lord – a discreet, strong and worthy governor, notably of the fine and noble land of Picardy, under the hand of my most revered and mighty lord Philip, by the grace of God duke of Burgundy, Lothier, Brabant and Limburg, count of Flanders, Artois and Burgundy, count palatine of Hainault, Holland, Zeeland and Namur, margrave of the Holy Empire and lord of Frisia, Salins and Mechelen – and since I myself, too, am a native of that same land of Picardy, I wish here to draw upon material I've found in the *History of the Belgians*, written and assembled by a most venerable doctor and master of theology, the Franciscan friar Jacques de Guise.[4] His history, compiled and composed at the command of the esteemed prince Duke Albert of Bavaria, count of Hainault, Holland and Zeeland,[5] gives reason to suppose that King Alexander was indeed lord of the abovementioned lands. I humbly ask all who read or hear this work of mine that, if they discover more details about his conquest of these countries, they will kindly add to this history accordingly and forgive any negligence of mine!

In any event, to explore this point we shall digress for a moment from our main theme and tell first how Alexander conquered the land of Albanie,[6] because it is after his victory over the men of Albanie that Jacques de Guise refers (as does Cresus[7] in his book) to Alexander bequeathing the Forest Carbonniere to

---

[1]   John of Burgundy: footnote 1, p.29.
[2]   See above, footnote 1, p.135.
[3]   This may be a reference to Guillaume 'aux Blanches Mains', the twelfth-century Archbishop of Reims to whom Walter of Châtillon dedicated his Latin *Alexandreis* (see note 1, below, p.302). Wauquelin seems to have accidentally taken him to be the author.
[4]   Jacques de Guise (1334-99) was the author of the *Annales Historiae Illustrium Principum Hannoniae* – the *Chronicles of Hainault* – which Wauquelin himself translated for Duke Philip the Good shortly before undertaking *The Deeds and Conquests of Alexander.*
[5]   Albert I, duke of Bavaria, 1336-1404.
[6]   As will become clear in the next chapter, this is '[the land] which we call Scotland'.
[7]   The name appears in the MSS as 'Orosius', who is shortly to be referred to correctly; but here it is almost certainly a mistaken transcription of 'Cresus'. Cresus (which itself may have been a corruption of 'Orosius') is the name of the 'able, shrewd and judicious scholar' commissioned by King Perceforest to record the Chronicles of England in the fourteenth-century romance of *Perceforest*. See *Perceforest*, tr. N. Bryant (Woodbridge, 2011), p.121.

a lady named Lyriope;[1] and in our own time this 'Forest Carbonniere' comprises a number of countries such as Picardy and Artois and especially Hainault, Flanders, Brabant, Liège, Hesbaye[2] and several other neighbouring lands.

CHAPTER II

How according to my sources Alexander conquered Albanie and a number of other lands.

So, then: after the noble King Alexander had overcome Darius and all the Medes and Persians, he wanted to take revenge upon King Porus of India. But he decided it would be better first to go and conquer the regions of the West, being well aware that Eastern parts are inhabited by many strange and fearsome beasts such as serpents, dragons, lions, bears, wild dogs and countless more; so it was far better, he thought, to initiate and toughen his men by confronting lesser challenges than those they'd face in the land of India – this applied especially to the Medes and Persians, with whom he'd reinforced his army in great numbers. So he prepared first to march into the land of Albanie, and mobilised his forces and entered the country at the start of spring.

His knights promptly began to roam the land, pillaging and plundering livestock and riches; and in response the brave, bold men of Albanie rallied together and came with their king to confront Alexander. A series of fierce battles followed, with victories and losses shared, but the Greeks steadily advanced, destroying and sacking towns and fortresses, cities and castles.

If you wish to know where this land of Albanie lies, Chapter 107 of the *Book of Properties*[3] begins '*Albania Asie est majoris provincia a colore, etc.*': Albanie, it says, is a province of Greater Asia, and takes its name from the colour of its people because they're generally born with white[4] hair (and also have eyes of black and white enabling them to see by night as well as day, according to Isidore).[5] The same book says that Albanie is a very cold region compared with the rest of Asia, and extends northwards from the Caspian Sea in the East along the Ocean[6] as far as the Sea of Azov,[7] and that many parts of the land were uninhabitable and full of fearsome creatures that proved quite a challenge to Alexander.

The dogs of that country in particular are greater, stronger and fiercer than any found in any land – the history says they would kill a bull, a lion or an elephant – and Alexander was often sorely tested by them. But he finally over-

---

[1]   See *Perceforest*, tr. Bryant, p.122, where the 'Forest Carbonniere' is referred to as the 'Selve Carbonneuse'.

[2]   '*Hasebain*' (from the Latin '*Hesbania*' used in many medieval documents). Hesbaye (or Hasbain) was part of the land centred on the city of Liège.

[3]   *Liber de proprietatibus rerum*, an encyclopaedic work covering all the sciences then known, written in the 1240s by the Franciscan monk Bartholomew the Englishman.

[4]   i.e. the Latin '*alba*'.

[5]   '*Ydore et Ysodore*'. The encyclopaedic histories of Isidore, Archbishop of Seville (c.560-636), were hugely influential throughout the Middle Ages and into the Renaissance.

[6]   i.e. the Ocean supposed by Ptolemy to encircle the earth.

[7]   '*Palus Martides*'.

came them by his cleverness: in the last battle fought against Alexander by the men of Albanie they brought these dogs with them, intending to launch them in a howling assault upon the Greeks as soon as they drew near and the Greek archers, as usual, began to loose volleys at the enemy bowmen and slingers; but Alexander, who'd been informed of their plan, had assembled a massive herd of pigs, and when the battle-lines were drawn and the horns and trumpets started blaring and the men of Albanie loosed their dogs, Alexander sent this herd of pigs straight across their path, and the dogs instantly chased the pigs and started savaging and devouring them. So the men of Albanie were outwitted; and the Greeks, who'd all been involved in the ruse, fell upon them with such force that the men of Albanie were overwhelmed in moments and started fleeing in a panic – spurs were of more use to them then than swords! Their defeat and their losses were so great that they surrendered themselves and their whole land to Alexander and accepted him as their lord. Alexander took immediate control of the country, sending embassies to all parts to secure oaths of fealty and homage – as is still customarily done in such cases, as you know. And a dog was presented to him then, a dog so huge and forbidding that in a single bout right there before him it killed a lion, a boar and an elephant: so says Isidore[1] in the eighth chapter of his book.

After these deeds and conquests Alexander advanced across the country to explore the islands in the Ocean to the West; and in short, he conquered so far and wide that he became lord of every western land including Britain, which we call England, Albanie, which we call Scotland, and (according to Orosius)[2] Hibernia, Denmark and many more.

CHAPTER III

How, according to written sources, the lands of Artois, Hainault, Flanders, Brabant and a number of others were given by King Alexander to Lyriope.

These lands were boldly, mightily, valiantly conquered by the noble King Alexander: so declares the historian Orosius in his history of the Scots (whom he calls – let us assume he is correct – the men of Albanie). In his account he says that Alexander, king of Macedon, having brought almost the whole world under his rule and dominion, had divided Britain between his knights[3] and others as he chose – ladies and damsels and all manner of people, to each according to his or her quality and worth; his many great, rich gifts included kingdoms, duchies,

---

[1]   See note 5, above, p.180.
[2]   Paulus Orosius, the fifth-century historian and theologian, author of *Historiarum adversus paganos libri VII* ('*Seven Books of History against the Pagans*'). But there may again be a confusion between 'Orosius' and 'Cresus', supposed chronicler of the adventures recounted in the romance of *Perceforest*.
[3]   In *Perceforest* he most importantly divides Britain between two characters taken from the *Alexander* romances: Betis and Gadifer. Betis (who comes to be known as Perceforest) is crowned king of England and Gadifer king of Scotland. See *Perceforest*, tr. Bryant, pp.37-40, 126.

counties, cities, castles, towns and fortresses. And then, just as he had organised his affairs and was ready to return to the East (where his true intent lay for
the reasons already made plain), a most noble virgin maiden, a damsel of royal
blood, appeared before him. Her name was Lyriope, and she had shared in no
part of the splendid, generous gifts bestowed by Alexander. She threw herself on
her knees before the king and with all possible humility begged him to extend
his grace to her – a noble damsel impoverished by the ravages suffered by her
next of kin in war against other foreigners – by granting her whatever land or
estates he chose. Alexander was moved to pity as he looked at this lovely virgin
girl, and asked his princes if he'd yet assigned all the lands he'd conquered. One
of them replied:

'Most excellent and mighty prince, beyond the sea, on the edge of Gaul, lies a
fair, fertile, prosperous land peopled by fierce and valiant knights, courageous,
bold and strong, and adorned with many fine, rich, strong cities and towns and
castles and abundant resources. The land is called the Forest Carbonniere, and
you've not yet ventured there. Most noble and esteemed prince, if you could
bring it under your subjection and it pleased you to give the land to the fair maid
Lyriope, it would be most profitably bestowed and you would have bequeathed
her a splendid, mighty domain.'

Hearing this, Alexander, in the presence of all the lords assembled there,
granted the whole of the Forest Carbonniere to Lyriope;[1] and he called upon
them all to join forces and assist her by conquering the land and installing her
securely there. They agreed, and made fitting and faithful vows to do so.

CHAPTER IV

*How Taron de Pierregort came to these lands for love of the fair Lyriope, to carry
out Alexander's command.*

After these solemn vows had been made the noble King Alexander departed,
leaving a number of his Greek knights to deal with the matter. Soon afterwards all the lords of those parts met on an appointed day to discuss the best
way to proceed. In the middle of their ruminations about how to fulfil their oath
to Alexander on behalf of the fair maid Lyriope, a most noble baron by the name
of Taron de Pierregort rose and, inspired by the deep love he felt for the girl and
out of respect for the noble King Alexander and to answer his bidding (and to
fulfil the oath he had sworn with the others), he vowed before them all that with
his own strength and might he would subjugate the whole of the Forest Carbonniere and swiftly and securely bring it under the maid's authority and into her
possession, if the gods granted that he live that long.[2]

---

[1]   Wauquelin took his account of the granting of the 'Forest Carbonniere' to Lyriope from
       Jacques de Guise's *Chronicles of Hainault* (see note 4, above, p.179); Jacques de Guise in
       turn had taken the story from the romance of *Perceforest*. See *Perceforest*, tr. Bryant, p.122.
[2]   See *Perceforest*, tr. Bryant, p.152, where the love-struck knight's name appears as Tor de
       Pedrac. All of the story that follows derives ultimately from this romance: *op. cit.*, pp. 156-
       61, 172-7.

Without further ado he left the company and started mustering all the troops he could. He had soon raised a great and impressive army, which he entrusted to a squire of his named Tholomeum. As commander of Taron's expedition, this able and resourceful man swiftly organised a fleet and saw to the boarding of the troops, not forgetting all the necessary gear and provisions; and as soon as all was ready they put to sea and the wind filled their sails and carried the fleet safely to port in the land of Neustrie, which we now call Normandy. They docked and began to make their way ashore, where they rested first for a little while.

CHAPTER V

How they besieged and captured the castle of Famars near Valenciennes.

But it wasn't long before they took to the field, sending raiding parties out across the land to take towns and forts and castles. Through the land of Picardy they advanced, bringing it entirely under their control, until they came before the Belgian city which we now call Bavay in Hainault. They mounted a fierce assault; but the author of the history doesn't mention whether they took it or not, saying only that they finally came to lay siege to the city of Famars, where they were stuck for six years before they managed to take it. The history tells that in that time there were many tough battles with much slaughter and fierce attacks by both sides; but in the end the king of Famars, leading a sortie against his foes, committed himself too rashly, and instead of defeating his enemies as he'd planned he was wretchedly slain along with most of his troops. With their king now dead the townspeople began to sue for peace, and finally, half by negotiation and half by force, they surrendered their city and all they possessed to the lordship of King Alexander. According to the history, the treaty involved the marriage of King Famars's daughter, named Clarmondine, to a noble lord named Carados, a close kinsman of Taron, prince of Pierregort; and with this marriage to confirm the treaty the whole land submitted to the maiden Lyriope, with control and government of the Forest Carbonniere being entrusted to Carados on Lyriope's behalf.

Their mission complete, the Britons and men of Albanie left the land with all their forces and returned in triumph to Scotland, from where they'd set out; and there they found Lyriope and told her of all their deeds and conquests in her name. She was overjoyed – with good reason! – and thanked them deeply and promised to reward them handsomely in due time and place.

CHAPTER VI

How the maiden Lyriope came to take possession of these lands.

We've discovered in our sources that during the siege of Famars the castle of Kievrain[1] was built by the aforementioned Carados.

---

[1]   Quiévrain, in Hainault.

So, then: the maiden Lyriope began to make her preparations, assembling a fleet to cross the sea when the gods were willing. Then she married Taron in a grand and glorious wedding of great solemnity and festivity. And after the rites and celebrations Lyriope and her husband the count of Pierregort put to sea, escorted by many eminent, noble barons from Albanie and Britain and a great company of men-at-arms; and they all made their way over land and sea until they reached the Forest Carbonniere where they were received with great joy, triumph and honour, all the cities, towns and castles opening their gates in welcome as obedient subjects. All the lords and knights and squires and ladies and damsels likewise accepted her as their lord with all possible joy and honour, holding their lands and possessions as her vassals, and acknowledging Count Taron as their king and lord and Lyriope as their lady and their queen.

Taron and Lyriope faced no hindrance or rebellion at all; they took peaceful, joyous possession of the gift bestowed upon the virgin damsel Lyriope by the noble and mighty King Alexander: all the territories, that is, that constitute the Forest Carbonniere. The History of the Belgians[1] says that the king reigning there at that time had been Leo, the second of that name, following Duke Justinus.

Let that suffice for now: our purpose was to show how Alexander was lord of the said lands and countries. We shall now return to our main theme, and tell first how Alexander made his way back to India where, as you'll soon hear, he engaged in many fierce and terrible battles against King Porus.

CHAPTER VII

How Alexander trapped a dreadful people called Gog and Magog between two mountains because they devoured all manner of flesh, human and other.

At this time there lived in a land to the East a people of hideous appearance and inclined to all manner of foulness: they ate every kind of meat including the flesh of dead humans. Word of them spread throughout the world; and when Alexander heard about these evil people he resolved to rid the land of them if he could.

So after his conquests of the Western lands he set out with his whole army and made his way to the land of Yraine, which he swiftly subdued, and then to Arcanie;[2] here he faced many stern battles but vanquished the people nonetheless, routing them on the field of battle. Next he confronted the Armis,[3] defeating and subjugating them likewise; and then he entered the land where these evil people lived.

As soon as he arrived and witnessed their foul practices, he feared that if they spread to other lands the world might be corrupted and befouled by their wick-

---

[1]   i.e. the Chronicles of Hainault: see note 4, above, p.179.
[2]   'Hyrcania' in the *Historia de Preliis*.
[3]   This is Wauquelin's transcription of '*Hermis*' in the Prose *Alexander*. At the same point the *Historia de Preliis* is referring to the Scythians.

ed example; so he swiftly herded them together, men, women and children alike, and drove them from this eastern land where they dwelt and into the north, to a place between two great mountains. When they reached there the good King Alexander, so full of all fine qualities, prayed to the almighty and immortal God that by His gracious mercy he would move the two mountains together – one was called Promunturium and the other Mount Boreum.[1] And God, seeing his intention was good, forced these two mountains so close together that the space between was only twelve feet wide; and Alexander had the gap sealed by mighty, looming iron gates covered with a kind of earth[2] that was proof against fire and impenetrable by iron or water, and from that day forth none of those people ever escaped and no one ever went in. According to some scriptures they will never be released until the Antichrist comes at the end of the world.

Alexander now set out with his whole army and made his way to the Caspian Gates.[3] Here he made camp, for it was a fair, fertile, abundant land, and he wisely ordered his men to gather all the supplies they would need, for he meant to march across deserts and into India – as indeed he did.

CHAPTER VIII

How Alexander's knights began complaining about the trials he was making them suffer.

Knowing, then, that the land of India was very wild and dangerous, Alexander ordered his troops to provision themselves as well as possible; then he began the march.

He passed into a vast desert where the sun was so blazing hot that whenever the Greeks filled a vessel with water it would almost instantly start to boil as if over a roaring fire. And as they crossed this land with its high, forbidding mountains, Alexander and his whole army were so beset by fatigue and exhaustion that they were nearly spent – indeed, a good number collapsed and died, to Alexander's grief. Much moaning and muttering now began, and not without reason – especially among the lords of the army, as they spoke together, saying:

'We've conquered so many lands and nations and brought them under our dominion – they should have been enough! And we're forgetting the sweetness of our homeland! Instead we go marching off to conquer India, where only wild beasts dwell! Why?' They were all thinking: 'If our lord Alexander is obsessed with fighting and subjugating lands and peoples to earn himself praise and glory, let him carry on and we'll go home! He's brought a great host of Persians with him – he can take them with him wherever he likes! We've supported and

---

[1]   These are the names as they appear in the *Historia de Preliis*. Wauquelin transcribes them as '*Promontoire*' and '*Boris*'.

[2]   The Prose *Alexander*, Wauquelin's source, struggles at this point to translate the '*asinthicum*' referred to in the *Historia de Preliis*.

[3]   Wauquelin follows the Prose *Alexander*'s '*Portes de Campis*', a transcription of '*Portas Caspias*' in the *Historia de Preliis*.

served him for a long while now: it's time for us to rest and let others help him complete his mission!'

These words and thoughts, or very like, immediately found their way to Alexander; and as soon as he heard what was in the wind he called a halt to the march and ordered all the Greeks and Macedonians to assemble to one side away from the Persians. Then he mounted a scaffold and addressed the Greeks more or less like this:

CHAPTER IX
How Alexander made his knights aware of their failings.

'Dear friends, sharers in prosperity and adversity, my fine and valiant knights of Macedon and Greece! You know these Persians have hitherto been our foes; and now, when your mighty prowess and valour have won us their submission and total obedience and you're near the end of your labours and the beginning of rest, you want to return home to your own domains and leave me here in a strange land with my former enemies! It seems you've soon forgotten the letters King Darius sent us, which so offended and enraged you all that I was hard pressed to control and calm you! Oh my! Don't you remember how when we met them on the battlefield I was always at the very front, the first to charge our enemies? And didn't I go alone to talk to Darius, the mighty emperor, risking my life to save yours? You seem to have forgotten all this! There's only one explanation, I'd say: your vows were made under duress, unwillingly, which can only ever end in grief! If that's the case and you mean to leave me, then I say to all who wish to go: take your belongings and be off, and may God keep you. I'll carry on without them to face my enemies – all alone if need be – with God's help, which has been with me hitherto and on which I've pinned all my hopes. And with the help of my good God in whom I've placed all my faith I shall vanquish and subdue them all! And I hope that as you head home without me and pass through enemy lands, you'll realise how an army fares without the guidance and direction of its leader.'

With that he fell silent. And all the Greek and Macedonian princes were so mortified, so overcome by shame at his words, that they cried aloud:

'Great, revered emperor, forgive our weak and wicked thoughts! Henceforth, truly, we place our lives in your hands: go where you will – we'll follow you until death! And with God's help we'll join you in conquering all your foes and winning their obedience to you!'

Then the supremely clever Alexander humbly and graciously thanked them.

With the matter thus settled, he ordered his army onward. And he made his way out of the desert and into the land of Philadelfie;[1] according to the history

---

[1]   '*Indiam Phasiacen*' in the *Historia de Preliis*. This is the region bordering on Colchis, in the southern part of the Caucasus; it was seen in the ancient world as the frontier between Europe and Asia.

it was now about the end of June. There he encamped to give his army time for rest and recovery, for there were few indeed who didn't need it.

CHAPTER X

How Porus sent a letter to Alexander, very hostile.

The arrival of Alexander and his army was instantly reported to King Porus by the people of the land. As soon as he received the news he had a letter written and sent to Alexander which read as follows:

'Porus, king of India, bids the thief Alexander, who wins kingdoms, lands and cities by robbery, not by chivalry, explain what a mortal man such as he can do against a people whose nobility is acknowledged by the gods? Just because you've vanquished men of scant and womanly strength, perhaps even deserving of punishment on account of their wretched failings, does your proud heart lead you to suppose you'll be endlessly victorious over all men? What overweening arrogance! Let me tell you: not only men but gods, too, bow before our empire! Don't you know that Dionysus Bacchus, deemed the father of all the gods, came to India to conquer her but returned in shame, unable to resist the Indians' might?[1] And I know for a fact that before Xerxes was king of Persia the Macedonians paid tribute to the kings of India – until they thought it was hardly worth their while and wouldn't deign to take it! After all, noble men prefer the fine, the great and grand rather than the paltry! So before your pride deludes you into this foolish enterprise, we advise – no, we command you absolutely – to go back to the land you came from and cease to set your outrageous sights on places where you know you've no authority and no cause whatever to claim it. Consider this very carefully, or your crazed ambition may lead you to repent too late!'

In such terms, or very like, was the letter couched. As soon as it was delivered by Porus's envoys it was opened and read in the presence of Alexander and all his knights; and when the knights heard the contents they were so enraged that they looked as if they were about to breathe fire and flame! Had it not been for Alexander they would have killed the messengers on the spot out of contempt for Porus and all who supported him. They thought how short his memory was of the entertainment and honour he'd received from Alexander. But Alexander, to pacify and cheer them, said:

'Oh, dear friends and companions! Don't be upset or angry at King Porus's haughty letter: remember how Darius's pr1ide and presumption drove him to write so offensively. I tell you, all barbarians are the same! They're like the bears and tigers and the other wild, unreasoning beasts that dwell among them – animals so sure of their own strength that even the weak with a bit of wit can hunt them down and kill them! So you've no need to worry: you often find the dog who barks the loudest has no bite!'

---

[1]   A reference to the ancient tradition that Dionysus's conquest of Asia ended at India.

So saying, he ordered that the messengers be supplied with their every need and presented them with rich and handsome gifts. Then he dictated a letter; and once it was written he gave it to the aforesaid messengers and bade them deliver it to their king Porus on his behalf. The contents were as follows:

CHAPTER XI

The contents of Alexander's letter to Porus.

'To Porus, king of India, from Alexander, commander of the Greeks, son of King Philip of Macedon and Queen Olympias, health and happiness. We have received and listened carefully to your letter, and this is our response: firstly, regarding your assertion that we win kingdoms, lands and cities through robbery rather than chivalry, we assure you we conquer and win them by chivalry in the open field. In any case, even if we did acquire them in the manner you suggest there'd be no reason to reproach us, for we challenge our enemies quite properly and adequately, and you surely agree that a man who's received a formal challenge has no right to pity if he loses. As for your comment that we've triumphed over feeble, womanly people, you're quite right! And our successes thus far have given us the appetite to carry on and complete our mission – especially against you, for we know you've witnessed our capacity and courage at first hand!

'On another point: you say there's nothing worth having in the land of Macedon while India abounds in riches; that's precisely why we, who have so little in our lands, wish with all our hearts to do battle with you and conquer your fine country, which we so badly need! You also say that men are bound to prefer the splendid to the paltry: that's why we, such paltry, petty folk in comparison to your greatness, wish to do battle with you to assume your glorious state – not, however, that we wish the gods to bow to us as you say they bow to you: no man should claim lordship over the one who made us. So we wish you to know that we're coming to do battle with you – and we won't be fighting a god, but a man stuffed full of vanity. And when sky, air, earth and water and all that exists within them cannot survive God's wrath for a single hour, how do you imagine we mortals can? That's why we assure you that your extravagant and senseless words don't daunt us in the least, but inspire and harden our resolve to achieve our goal. We trust this reply is clear enough.'

The messengers immediately took their leave of Alexander and his barons and set off; they made their way swiftly to King Porus and delivered the letter, which he bade be read at once. When the reading was complete he was beside himself with rage; without a moment's delay he ordered ten thousand of his finest men to arm, and sent them to do what they could to slow Alexander's advance and to stop the enemy's raids and foraging, while he assembled all his forces – men-at-arms, elephants and all the rest.

Chapter XII
How Porus married his daughter to the son of Queen Candace, named Carador.

So, then, realising Alexander's fierce resolve, King Porus began to make his preparations to resist him if he could. Our history says he had a beautiful daughter (it doesn't say whether she was the child of the lady Phesonnas of whom we spoke when telling of the vows of the peacock, though it does say that by this time the lady had passed from this world); and Porus, not wanting his daughter to fall into the hands of Alexander or his men, sent her to be looked after by Queen Candace. The girl then fell in love with one of Candace's sons by the name of Carador; it led to them marrying with the consent of both parties, their union being marked by lavish rites and celebrations.

But to return to the point: in less than twelve days Porus, having summoned his forces from far and wide, had amassed four hundred and fifty thousand men-at-arms, along with eighty chariots armed exactly like King Darius's in the battles we described before. And Porus had an even more awesome weapon in the shape of four hundred elephants: they carried wooden towers on their backs, with thirty men-at-arms in each tower equipped with all manner of bows and slings and missiles. Porus, indeed, was able to deploy these various forces in so many squadrons that, as all the histories agree, when battle was joined it lasted twenty consecutive days.

It was the most awesome, dreadful battle ever seen. Our sources say that on the first day the Garamantes were routed, on the second day the Salaties, on the third the king of Valbrune, on the fourth a king named Madeus des Desiers, on the fifth Moab, a Phrygian king, on the sixth Aumadab de Pois and so many more whose names I've not discovered that it would be amazing to relate. After the successive defeats of all these forces, Porus ordered the rest of his mighty host to advance on Alexander, who had already drawn very near, so that the two armies could clearly see each other's clouds of dust and steam. Then both sides halted for rest and refreshment; and King Alexander, so diligent and attentive to his men, mounted Bucephalus and rode among his troops to hearten and exhort them all as winningly as could be. He'd also sent spies into the Indian camp to find out what they could; they were already back with precise details of their forces – and especially of the elephants, whose custom in battle was to crush and throttle men and swallow them whole in their bellies. He clearly needed to think of a way of dealing with these beasts.

Chapter XIII
How Alexander had men of brass built and filled with fire to deal with the elephants.

As soon as Alexander heard what these elephants were like he summoned a band of master craftsmen. He bade them forge and fashion, swiftly and without delay, two or three hundred brass statues in the forms of men, hollow inside. This was done at once. Then he had these figures filled with red-hot coals and ingeniously mounted on wheels and positioned in front of his army, guessing that Porus would have his elephants make the first charge and that they'd be bent on throttling and swallowing his men.

It turned out exactly as he thought; for when all the battalions on both sides were assembled – with the Medes and Persians at the front of Alexander's – the elephants were first to come storming forward, with towers on their backs just as you've heard. To the sound of trumpets the battle began with hails of missiles, and the elephants, stung by the barbs of the archers before them, came charging down and whipped up the fire-filled brass men with the trunks they have as mouths and thrust them in their maws and swallowed them whole; and convulsed by the heat now roaring in their bellies they plunged to the ground, breaking necks and arms and legs of the men they carried. No one could describe the hideous, fearful chaos they created; indeed, the elephants did more damage to their own side than they did to the Medes and Persians. Porus was aghast and baffled: he couldn't understand what had caused this great convulsion in the beasts.

With the elephant squadrons wretchedly undone the armed chariots charged next; but they met with such a reception that hardly a single one escaped: they were engulfed in Greek fire launched by Alexander's men.

The history now insists that in every passage of the battle that followed Alexander was at the forefront; many times the Medes and Persians would have broken had it not been for his courage and daring, for the Indians were so vast in number and launched so many different attacks that a full account would take an age: as we've already said, the history assures us that the battle lasted twenty consecutive days. Each day as night fell the armies withdrew to their tents and declared a truce till morning when they returned to the fray.

CHAPTER XIV

How according to the history Alexander defeated Porus and captured his city.

You may well suppose that in a battle so fierce and long there was an appalling loss of life on both sides, and that many brave and mighty men-at-arms must have fallen; and so it was indeed. But in the end, through Alexander's awesome resolve and valour, the battle turned against the Indians and they began to flee in countless numbers, some the way they'd come and others whichever way they could. When Porus saw disaster looming he decided that staying could be fatal, and he turned and fled from the battle, riding into a dense forest to take refuge and make his escape with some of his barons. But Alexander wouldn't let his men give chase: he wanted them to rest instead – for as he said, it was high time. So he made camp there on the field, and in that very spot gave thanks and praise to God for the glorious victory He'd granted him by His mercy. This sacrifice made, he had a number of great barons who'd died in the battle, Greeks and Indians alike, buried with great honour; likewise all the rest, each according to his rank and as he guessed had been their worth.

Then he headed to the city and ordered an assault, and swiftly took it by force of arms. The fact is that the citizens didn't know what had become of their king, so they soon decided it was best to surrender the city or let it be taken.

As soon as the city fell, Alexander rode straight to King Porus's palace. There he found riches on a wondrous scale. Their description strains credulity: the history says the palace housed four hundred pillars of fine gold, between which hung a vine, of gold likewise – leaves, branches and roots alike were all of purest gold, enamelled in fitting colours; and the vine bore great, fat bunches of grapes: some were made of crystal but others were pearls as big as a man's thumb, and others were emeralds and others fine sapphires. The palace walls, too, were laminated in gold and adorned with pearls, carbuncles, emeralds and amethysts, astonishing to behold. And that's not all: there was another palace, the Queen's Palace, built entirely of ivory, with a chamber lined with cypress and cedar and closets of brazil wood. Opposite this palace stood tall and mighty golden statues supporting a tree of many branches, and on every branch were all manner of birds, each one made of purest gold and painted according to its nature, but with crystal feet and beaks and claws and richly adorned with scatterings of pearls and precious stones; and they'd been made by magic so that, when King Porus wished, he could make them sing together, each in its own song. And in this palace Alexander found so many vessels of gold and silver, so much crystal, so many jewels, that no one who hadn't seen it would believe it.

Our history in conclusion says that he found such abundant wealth in the city that when he'd given his army – his knights and his men, each according to his rank – a share so generous that all were more than satisfied, there remained so much that he couldn't believe any king in the world had riches as great as he. And that was just what was left after he'd given his knights their portion.

Chapter XV
How Alexander sent knights to the queen of the Amazons.

After all this sharing of spoils King Alexander commanded two of his barons, Ptholomer and Philotas, to take ten thousand troops and go and reconnoitre the surrounding cities and find out if they were inclined to surrender or meant to resist his majesty; those that intended to rebel they were to attack and destroy utterly.

But in the event the two barons found no resistance in any city, fort or castle; everywhere they went the people surrendered to Alexander and placed themselves and their possessions under his dominion and lordship. And they, valiant knights that they were, in the manner of all good masters showed them kindness and favour and accepted them in love and peace; and indeed the people gave them such a noble welcome, showing them all possible goodwill, that they had no cause or reason to do otherwise.

With all this settled, Alexander, seeing the land's obedience was secure, decided to send messengers to the realm of the Amazons, which wasn't far from there. He dictated a letter and entrusted it to his envoys, insisting that they shouldn't stop till they reached the Amazons.

They followed his instructions and made their way to the Amazon queen Calistrida and presented his letter to her. She accepted it and had it read, and found it contained the following or very like:

'From Alexander, commander of the Greeks, son of King Philip and Queen Olympias, to the most noble queen of the Amazons, health and happiness. We wish you to know that with the help of power divine and through the efforts and the courage of our men we have brought the kingdom of Persia under our dominion, and part of India likewise; so we bid you, as soon as you receive this message, send us tribute and acknowledge that you hold your land as our vassal. If you fail to do so, be assured that we shall come against you in such force that we shall win your land's subjection to your detriment and harm.'

CHAPTER XVI

The queen of the Amazons' letter to Alexander.

When the queen of the Amazons heard the letter's content she was rather troubled, and immediately summoned her full council – a council consisting solely of ladies and damsels, all of them maidens of great valour, wisdom and fine breeding. She informed them of the letter, and they decided to return a letter of their own to Alexander, which read as follows:

'Greetings and good wishes to the victorious and mighty prince Alexander of Macedon, king of kings and lord of lords, from Calistrida, queen of the Amazons, who surpass all people in the world in strength, valour, courage and all chivalrous qualities. We wish to enlighten your victorious majesty about the state and nature of our realm, so that you are better informed before you proceed with your apparent plan.

'Know, then, that we dwell on an island surrounded by a river which has no beginning and no end, with just a narrow entrance on one side by which we can ride out to the mountains that lie before you. We are women, fully eight hundred thousand in number, and have never shared the company of men, and no men have ever dwelt here – only on the other side of the river. This state of affairs began when a former king of our land took all the men of our realm to war against another king, and he and all our men were slaughtered. When we women heard that our men and lords were slain we decreed that no man would ever enter our land, and this ruling is now so long established that all memory of the former state is lost. But you should know that when we celebrate the feast of Jupiter we cross the river and spend thirty days with the men; then we return to our land, and if any of us are pregnant and the child proves to be a son, the mother nurses him for seven years and then sends him to the father, and if it be a daughter she stays here with her mother all her life.

'And because we are often at war with our neighbours and many others, we cut off our left breasts so that we can better bear our shields when we are armed; that's why people call us Amazons, meaning women with one breast. And when we go to war we choose five hundred thousand[1] armed cavalry and the rest we leave here to guard the island. Then we leave our land and ride into the mountains because of the protection and defence they give. Those men of ours – the men I mentioned earlier – follow us, and if we return victorious they worship us. If any of us dies in battle (or otherwise), her closest kinswoman inherits all she owns.

'In view of all this, we advise you not to engage us in battle: for even if you defeated us it would earn you no credit: people would say you had only beaten women; but if we succeeded in defeating you, the mightiest man in the world, what triumph and glory we would win! You would surely do better, we suggest, to refrain from war with us than risk such shame! But give us a prompt decision: you may be sure that if you choose to do battle, we will meet you in the mountains to fight you and all your might.'

As soon as this letter was written they gave it to Alexander's messengers and bade them deliver it to their king. And this they did, not stopping till they reached their lord and presented him with the letter.

CHAPTER XVII

How Alexander sent another letter in reply to the queen of the Amazons.

As soon as Alexander received the queen's letter he had it read in the presence of his knights; and when he heard the content he began to smile and asked some of his knights what they made of it. Each gave his own opinion; and at last the king, to whom most of the world was now subject, said it would be a cause of sore reproach if he failed to be obeyed by these women as he was by so many noble, strong, bold and powerful men – many by force but others willingly. So he dictated another letter to the queen and sent it by her messengers who delivered it to her on his behalf. She had it read at once, and this in essence is what it said:

'From Alexander, commander of the Greeks, son of King Philip and Queen Olympias, health and happiness to the noble queen of the Amazons and to all their allies. We have received and carefully considered your letter. Our reply to you is this: since by the will of God we have brought the three parts of the world under our dominion – that is, Europe, Africa and Asia – it would be shameful if we failed to do the same with you: it would stand as a disgrace for evermore. But it seems from your letter that you would settle matters between us peacefully rather than by war; so we advise you not to come into the mountains to confront us and risk losing your land and your lives, but cross the river if you will and come and meet us and speak with us. I promise and swear that neither I nor any of my men will inflict harm upon your persons or deprive you of anything you own; and whatever tribute you send us, be it of damsels or of horses, we shall re-

---

[1]   The MSS (and the source, the Prose *Alexander*) all read '*cent fois .C. m'* – 'a hundred times a hundred thousand'. This is a formidable number to say the least, and doesn't tally with their stated population: the likelihood is that '*cent*' was originally meant to read '*cinq*'.

ceive and treat with honour out of respect for you, with the clear understanding that they may leave our company at any time of their own choosing. Consider this and decide what you wish to do; and let us have your answer swiftly.'

Having read the letter the queen discussed it with the ladies present, and it was decided that they would send him gifts by way of tribute. She summoned two of her maidens and had them gorgeously attired; and once they were ready she bade them go to Alexander with a magnificent array of gifts entrusted to them.

CHAPTER XVIII

How the queen of the Amazons sent gifts to Alexander.

The two damsels soon reached Alexander's host, where their beauty and noble apparel attracted the admiring gaze of all. With great honour and reverence the lords of the army led them directly into the king's presence, and they greeted him on their queen's behalf and presented him with the gifts they'd brought. These gifts consisted of forty wild horses and thirty packhorses laden with silk and cloth of gold, and ten more laden with gold and silver. Alexander accepted them with fulsome thanks to the queen, and bade that the damsels be lodged and entertained with all honour so that they should have no cause for complaint. The Greeks saw to this; and the damsels rested till the first hour[1] next morning when they dressed in splendid, rich attire once more and came to present themselves again to Alexander at the palace. Then the elder, whose name was Flore, began to deliver her queen's message thus:

'Mighty emperor, we understand that, through the great prowess of your barons, knights and men-at-arms – and the vast support that you have earned by your generous nature and have always commanded with true acumen – you have brought every part of the world under your dominion except the land of the Amazons, ruled at present by my esteemed queen Calistrida. Aware of your intentions, she has consulted the good ladies of her realm, and their unanimous opinion is that they could have no greater honour than to forge an amicable alliance with such a worthy man as you. That is why my noble lady has sent us to you with her offer to hold her realm as your vassal as long as you live. To assure you of her sincerity, mighty emperor, she sends you now, and will send you every year, such a gift as a lady should send her knight – the ring from her own finger.'

So saying, the damsel took the ring from her purse and gave it to the king. He was ravished by the sight, and with good reason, for it was so exquisitely beautiful that no eye could tire of beholding it. And he happily replied:

'We thank your queen for her goodwill towards us, and accept her in love and companionship. As for the tribute she has sent us, we consider ourselves well paid; and if it be her gracious pleasure let her come to us and confirm the terms outlined by ourselves and her.'

---

[1]   *'prime'*: the first canonical hour of the day, around 6 a.m.

Chapter XIX

How the queen of the Amazons came to Alexander accompanied by a host of ladies and damsels.

Once the damsels had heard the king's response they took courteous leave and departed, the king appointing an escort to accompany them a fitting distance, and they rode on till they reached their land. They went straight to their queen and relayed the king's wishes, and when she realised he wanted her to go and meet him she prepared as grandly as possible.

Once all was to her satisfaction she set out with more than a thousand maidens and made her way to Alexander; and when the barons heard of their arrival they came to greet them with all possible courtesy and splendour and escorted them to the king. The moment their coming was announced he came down the palace steps to meet them and received them with the utmost honour, and led them up to the palace amid great joy, pomp and ceremony. The king and all the lords of his court were amazed beyond measure by the exceptional beauty, elegance and grace of the whole company of maidens, and their attire, too, was so gorgeously rich that they were truly a feast for the eyes. And if the knights were astonished by their beauty, elegance, bearing, dress and adornment, they were even more stunned by the way the queen and all the maidens rode with poise and skill and mastery on mighty horses handsome to behold: no man anywhere could have ridden – or galloped indeed – in more accomplished style.

Their arrival prompted a glorious and joyous feast, for the king had commanded that they be shown all possible honour. The festivities lasted for three full days, in the course of which you may be sure there was a good deal of amorous banter and sweet repartee between the knights and ladies; but we needn't give you details: anyone with experience of such matters knows exactly what tends to happen!

On the fourth day the queen came to the king and asked his leave to depart, promising that if he ever needed their aid and support she would send him a thousand cavalry – a thousand maidens on horseback – as part of the homage she owed him for her realm. Alexander thanked her deeply for her words and pledges and gave her abundant gifts of great worth and magnificence. With promises given and accepted by both sides the queen departed; the king escorted her out of the city before returning to his palace, and the queen made her way back to her country. But we shall leave these ladies now and return to King Porus of India.

Chapter XX

How Alexander set out in pursuit of Porus who had retreated into the desert.

At this point our history says that after the queen of the Amazons had gone, Alexander learned that Porus of India had fled with a large company into the Indian desert, where he was gathering all his forces to do battle with him again. So Alexander took forty knights of the region to act as guides in the desert, and set out with his whole army.

They marched on until, at the beginning of August, when the sun is extremely hot, they entered a sandy, barren land where they found the going very tough, especially with the blazing heat of the sun and the fact that they found no water. What they did find was a multitude of scorpions, snakes and other vile and venomous creatures; and because of their vicious, tormenting attacks they had to ride fully armed. Plagued by the heat, made all the worse by having to ride in armour, many were so tortured by thirst that they were driven to drink their own urine, and some even sucked on pieces of iron in an attempt to slake their dreadful thirst.

Amid this trial and tribulation the king and his army came upon the bank of a river. They followed it till they saw a little island in the middle; it was fortified by a castle – or at least, a kind of bulwark built of oaks – and surrounded by the river which was four stages wide, which is to say a quarter of a league. It was now about eight in the morning. As Alexander neared the fort and turned to look he saw it was filled with men, and ordered someone to ask them in the Indian tongue where they could find good water, for the water of the river was acrid, undrinkable. But when the men in the castle's barbican heard voices calling they all hid and made no reply, much to the puzzlement and annoyance of Alexander and his men. And seeing no bridge or plank to provide a crossing – and no sign of farming on the island to suggest how the men sustained themselves – he wondered what they lived on. He ordered a band of knights to swim over to the fort and find some answers.

CHAPTER XXI

How Alexander lost some of his knights to dragons, scorpions and hippopotami.

No sooner had Alexander issued the order than some forty knights stripped off and, sword in hand, dived in the river and began to swim towards the island. But when they were about a quarter of the way across, a herd of creatures called hippopotami came surging from the water and devoured them all except four who were slower than the rest; they saw the slaughter of their companions and swam back as quickly as they could. Alexander was shaken by the sight, but even more upset by the loss of his fine knights. He left the place at once, taking all his men with him.

On they marched until, about eleven o'clock, they came upon a great pool fully twenty-four stages long – that's to say a league and a half. The water looked clear, clean and undisturbed, so Alexander ordered his army to halt and take refreshment; but before they settled down to rest he bade them fell a large number of oaks and other trees that stood nearby and lay them all around their camp, and when it grew dark he ordered them to set them ablaze and to light more than three thousand lamps as well. Only when all was done did he give orders for supper to be prepared. They did as bidden and then sat down to eat. But as they took refreshment, a vast horde of scorpions started swarming up to the pool to drink as was their custom; and they were followed by other kinds of creatures: big, fat, hideous frogs; then huge and monstrous dragons of alarming colours – and these dragons or serpents had crests on their heads as sharp as razors, and uttered terrifying hisses as they came; and they belched forth such a toxic stench that Alexander's men could hardly bear it – in fact a good number choked to death, and the whole army thought their time had come. But there in their midst was Alexander with cheering words to give them heart:

'Oh, my valiant knights and companions! Don't despair: do the same as I!'

And so saying, he took a shield and a spear and boldly strode towards the hideous beasts and started fighting them with wondrous might. His knights, seeing his awesome courage, snatched up their weapons and ran to join him and slew a horde of the creatures with their lances; and many more of the beasts were consumed in the burning ring of trees, being so crazed with thirst that they were reckless of fire or lance or anything else. In the end Alexander and his men overcame them all and slew a huge number – though the history says it cost Alexander twenty knights and thirty foot soldiers.

But after this battle, just as the Greeks thought they'd be able to rest, up swarmed another horde of creatures with backs so hard that it was like striking an anvil: the knights couldn't cut through their hides, much to their rage and bewilderment; but so many of the creatures were burnt in the fire that the remainder were no great trouble to the men – as soon as they managed to reach the pool they plunged in and stayed there just as if they'd been fish.

CHAPTER XXII

How Alexander fought white lions the size of bulls, and then boars with teeth a cubit long, and wild men and women with six hands and a terrible beast with three horns.

When these hard-backed creatures – which they called 'cancers', or crabs – had been destroyed, the army thought they could rest at last; but about the fifth hour of the night a band of white lions came to drink at the pool, as fearsome and as huge as bulls, and they savagely attacked the men. All ranks leapt up to confront them and battle began; and the beasts were swiftly overcome as Alexander's men – and above all Alexander – thrust their lances clean through their bodies.

But no sooner had they dealt with these dread lions than a herd of terrifying wild boars appeared, with tusks jutting from their maws, exceedingly sharp and very long – a cubit[1] in length, the history says. And with these boars came wild men and women with six hands; and boars and men and women together came charging into the camp and started killing and maiming horses and cattle – and men-at-arms, too. The army recoiled before this terrifying onslaught of pigs and savage beings. But then Alexander, epitome of prowess that he was, cried out

---

[1]   A measurement based on the length of the arm to the elbow – i.e. roughly half a yard (50cms).

to his men and strode to the fore with his shield braced and, the history says, displayed such valour that his men found their courage once more; and these awesome monsters were defeated with countless numbers slain – though many men, too, were killed and innumerable wounded.

But straight after these two dreadful battles they were attacked by an appalling beast of astounding size, bigger, stronger and more daunting than an elephant, with a pitch-black head from the front of which jutted three horns as sharp as any sword; the Indians called it 'the toothed tyrant'.[1] It was coming to the pool to drink, but as soon as it saw the army it charged at them like a crazed thing and tossed and scattered the men-at-arms like seed, with broken legs and arms and necks, and some it threw dead to the ground. The havoc it wrought was astounding: the history says that before it was finished off it had killed twenty-seven men-at-arms and wounded fifty-two. But it was finally slain by that valiant knight Emenidus, duke of Arcadia, much to the joy of Alexander and all his men.

But no sooner had this beast been killed than there emerged through the sand from underground, right where the army was encamped, rodents bigger than foxes,[2] which feasted on carrion, human and animal alike; if they attacked any animals their bite would kill them instantly, though they did no harm to men. And with these creatures came bats the size of doves, with teeth that looked like human teeth, and they plagued the men by flapping and beating them in the face. And finally, as dawn approached, came a flock of birds as big as goshawks, red in colour with beaks and feet of black; they perched around the pool and started catching fish, but they didn't trouble Alexander's men.

CHAPTER XXIII

*How Alexander came out of the desert and advanced on King Porus
who was massing his forces for battle.*

As soon as the king saw day break he ordered all his forces to move on, and they kept marching till they were out of the desert. They entered a region known as the land of the Bactrians,[3] a fertile land of abundant wealth: gold,

---

[1]   The MSS read *'arine hayant le tirant'*, following the *'arine qui het le tirant'* in the Prose *Alexander*. This is a (perhaps understandably) strange transcription of the *'Odontetiranno'* that appears in the Latin *Historia de Preliis*. Along with many of the other Indian wonders we're about to encounter, it ultimately derives from *The Letter from Alexander to Aristotle about India*. This work, originally written in Greek and later absorbed into the Greek Alexander romance and later still translated into Latin, was very popular in the Middle Ages. Of the 'odontotyrannus' Richard Stoneman comments that it 'might be derived from the giant fanged worm of the Indus [called] the Monoceros; other candidates have included the mammoth, the kraken, the rhinoceros and the crocodile… It may be a description of a monster portrayed in Indian sculpture, of a type going back to at least the mid-fourth century BC.' Stoneman, *Alexander the Great, A Life in Legend* (Yale, 2008), pp.75-6.
[2]   I have taken the liberty of emending Wauquelin's text here. He curiously writes 'creatures which the Indians call foxes', an uncharacteristically poor rendering of the Prose *Alexander*'s 'mice bigger than foxes'.
[3]   *'Bastimens'*. Wauquelin has followed the Prose *Alexander*'s *'Bastiniens'*; the Latin of the *Historia de Preliis* reads *'in loca Bactrianorum'*.

silver and many other riches. When the people of the country learned of Alexander's coming they came to welcome him most amicably and he accepted their submission in like spirit. The history says they are a short people of little physical strength and their only occupation is the production of silk.

Alexander stayed there for twenty days to let his army rest and take on all the fresh supplies they needed. Once they were fully rested he smartly organised all ranks in their divisions and under their banners, the vanguard before and the rearguard behind, knowing as he did that Porus was quite nearby in a high state of readiness. With his battalions formed to his utmost ability, Alexander ordered them to advance; they did so, and with such bold purpose that they were soon within three miles of Porus's army, and the two sides could clearly see each other's clouds of dust and steam – and could hear each other, too, for truly, the din they created could be heard three Lombard leagues away.

Porus, king of India, was awestruck as he realised the extent of Alexander's courage: he'd followed him relentlessly over vast and fearful deserts; and he decided now, since some of his forces were still to arrive, to send a message to Alexander proposing a truce for twenty days. He dispatched his heralds at once; they followed his instructions and came before Alexander and told him on their king's behalf that if he was brave enough to bide there and wait for battle for twenty days they would supply him and his men with bread and meat and wine and everything else they needed, and guarantee safe conduct to visit whichever cities he pleased; and Porus would send him a thousand coursers[1] fully harnessed and five hundred packhorses, a quarter laden with silken cloth, a quarter with leopard and lion skins, a quarter with fine Arabian gold and a quarter with purest silver; he would also send two thousand maidens, two thousand moulted falcons and too many other gifts to name! Alexander replied that he would willingly agree to the truce, not because of these promised gifts but simply so that his men would have adequate provisions, which indeed was all he wanted; for he had so little fear of King Porus that he was quite happy to wait till he'd mustered all his forces.

'The more of them there are involved,' he said, 'the sooner we'll be rid of them!'

CHAPTER XXIV

How Alexander went in disguise to see King Porus,
to purchase food and other goods.

With the truce agreed and pledges exchanged, Alexander had a mind to go to Porus's city and pay him a visit. He promptly removed his royal garb and dressed in some clothes he found that looked like a poor workman's or a lowly trader's. Once he was happy with his disguise he picked up a sack and

---

[1]   The courser ('*coursier*') was a good class of horse, fast and strong, used both for warfare and hunting.

climbed on a mare and set off, and kept riding till he reached the city where Porus was residing, a city named in the history as Bactra.[1]

Just as Alexander arrived King Porus was on his way somewhere and was passing down a street and saw him, but didn't recognise him at all; and he sent for him, assuming him to be one of the suppliers or quartermasters from Alexander's army. Alexander was led before him; he bowed and paid his respects rather gauchely, playing the part of a simple man, and when Porus started plying him with questions he answered as best he could while maintaining his disguise. Among the questions was whether he knew King Alexander.

'Oh yes!' he replied. 'Very well! As well as any man alive! In fact he confides in me as much as any man at court: my line of business has brought me close to him for years – we've come to know each other intimately!'[2]

'Since you know him so well,' said Porus, 'kindly send him my regards and tell him from me that, if Fortune and the gods bring us face to face on the battlefield, I'll behead him with my sword like the false, thieving bastard that he is!'

Alexander, much offended by this insult, answered: 'Mighty emperor, no man benefits or enhances his honour by slighting and abusing his enemy. But if it please the gods I hope the two of you do meet as you say.'

With that they parted, and Alexander went into the city and bought wax and other goods and packed them on his mare and returned to his knights who were overjoyed to see him back. He told them all about King Porus and his words and how he'd threatened to his face to behead him if Fortune and the gods gave him strength.

CHAPTER XXV

How King Porus called Alexander from the field in their mighty second battle.

The knights began to laugh about this and pull his leg, claiming he was starting to shake with fear already; the banter continued for a fair time. But all the while Alexander, shrewd and prudent man that he was, was making thorough and meticulous plans, and continued to do so throughout the twenty days of truce. So indeed on the other side did Porus, both parties well aware that honour demanded they observe the day.

According to the history Porus had assembled so many men from far-off lands that they were near-impossible to number; and when the time came he boldly formed them into battalions and advanced to meet the Greeks, who responded not like children but like men of the utmost valour: they met the

---

[1]   'Bautre'. The 'history' in this instance, Wauquelin's source for this episode, is the verse *Roman d'Alexandre*, where the name appears as 'Bastre'.

[2]   Wauquelin has chosen to use this irony to create a comic touch, instead of following the verse romance's somewhat curious idea that the disguised Alexander tells Porus: '"[King Alexander's] body is cold and shrivelled with age and his health is poor... And he's lost so much blood from his numerous wounds that he won't live much longer..." Porus beamed with delight to hear that Alexander was old whereas he was so young...' (Branch III stanzas 93-4).

Indians with lance-heads and sword-blades with such ferocity that in this first charge so many were killed and felled that the living could hardly get at each other. And the history says that Porus and Alexander were the first of each side to clash, charging to meet one another with a force that shattered their lances into shards; then they gripped their swords and exchanged such blows that flames and sparks leapt from their swords and helms. If their knights hadn't charged to the rescue neither party would have left that place until one was dead and finished. But the knights and men-at-arms raced to support their respective lord in a storm of blows so mighty that the two kings were driven apart whether they liked it or not.

The battle proved how little love was lost between those armies: they were savaging each other pitilessly like feral beasts. The Greeks were afire, ablaze, hewing and pounding the Indians like carpenters hacking timber or blacksmiths hammering iron. But if the Greek assault was bold and brutal, the Indian defence was no less fierce: it can truly be said that the carnage and the slaughter were immense.

From dawn to noon they were locked together, with neither side gaining a clear advantage. Then Porus, a man of valour indeed, seeing his men – including Aminada, one of the greatest lords of his army – being slain on every side, fought his way towards Alexander, felling knights and horses as he went; and as soon as he saw him within earshot he cried to him:

'No emperor should have his people lose their lives in vain! If he's the cause of the loss he'd do better – and he'd earn more praise – to display his own strength. So if you're brave enough, let's prevent more deaths in this battle in which so many have already died: let's bid our men withdraw and meet in single combat, you and I, on condition that if you defeat me my people and my whole kingdom will be yours, and if I succeed in defeating you, your people and all your dominions will be mine.'

Porus was only saying this because of his disdain for Alexander's short stature; for he was a small man indeed, by all accounts only three cubits tall,[1] while he, Porus, was a knight of tall, strong, fine physique. But he clearly hadn't taken heed of the poetry of Cato and the line: '*Corporis exigui vires contempnere noli*';[2] Alexander might have been short, but his wisdom and ingenuity were peerless.

CHAPTER XXVI

How Alexander met Porus in single combat.

Hearing Porus's words Alexander, a man brimful of prowess, granted his request. And there and then, without a moment's delay, they called a halt to the battle and exchanged pledges to meet in single combat. Then they parted till next day, when the two kings were to meet and fight.

---

[1]   An exaggeration perhaps, but this is indeed the height given in the Prose *Alexander*, making Alexander little more than four and a half feet tall (less than 150cms).
[2]   'Never underestimate men of small physique'!

Morning came, and they armed as each thought best and went straight to the appointed place. But truly, when they arrived at the field and saw each other they were both filled with trepidation, knowing that one of them would be leaving there either dead or vanquished. But they knew they were there of their own volition, and that all their men had gathered in their honour and would have to give obedience to whichever man God gave victory; so they put all their fear behind them, gripped their shield-straps, levelled their lances and thrust in their spurs, and their horses, swift and strong, launched into a charge so fierce that the earth seemed to quake beneath their hooves. As they clashed King Porus delivered a blow to Alexander's shield that sent it flying from his neck across the field, while Alexander's lance-head found its target right on the chin-plate of Porus's helm, pitching him willy-nilly from his saddle and sending him tumbling to the ground. And as their horses met, Alexander's collided with Porus's and brought it crashing down on top of its master with its legs in the air, while Alexander galloped on past as far as his momentum took him. As he completed his charge and turned his horse about he saw Porus lying on the ground; he thought it would be shameful to attack him on horseback, and dismounted at once. Porus, now back on his feet, realised his helm had flown from his head as he fell, so he ran to pick it up and put it back on his head. While Porus was seeing to his helmet Alexander ran to recover his shield and slung it round his neck once more; then they drew their swords, razor-sharp, and with shields braced before them they came to meet each other. They proved they were two warriors of the highest calibre, exchanging such blows that no one who witnessed them could have denied they were valiant men indeed. They sent flaming sparks leaping from their blades and their armour – it was fearful to behold; and in this mighty, awesome combat Porus raised his sword and brought it crashing down so fearsomely on Alexander that, as he raised his shield to parry the blow, he smashed half of it clean away and sent it flying to the ground and dashed flowers[1] and jewels from his helmet; the weight of the blow drove Alexander to his knees. Porus thought that with that blow he'd won the day, and when the Greeks and Macedonians witnessed it they were beside themselves with horror and started wailing uncontrollably, while the Indians were ecstatic: the history says that when they saw Alexander fall the surrounding country rang with their cheering roars. Hearing all the clamour, Porus thought the watching troops had joined in battle and turned to look; and as he did so Alexander, now back on his feet with sword on high, brought it scything down through Porus's helm: neither helm nor mail hood could stop it cleaving through his head and scattering his brain across the field.

This is how Vincent le Jacopin[2] describes Porus's death in his history, and another historian named Guillaume[3] agrees. But the history we've been following in this part of our work – it's untitled, so we don't know the author's

[1]   i.e. enamel decorations.
[2]   See note 1, above, p.135.
[3]   See note 3, above, p.179.

name[1] – says that Porus wasn't killed then by Alexander but surrendered to him, and spent a long while riding with him across the deserts to the place where (as you'll hear in due course) Alexander spoke to the Trees of the Sun and the Moon. According to that untitled history, it was after this conversation with the trees that Porus, having heard that Alexander hadn't long to live, attacked him but was killed in the combat that followed.[2] I leave the matter to the reader's discretion; but in any event, all the histories agree that Alexander killed King Porus on the field of battle in single combat. Let us now return to our story.

Chapter XXVII

How the Indians wanted to attack Alexander to avenge their lord's death.

When the Indian barons saw their lord slain they began to lament and wail in bitterest anguish and said to each other:

'It would be better to die with our lord than live to see the destruction of our people and our lands!'

And like men deranged they thrust in their spurs, meaning to attack Alexander and avenge their lord. Seeing their wild charge Alexander, already remounted on Bucephalus, turned to face them and cried:

'Ah, lords of India! What are you thinking of? You know your lord brought his death upon himself through his own pride and folly, not through any advice of yours! You had no part in his decision, so you've no reason to share his punishment! Far from it: I wish you and all that is yours to be secure, unharmed, and if any of you wish to return home to your lands you may do so in total safety. And any who wish to join my company will be honoured by me and my men and will find themselves well pleased with their reward!'

When the Indians heard Alexander's courteous words they instantly threw down their arms and knelt before him and begged him to forgive their actions; he granted pardon most graciously, which earned their admiration and esteem – indeed they worshipped him as if he were a very god. The Macedonians now joined him, hailing their king with fulsome adulation; and he bade them pitch their tents there on the battlefield, with his own on the very spot where Porus had been killed, for he wished to make a sacrifice there to Our Lord in thanks for his great victory. They carried out his command at once, calling the troops to come and pitch all manner of tents and pavilions, great and small; and the king's own tent, the finest then to be found in all the world, they erected over Porus's body, which lay there stretched out still.

---

[1]   Wauquelin is referring again to the verse *Roman d'Alexandre*, though he is drawing on both that source and the Prose *Alexander* throughout this section of his work.

[2]   In Branch III stanza 235, where Alexander kills Porus and his horse together with an even more awesome blow that leaves him 'lying in the field cut in two halves'.

CHAPTER XXVIII

*How Alexander had King Porus buried with honour
and made a sacrifice to Our Lord.*

When all was ready the noble and valiant King Alexander set about making
a sacrifice to Our Lord as was his custom, in the course of which he saw
King Porus buried with all honour. And when the offering had been made to his
satisfaction and the burial was complete, he ordered an assembly of carpenters,
masons, labourers and all required materials, for out of respect and honour for
King Porus he wished to build a city in that place. This was duly done; and
our sources say that Alexander stayed there till the city was built and occupied.
When it was complete and he'd given it a name[1] he entrusted it to one of his
Macedonian lords named Ariscé.

Once all this had been settled Alexander, wishing to seek out and see all the
wonders in the deserts and forests and waters of India, ordered his men to assemble copious supplies of food and water and to prepare their arms and gear
meticulously. Any who found himself wanting was to come to him at once and
he would be given whatever he lacked. What preparations you would then have
seen, for those men knew they were going to face their greatest dangers yet!

When he could see that all was ready, Alexander strengthened his army by
enlisting many Indian lords to be their guides. Then they took to the road. Into
the desert they passed, and encountered first two[2] statues: the history doesn't
say of what material or metal they were made, only that they were twelve cubits
high and two cubits wide.[3] When Alexander saw them he gave orders that they
be pierced with holes; they were found to be hollow, and he had them packed
with fifteen hundred gold bezants[4] and the holes refilled, though I've not yet
discovered why he did this.[5]

Alexander now pressed on and came to a lofty mountain. To its heights had
fled a large band of people known as Confides: they numbered fully two thou-

[1]   The *Historia de Preliis* gives the name as Alexandria Yepiporum.
[2]   The text reads 'some', but see the inserted passage below from the verse *Roman d'Alexandre*.
[3]   i.e. roughly eighteen feet by three (six metres by one).
[4]   See note 2, above, p.138.
[5]   Wauquelin was at a loss because his source, the Prose *Alexander*, does not translate the
phrase in the *Historia de Preliis* which makes it clear that Alexander wanted to know
whether the statues were of solid gold or hollow. The origin of the episode is almost certainly *The Letter from Alexander to Aristotle about India* (see note 1, above, p.198), in which
Alexander comes across gold statues to Hercules and Dionysos at the eastern edge of
Porus's kingdom and, finding them to be hollow, stuffs them with more gold to appease
the gods. The verse *Roman d'Alexandre* interestingly replaces the statue of Hercules with
a statue of Arthur, and stresses Alexander's daring in going further than his predecessors: Alexander is told that '"when Arthur and Dionysos came to the East and had gone
as far as they could, they erected two statues of themselves in gold... No man alive has
gone beyond them. Make a sacrifice to them, King, to avoid their anger..." Hearing this,
Alexander laughed and replied: "The people of this land are cowardly fools to believe in
these idols and worship them... In the morning you'll all see me ride on beyond them."'
(Branch III stanza 141).

sand men-at-arms. When they saw Alexander advancing on them they came to meet him, determined to defend their mountain refuge, and launched such a hail of missiles that they brought down a good many Greeks. Then Alexander, man of boundless strength that he was, ordered all his troops to cover themselves with their shields, draw their swords and follow him up the mountain, and at the forefront of them all he clambered up to meet the foe. But the battle, fierce though it was, was short, for the Confides were few in number compared to the Greeks and were swiftly crushed.

CHAPTER XXIX

Here follow the great wonders found by Alexander in the deserts of India.

After conquering these men and their mountain refuge Alexander rode on, and he hadn't gone far before he came upon strange and massive stones which the people of those parts called the Bounds of Hercules. Determined to surpass Hercules's feats, Alexander resolved to go beyond these bounds and rode on past with his whole army.

There he found a people whom he subjugated with ease, for they were feeble and unarmed.

Then he entered the land of the Orasinis and the Dasques and overcame them likewise, for they were all but savages. And as he passed through the forests and the deserts where tribes called Aristiens, Cancestiens, Parsidiens and Gangratiens dwelt he brought them, too, under his dominion, and little wonder, for they were hunter-gatherers clad in animal-skins and tree-bark – that was their only armour; and their only offensive weapons were sticks torn from trees, and rocks and stones and the like.

Having conquered these various peoples Alexander left the wilds and entered a kingdom of vast expanse, boasting many fine cities. It was called Confite;[1] and when the people of the land learned of Alexander's coming they massed their forces and advanced to meet him with two hundred thousand men; but they were routed utterly and most of them were left slaughtered in the field. The reason they were so quickly vanquished was their inexperience in battle.

Having crushed them and captured all their cities Alexander marched on and came to the land of Parapomenos;[2] here too he swiftly won the submission of its people and their cities likewise: they surrendered without a blow being struck.

The king left this land and entered a region uninhabited by man or beast: it was bitterly cold and desolate, and so dark that the knights could barely see one another. They suffered and struggled through this waste for seven days; but on the eighth day, to their utmost joy, they left it and found themselves on the bank of a hot, hot river. On the opposite bank of this river, which teemed with huge and horrible snakes, were women of foul and ghastly appearance and attire; but

---

[1]   The Prose *Alexander* says that Alexander '*returned* to Confite', implying that this is the homeland of the 'Confides' mentioned at the end of the previous chapter.

[2]   This may be a corruption of 'Paropamisus', a name given in antiquity to the Hindu Kush.

in the eyes of Alexander's men they were beautiful, and they could see no men accompanying them. They seemed to be holding swords and axes made of gold and silver rather than of iron – and indeed, according to the people round about they had no iron in their land. Alexander wanted to cross the river and make contact but it was impossible, partly because of the water's heat but especially because of the huge and terrible snakes that swarmed there. Realising there was no way across, he left the women and rode on.

He came now to a place on the left-hand side of India, a wilderness of swamp and dense and lacerating thorn. As they crossed this waste there emerged from the swamp a monstrous creature which might be called a hippopotamus – it wasn't exactly a hippo but was similar in some respects, though it had a breast like a crocodile and long, pointed, razor-sharp teeth. At the moment when the Greeks caught sight of it this creature was crawling along like a slug; but when it saw the men it swept to the attack and killed two knights. There was no way of stabbing it with lance or sword, so tough was its hide, so they snatched up sticks and battered the beast to death.

Then they set off into the furthest forests of India, where they rested for a long while beside a river called the Beumar, having done nothing but trek and toil without a moment's rest for the best part of a month.

CHAPTER XXX

*How Alexander encountered herds of huge and terrible elephants
and hairy, horned women and many more.*

One day while they were resting there, just as they were seated at dinner, out of the forest came a great herd of elephants, heading for the river to drink as was their custom; and the moment they saw the Greek army and the hordes of men and horses they let out such a blasting cry that the army almost fled in terror. Alexander, sitting at the table and hearing the animals' awesome bellows and seeing his men in disarray, rose at once and leapt on Bucephalus and rode, sword in hand, to where his troops – even those closest to him – were stricken with panic, and cried to them:

'Oh, dear friends and companions! Valiant knights! Don't be alarmed by these creatures, despite their numbers: we'll deal with them as easily as we did the dogs of Albanie![1] Go and round up the army's pigs and beat them to make them squeal, and sound the trumpets and clarions, and let each man roar his battle-cry as loud as he can! That'll make them run, for sure! And follow me and do as I do.'

With his orders promptly carried out, the elephants heard the army's din and all turned tail and took to flight. Then Alexander and his knights gave chase and slew a good number, though others escaped; and when the slaughter was done Alexander had the dead beasts' tusks removed, for he'd never seen finer ivory.

[1]   Above, p.181.

As soon as he'd rested long enough Alexander took to the road again, and marched on till he entered a forest where he found great bands of women with horns, and beards down to their breasts, all dressed in animal skins. With them were dog-like beasts that these women bred and raised, training them to hunt the game on which they lived. But when they saw the horses and men-at-arms they plunged deeper into the forest. Seeing this, Alexander ordered a band of his knights to go after them; they did so, and caught three and brought them back to him. He had an interpreter ask them in the Indian tongue how they lived in those forests with no apparent homes; they replied that they roamed the forest and lived on game which they hunted with their dogs. The king let them go in peace.

He moved on and left the forest and found himself in a stretch of open country – pleasant enough, but uninhabited. They hadn't gone far before they found a river running through it. In the river were a number of big rocks, and scattered over them they saw a host of women who were naked but covered in hair. As Alexander – riding as ever at his army's head – drew near, these women, seeing this horde of men approach, all dived in the water and stayed there as if they were fish: they never reappeared as long as the army was there.

When Alexander realised they weren't going to show themselves he carried on along the river and found another tribe of women with amazingly long teeth and hair growing down to their heels. The rest of their body was covered in bristles rather like a camel's or a hedgehog's, and from their navel sprang a tail[1] like a cow's. And they were easily twelve feet tall. But these women, like the others, vanished into the water.

Alexander left the river and entered another forest. As he passed through he found more women, known in those parts as Janitres: they were of fabulous beauty, with gold-hued hair flowing down to their feet – feet in the form of horses' hooves. And they were about seven feet tall. When the Greeks and Macedonians caught sight of them they began to give chase, and captured a fair number and led them back to Alexander; he marvelled at their beauty, especially the way their hair parted and fell, so perfectly that it was gorgeous to behold. Alexander had questions posed in the Indian tongue, asking them all about themselves, and they replied:

'We never leave the forest and eat nothing but flowers – roses, for instance, and violets – and drink only the dew that falls upon them. And we're never too hot or too cold. And nothing takes away our beauty – neither growing old nor anything else.'

Alexander left them then, and passed out of the forest and into a fair and pleasant plain to give his army rest and refreshment.

---

[1]   The text reads *'cornes'* – 'horns'; this is surely an unintended misreading of *'coues'* in the Prose *Alexander* ('*caudam*' in the Latin *Historia*).

CHAPTER XXXI

How Alexander and his men were tormented by fire from the sky and storms and blizzards.

By the time they'd reached the open ground and pitched their tents Alexander saw that night was drawing in, and he ordered fires to be lit right round the camp to ward off attacks from wild beasts. Once this was done they sat down to eat and drink and take their ease.

But about eleven that night, after they'd eaten and were about to lie down and rest, a wind struck up, so mighty and so fearful that it blew down all their tents, and it was a sorry sight to behold as the men fought to hold them down by force and stop the gale sweeping them away. And it wasn't their only problem: the wind was whipping up coals and sparks from the fires and blasting them in their faces so violently that it was unbearable: they were wretchedly scorched and seared. Then a great murmuring arose and spread through the army as they said to each other, in the words of the Scripture:

'Merito hec patimur:[1] we're suffering this loss and torment with good reason! We, mere mortals, have entered the land of the gods against their will – we shouldn't have done this!'

Alexander heard their words and began to cheer them and give them heart, saying: 'Oh, valiant knights! Faithful companions! Don't be alarmed or afraid of this scourging wind! It's not a sign of God's wrath, I promise you: it comes from the clash of day's heat with night's cold.[2] It sometimes happens, and has happened now.'

And as Alexander spoke these heartening words the wind began to drop until it ceased to blow. Then the men gathered up their flattened tents and pavilions, and moved down into a valley where they set up camp afresh.

On the way Alexander found one of his knights lying on the path all shrivelled up, through cold and age and sickness. As soon as he saw him he dismounted and managed to lift him on to his horse's back, and then took him in his arms and carried him to his tent. There he laid him in his own bed, and took such good care of him that his body warmed again and recovered strength and vigour. And when he was restored to health, Alexander treated him to splendid gifts before giving him leave to rejoin his companions.

Once they were all encamped, Alexander sensed the air was turning cold, and gave orders for big fires to be lit all around the camp and outside every tent. And just as they were seeing to this, it began to snow so heavily that it seemed it would bury everything; Alexander, fearing the snow would get too deep, ordered everyone to start tramping it down and to bring in all the army's livestock to trample and crush it all the more. The fires they'd built helped a good deal, as the heat from the blaze made the snow melt in many places; but the cold of

[1]   'We are suffering this deservedly': Genesis 42:21.
[2]   Literally 'it comes from the inequality of the day and the night'.

the snow still caused the deaths of five hundred of the army, and Alexander had them buried there with much honour. The snow now began to thaw and disappear; but suddenly rain came down in torrents: it seemed the world would end in flood as the downpour turned all the fallen snow back to its original state. After the rain came clouds filled with fire and flame – they looked as if they'd set all the fields ablaze; and Alexander, seeing this, fell to his knees and prayed to Our Lord with the utmost devotion, imploring Him in His gracious mercy to bring an end to all this tumult; and no sooner had he uttered the prayer than the turmoil came to an end. Without a moment's delay Alexander ordered his men to decamp and leave that place.

They journeyed on till they came to a land called Oxidraces,[1] inhabited by a people devoid of pride who never engage in any conflict. They go about entirely naked and dwell only in mountain caves; their neighbours call them Gymnosophists,[2] which in our common tongue means 'people who go naked'. They have a king, but he is no more a master than the lowliest among them: all he has is the title. And when any news arrives in the land, they all gather around their king and jointly discuss what to do for the best.

CHAPTER XXXII

How the king of the Gymnosophists sent messengers to Alexander to explain the customs of their land.

When the king of this country heard of Alexander's approach he summoned some of his closest companions and entrusted them with a message for Alexander. They set off and arrived at the Greek camp entirely naked, making no attempt to hide their manhood. Into the king's presence they came and addressed him thus in the Indian tongue:

'From the mortal beings that are the Gymnosophists, to the man Alexander, greetings. We hear you have lately resolved to do battle with us to win our submission; we wish all here present to understand that you have nothing to gain thereby, for our custom is to gain through suffering, which we are committed to enduring until death. Since our suffering is voluntary, you can clearly see there'd be no honour in fighting us – and even less profit, for there's nothing to be won

---

[1]   Wauquelin writes 'Oridrascés'; I've adopted the spelling 'Oxidraces' from the *Historia de Preliis* to bring it closer to its derivation. Richard Stoneman tells how 'the author of the [Greek] *Alexander romance* writes…that, following the conquest of Porus, "Alexander took all the treasure from the royal palace and marched on the Brahmans, or Oxydorkai. These were not for the most part warriors, but philosophers who lived in huts or caves." Oxydorkai…is the Greek form of Khshudrakas, a warrior people of the Indus region who are mentioned in the *Mahabharata*.' Stoneman, *op. cit.*, p.93. It is interesting to note therefore that the Greek romance, the ultimate source of the French material, confused two historical episodes: Alexander's campaign against an Indian warrior people and his meeting with Indian ascetics.

[2]   'Nocefices'. The 'Gymnosophists' were an influential sect of Indian ascetics who lived naked, ate only fruit and vegetables and were devoted to all manner of self-denial and mortification of the flesh.

or taken from us: all we have is what Nature gives us, which none but Divine Providence can ever take away.'

They said no more. And when their words were interpreted for Alexander, he asked that it be made plain to them that he'd no wish to fight, only to pass peacefully through their land and observe their way of life. On hearing this they returned to their king who was delighted by the response.

Alexander now entered their land, and was amazed to see that they dwelt in caves and rocks; and the women stayed apart from the men, living with the animals. Then he asked them where they buried their dead, and they replied that they had no other sepulchres but the bodies they stood in, for if they were good enough to house their souls they surely sufficed when the soul was gone.

Seeing the extent of their self-denial, Alexander bade his interpreter tell them they could ask for anything and he would give it. So they asked him to give them immortality, as they were rich in everything else. His response was this:

'As I am a mortal man, how can I give immortality?'

To which they answered: 'Since he says he's mortal, for what possible reason does he march through the world doing all manner of harm?'

'That,' he said in reply, 'is my destiny, ordained by Sovereign Providence, whom I obey as its minister. The sea is rough only when the wind blows upon it; I likewise stir only when Divine Providence drives me to act as you say: I'd be only too pleased to rest, if almighty God permitted it. And you'd surely agree that if everyone in the world was alike in nature and outlook, there'd be no way of recognising goodness and valour.'

So saying, Alexander let them go. And he and his army left their land behind and marched on till they came to a river referred to in the Old Testament as the Epheison,[1] and there they made camp.

Chapter XXXIII
How Alexander sent a letter to the king of the Brahmans.

On the far side Alexander could see large numbers of people. He sent men to call across and ask them who they were, and the reply came that they were called Brahmans. At this, Alexander was very keen to cross the river, but no one could find a bridge of any kind, and the water was so full of snakes that no one would have dared step in unless he wanted to be devoured on the spot. Realising there was no way for his men to cross, Alexander bade them call to the Brahmans and see if any were bold enough to make the crossing to him; one of them did so, jumping in a little boat and coming across to parley. When he arrived, Alexander gave him a letter and asked him to take it to his king; he promised to do so, but first Alexander asked him his king's name so that it could be inserted in the superscription. Then, once he had the letter, the man stepped back in his boat and returned to his side of the river. He made his way to his

---

[1]   'Phison' in the Prose Alexander, so this is probably the Pishon, one of the four rivers that flowed from Eden according to Genesis 2, 10-14.

king and delivered Alexander's missive. The king had the letter read to him; its contents were as follows:

'Alexander, commander of the Greeks, son of King Philip of Macedon and Queen Olympias, wishes Lindmo,[1] king of the Brahmans, health and happiness. We have often heard that you live quite divorced from other men, and seek help neither by land nor by sea. We find this hard to believe, but if it's true it is most remarkable! We were brought up by our tutor not to disparage your way of life,[2] and ask you in all sincerity to let us see that your life lives up to its great reputation and renown. We feel you should grant our request: you have nothing to lose in doing so and a good deal to gain. After all, a burning candle can light many others without diminishing its own flame; likewise a worthy man can improve many men without lessening his own goodness. We hope we may be given such enlightenment; for if your life matches all reports, I for one am ready to follow your example: since childhood I have been striving to learn it and to live according to right and reason.'

Chapter XXXIV

How the king of the Brahmans returned a letter to the noble King Alexander.

After hearing this message and discussing it with his barons and companions, Lindmo wrote a letter in reply and sent it to Alexander. It read as follows:

'From Lindmo, master of the Brahmans, health and joy to King Alexander. We see from your letter that you wish to learn the nature of true wisdom; this clearly shows your appreciation of knowledge and perfection, and we are very pleased to see it – we always say that the valuing of wisdom is a step towards perfection. Nonetheless, it seems to us that you're in no position to adopt our way of life, and our doctrine is very different from your own – the god you worship we do not and your life is wholly unlike ours. So forgive me if I don't answer all your questions, but it strikes me as a waste of time, though I'll tell you a little about our life and customs – not much, however, because you're so busy with your battles that you wouldn't have time to read much more! But I wouldn't have you think I begrudge you knowledge that is willingly shared, and the following words I send with all respect.

'We Brahmans live our lives in purity and simplicity; we commit no sins and wish for nothing more than life's essential needs. All else we disregard and consider superfluous, and we happily bear our self-denial.'

After reading Lindmo's letter Alexander decided to send him another. This he did, dictating it at once and giving it to the messengers to take back to their king. It read as follows:

---

[1]   In other accounts of Alexander's meeting with the Brahman king, the name usually appears as Dindimus or Dandamis.

[2]   If this phrase seems strange, it's because it's Wauquelin's rendition of a somewhat contorted passage in his source at this point (the Prose *Alexander*) which implies that Alexander had been instructed to live in a manner 'blameless in the eyes of the good'.

'Alexander, commander of the Greeks, son of King Philip of Macedon and Queen Olympias, wishes Lindmo, king of the Brahmans, health and happiness. You say you lead a good life, not least because you live in a part of the world where strangers cannot venture. But nor can you venture abroad! This strikes us as a great misfortune; yet you value and cherish your isolation, as if – in your eyes – men in prison are fortunate, or should think themselves so: after all, what they endure for just a while is your permanent state! What malefactors are condemned by our law to suffer, you suffer as your natural way of life! What you deem admirable we'd say was damnable! We've surmounted the misfortunes you endure, and are the better for it: we've more reason to rejoice, we'd say, than men in endless captivity! By enduring what you're powerless to change you call yourselves philosophers, but no reasonable or honest man could deem your life a happy one: it can only be thought a punishment and affliction!'

Once the letter was written and sent, Alexander summoned the workmen from his army and ordered them to erect a marble column on that spot without delay; upon it were to be inscribed the words exchanged between him and the Brahman king, to record them for anyone who ever passed that way.

When this had been duly done he departed with all his army, and journeyed on till they came to a plain called Arrea where they stopped to make camp and rest.

CHAPTER XXXV

How Alexander fought with giants and encountered a wild man.

A round the plain where Alexander and his men encamped stood a forest of colossal trees. The fruit they bore fed the people who dwelt there – men of enormous height and girth called giants, who dressed themselves in the skins of animals they caught in the woods. As soon as these forest giants spotted Alexander's army they flocked together till they numbered a good three thousand; and once they were all assembled, clad in their furs and pelts and armed with stones which they flung with such force that every throw felled a horse or a camel, they surged from the trees in a thunderous attack upon the army. The knights and pickets saw them coming and strode out to meet them with volleys of arrows and darts. But the giants responded with a hail of stones that wrought appalling slaughter, their fearsome blows bringing horses and knights crashing down in heaps. And when they joined battle hand to hand the Greeks were overwhelmed, the wild men scything them down like August corn. So ferocious was this first onslaught that they were forced to flee.

When Alexander saw his men in flight he made them rally round him, and ordered them to yell with all their might. They did so; and when the giants heard these human voices, unlike any they'd heard before, they were stricken with terror and all turned and started running back towards the forest. Seeing this, Alexander spurred after them and his knights followed; they cut down a huge number – our source says six hundred were killed, though another says one hundred and forty-four. Our history adds that Alexander lost three hundred knights (not counting the foot soldiers killed), but the other version says it was only one hundred and twenty-six: I leave it to the reader to decide.[1]

Alexander stayed here with his army for four days, during which his men gathered a great hoard of the forest fruits to eat: they were truly delicious, and the history says they lived on them for a very long time.

At the end of these four days Alexander and his army set out once more, and next made camp beside a river beyond the forest. But while they were busy pitching their tents a man of amazing size appeared; he looked like a wild man, and so indeed he was, covered in bristles like a wild boar.

CHAPTER XXXVI

How Alexander had the wild man burnt, and how he entered the Perilous Valley.

When the men of the army saw this man coming they took up spears and lances and went to confront him. But the moment he saw them he stood as still as a statue: they began to talk to him, but he made no response of any kind – indeed, he'd never heard a man speak before. Alexander was informed of all this and went straight to see. He told his men to take the man in hand, and they strode forward together to do so. But he wouldn't budge: no matter what they did he stood there rooted. In case he was up to something Alexander had him bound hand and foot; then they took him into camp.

When Alexander was rested and refreshed he bade them bring the wild man to him, which they did; and Alexander had him plied with questions in a number of tongues, but he made no answer to any: he didn't say a single word. So Alexander had him presented with the kind of food eaten by civilised men, but all he ate was a fruit or two that happened to be included. To test his reactions further, Alexander had a girl stripped naked and led before him. The moment he saw her the man seized her in his arms and made to haul her away; Alexander ordered them to pull her from his clutches, which they did, but according to the history it was quite a struggle, the man uttering such fearful howls that everyone was terrified: he sounded like a demented beast. So alarming was he, both in looks and nature, evidently devoid of wit and reason, that Alexander called at once for a strong stake to be erected and for the wild man to be bound to it and burnt in a fire. His knights carried out the order, and when the flames began to make themselves felt, the din he made was truly fearsome, hideous.

After the death of this grisly, monstrous being, the valiant King Alexander set off once more with his whole army. They'd been marching for about half a day when they came upon a mountain, and crossed it and descended into a valley; and if the history is to be believed it was a wondrous place: according to our source –

---

[1]   Wauquelin's claim that he has two sources for these figures is intriguing. The precise numbers of 144 and 126 come from the Prose *Alexander*, but there is no reference to the other numbers in any surviving version of the verse *Roman d'Alexandre*.

which has no title[1] – a most beautiful river ran through it, the loveliest imaginable, so delightful that Alexander gave orders for the army to make camp there in the pleasant meadows.

But when they were all encamped and midnight drew near, the weather turned so dreadful that it seemed the world was about to end in a turmoil of thunder, lightning, tempest, rain and a storm of hailstones so immense that it felt like an avalanche of rocks – and with the hail came flames, appalling, ghastly, so terrifying that their legs gave way and they collapsed and lay prostrate upon the ground. They suffered this ordeal till daybreak, and it cost the lives of many.

Chapter XXXVII

How Alexander, according to our history, stayed in the Perilous Valley all alone.

When day came and the terrible storm abated, Alexander gave orders to strike camp. Then they began to march. They marched till midday – and got nowhere: around noon they found themselves back where they'd camped the night before. They were bewildered, and couldn't understand what was happening. Alexander issued orders to find another route, but after marching till about two hours after the ninth[2] they once more found themselves in the same place: they were more than perplexed, and little wonder. Alexander now bade them rest and eat, and said he would head for the mountains on his own to see if he could find a path or track that would take them out of the valley. He set off at once, though some of his knights followed him to see how he fared.

Chance brought him to a stone that bore the following inscription:

'Anyone who comes to this valley may be sure he will never leave.'

Alexander was horrified, completely at a loss; and as he gaped and stared at what was written he noticed there were letters carved in the other side of the stone. They said:

'If a company of men enter this valley, they can leave if one will volunteer to stay.'

When Alexander read this he felt a measure of comfort, fearing less for himself than that his men would die of hunger there. He rode straight back to rejoin his companions, who were waiting for him in a state of fearful agitation. When he arrived and saw his men he began to weep, and tearfully reported what he'd found. Hearing what he had to say his knights were utterly dismayed: it was a tall order to find someone who'd willingly commit himself to death, and they launched into frantic debate. Seeing his men's alarm at what he'd told them, Alexander climbed upon a scaffold and addressed them thus:

---

[1]   i.e. the verse *Roman d'Alexandre*, the source for the following episode (though in the MS edited by Armstrong, Buffum *et al.* it doesn't mention the river referred to in the next phrase, merely saying that 'the meadow was beautiful, the grass very lush; no man ever saw a fairer valley' – Branch III stanza 148).

[2]   The ninth canonical hour, about 3 p.m.; so in modern terms they'd been marching till five o'clock.

'Oh, my valiant men – all of you, great and lowly alike! You've been my good and faithful companions, and I thank you deeply for your fine fellowship. I wouldn't be a good shepherd if I didn't risk my own life for my flock, and because I want to repay your service I mean to save your lives. I command you now to go and leave me, for I shall stay here all alone and hope for the favour of the Sovereign God. But when you go, I beg you, stay together in love and peace till you all reach your desired destinations.'

CHAPTER XXXVIII

How Alexander's army left the Perilous Valley and he stayed there all alone.

On hearing Alexander's words, the valiant knights Emenidus, Ptholomer, Danselin and many more protested, weeping:

'Ah, mighty emperor, it isn't possible! How can we leave you here after the countless blessings you've showered upon us? Truly, we'd rather die at your side than leave without you. We can surely find one among us who'll be less terrible a loss than you – the moment you leave us will be our end! You know yourself a body cannot live without a head – so how will we live without you when you're our life and our provider, the source of all our wealth and the reason that we're feared by other men? Alas, lord, what will they do now, the poor knights you've always nurtured and promoted when you've found them able and worthy? They'll have every reason to say their days are done!'

They had much more than this to say, but I'll move on. Alexander, seeing their distress, replied: 'Ah, beloved friends! It cannot be otherwise, truly. But I tell you, your anguish and pain are harder for me to bear than the death to which I sense my foolish action has brought me – for I'd endure death well enough if it caused suffering to myself alone. So go now, and quickly, for evening's closing in, and you must avoid the perils of the dark that you faced last night!'

With that all ranks began to turn away and leave; but there's no need to ask if they were stricken with grief: indeed, no man could express in words how desolate they were, for as you can well imagine, when a people love a lord as utterly as they loved King Alexander, it's no wonder they grieve bitterly if they lose him.

But when something can't be changed you must move on – and they moved on and left that terrible valley, and crossed a mountain and came to another vast plain bordering a gulf of the sea into which a river of sweet water flowed. There they made camp, pitching their tents and even the king's pavilion. But they did so amid tears and lamentation; and their spirits didn't recover all night – not indeed till the evening of the following day when Alexander returned to them as I'll explain, trusting our untitled source is to be believed.

CHAPTER XXXIX

How, according to our source, King Alexander returned to his companions.

And so it was that Alexander stayed behind, all alone, in the Perilous Valley. He was in anguish, quite distraught, and little wonder; for as he recalled the noble, glorious triumphs he'd achieved and the soaring honours that he'd won, and now found himself held captive as if by some phantom – and unable to discover or comprehend why, unless it was the work of the Enemy[1] – you may well imagine that it was a knife through his heart: it cut him to the quick. But like a truly wise and valiant knight he went down on his knees and prayed to his true Creator to have pity at least on his men – since it was evidently His wish that he should die a wretched death there all alone, devoid of human company – and guide them to a place from which they could safely return. Alexander's trusty horse was at his side, and seemed distressed by his master's woe.

And then, with Alexander in this dismal plight, thunder and lightning began to peal and strike so mightily that it seemed the sky and the celestial bodies were about to crash down to earth, and not just fall but destroy the earth entirely – an earth that was quaking and shaking so fearfully that Alexander expected to be swallowed at any moment. And to cap it all the earth seemed to be bursting into flames, and the blaze was accompanied by such a stench that any man who smelled it would have struggled to fend off death. Throughout this night of torment King Alexander kept his hands clasped heavenward in prayer to his true Creator, imploring Him in His gracious mercy to have pity, saying:

'I see, Lord, you want me to pay before my death for my misdeeds!'

And although he had his hands clasped and kept kneeling as much as he could, the convulsions of the earth often laid him out prostrate and made him struggle to stay face up. And that's not all: in the midst of all this turmoil he saw evil spirits locked in dreadful battle, and the sight filled him with such horror that he wanted to die then on the spot and almost lost his mind – his horse Bucephalus, too, collapsed in terror at these awesome sights and sounds.

But suddenly, after all this appalling horror, day broke and the sun began to shine, and with its shining all the terrors disappeared – according to our history they were gone in the blinking of an eye. No one could describe his joy at being relieved and free of that mortal torment, and he resolved to do all he could to find a way out of that accursed valley. Without more ado he jumped on his horse Bucephalus and spurred him forward to see if he could find and follow his army's tracks. But he hit upon no way out at all, much to his frustration and dismay.

At last, after riding for a long while, he came upon a crag where a tunnel like a cistern had been hollowed from the rock. And in this cistern sat a stone in which was trapped an evil spirit, imprisoned there by the gods long ago to prevent the world's destruction. The king rode up to the cistern and went in; but he could see neither man nor woman in the place, broad and spacious though it was. As he sat there looking this way and that, he was startled and alarmed to hear a voice – but what a source of comfort it proved to be, for it told him how to get out of the valley in return for his promise to free it from the stone. Alexander did so; but what emerged was a stinking reek so foul and overwhelming that he

---

[1]   i.e. the Devil.

thought he'd choke to death. He was out of the tunnel in a flash; and he spurred his horse on till he came to a stone gateway, where an inscription gave directions to the way out of the Perilous Valley.[1]

CHAPTER XL

How Alexander's return was celebrated by his barons, and a number of other matters.

As soon as Alexander had read and taken in the inscription he set off along the way it pointed. He immediately found a path and began to follow it, and hadn't gone far before he spotted his army's tracks leading down a mountain. Greatly cheered he spurred Bucephalus forward, and the horse bore him on with joyful speed, apparently as happy as his master. Why should I lengthen the story? Alexander rode on until, late in the evening, he caught sight of his whole army, who hadn't moved from the place where they'd made camp the previous day. And indeed he could see his own tent, which according to the histories was one of the most handsome pavilions that ever housed a prince or king. He rode right through the camp and up to his tent, and as he passed you can well imagine the welcome he received: truly, they came in such a cheering throng to witness his return that he didn't know which way to look and whom to acknowledge first, and such was their elation that it was hard to believe they'd ever known a moment's suffering or sorrow in their lives. Indeed, our history says that in their jubilation they forgot all about eating and drinking – all they did was light bonfires and celebrate like men new-freed from slavery, and their joy and celebration lasted all night long.

As soon as Alexander was recovered and refreshed he went – being supremely shrewd in understanding how to act – to every lodging in the camp to visit and reassure his captains, barons, knights and men-at-arms, giving each such generous attention that they thought they'd gone to paradise! Then he returned to his pavilion and rested till the morning.

When day broke and all the barons were up, Alexander made a sacrifice to God, who in His gracious mercy had freed him from his dismal plight; and as he made the sacrifice he gave his men to understand that no one with true faith in immortal God could ever come to a bad end. Then he ordered them to strike camp and pack up all the tents and pavilions and take to the road once more, and this they duly did.

They hadn't gone far before they saw four men approaching, very aged and

---

[1] Wauquelin simplifies the episode he found in the verse *Roman d'Alexandre*, in which the demon initially gives Alexander false information but fails to deceive him. The demon, amused and full of admiration, then tells him the proper way out; Alexander goes to check that it's true before honouring the deal and returning to free the demon from the stone; then, rather than a 'stinking reek' that nearly chokes him to death, Alexander is greeted by two appalling shrieks that 'all but drove him insane; but he held himself together like the valiant knight he was and mounted his horse and rode off at once'. (Branch III stanzas 160-2).

very tall: they were fully fourteen feet in height; and they were covered in hair like bears, had horns like antlers sprouting from their foreheads, and were berry-black, with eyes that shone like carbuncles. When these four men saw the army coming they took to their heels, at such a speed that, according to our history,[1] there wasn't a horse in all the army that could catch them – except Bucephalus. Mounted on Bucephalus Alexander caught up with one and seized him by the head; the man started screaming hideously, and the other three, hearing this, turned and saw him in Alexander's clutches and raced back to the rescue. They would certainly have killed Alexander and his horse together if the king's knights hadn't come so fast and swiftly surrounded them; one knight thrust his sword at them and the others spears and lances, striking them to the ground where they were seized and bound and taken captive. All four were led to Alexander's tent, already pitched and prepared.

CHAPTER XLI

How Alexander found a spring where, if the history is to be believed,
cooked fish came back to life.

Once Alexander had eaten and drunk he called for these wild men they'd captured to be brought to him. This was done; and when they arrived the king had them addressed in several tongues until there was one they understood. They responded to this and explained that they were four brothers and came from the Orient, from a region whose name I haven't found in the history.[2] The king asked them what had brought them to the present land, and they replied that back in their own country lived a master astrologer who'd told them that in those deserts of India were a hundred springs, three of which were of exceptional power. The first was such that any man, however old, who drank and bathed in its water would return to the state he'd been at the age of thirty. The second was such that no man or woman who bathed in it would ever die, but this spring appeared on only one day each year.

'And the third is such that it restores life and all bodily health. These three springs are what brought us to this desert land.'

Alexander was astonished by their tale, and began to wonder if it could be true; but it seemed very possible, for the one who'd created all things from nothing could surely then make something out of something! So he gave orders for the army to set out and see if chance might lead them to these springs. He also had the old men unbound, and told them they could go with his men in safety and bade them do all they could to find the springs.

So the whole army set off. Across the desert they ranged, riding all day without finding anything worthy of note. But as evening drew near they came upon a little stream of crystal-clear water and guessed it must be straight from a spring,

---

[1]   The verse *Roman d'Alexandre*, beginning at Branch III stanza 167.
[2]   Wauquelin's source at this point continues to be the verse *Roman d'Alexandre*.

so they carried on upstream until they found a beautiful, shining spring and stopped there to make camp.

Soon the whole army was lodged and supper was ready. Now, it so happened that the cooks had boiled a cauldron full of fish, and by chance had left it right beside the spring. A dog had seen the fish in the cauldron and fancied nabbing one for his supper; a cook spotted him and started yelling, and the dog took fright and went bounding round the cauldron and in doing so sent it toppling over, and some at least of the cooked fish fell into the spring. Then the cook, running up to recover the spilled fish, came to the spring and saw them swimming about in the water! He was dumbfounded, and went straight to the king and fell on his knees and said:

'Mighty emperor, if it please you, come and see an amazing sight! I'll show you something I'll swear you've never seen in your life before, but it's really happened!'

Hearing this, Alexander and his barons went swiftly to the spring and saw the fish, all very much alive, and couldn't believe they'd previously been cooked! So the cook took another fish that was left in the cauldron and threw it in the spring, and it instantly started swimming like the rest: it was just as if they were playing there together! When Alexander witnessed this he summoned all the army's masons and bade them build a tower around the spring right there and then, and so they did.

Once the tower was finished Alexander departed. But our history says that before he left, while the tower was being built, he had his men scour the desert to see if they could find the other springs described by the old men. According to this version, one of his knights did find one of the springs, the one that appeared only once a year; but the knight could never find the way back to it, which angered Alexander so much that he had the knight walled up in a tower, the only way he could think of killing him.[1] If this is true, so be it. But neither Vincent's history nor Guillaume's[2] mentions it – though they do admit that they haven't recorded all the wonders that Alexander encountered in India, so I leave it to the reader's discretion.

CHAPTER XLII

How, according to our history, Alexander discovered the fountain of youth.

After seeing the tower completed, Alexander set out with his whole army and rode through the deserts of India for several days before he found anything worthy of record.

Then he entered a plain of the strangest kind: he arrived there in the fairest

---

[1]   According to the verse *Roman d'Alexandre*, 'he told him he'd pay dearly for his bath. "Enoc,' said Alexander, "I can't torture you or kill you, burn you or maim you; I'll make you live out your life in misery." He summoned his masons and ordered them to build a pillar and seal Enoc up within it. No one could free him from it till the world's end.' (Branch III stanzas 177-8).

[2]   See footnote 1, above p.135, and note 3, p.179.

weather, but the moment he and his men stopped to make camp, the ground beneath them started belching fire. Awed by this perilous wonder they struck camp again and moved on. But they came then to a plain as alarming as the first, the ground quaking so violently that it seemed about to collapse beneath their feet. They didn't dare stay, and rode on all night as chance took them – and right through the night they were assailed by serpents and dragon-snakes: never had they endured such an ordeal. And then, after all these attacks by snakes and serpents, when day broke and they found themselves in a field where they thought they could get some rest, a mighty storm struck up. The sky grew dark and dense with cloud, thunder and lightning raged and flared and rain fell in fearful torrents; and this rain was as red as blood, so red that the army and everything in it – humans, animals and all their gear – looked as if they were covered in gore. Alexander was appalled and aghast at the sight, and jumped down from his horse and prayed to God in His sweet mercy to make this torment cease; and hardly had he finished his prayer before the terrible storm abated. Seeing the elements suddenly stilled Alexander was overjoyed, and not without cause; and he went among his knights and men and began to cheer and reassure them – for they were muttering against him, saying:

'If we keep following this man, whose rash daring has enraged the gods by trespassing on their domains, he'll lead us all to our doom!'

So he went among them with words of comfort, saying: 'Oh, my valiant knights and companions, don't be afraid! My hope is that, God willing, after these torments will come relief: you know it's in the natural way of things that drear drizzle is followed by shining sun! So if we've suffered this storming turmoil there's no cause to be alarmed: so vast is Nature's God-given power that it has to be released somewhere!'

Once he'd reassured his men and they'd eaten and rested awhile, Alexander issued orders to take to the road again. They did so, and found themselves passing now through many a pleasant place – but we'll say nothing of them, as there was little worthy of note.

They rode on till they came at last to a beautiful stretch of grassland covered with fair and fragrant flowers, and little trees laden with fruit of a scent so sweet that balm and incense could not compare. Their delight knew no bounds, and they all went roaming across the plain picking violets, roses and all kinds of flowers whose fragrance was so reviving that all the hardship, thirst and hunger they'd suffered were forgotten. Alexander issued orders to make camp there, which they did very readily, the place being so ravishing; and they started preparing their ground and pitching their tents, including the king's pavilion.

When all was done Alexander bade some of his knights explore the full extent of this delightful stretch of land. They duly set off; and right in the middle, hidden among a mass of huge trees, they came upon a beautiful spring, a surging gush of clear and shining water. And the history says that before this spring stood a lion of pure gold through which the water passed through a kind of pipe, and around the lion were four more as if to guard him, along with two dragons. They'd have been a terrifying sight if they'd been alive, but they'd been turned to stone by some magic art and for a very special reason: according to the history it was because they'd angered the gods by killing the son of a goddess while he'd been bathing there.[1] The history goes on to say that the water from this spring protected men from venom and toxin of every kind, and adds that it was enclosed in a crystalline stone with a border of finest gold. They reported their discovery to the king at once, and he rode straight there to see it. He gazed at the spring and its surroundings in awe and delight, and bade that his pavilion be brought there and that the army come and camp there right beside it, and this was done. And the history says he decreed that, on pain of death, no one should damage the spring or plunder it in any way – he was thinking of the abundant gold that adorned it; but, following the advice of two of the old men who were acting as his guides, he let his men pick as many of the flowers and fruits from the trees as they wished.

Now, in this beautiful tract of land the weather was fine and very hot, and it so happened that a number of men from the army went to wash and bathe in the stream from the spring. And our history says that among them were some who were very old, but the moment they'd washed and bathed in the water they were restored to perfect bodily health and seemed no older than thirty! Seeing this, everyone in the army suffering from sickness or infirmity or age came and bathed there – even those who weren't unwell and didn't need a wash: in fact everyone! – until the whole army was so newly filled with health that there wasn't the slightest trace of illness to be found. According to our history, this spring came from the earthly paradise that lay between two rivers called the Tigris and Euphrates.[2]

When Alexander and all his followers, men and women alike, were thoroughly refreshed, he summoned the old men who were accompanying him and asked them if they knew of anything in those forests and deserts that they hadn't yet seen and was worth seeing. They replied that not far away was a marvel indeed, in the shape of two trees that gave answers to any questions: they were known as the Trees of the Sun and the Moon.

Chapter XLIII
How Alexander made his way to consult the Trees of the Sun and the Moon.

Alexander was amazed by this, wondering how two trees could talk! But then it struck him that it might well be possible: he knew of many man-made idols in the world – of brass, for instance, and copper and wood and other things – that answered people's questions, so there was surely every reason to

---

[1]   This is a clarification of Wauquelin's phrase 'because the son of a goddess had once bathed there against the will of the gods'. In a convoluted passage which may well have confused him, his source, the verse *Roman d'Alexandre*, concludes: 'for poisoning a goddess's son they ['four crested serpents and two dragons' who were 'guarding the lion'] were all killed together by a lightning bolt' (Branch III stanza 203).

[2]   Along with the Pishon (see note 1, above, p.210), the Tigris and Euphrates were rivers that flowed from Eden according to Genesis 2, 10-14.

suppose that these trees, made by no less a being than the Sovereign and Eternal Majesty, were far more likely to have such power. And so, earnestly wanting to know how his reign would end, he immediately gave orders to strike camp, for he wanted to press on; but you may be sure that many of his army were most reluctant: they would gladly have stayed there in that land of so much bounty. But in obedience to the king's command they had to go, and after striking camp they all set off.

They kept marching till they came upon a colossal mountain known by the local people as Mount Damastice. Steps led up the mountainside – without them it would have been unscalable. And as they drew closer they noticed there was a huge golden chain that ran down the length of the steps to the mountain's foot, evidently placed there to provide a grip and support to the climber. According to Vincent's history[1] there were three thousand five hundred steps, every one made of precious sapphires.

Alexander, seeing the mountain's size, didn't want his army taxed by such a climb, and ordered them to make camp and pitch their tents. This was done; then when they were encamped Alexander gathered a handful of his barons, those closest to him, and told them he meant to climb the mountain where the old men had told him there were two trees that answered people's questions.

'Only those of us here,' he said, 'will go and explore the mountain top, so that if we find it's true about the trees, our men can't get in the way of our discovering what adventures and events God has in store for us.'

So saying, Alexander began the climb and his barons with him – but only three, it seems. They kept climbing till they came upon a magnificent palace with doors and windows of fine gold: it was called the Palace of the Sun. And close beside it stood a temple wholly built of gold, with a golden vine outside its doors bearing great, fat bunches of pearls and onyx, ravishing to behold. As Alexander gazed at these beauteous buildings, he decided to enter the palace first. In he went; and the moment he entered he saw a man lying in a gorgeous bed made all of gold and covered with rich golden cloth. The man was very big of build and his hair and beard were white; and lying in bed though he was, he was dressed in a robe of purest white, most fine and splendid. And according to our source he lived solely on incense and balm. When they saw him Alexander and his barons went down on their knees and worshipped him as if he were God – and a divine being he seemed indeed. And when the old man became aware of them he said:

'Have you come here, friends, to see the sacred trees of the sun and the moon which forewarn us of what is to come?'

And Alexander, suffused with joy, replied: 'That is indeed why we have come, sir, truly, and we would be very glad to see them if you approve.'

Then the worthy man said: 'If you and your princes are born of male and female, it is right that you should enter this place.'

---

[1]   Wauquelin has now returned to following the Prose *Alexander*, the French translation of the *Historia de Preliis* which he took to be the work of Vincent of Beauvais: see note 1, above, p.135.

And Alexander answered: 'We are born of male and female.'

At this the old man rose from the bed where he lay and said to them: 'Come then, sirs. You must remove your clothes and shoes.' So they began to undress, and when they were done he said: 'Follow me.'

And they set off after the old man, Alexander at the front and Ptholomer, Antigonus and Perdicas behind, and followed him. He led them into a forest enclosed by a mighty wall. Here they found trees akin to laurels and olive trees, but they soared to more than a hundred feet and yielded abundant balm and incense. Deeper into the forest they went, and came upon a tree of astonishing height devoid of leaves and fruit, on which sat an enormous bird with a crest on its head like a peacock's and feathers on its neck that shone like fine gold; the rest of its plumage was purple or rose. When Alexander and his barons caught sight of it they asked the old man to tell them the name of the bird in the tree, and he said:

'That bird is called the phoenix, and it's the only one in the world. But don't imagine it's immortal; no, it dies; but as soon as it does so another is reborn from it by the Creator's will, and I'll tell you how. When this bird has run its natural course it gathers a bundle of dry twigs on a high mountain in Arabia, and beats its wings to fan the sun's heat on the wood till it catches fire. And there, upon the pyre it's built, it destroys itself in the flames. But the day after the bird has burnt, an egg appears in the ashes and stays there throughout that second day. And on the third day the egg cracks open and another phoenix emerges, which takes to the air that very day and flies here to this place, where it lives on what it finds in these lofty trees.'

CHAPTER XLIV

*How, according to the history, Alexander spoke
to the Trees of the Sun and the Moon.*

After hearing the worthy man's story of the bird they went deeper still into the forest, until they neared the trees they sought and could clearly see them. Then the old man stopped and said:

'There are the sacred trees, my friends. Approach them in all humility and look upward, and make sure you do not say a word. Then, once you have worshipped them and kissed them, ask your question inwardly but do not utter it aloud. The Tree of the Sun will answer first, in the Indian tongue, and then the Tree of the Moon will speak. Go now, and do what you must.'

So Alexander went forward on his own and walked up to the trees, and worshipped and kissed them in all humility. Then he began to pose the questions in his mind: whether he would conquer the whole world, and if he would ever return to his homeland of Macedon. His thought was answered by the trees, the Tree of the Sun first saying:

'Alexander, you will indeed be lord of all the earth, but you will never see the land of Macedon again, for as soon as you have achieved your conquest you will pass from this world.'

With that the tree fell silent, and the Tree of the Moon spoke then, saying: 'Al-exander, you are nearing the end of your life, and you will be parted from this world by one you least suspect.'

Then Alexander began inwardly to say: 'Most sacred tree, who is he who will part me from this world?'

And the Tree of the Sun replied: 'If you knew that, you would kill him, and your destiny would not be fulfilled!'

And the Tree of the Moon said: 'No man needs to know the hour or the man-ner of his death: he would never be happy from that time forth; and it would be much to the displeasure of the three goddesses of destiny, the three sisters Cloto, Latesis and Antropos, if we obstructed what they'd planned and ordained for mortal lives. But I'll tell you this much: your death won't be from blade or spear-head[1] as you may imagine, but from poison, and suddenly, and soon.'

Then the worthy man came up and said: 'Alexander, my friend, that's enough. Don't press the trees any further or it could make trouble for you. I'd advise you to go back now.'

Alexander said he was ready, though he was much dismayed by the news that his death was so near. They returned the way they'd come, and when they reached the Palace of the Sun the worthy man gave them leave and disappeared inside. Alexander and his companions made their way back down the steps to rejoin the army at the mountain's foot and were received with jubilation.

But it wasn't long, the history says, before word of what the trees had said about Alexander's death had spread like wildfire through the army and every-one was talking of it. That's why our untitled source refers at this point to the death of Porus,[2] suggesting that when Porus learned that the king hadn't long to live he challenged him anew, thinking it was his prowess that was destined to bring Alexander to his death – but his interpretation was very wide of the mark, for Alexander put paid to him as you've heard above. So we'll leave that now and return to our story.

CHAPTER XLV

How according to the history Alexander sent a letter to Queen Candace.

Back now with his army, Alexander decided it was time to go and find Can-dace, the queen I mentioned earlier,[3] for he longed to see her on account of her great beauty and, above all, her outstanding wisdom. He gave orders for everyone to strike camp and take to the road.

They did so, and according to the history they marched for fifteen days with-out stopping anywhere or finding anything worthy of record. But at the fort-

---

[1]   Literally 'from iron'.
[2]   The verse *Roman d'Alexandre*, which (as Wauquelin notes above, pp.202–3) deals differ-ently with the end of the conflict between Porus and Alexander, does indeed digress at this point to recount at length the death of Porus.
[3]   Above, p.73.

night's end they entered a land then known as Tradiaque,[1] and there they halted and made camp. As soon as the people of the land heard that King Alexander, conqueror of all the world, was so near at hand – indeed, was already in their country – they came to meet him, having no mind to rebel, and welcomed him with honour and celebration, presenting him with gifts of gold and lions and dragons and leopards and other wild beasts.

Our history says that in this land lay a mountain of great fertility and abundance on which stood a rich and magnificent city, shining with all manner of precious stones; and the lady and queen of this city was a most beautiful lady of great power and wisdom named Queen Candace, of whom we spoke before. This lady Candace, surnamed Cleophis, had three sons: the eldest was named Candaculus, the second Marsipius and the third Carador, who had married the daughter of King Porus of India.[2] When Alexander realised he'd entered this lady's land he wrote her the following letter:

'From Alexander, commander of the Greeks, son of King Philip of Macedon and Queen Olympias, to Candace Cleophis, queen of Meroe,[3] health and happiness. We wish to inform you that we are to make a sacrifice in the mountains to the god Ammon; which is why, your fine reputation having fired our desire to make your acquaintance and enjoy your company, we most cordially entreat you to come and join us at the sacrifice there.'

When the queen received and read Alexander's letter she dictated a reply and sent it to him at once. It read as follows:

CHAPTER XLVI

Queen Candace's letter in reply to Alexander.

'From Candace Cleophis, queen of Meroe, health and joy to the most mighty and illustrious emperor Alexander, king of kings. We have received your cordial invitation to join you in the mountains to make sacrifice to the god Ammon. In reply, we have to inform you that it does not behove us to make such a sacrifice, for we hold to a different faith to yours, believing as we do in God the Omnipotent. You may believe that you owe your victories over the Persians, the Indians and all the rest to your god Ammon, but we are certain that it was not Ammon who granted you those triumphs, for he has no such power; no, your debt is to God the Omnipotent, source and creator of all things,[4] for without His sanction you would have achieved nothing. But to please you, who are well worthy of such a favour, we send to your god a golden crown adorned with pearls

---

[1]   See note 1, above, p.73.
[2]   As mentioned above, p.189.
[3]   '*Moree*'. As ever, it's unwise to look too hard for geographical logic or consistency: Meroe was a land beside the Nile, not far from present-day Khartoum, at the heart of the ancient kingdom of Nubia – hence the reference shortly to 'Ethiopian children'.
[4]   Literally 'from whom all things come and are born'.

and emeralds, along with a hundred Ethiopian children,[1] two hundred women, four thousand elephants and four hundred leopard skins; and we would ask you to let us know whether you have truly conquered the whole world and brought it under your subjection. God grant you continuing joy and triumph.'

Among the embassy sent by the queen to Alexander was a painter, whom she ordered to bring back a portrait of the king, and to take great care in the making of it, so that when he returned he could recreate his image in marble. The painter did as bidden. And the envoys came to Alexander with the letter from their queen and all her gifts, and were received with the utmost honour at his pavilion. They made their presentation to him – the letter first and the gifts after – and when Alexander had read the letter and received the presents with great civility and joy, he responded thus:

'My friends, tell my lady your queen that we are very well disposed towards her and most grateful for her gifts, and if she ever has need of us she must let us know and we shall assist her to her utmost satisfaction, for we wish to be of service to her and her people in every feasible way.'

Then he bade that the envoys be provided with their every need, and presented them with a wealth of rich and handsome gifts, as was his custom. When they were ready they took their leave of the king and his barons who bade them a gracious farewell; then they set off and returned to their lady and reported all that had been said and the honourable reception accorded them by Alexander.

Soon afterwards the painter came to the queen and presented her with the image he'd made of the king, carved in marble. She was delighted with it, for she had no greater desire than to see what Alexander looked like; and to be certain of its accuracy she summoned a number of people who'd seen the king many times and took them to her chamber where she'd placed the image, and asked them which of her children it most resembled: she was doing this to verify the likeness. Some of them replied that the image looked nothing like her children, but resembled no one as much as King Alexander! The queen was overjoyed by this, and treasured the image more than ever. And it enabled her to recognise Alexander when he went in disguise to rescue the wife of her eldest son who'd been abducted by another king, as you're about to hear.

CHAPTER XLVII

How the king of the Belices abducted Candaculus's wife and killed a great number of his men.

While King Alexander was in this land, allowing his army to take rest and refreshment and to provision themselves with all they needed, many of the country's people, following their annual custom, gathered to make sacrifices

---

[1] The text reads *'cent pourpres petis'* – a hundred short mantles (of fine 'purple' cloth) – which makes a kind of sense, but Wauquelin was working from an odd rendition in the Prose *Alexander* (*'.c. Piopes petis'*) of the Latin *'Ethiopes infantulos centum'* in the *Historia de Preliis*.

to their god, who was God immortal.[1] Among those preparing for the assembly was Candaculus, Queen Candace's eldest son, accompanied by his wife and an escort of thirty knights, not to mention pages and foot soldiers.

Now, the king of the Belices,[2] well aware of the custom, was informed by his spies that Candaculus was taking his wife to the feast; and this king loved her passionately, desiring nothing so much in all the world as that lady's love: she was indeed reputed to be one of the most beautiful women on earth. So as soon as he learned of this he mustered a great body of men-at-arms and lay in wait along the route Candaculus would have to take.

So Candaculus, suspecting nothing, came with his wife to make his sacrifice to God immortal, and ran straight into the ambush. The king of the Belices and all his men suddenly sprang forward crying 'To the death! To the death!', and started striking and felling knights and horses, taking them completely by surprise. They came straight to the lady and seized her on their king's behalf, saying 'You're going no further, lady!', and Candaculus, seeing them accost his wife, drew his sword and charged to the attack. A number of his men came to his aid, but it was no use: they would all have been killed if they hadn't fled, and Candaculus, seeing disaster imminent, thrust in his spurs and valiantly fought his way out of the press and escaped.

Once he'd reached safety he stopped to think what to do next; and knowing that Alexander was close at hand with his whole army, he decided to go and seek his help, feeling sure he'd grant it out of love for his mother.

With a very small band of followers he made his way to Alexander's camp. As soon as he was spotted by the guards they jumped up and stopped him and asked where he was going; he told them he'd come to see King Alexander. So they led him to Ptholomer's tent, for at that point it was always to him that people arriving at camp were first taken. After he'd spoken to him, Ptholomer told him to wait there at his tent while he went to seek advice. He came to the sleeping Alexander and woke him, and told him of Candaculus's plight and how he'd come in search of help. Alexander listened to the tale and pondered awhile and then said:

'Ptholomer, stay here in my tent and wear my crown and pretend to be King Alexander. When you're ready call for Candaculus and invite him to tell you what's befallen him. Then say you're sending for Antigonus; but whoever you send is to come and fetch me and bring me before you, and you must ask me for advice as if I were Antigonus, and I'll respond as I see fit.'

So saying, Alexander left his pavilion and went to Antigonus's tent and told him what was to be done. Meanwhile Ptholomer stayed in the king's pavilion and donned the crown as he'd bidden him. His men were informed of the plan, and once he was in royal apparel he told them to bring Candaculus to him. They

[1]   In the verse *Roman d'Alexandre* these people worship a pagan deity, the goddess Lucina, while the god is not specified at all in the Prose *Alexander* – he is simply 'their god'. In this episode, incidentally, Wauquelin draws on both sources.

[2]   The Prose *Alexander* gives 'rois des Eblicos', the *Historia de Preliis* 'rex Bebricorum'.

did so; and when Candaculus entered the tent he was amazed: never in his life had he seen such a handsome pavilion. And when he saw Ptholomer he went straight down on his knees – thinking he was the king – and begged him by his gracious mercy to lend him aid against the king of the Belices who had criminally, cunningly and without any warning attacked him and killed his men and, worse still, had robbed him of his wife by cruel force and carried her off to his city of Palatine.[1] Then Ptholomer, casting his eyes about him as if he were Alexander, commanded that Antigonus be summoned. One of those who were in on the plan went to Alexander and said:

'Antigonus, sir, come and speak to the king!'

And Alexander, pretending to be Antigonus, went to the royal pavilion, pushed his way through the crowd and came before Ptholomer, who was playing the role of the king, and said:

'Great emperor, what is your majesty's wish?'

And Ptholomer replied: 'Antigonus, this is how it is,' and so forth, 'and I pray you advise me how you think we should proceed, to our honour and the honour of our friends.'

Alexander, in the guise of Antigonus, answered, saying: 'Mighty emperor, if it please your majesty, I shall go to this young man's aid, and before two days are out I shall lay siege to the king of the Belices's city and issue an ultimatum: either he returns this young man's wife to us or I shall break down his walls and destroy or burn his city.'

Then Alexander – that is to say, Ptholomer – replied: 'Let it be as you say. Go and act as you see fit: we leave it entirely to you.'

CHAPTER XLVIII

How Alexander, pretending to be Antigonus, took the king of the Belices's city by storm and, having conquered the city, returned Candaculus's wife to him.

Hearing the king's words, but believing him to be Antigonus, Candaculus said: 'Oh, good Antigonus, you're endowed with such valour! I'd say you're worthy to be a mighty emperor!'

Then Alexander bade Candaculus go back to his city and muster his forces, for if it pleased God, by the time he'd done so he'd find him laying siege to the city of Palatine. To help him on his way Candaculus left a party of his men to guide him to Palatine; then he set off and rode back to his mother and told her all that had happened. She was distressed at her son's loss but overjoyed to hear that Alexander was sending help, and immediately called to arms all the men of her city and the surrounding land and commanded them to go and support her son.

But by the time they arrived Alexander had already taken the city, rescued the lady and had the king of the Belices hanged! This is what happened: as soon as

---

[1]   'Palestine'. 'Palatine' is the name given in the verse *Roman d'Alexandre* to the land of the king of the Belices.

Candaculus had departed from camp Alexander set off with twenty thousand troops, and with the help of the guides left behind by Candaculus he arrived at sunset next day before the walls of Palatine. He encircled the city and laid siege to it, and without waiting for any response he ordered an immediate assault. When the men of the city saw this they ran to arms to mount a defence, and from the city walls they cried out to their attackers:

'Who are you that attack us without issuing a challenge?'

They replied that they were on Candaculus's side, and that the defenders had no right to expect a challenge because they'd shown themselves to be traitors and murderers, to whom no challenge is due. But they'd come to give them warning that unless they quickly surrendered the city to Candaculus – along with his wife – they wouldn't leave till they'd taken it, and if it had to be taken by force then their lives and all they possessed would be lost: they would destroy them utterly. But the men of the city replied that for all these bold threats they'd no intention of returning the lady, and that if what they'd done was still to be done, they'd do the same again! At this, Alexander issued orders to storm the city.

And storm it they did: according to the history their siege engines launched such a bombardment of rocks and stones that no one in the city dared step out of doors, and the archers loosed such a hail of arrows at the barbicans and battlements that the defenders didn't dare show their heads – in any case, they were poorly armed and had little experience of such an assault. The history says the attack lasted till noon next day; at that hour exactly Alexander scaled the wall and entered the city, and as soon as the defenders saw men-at-arms breaking in they started to flee – but couldn't see which way to go, for the city was completely surrounded. And so it was that few if any escaped.

When the king of the Belices saw his city was taken he was aghast, and would willingly have surrendered the lady – but it was too late: the Greeks were already in his palace. They found him in a corner trying to hide; they seized him and delivered him to Alexander, who promptly had him hanged from his palace's highest rooftop. Then the lady was recovered and entrusted to Alexander, who was still pretending to be Antigonus. Once the city had been looted from top to bottom he commanded that it be put to the torch. In moments it was ablaze, and the fire raged on till the city was reduced to ash and total ruin.

According to the history, just as Alexander was about to leave Candaculus appeared with his reinforcements; and when he arrived and saw that all was done he was overjoyed. He rode with all speed to Alexander, who he believed to be Antigonus; and as soon as the king saw him he gave him back his wife. Candaculus fell to his knees before him and said:

'Truly, Antigonus, good and valiant knight, you deserve all praise and commendation! So I pray you come now to my mother, that she may reward the honour and the service you have done me.'

CHAPTER XLIX

How Alexander went to see Queen Candace while pretending
to be Antigonus, but was recognised by her.

Hearing Candaculus say this, Alexander, so eager to see Queen Candace and her city, replied: 'Truly, sir, I wouldn't dare go without the king's leave.' He did this so that his men would know where he was, and so that he could first take his troops back to camp. 'Let's go to the emperor Alexander,' he said, 'and ask if I can go with his blessing: if he approves I'll gladly come.'

So they all returned to the king's camp, and Candaculus went to Ptholomer and asked that the good knight Antigonus be allowed to visit his mother to receive reward for his fine service. Ptholomer, pretending to be the king, and knowing it was Alexander's keenest desire, gave him permission to do as he pleased. So Alexander took his leave of Ptholomer – as if he had been Antigonus and Ptholomer Alexander – and set off alone with Candaculus.

They started to climb a high mountain called Adidalas – and high it was indeed: it seemed to soar to the very heavens. The mountain was thick with handsome, lofty trees like cedars that bore enormous apples, much to Alexander's wonderment. And he was even more amazed by the sight of vines of astonishing size bearing bunches of grapes so huge that each bunch was as much as a man could carry; and in the trees were more snakes and apes than he imagined could be found anywhere in the world.

They crested the mountain and drew near the city, and when Candaculus saw the time was right he announced his arrival to his mother, letting her know he was returning safe and sound and had won back his wife by the will of God and through the courage of the knight Antigonus; and he was bringing the knight back with him, so he prayed her most fondly to prepare to receive him with all honour, saying no welcome could match his deserts.

When the queen heard this she was overjoyed, and without a moment's delay she went and donned her finest clothes – her royal vestments indeed – and on her head she placed a splendid crown encrusted with rich jewels. Once she was duly attired and thought the time had come, she came to meet her son at the foot of the palace steps. Alexander was right behind him, and Candaculus showed him all honour as he led him by the right hand and his wife by the left. And the moment that Alexander saw the queen, so fair and elegant and wondrously adorned, he was reminded of his mother Olympias – indeed he was convinced it was her, and couldn't take his eyes off her. Queen Candace was gazing just as fixedly at the knight: she'd been told he was Antigonus, but the memory of the portrait made her sure it wasn't him but Alexander. She took him by the hand and welcomed him with all honour, along with her son and fair daughter-in-law.

They went up to the palace hand in hand. It was dazzlingly beautiful, roofed entirely in gold – indeed every part of the palace from top to bottom, the masonry and everything else, was made of nothing but gold or silver or precious stone. Holding Alexander by the hand, the lady entered a gorgeous chamber in which stood a bed made of pure gold inlaid with onyx and chalcedony, and all the chairs, benches, trestles and tables were made of precious stone and the pillars of a stone like porphyry, the richest and most splendid imaginable. And underfoot the room seemed to be borne on chariots – though it wasn't moving! – with a river flowing beneath, of golden hue.[1]

CHAPTER L

How Queen Candace called Alexander by his own name, much to his annoyance.

Alexander was stunned by the chamber's wondrous splendour; and the queen sat down and seated him at her right hand and her son at her left. They began to talk of many things while the tables were set and food was prepared; and when all was ready they washed and took their places at the table. Our history says that Alexander was seated opposite the lady, for she was keen to see his face – and he was only too pleased to be seated so, for he wanted nothing so much as to be free to gaze at her as long as he wished.

And she was well worthy of his gaze, for in every respect she was beautiful, gracious and pleasant, being open and most attractive in her manner and good-humoured and charming in her speech. She had a high and quite unblemished forehead, a milk-white space between soft, neat brows, and eyes as bright as a falcon's, winningly merry; in her dimpled cheeks the white rose and the red competed without either holding sway – the balance of red and white was simply perfect. Her shapely nose turned up a little at the tip (rather like an iron foot beneath a cooking pot!); her lips were full and red and flawless, and when she parted them to speak or laugh she revealed delicate, white teeth that were a perfect picture – as were her soft and slightly dimpled chin, her neck and as much as could be seen of her white but exquisitely rose-tinted breast. Her garments were enchanting, revealing enough of her body to leave little doubt that what lay beneath was of absolute perfection. Alexander was enjoying the supper immensely! And the queen kept casting her eyes at him, and all the while her heart was telling her that he was not Antigonus but King Alexander.

Attending this supper, to honour the knight all the more, were all three of Queen Candace's sons and their wives – though the wife of Carador, the youngest, had stayed away because she hated Alexander and all his knights, knowing they were responsible for her losing her father Porus and his whole kingdom of India.

After supper the tables were cleared, and when it was time to sleep they took to their beds and slept till morning. But you may guess for yourselves whether the queen and Alexander had trouble sleeping: according to the history they

---

[1]   This image is unclear (as is another in the next chapter) because Wauquelin's source, the Prose *Alexander*, fails to translate the crucial word '*sculptos*' in the *Historia de Preliis*: the intended image is probably of a sculptured trompe-l'oeil effect beneath a transparent floor. For an illusion created by a similar amazing floor, see the adventures of Alexander and King Perceforest at the 'Perilous Temple' in *Perceforest*, tr. Bryant, pp.53-4, 82-3.

were both disturbed by a stream of thoughts that night; whenever they tried to go to sleep their memories pricked them with images that made them turn this way and that and gave them little rest. I leave it to the imagination of those with like experience.

When morning came and the king rose, he came to the hall of the palace where he found the queen already up and leaning at a window talking to one of her maids. As soon as she saw him she came to meet him and took him by the hand and paid him all honour in her eminently gracious way. Then the king and the queen withdrew alone to a chamber, and from there into another, built all of cedar wood and seated by some magic art on wheels and pulled by twenty elephants – though they didn't make it move![1] Alexander was filled with awe; and while they were there together talking and enjoying each other's company, one of the things he said was:

'Would to God the Greeks and Macedonians possessed such wonders: they're well worthy of such riches, and if they knew of them I'm sure they'd be amazed.'

And the queen replied: 'You're right, Alexander: they're more fitting for the Greeks than for us!'

When the king heard her use his proper name he was completely wrong-footed and flushed bright red. Seeing his colour change she thought her words had upset him, and said:

'Ah, sir, are you angry that I've called you by your name?'

'Truly, lady,' he replied, 'my name's Antigonus!'

'Honestly, sir,' said the queen, 'there's no point trying to hide it from me – I can prove you're Alexander: come with me!'

And she took him by the hand and led him to the chamber where she kept the image carved in his likeness – the one you heard about earlier. Then she said: 'Do you see this image?'

Alexander looked at it and saw his plan was foiled! He began to fume with rage, and the queen, seeing this, said quite brusquely: 'How can it be that you're so easily provoked and so dismayed? You've conquered all the world, not least those two noble, mighty kingdoms of Persia and India, and now, with no armies to contend with and no battle to endure – faced only by a single woman – you're quite unmanned! It just goes to show, Alexander: however much success a man enjoys, he shouldn't get carried away – he should always bear in mind that he may yet meet someone who'll surpass him in power and resolve!'

Then Alexander, seeing himself on the receiving end of a woman's wiles, shook his head and ground his teeth in rage and frustration.

'Oh, king!' she said. 'Why are you so angry and upset? What price now all your glory and your valour, your power and your might?'

'What upsets me most,' he replied, 'is that I haven't got my sword!'

'And if you had,' said the queen, 'what would you do?'

---

[1]   See note 1 above, p. 231. The intended image is again, in all probability, of an amazing trompe-l'oeil effect, but in this instance there is nothing in either the *Historia de Preliis* or the Prose *Alexander* to make this clear.

'Truly, if I had my sword,' said Alexander, 'then, because you've outwitted me, I'd kill you first and myself after!'

There was a moment's pause while the queen took this in before saying: 'Are those the words of a wise man? But never mind that; listen: don't be upset or angry now; concealing your name will save you from harm, that's certain, and rescue you from danger – as surely as you freed my son Candaculus's wife from the clutches of the king of the Belices! For I tell you truly: my son Carador is now lord of the Briennes[1] through his wife, a daughter of King Porus of India whom you killed and destroyed through your chivalry; and if the Briennes knew you were here they'd kill you to avenge their lord Porus: they hate no one in the world as much as you.'

Chapter LI

How the two brothers Candaculus and Carador tried to kill
each other on account of Alexander.

While Alexander and Queen Candace were in the chamber together, her two sons Candaculus and Carador arrived at the palace. Candaculus came first, to entertain and honour Alexander – who he believed to be Antigonus – and a moment later came his brother Carador. The latter was fully armed, and when Candaculus saw this he asked him why. He replied that he meant to kill the knight in the chamber to spite Alexander at the prompting of his wife, because Alexander had killed her father and destroyed her homeland. To this Candaculus answered saying:

'Oh, dear brother! Think before you act! You'll incur the utmost blame – the shame will never be erased! I won't allow it, I tell you!'

'I promise you, brother, whether you like it or not my mind's made up: I'm going to kill him if I can.'

'Antigonus saved me and my wife!' said Candaculus. 'It's thanks to his courage that we're here in safety and with our honour intact. So if it please God I'll lead him back to Alexander's camp alive and well or die in the attempt – I'll prove it before any man!'

'Then there'll be battle between us, I swear it!' said Carador. 'I'll kill him even if I have to kill you, too!'

In the midst of their quarrel, just as they drew their swords ready to exchange blows and the cry went up in the hall that the two brothers were about to fight, the queen appeared from her chamber holding Alexander by the hand. Seeing them poised to strike she left Alexander at the chamber door and strode forward to ask her children what was wrong. When they told her the matter she said:

'Ah, dear sons! You must honour and show gratitude to this knight, Antigonus by name! He has shown you such kindness, risking his life in your cause to secure your happiness!'

---

[1]   This is presumably meant to indicate a particular Indian people. The Prose *Alexander* reads 'barbarians' ('*barbariens*').

'Truly, my lady and my mother,' said Carador, 'he will die! And all to spite King Alexander, who cost my wife – who has urged me to this – her father and her kingdom!'

Then Candaculus sprang forward to strike his brother, and his brother struck back. And indeed, if some of those present hadn't intervened, they would have killed each other.

CHAPTER LII

How King Alexander cleverly made peace between the two brothers.

Seeing her two sons on the point of killing one another, Queen Candace ran to Alexander and said to him:

'Ah, dear lord! I've heard how shrewd and clever you are – and seen it for myself! Why don't you make peace between my children when they're trying to kill each other because of their conflicting love and hate for you? Bring your wiles to bear now, and reconcile my sons with your subtle skills!'

And Alexander said: 'Lady, let me speak to them.'

So the lady let him go; and he strode right up to the fighting youths and called first to Carador, saying: 'Carador, dear friend, if you were to kill me now you'd win scant praise, for King Alexander has many princes finer than me – I'd be of little concern to him! If you really want to exact revenge upon the one who killed your lord, I'll stand him before you here in your palace, I promise you, if you swear you'll give me what I ask.'

When Carador heard this he was elated, and left his brother and came to Alexander and offered him his hand, saying: 'If you'll do that for me, friend, ask whatever you want and I'll grant it if I can.'

So vows were exchanged and a deal struck, and thus peace was made between the two brothers. And when the queen saw her sons reconciled she took Alexander by the hand once more and drew him aside to her chamber in private; and there she said to him:

'Mighty emperor, wise and valiant! I'd think myself fortunate indeed if I could have you beside me all the days of my life! Truly, I'd love you as much as my own children – or more! I tell you, as long as you were at my side I'd feel I'd vanquished all my foes.'

Then she opened a rich and handsome ivory coffer and from it drew a crown of fine gold encrusted with diamonds and adorned with a sumptuous, gold-embroidered fabric spangled with blue stars and precious stones; and this magnificent crown she presented to King Alexander who accepted it most graciously, thanking her deeply.

CHAPTER LIII

How Alexander spoke to the gods of the cave, and how he rejoined his army.

After receiving this most precious crown Alexander took his leave of the noble Queen Candace. She led him to the hall and returned him to her son

Candaculus to escort back to 'the army of the king named Alexander'. Then he took leave of Carador and the other lords and set off with Candaculus.

They rode on until, at evening, as they made their way to the mountain's foot,[1] they camped for the night not far from a cave. They'd just dismounted and made camp when Candaculus came to the king and said:

'Antigonus dear friend, the gods once feasted in that cave at a banquet they held together.'

Hearing this, Alexander straightway made a sacrifice to God and entered the cave alone: Candaculus waited for him outside, not daring to venture in.

Once he was inside he saw a dense, dark cloud, in the midst of which was something like a constellation of bright and glittering stars, and among them a man of wondrous appearance, with eyes that shone with a piercing light. Alexander was stunned by the sight; and as he stood there wondering, the great god of the place said:

'Greetings, Alexander!'

When he heard his name uttered Alexander, wondering who on earth had spoken, said: 'Who are you, sir, addressing me?'

To which the voice replied: 'I am the one who reigns over all the world – the whole world is subject to me.[2] Yet I cannot match your renown: you have a city named after you! But come now: enter boldly and with confidence, and you'll see things worthy of wonder.'

So Alexander stepped deeper in and found the swirling darkness denser still; and there in the cloud he beheld a god named Serapis[3] seated on a royal throne magnificently adorned with all manner of riches. When Alexander saw him he spoke up boldly, asking:

'Who are you, sir?'

'I, Alexander,' came the reply, 'am the wellspring of all the gods. I am the one who saw you in the land of Libya,[4] and now it seems I find you here.'

Then Alexander, eager to know of his end, said: 'Ah, lord! Since it's you and I believe you know the future, I pray you in your mercy tell me how many years I have yet to live.'

To which the god Serapis replied: 'You have asked me the same question before[5] and I shall not give a different answer; for you should know that no man

---

[1]   i.e. Mount Adidalas: see above, p.230.
[2]   In the Prose *Alexander* this figure identifies himself as '*Cesangnotis*', a transliteration of '*Sesonchosis*' in the *Historia de Preliis*. Sesonchosis (or Sesostris) was the Ancient Egyptian king who, according to Herodotus, led a mighty, conquering expedition through Asia Minor and into Europe.
[3]   '*Seraphin*'.
[4]   I have emended the text here. It reads 'I am the one who *sent you to* the land of Libya'; Wauquelin directly copied the line from the Prose *Alexander* ('*je t'envoiai en la terre de Libe*'), but this was a mistranslation of the *Historia de Preliis*, which reads '*ego vidi te in terra Libie*' ('I saw you in the land of Libya') – Hilka's edition, p.221. The passage is of course referring to Alexander's encounter with Serapis before the founding of the city of Alexandria, above, p.139.
[5]   Above, p.139.

should have knowledge of the hour of his death or he would lose all joy in life: the truth is that a man daily tormented by such anxiety would find pleasure in nothing again! But I'll tell you this: in the city you've built in your name, a glorious city whose fame will spread throughout the world, where many an emperor, king, duke and lord will risk his life to win such a prize, your body will soon be entombed and buried, and there it will rest. Let that suffice.'

Then Alexander took his leave of Serapis and left the cave. He found Candaculus still waiting outside and told him that since they were now at the mountain's foot he was free to return home, so they took their leave of each other. In doing so, Alexander asked Candaculus to give his respects first to his mother and then to his brother Carador, to whom he was to say that he should consider himself satisfied, for he'd kept his word: when he'd promised to show him Alexander in his palace 'from the moment I introduced myself I was presenting him with Alexander'.

Candaculus was dumbfounded by this, and fell to his knees and said: 'Oh, most noble emperor! Why did you wickedly deceive my mother and me by concealing your identity? If we'd known who you were we'd have shown you the honour and respect befitting your majesty!'

'Truly,' Alexander replied, 'you've shown me so much honour that I consider myself well satisfied, and indebted to you and your mother for the rest of my life.'

'Ah, great emperor!' said Candaculus. 'You know the outrageous wrong my brother Carador meant to do you! I pray you, in God's name, have pity and overlook his folly!'

'Truly, friend,' Alexander replied, 'I don't think of it as folly. His intentions sprang from a fine and valiant heart, for you surely know that a good heart doesn't easily forget a suffered shame. And although he shouldn't have been trying to avenge the deed by attacking me (since he didn't know I was Alexander), in return for the love your mother and you have shown me I forgive him everything.'

With that they parted, and Candaculus made his way home to his mother and told her all that had been said. She pretended to be upset at not having known he was Alexander.

But we'll leave her and her children now and return to the king, who rode on after leaving Candaculus until he reached his army and appeared before his barons. They'd been very worried about him in his absence, and the moment they saw him they leapt up to greet and honour him with the utmost joy, the more so when they saw him safe and sound.

CHAPTER LIV

How Alexander fought serpents with emeralds in their foreheads,
and other beasts with the heads of boars and the skins of lions.

Back now with his army, much to their joy, Alexander gave orders for everyone to prepare to march next day as he meant to press on. They did as bidden, and struck camp and took to the road and made their way out of the land of Tradiaque.

As they left that country they descended into a valley where they found serpents in countless numbers, each bearing in its forehead a precious stone called an emerald. The history says these serpents live on white pepper and cumin, which grow there in the valley; and their nature is such that once every year they do battle with each other, in the course of which a vast number die. The moment they saw Alexander ride down to the valley they launched a vicious attack, crippling and wounding a good few of his men; seeing this, Alexander and a band of his barons charged forward and started assailing them with their swords, hewing and slashing till they overpowered them utterly: most of the serpents were killed in this battle, and the rest fled across the desert and never again dared attack any man.

Once he could see he was rid of the serpents Alexander ordered his men to march on. They did so, until they came to a place where they found wild beasts of an amazing kind: they had two sharp claws on their boar-like feet, each of these claws fully four feet long; and they had great fat heads like boars but their skin was like a lion's. And with these amazing beasts were huge birds called griffons. When these birds and beasts saw Alexander's approaching army they attacked them in a wild fury. With their clawed feet the beasts struck the men-at-arms so ferociously that with every blow they brought one crashing to the ground; and the griffons pounced on knights and horses and clung on till they'd throttled them. Alexander, seeing this slaughter, summoned his men to show courage and sent his archers and crossbowmen forward to shoot at these birds and beasts, which they did; and when the creatures felt the volleys strike it was as if they'd been hit by a lightning bolt: many of them loosed their grip and the knights started cutting them to pieces and swiftly overcame them. All the same, the battle cost Alexander one hundred and eight men-at-arms; he was very upset, but he couldn't bring them back.

They took to the road again and left this place, and carried on till they came to a great river, colossally wide – the history says it was a league and a quarter across. They made camp along its bank, to rest and recover.

Chapter LV

How Alexander discovered women who make men lie with them till their souls leave their bodies, and how he found the Pillars of Hercules.

Once they were encamped along the riverbank Alexander sent parties to see if there was any bridge or plank to take them to the other side. But they found none, much to their vexation, for they were very keen to cross.

Now, the banks and the water were thick with reeds, exceptionally long and broad, and Alexander gave orders for some to be picked to make boats to cross the river. It was in doing so that they encountered an unforgettable adventure; for all accounts say that among the reeds in this river dwell the most beautiful women (in every respect) that any man in the world could ever see. And they came to Alexander's men stark naked – as they always were[1] – and offered themselves to them; and many of the men, roused by the gorgeous sight of their shapely natural assets, flung off their clothes and lay with them among the reeds. But the nature of these women was such that they kept the men rapt in carnal pleasure until they died on top of them.[2] When others in the army realised this and saw they were losing great numbers of their men they reported the news to Alexander, and delivered two of the women to him. The king commanded an end to the business, on pain of death. These women had hair flowing down to their heels, and they were of amazing height: the shortest apparently was more than ten feet tall. But they had feet like dogs' paws.[3]

Once Alexander was across the river and all his army after him, he set out once more and rode on till he came to where the land met the Ocean and the sea seemed to merge with the sky. And there on the sea's edge they found the pillars erected long ago by Hercules to mark the end of the earth.

Then Alexander turned aside and rode for many days along the margin of the sea until they came to an island close to the shore inhabited by men and women who spoke perfect Greek. Alexander talked with them and asked them where they'd come from. They told him they were natives of Greece but had come there at the gods' command after the destruction of Great Troy.

He stayed there on the isle for a long while. Then he departed and carried on along the sea's edge till he caught sight of another island inhabited by people; but he couldn't reach them because of savage fish in the sea which dragged under and drowned anyone they caught. Alexander was most distressed and reluctant to follow advice – indeed, had it not been for some of his men he would have put himself in danger when he saw a knight die there, a knight he loved dearly on account of his prowess. He lost a great number of his men to this dire adventure; and according to the history these fish were of human shape,[4] and dragged Alexander's men to the very bottom of the sea.

---

[1] The treatment of this episode in the Prose *Alexander* is curt and flat, and makes no mention of the women's nakedness. Wauquelin, evidently dissatisfied, clearly turned to the verse *Roman d'Alexandre* at this point, where he would have read that 'they were cavorting in the water like fish, and were completely naked – everything supplied by Nature was plainly visible from head to heel. Their hair shimmered like a peacock's feathers – and was their clothing indeed, for they had no other garb...' (Branch III stanza 164).

[2] The method of killing is clearer in the verse *Roman d'Alexandre*: 'When the men were so tired that they couldn't carry on they would gladly have left them, but the women clung on...and pulled them down into the water where they held them clasped on top of them till they expired...' (Branch III stanza 165).

[3] It is hard to trace Wauquelin's use of his sources here: this bizarre detail seems to be a variation on the Prose *Alexander*'s description of two of the women being taken captive and proving to be 'white as snow and ten feet tall with teeth like dogs' (Hilka's edition, p.225).

[4] Wauquelin may have misread an inelegant line in the Prose *Alexander* in which the words 'men' and 'fish' awkwardly follow one another; his source in fact says that Alexander's men are dragged to the bottom by 'fish bigger than crabs' (ed. Hilka, p.226).

Chapter LVI

*How Alexander overcame a people called the Mardissibardis,
whose king told him his death was drawing near.*

After this woeful adventure Alexander and all his army left that place and moved on, still following the sea's edge, until they came to a country inhabited by a people known in their tongue as the Mardissibardis;[1] their king was one by the name of Calammus. As soon as they saw Alexander's army these people, realising he'd come to conquer them, assembled in a single mighty host, being men of great valour; and arming and equipping themselves as well as they could they advanced with their king at their head to meet the Greeks and Macedonians and attacked them with the utmost will. A fierce and terrible battle ensued, valiantly fought and sustained, for these people were big and strong, and though they were very poorly armed they inflicted grievous losses on Alexander; indeed I believe that if they'd matched the Macedonians' numbers Alexander and his men would have been in deep trouble. But it wasn't to be; for when they assembled they found they numbered only ten thousand, while Alexander at that point still had fully sixty thousand troops; nor were the Mardissibardis as experienced in warfare as the Greeks. And as you know, the saying goes that might will carry the day, and they were utterly routed and put to the slaughter.

In the course of this their king was captured alive and taken before Alexander who, when the rout was complete, ordered that a great fire be built and lit and that King Calammus be burnt upon it for inflicting so much damage – for according to the history, Alexander had lost fully six hundred knights and four thousand[2] foot soldiers, not to mention countless horses. And it so happened that when the fire was built for the burning of this King Calammus and they were ready to throw him in the flames, Alexander asked him if he wanted anything to eat or drink; and the king's response was to turn and look at him and say:

'Alexander, I'll be seeing you soon!'

And what he said came to pass, for Alexander was not to live much longer.

Once Calammus was dead Alexander set off towards his city, intent on taking and destroying it. But when he arrived before it he saw no one on the walls or gates: they were all hidden behind the ramparts. Thinking the city was undefended, Alexander had ladders thrown up against the walls at once, and like the daring man he was he started clambering up on his own. And the moment he was atop the wall the defenders hidden behind the battlements attacked him in a fury with a fearsome hail of darts and spears. But Alexander was quite undaunted, and like the worthy, valiant warrior he was he set his shield against their blows and brandished his sword and struck back at them, slicing through their spears and darts in astounding fashion and sending a

---

[1] The *Historia de Preliis* cites two peoples, the '*Mardos et Subagras*'; the Prose *Alexander* transcribes this as '*Mardos Subardis*'.
[2] The text gives the more modest and improbable 'four score'.

good many tumbling from the walls. But one thing did trouble him: a band of archers were peppering him with arrows, and although they didn't pierce his armour and he presented an ever-moving target, they were a serious hindrance nonetheless. But he stood his ground long enough for his men-at-arms to breach the wall; indeed, a great chunk of the wall collapsed taking Alexander and some of his enemies with it, and one of the defenders took the chance to deal him a blow that brought him to his knees. But he carried on fighting on his knees and valiantly held out till hordes of his men came storming through the breach; they came straight to their king's aid and helped him back on his feet, and once he was up he cut such a swathe through his enemies that anyone who saw him would have declared him a figure of valour indeed. And the history records that with his own hand, while he was still on his knees, he killed the one who'd dealt him the blow.

The defenders now began to break and flee in all directions – but to no avail: they were all slaughtered, women and children too. According to the history every living creature found was put to the sword, and at the end of it all the city was utterly destroyed. Alexander had the very foundations dug up and dragged away, a fearful vengeance indeed.

Chapter LVII

How Alexander defeated King Ambria and destroyed his city.

Having taken and destroyed the city, Alexander left those parts and marched on till he came to another isle nearby where there stood a mighty and imposing city ruled by a king named Ambria. Once on the island Alexander came before the city and laid siege to it, surrounding it with all his forces, and when it was completely encircled he ordered an assault. And attack it they did, but Alexander achieved nothing in the first assault but a sound beating for his men and a fair number of dead, for the men of the city fought back valiantly, determined to defend their lives and possessions. Alexander's troops withdrew to their tents, and he went to visit and encourage them, bidding them stay armed as he meant to renew the attack next day. Then he had the wounded treated and the dead buried.

Morning came and Alexander set up his siege engines. A fearsome assault of the city began as they launched a vast barrage of stones; but the men of the city fought back bravely like the valiant men they were. Attack and defence were equally unsparing, and for the second day the Greeks gained nothing, and suffered even greater numbers killed and maimed. Alexander was so enraged that he swore upon his honour that if he could take the city he would destroy it utterly.

Night fell, and all retired to their lodgings. Alexander, pondering on his affairs and especially this current siege, fell asleep in bed in his pavilion. But hardly had he done so when the god Ammon appeared to him, saying:

'Dear son Alexander, have no fear: tomorrow the city will be in your hands. To convince you, let me tell you that I am the god Ammon, and I give you this herb with which tomorrow, as soon as you rise, you will treat all those of your army who are wounded. Then they will all be as fit as they ever were!'

With that he vanished, and a moment later the king awoke and found the herb lying on his bed. He rose and dressed, and had an infusion made of the herb and sent throughout the camp to all who were suffering; and the history says that all the sick and wounded were healed by the potion, even the many who had mortal wounds.

Having treated and cured his men Alexander exhorted them to go and attack the city once more; but in truth they were less than eager, and seeing their reluctance he said:

'Oh, my dear, valiant companions! It would be a grave dishonour to leave this city when it's already cost us so much. And I tell you truly, the god Ammon has promised me it'll be ours today – the medicine he gave us is proof of it!'

And thereupon they all cried with one voice: 'Long live King Alexander!' and 'We'll never stop till his will is done!'

With that all ranks were off to begin bombardment and to storm the city. And truly, this time they mounted such a fearsome assault that around noon they broke in despite the citizens' efforts and started slaughtering them on every side. King Ambria was in the thick of it, fighting with all his might, but finally Perdicas slew him in combat. And after that his people were utterly crushed and put to the sword and the entire city destroyed.

CHAPTER LVIII

How Alexander came before an ancient city which he didn't take, but where he received tribute in the form of a wondrous stone.

After destroying King Ambria and his city, Alexander, intent upon conquering all the world, left that land and rode on with his army between two great rivers – so great indeed that they looked like seas.

After about a week he arrived before a city built deep in the water – that's to say, very far out. And there was no way of reaching it: it was completely surrounded by the waves which appeared to wash against its walls. It was an ancient city, so it seemed to Alexander: well endowed with towers and ramparts, but it looked as if age had covered them in moss. Alexander, intrigued by the sight, ordered one of his knights to climb into a boat he'd had made and to row out to the city and demand its surrender and receive tribute. Worthy servant that he was, the knight boarded the little craft and made his way – with a good deal of difficulty – close enough to the city's walls for the people inside to hear him clearly. He started hailing them at the top of his voice, calling for someone to make himself known; and to a window of a tower ahead of him came a man of very great age with snow-white hair and a handsome beard of like colour, and his face suggested he was a man of notable wisdom. He opened the window and leaned out, head and shoulders, and called out to the knight, asking what he wanted. The knight looked up and answered, saying:

'Truly, sir, I have come from King Alexander, at the gods' bidding master and conqueror of all the world, to take possession of this city and receive tribute on his behalf, as befits his glorious majesty.'

To this the old man replied: 'Wait there; I'll be back in a moment.' And he ducked inside and shut the window; but it wasn't long before he returned and called down to the knight: 'I'm back, my friend. The city's barons have discussed your request and reached the following decision: because God omnipotent, creator of all things, has ordained that King Alexander should be lord and master of all the earth, they, not wishing to disobey the divine will, have decided to render obedience to him. And so that he need not labour to subjugate and overcome this ancient city – the very first in all the world – here is the tribute they have sent him.'

And so saying, he thrust his arm through the window and threw a little stone to the knight in the boat, and the knight caught it. Before turning back he asked the old man the name of the city, but his answer was that he should leave it at that – for the moment he would know no more – and he shut the window once again; and the waves struck up with such force, so the history says, that the knight was soon driven back to the army and the city was lost to sight.

Alexander was delighted to see his knight return and asked him what had happened; and the knight gave him the little stone the old man had thrown him and reported all that he'd said. Alexander took the stone and looked long at it, but couldn't think what purpose it served. So he summoned all the oldest men in the army to see if any knew its special properties.

It so happened that among his men was an elderly Jew who came as bidden and, the moment he saw the stone, said: 'Ah, mighty emperor! Whoever sent you this is clearly a friend of yours! And it's a clear sign that he knows you well! To prove it, call for a pair of scales and I'll show you the point of this little stone.'

The scales were duly brought, and in one pan was placed the stone and in the other a tiny feather. Then the Jew called for a great sod of earth and added it to the second pan, but it didn't make the stone move in the slightest: it seemed no earthly thing would outweigh it, and Alexander and all those watching were amazed. Then the Jew took the sod of earth and laid it on top of the stone, but the sod and stone together couldn't make the feather rise – it was apparently too heavy! – and Alexander and his men were more amazed than ever. He bade the old Jew explain the meaning of it all, and the Jew replied:

'Lord king, this little stone represents yourself: of no great size[1] yet the whole world, represented by the feather [and the earth], could not outweigh it. But understand that when you leave this world and are covered by the earth, as your stone just now was covered by the sod, you'll not outweigh the lowliest being in the world.'

Alexander declared that this was well said, for nothing remained of a man in this world but the reputation he'd won; and he had the stone kept in a sacred place to be revered and preserved as he wished.

---

[1]   See note 1, above, p.201.

Chapter LIX

How Alexander was borne into the air so high that he lost sight of the earth.

After this King Alexander led his army in a different direction, southward now, until he came to the Red Sea. But it took him the best part of a fortnight to reach it, and when he arrived he ordered his men to make camp and take on all the fresh provisions they needed, for it was a region abounding in all things.

Then one day he was standing at the door of his tent looking out towards the Red Sea, which was very near, and saw that beside the sea was a mountain so high that it seemed to touch the sky; and looking at this, it set him wondering how he could climb above the clouds and discover what was there. So this is what he did: he summoned carpenters and bade them make a cage big enough to hold him comfortably; and when it was finished he took eight griffons – there were a good few among his collection of all the strange wonders he'd encountered in India – and had them securely fastened to the cage with iron chains, two on each side. Once this was done he told his barons to wait for him there till they had news of him. Then he climbed into the cage, taking with him sponges full of water; and when he was inside he took a lance and stuck a piece of meat on the end and thrust it upward through the roof of the cage. Then the griffons, being hungry, took off into the air to go after the meat, and in doing so bore the cage and meat up with them.

And they kept on going. They soared so high indeed that the barons of Alexander's army lost all sight of their lord and the cage and the birds, as Alexander did of them; and finally they'd reached such a height that Alexander had gone beyond the pure air and was very near the fire. Then he began to mop the birds' feet with the sponges to cool them down, and doused himself with them, too. Having reached the point where he could feel the fire's heat he turned to look back down; and the history tells us that the earth appeared to him now like a tiny garden bounded by a little fence, and the sea that surrounds the earth looked like a little snake. Realising how high he was, and fearing the birds' feathers would burn, he prayed to almighty God in His gracious mercy to let him return to his army safe and sound, not for his own sake but to see them safe. Then power divine provided shade for the birds and the cage and saw them safely back to the ground – though they landed more than ten long days' riding from the army. Alexander climbed out of the cage and gave thanks to Our Lord for the honour and the favour he had shown him in mercifully seeing him safe back to earth.

Then he left that place and wandered in search of his army, until on the eleventh day, after much toil, he found them at last. Needless to say he received a glorious and joyful welcome: as soon as his barons saw him they came to meet him with all possible pomp and celebration, and praised and exalted him, crying:

'Long live King Alexander, lord and master of all the world – of air and earth alike!'

Chapter LX

How Alexander was lowered to the bottom of the sea in a glass barrel.

Not long after, Alexander was gripped by the desire to plumb the depths of the sea and to see its wonders, just as he'd explored the sky. So he ordered glass-workers to come at once, and commissioned them to make him a glass barrel, big enough to allow him to turn round inside, this way and that as he pleased, and clear enough to give full visibility. They built it exactly as he asked; then they bound it round with good iron chains, and fixed a big ring beneath to which they fastened a strong hempen rope. When his barrel was arranged to his satisfaction he clambered inside, taking with him an ample supply of burning lamps, and then stopped up the hatch so fast that not a drop of water could enter. Then he had himself towed out to the high sea and lowered down on the rope.

The things he reported when he surfaced are quite beyond belief: had he not seen them with his own eyes he wouldn't have believed them himself! He saw fishes of the strangest shapes and colours, and whales of quite gigantic size and countless other things amazing to relate. He saw fishes in the shapes of the animals that walk on land, roaming on foot across the bottom of the sea eating fruit from the trees that grew on the sea bed – trees that bore fruit just like those on land, and had leaves and blossom, too. And he saw whales of barely credible size, but when they came near him they fled in terror from the light of his lamps. In the end he wouldn't reveal half of what he'd witnessed – it was too amazing; but he did describe having seen men and women – or fishes in human form – that went about on foot and hunted other fish to eat, just as men hunt game on land.

Once he'd seen all he wished of the wonders of the sea, Alexander signalled to the men above to pull him back to the surface; they did so, bringing him safely back on board, and he broke through the glass and clambered out. Then he returned to his pavilion where his barons were awaiting him in great trepidation. They were alarmed at the way he was taking so many risks, and as soon as he arrived at the tent they began to reproach and berate him for exposing himself to such needless danger. Alexander's reply was this:

'Sirs, a man who means to repair his shame or increase his honour and power and improve himself must often submit to the perils of Fortune, and not rest content with being the equal of his rivals – but neither should he abuse them, for there's no prowess or honour in abusive words. So don't be surprised if I've exposed myself to danger here: I'd say I've gained a vast amount, and will be a better leader of my army for it, all the days of my life; for I've learnt that, although strength is truly a great advantage, it's sometimes of little use without cunning. I'll tell you why I say so: it's because in the depths of the sea I saw tiny fish overcome much bigger fish by outwitting them when they could never have matched them for strength at all.'

CHAPTER LXI

How Alexander overcame beasts with sharp horns on their foreheads, and then fought dragons with rams' horns.

After Alexander had returned from the sea and told his barons about many of the wonders he'd witnessed, and once he was fully refreshed in mind and body, he left that place and set off once more with his whole army, still following the sea's edge.

They journeyed on till they came to a wild spot indeed, inhabited by savage beasts with horns like swords jutting from their foreheads, the edges jaggedly toothed like saws. These beasts did a good deal of damage to the army: the moment they saw them approach they attacked them in a rabid fury, killing many before the knights had time to rally; according to the history[1] their horns went clean through the Greeks' shields and all parts of their armour as they charged as rams would do, battering down two or three or four men-at-arms at a time. But as soon as the archers started shooting at these creatures at Alexander's command, the tide turned; in the end they were assailed from every side, and left eight thousand, four hundred and fifty dead there in the field.

After this great rout the king and all his men moved on, and kept marching till they came to a remote place where vast quantities of pepper grew. Here dwelt serpents or dragons of wondrous size, with rams' horns on their heads; and with these they inflicted great harm indeed, attacking the army as soon as they saw them. It seemed they would surely destroy all in their path; but the knights, setting their shields against them, started fighting back so fiercely that they utterly crushed these serpent beasts, slaughtering them in countless numbers.

CHAPTER LXII

How Alexander fought men with horses' heads that snorted smoke, and then battled with one-eyed giants.

Such was the stench of these foul creatures that Alexander had no desire to linger, and soon moved on with all his men.

On they rode till they came to make camp in a place near a forest inhabited by people of amazing kind: they were of human shape except for their heads, which were just like the heads of horses; and these people were immensely tall and had long, sharp teeth – indeed, when they fought their teeth were the only weapons they used. And as soon as they saw Alexander's army make camp, they swarmed from the forest in huge bands and fell upon them, inflicting grave damage: according to the history they spouted fire and flame from their mouths, much to the horror of the Greeks. But Alexander's prowess and valour, as he strode sword in hand ahead of his knights, won the day for the Greeks, and these

---

[1] Wauquelin is principally following the Prose *Alexander* again, as he has for the two preceding chapters telling of Alexander's exploration of sky and sea.

terrible creatures were routed and forced to flee back to the forest, leaving a vast number of dead.

The army were left in peace that night; and next morning, as soon as the sun rose, they left there and journeyed on until, on the fourth day after, they came to a broad expanse of land and halted there to rest. But as they lay resting, there emerged from the surrounding mountains men of colossal size in every respect, with booming, strident voices and just a single eye in the middle of their foreheads. They launched a terrible assault on the army and slaughtered great numbers, forcing them to give ground and abandon their camp. Alexander, seeing his men in retreat, was distraught beyond measure; but like the daring man he was he placed himself in Fortune's hands, slung his shield from his neck and clasped a stout lance, thrust his spurs into Bucephalus and galloped ahead of all his knights; and he put up such a fight that the horde of giants began to flee him, and his barons, witnessing their king's display of prowess, recovered strength and resolve and mounted such a charge against the giants that they forced them to flee and chased them right off the field – and all because of Alexander's courage. In this pursuit a great many giants were killed and captured, and the rest fled away into the mountains.

Chapter LXIII
How Alexander met people of golden hue with mouths and eyes in the middle of their chests; and how he battled with beasts like horses, except they had lions' feet.

After fighting off these giants the Greeks moved on again, until they came to a mighty river which they crossed only with the utmost difficulty. They found themselves on an isle where they came upon people of wondrous kind: they were yellow and shining like gold, and although they were about six feet tall they had no heads; instead their eyes and noses and mouths were in the middle of their chests, and their beards grew from beneath their navels and covered them down to their knees. They seemed reasonable enough, not harming the army in any way but offering them produce from their land in abundance; and Alexander, finding them so wondrous to behold compared with other peoples of the world, took thirty of them and kept them with him in his army for the rest of their days.

They came now to a forested part of the land, where they found beasts some thirty feet long and twelve feet in girth that looked just like horses except they had feet like lions' paws. They did grave harm to the king and his army, killing great numbers of his knights and men-at-arms, and in particular slaughtering countless horses, for they were stronger even than elephants. Finally, after much effort and a fearsome struggle and heavy losses, they were defeated and many were killed, while the rest fled, charging away into the forests.

Chapter LXIV

How Alexander's good horse Bucephalus died, to Alexander's great sorrow, and how he had him solemnly buried and a city built upon his grave.

After overcoming these savage beasts Alexander and his army left there as soon as they could. He marched on till he came to a wide and pleasant sward where he immediately gave orders to pitch tents and lodges and pavilions so that they could rest, for some of the men were very weary. His horse Bucephalus was notably tired and sick, as were many other horses, much to the distress of Alexander and all his knights. But it's no wonder they were sickening, having endured such hardship and exertions in crossing those terrible deserts. When Alexander saw his horse getting no better, but rather ever weaker, he was as downcast as could be.

And in the end Bucephalus died. Alexander was utterly distraught, needless to say; indeed, if ever a man had cause to grieve the loss of a horse it was he, and I'll tell you why: it was truly a terrible blow because Bucephalus had the power, when Alexander rode into battle, to give signs of what the outcome would be – victory or defeat; what's more, the horse would allow no man to mount him but his master, and in combat would defend him, biting and buffeting and stabbing with a horn he had in his forehead, felling anything that stood in his way. And another wondrous gift he had: he could sense impending danger and would avoid ever getting into a spot from which there'd be no escape. And he could recognise traitors and wicked men: if ever he was present he wouldn't let them near his master. And no other horse, however strong, could catch or overtake him. So it's no wonder Alexander was distraught.

And so it was that, as a permanent memorial to that valiant horse, he arranged a most noble burial. As the horse was interred Alexander wept so bitterly that any man who saw him would have felt pity; and through his tears he uttered these words of grief, or very like:

'Alas! Woe and misfortune are upon me! I see now that my end is near, for without a doubt the death of my good horse portends my own. May it please God,' he said, 'that I die today with him! I know I'll never find his like again.'

And indeed that was the truth. In the end, Alexander's grief and depression were such that he didn't eat or drink for more than three days, so the historians say. But after all this grieving he recovered a little, and ordered the building of a splendid monument to be erected on Bucephalus's grave, with an inscription explaining its purpose and proclaiming the horse's virtues. And not content with honouring him thus, he summoned an army of workmen from far and wide and ordered them to build there on that very spot a most handsome, strong and impressive city with towers and walls and fortified gates, surrounded by wide, deep moats; then he saw it well colonised by men and women, and told them that from that day forth the city would be named Alexandria Bucephala.[1] He ended by granting the city and its citizens a host of privileges.

---

[1] '*Alixandre Bucifal*'.

When all was done he bade his whole army prepare to march, his prime goal now being to go and conquer Babylon, the principal city in all the world, and to hold court there. To this end he sent word to all the lands he'd conquered bidding the governors come to him in Babylonia, before the said city, on an appointed day, bearing him tribute.

CHAPTER LXV

How Alexander left his new city of Alexandria Bucephala and rode to a palace named the Palace of King Xerxes.

Once the city had been completed to his satisfaction and his army and his men-at-arms were back in proper shape, Alexander mobilised all who'd been serving him and took to the road.

He rode ever further from the city until he came to a region where he found a great and magnificent palace of most admirable design which was known as the Palace of King Xerxes. As he drew near he could see no one appearing to defend it, so he rode straight in; and all accounts say that he found more abundant riches there than he believed existed anywhere in the world: there were so many extraordinary sights to see that he hardly knew which way to turn first to view the wonders on display.

Among the marvels he beheld was a kind of bird, about the size of a dove, which the people of the land called the caladrius.[1] According to the scriptures, these birds announce to ailing people who come into their presence whether they're to die of their sickness or recover in some way: if it's the case that the invalid is to live and regain his health, these birds will turn and look him in the face; but if he's to die they turn away and won't look at him. Some philosophers say this power has been bestowed upon them by Our Lord, and that as they look on one who's to be restored to health these birds take his infirmity into themselves and carry it away into the skies, right up to the fourth element of fire; and there, in that element, they burn away all ills and maladies. But of all the palace's other wonders the histories say little.

CHAPTER LXVI

How King Alexander entered the land of Babylon, at the edge of which he met with serpents and beasts which did him great harm.

When Alexander had seen all he wished of the palace's wonders he rode out and rejoined his army. Then he began his onward march, riding on till he reached the edge of Babylonia. It was a land to which he'd long desired

---

[1]   'sallandre' ('calandres' in the Prose *Alexander*). From the Latin 'charadrium'. In Deuteronomy 14:18 the 'charadrium' is listed among 'unclean' birds which are not to be eaten. Its healing properties and assumption of a sick person's ills give it a self-sacrificial, Christ-like significance.

to come; but I think if he'd known what was to befall him there he would never have gone.

As they came to the edge of that land they had to cross a desert; and here in this desert they found huge and terrible serpents, strong and vicious, with two heads, each with a pair of eyes that shone like mirrors. And these creatures inflicted grave harm before he overpowered them, killing countless numbers of his men. Indeed the history says that but for Alexander's own valour the Greeks would have been destroyed; and certainly, by all accounts he'd never been in such trouble – and little wonder, for he no longer had his good horse Bucephalus who'd given him so much help in all his deeds. Our source[1] assures us he had a fine new mount indeed, sent to him by a great lord from India, with a red head and handsomely dappled crupper and flanks and neck as white as snow; it was a wonderfully strong and powerful horse, but still it could never compare with Bucephalus. And among these serpents confronting Alexander were creatures no bigger than monkeys but of ghastly kind, with eight feet, eight eyes and two horns of awesome sharpness on their heads. Alexander lost many of his men to these beasts, for with razor-sharp teeth and claws and horns as sharp as daggers they ripped through the bodies of knights and their mounts alike. Never had Alexander been so afraid of defeat as then; never, according to the histories, in all the mortal battles he had fought and endured in his life had he experienced such dread. But for all that, in the end, through his own mighty courage he was victorious, and joyously gave thanks to Our Lord.

Chapter LXVII

How Alexander advanced to lay siege to the city of Babylon.

Crossing deserts and narrow passes, the king drew ever closer to the city of Babylon. And though Vincent's history[2] says that the conquest of this city involved no deeds of arms worthy of note,[3] the account we've followed at this point[4] says:

When Alexander entered the kingdom of Babylon he deployed his troops to form a fine, imposing vanguard commanded by two valiant barons named Licanor and Philotas, entrusting them with ten thousand men-at-arms superbly equipped for battle, and an equally fine, strong rearguard of which he made two other barons, Ariscé and Perdicas, the captains. Then he sent word throughout

[1]   Although Wauquelin has been continuing for the most part to follow the Prose *Alexander*, he takes this description of the new horse from the verse *Roman d'Alexandre* (Branch III stanza 286).

[2]   i.e. the Prose *Alexander*; see note 1, above, p.135.

[3]   The Prose *Alexander* does indeed say that Babylon 'soon surrendered to him without any feats of chivalry being performed by either defenders or attackers that ought to be told' (Hilka's edition, p.241). This is bizarrely anti-climactic, given that the conquest of Babylon is Alexander's last great triumph; no wonder Wauquelin was dissatisfied and turned to another source.

[4]   Wauquelin is about to return to the verse *Roman d'Alexandre* as his main source, beginning at Branch III stanza 288, though he is highly selective and adapts it freely.

the army forbidding any man, on pain of death, to cause trouble to any of the people of that land; he could see how fearful and alarmed they were, having not seen such an awesome army for a very long while. And that wasn't all: a rumour was spreading through the land that Alexander and his men were cruel and terrible; that he was out to destroy all human kind; that he and his army were nothing more than robbers and murderers, destroyers of towns and cities, of men and women; that they were pitiless, bent on destroying all the world. Aware that this was his reputation in the land he issued the aforesaid order to all his troops. Nor did they take any food without paying the price demanded by the seller – and the truth is, he and his men were indescribably rich in gold and silver and precious stones: they had cartloads and wagonloads beyond all counting. And they were so magnificently equipped with arms and harness that they were a joy to behold, their wealth clearly apparent as every part of their gear seemed to radiate gold – they appeared to be parading all the riches upon earth.

In Alexander's own company and battalion were Danselin, Ptholomer, Emenidus and many other noble barons in superb apparel and array, all of them ready to do his will and serve him. He also had a number of sound, courageous men from those parts who were guiding him to the city by the best and safest roads; these guides very ably led him to a fine plain beside a river called the Cobar, great and deep, which flowed into the Euphrates, the river that runs through the city of Babylon.

CHAPTER LXVIII

How King Alexander and his whole army crossed the river.

When he reached the river he ordered tents and lodges and pavilions to be pitched so that everyone could relax and rest. And while the army made camp he sent parties to explore and test the river to see how they could cross, for the country on the other side looked very fertile – as indeed it was, full of fine castles and fortresses and prosperous towns, all of them subject to the sultan of Babylon, named in our history as Nabugor, emir of Babylon.

The river was found to be deep and dangerous, and Alexander wondered how to get his men across in safety. He summoned a huge band of workmen and bade them dig an immense, deep ditch in a semi-circle from a point on the bank to another point further upstream: from one end to the other it was about a thousand paces long, and at its widest about four hundred paces across. Then when it was finished Alexander ordered his whole army to position themselves in the enclosure created by the ditch; they did so, and once they were all inside he gave orders for the dyke that held back the water to be broken so that it flooded through the ditch. Now all his forces could cross the river, for it was flowing round behind them rather than in front; so little water remained that they made their way to the other side and hardly got their feet wet.

As soon as they reached the further bank Alexander ordered some of his captains to go and forage. They did so, to the astonished alarm of the country folk who couldn't understand how Alexander had crossed that great, deep river which they'd trusted to protect them. And from the crossing-place to the city of Babylon it was now a mere three leagues.

CHAPTER LXIX

How Nabugor, emir of Babylon, sent a letter to Alexander.

The scouts and foragers set about their business with a will, and in a very short time had supplied the king's army with fresh victuals and provisions in abundance. The people round about, seeing they had Alexander and the Greeks and Macedonians for neighbours, were terrified, and started fleeing to wherever they thought they'd be safest, some to castles and others to cities and the major towns.

Many of the wealthiest and most eminent took refuge in the city of Babylon, assuming it to be strong and secure for a number of reasons: firstly because of its mighty walls and towers and defences, and secondly because the emir, long alerted to Alexander's all-conquering progress through the world and fearing he would move against him as he had the other kings, had massed a great army in the city with a vast store of supplies: that's why the people retreated there.

When the emir heard that Alexander had come he was deeply worried and alarmed, and immediately assembled his council to decide how to deal with the Greeks. The council duly gathered; and after much debate it was proposed they should send an embassy to ascertain Alexander's intentions, for, as they pointed out, he tended not to issue challenges: anyone who failed to pay him tribute he deemed to be an enemy. So two knights were chosen to take him a letter from the sultan; it read as follows, or very like:

'From Nabugor, king and lord of the great city of Babylon, built long ago to evade and escape the wrath of the sovereign,[1] to Alexander the conqueror, greetings. In view of the fine upbringing you must have received from the wisest of philosophers, we are amazed by your presumption: we are reliably informed that your aim is to crush and subjugate every king and prince and lord in all the world! You evidently feel that all things should be yours! This comes from your overweening pride and the appalling company you daily keep – thieves, murderers, butchers. What a vile and unseemly image for a man of such fine, illustrious, noble blood as yours! Whatever the truth about your conception, everyone agrees you are a king's son. Philip of Macedon was a king, and you take him to be your father. But rumour has it that you were sired by Nectanebus, and he was a king of our domain of Egypt, so it seems to us that you should at least have given notice that you were coming rather than enter our lands without our leave and licence. But we put it down to mere ignorance, and so bid and command

---

[1]   i.e. the wrath of God: the word 'God' may indeed have been accidentally omitted after 'sovereign'. God was eventually to be the destroyer of Babylon according to the Book of Revelation, chapters 16-18, supposedly as predicted by Old Testament prophets (for example, in Jeremiah, chapters 50 and 51).

you, on receipt of this letter, to leave our lands and kingdom; if you fail to do so, be assured that you will soon feel our ferocity.'

CHAPTER LXX

How Alexander sent a letter in reply to the sultan of Babylon.

When the letter arrived and it was read to Alexander it made little impression on him; but some of his knights were deeply offended – indeed, they wanted to kill the messengers there and then, in Alexander's presence – because the letter had said he was accompanied by 'thieves and murderers and butchers'. But Alexander forbade them to harm the messengers, saying:

'It would send the wrong signal to a dog whose bark is so much worse than his bite. I'm confident,' he said, 'that before the year is out we'll make him change his tune.'

Then he dictated a letter and gave it to the messengers and bade them take it to their lord the emir of Babylon, and after presenting them with handsome gifts he sent them on their way. They set off and rode straight back to the emir and delivered Alexander's letter, which read as follows:

'From Alexander, commander of the Greeks, son of King Philip of Macedon and Queen Olympias, to Nabugor, emir of Babylon, greetings. We have received your letter and seen and read its contents and given them due consideration; and our response to you is this: with the help of God first and then of the valiant men-at-arms and fine worthies and barons and princes and noble lords in our company, we shall win lordship and mastery of your land just as we have of the other kings and princes we have brought under our subjection. You have threatened to make us feel your ferocity unless we leave your land; but since we consider it ours henceforth, we hereby inform you that if you fail to hand it over peaceably we shall show you our humanity, which you'll find more potent – and more painful – than your cruelty.'

The emir was utterly taken aback by this, and began to debate whether to do battle with Alexander in the open field or wait till he'd camped outside his city. It was finally decided that next morning, without waiting any longer and before Alexander was any nearer, they would ride out and gauge his army's strength, and test them and see how brave they were. So the emir summoned Nabusardan, a mighty baron who was with him in the city, the marshal and commander of all his forces, and gave him urgent orders to have ten thousand of their staunchest and bravest men-at-arms, the fittest possible for such a task, ready as early as could be, for he planned to pay Alexander's army a visit and give them an uncomfortable wake-up call.

Nabusardan set about it. He was a veteran, a wily warrior indeed, and that very night he sent scouts from the city to reconnoitre and spy on the enemy, insisting they be back good and early to show them the way if necessary. With all arranged he went to every house in the city where he knew the bravest men were lodging, and ensured that before he retired to rest they were all ready to answer the emir's bidding.

CHAPTER LXXI

How the emir of Babylon came and skirmished with Alexander's men.

By the time night had passed and dawn approached, a whole array of companions were armed and equipped, mounted and ready, and the emir rode from the city with a great number of knights: first and foremost Nabusardan, and another named Johaies of Egypt, and Amillas de Millat, and Cabamis, who was king of Belleme, and Rodoan des Pois and many more whose names I don't know.

Setting out in serried ranks, they hadn't gone far before they met the spies sent out by Nabusardan the previous night. They told them they'd found the enemy quite near, but that Alexander wasn't there: he'd gone somewhere else but they didn't know where. What they did know was that there were some very valiant men among his army: they'd heard mention of one named Ptholomer who was held in high regard by the Greeks. The emir was delighted by the news that Alexander was away from camp and said:

'Come then, friends! A mission bravely undertaken can only turn out well! So I pray you, make this mob of foreigners, who mean to rob us of our strength and all we own, feel the power of your blows this day, to your everlasting praise and honour!'

After these exhortations the emir ordered his spies to guide them and show them the best way to spring a sudden and surprise attack on the Greek camp. So the spies turned back and led the emir to within a quarter of a mile of Alexander's army – that's to say an eighth of a league – without being seen. Then as soon as they caught sight of the Greeks they lowered their lances and thrust in their spurs; their horses bore them with such fury that the very earth seemed to quake beneath their hooves, and they charged into Alexander's camp smashing everything in their path. They brought pavilions, tents and lodges crashing, slashing ropes and felling posts: it seemed they would flatten everything, and raised such a howling, wailing din that you'd have thought it was the end of the world. The Greeks were running hither and thither in total disarray. Then Ptholomer, who'd been left in charge that night but had retired to his tent with the coming of dawn, heard the clamour and leapt up at once; and rushing to his tent came Danselin first, his companion in arms, and then Emenidus and Perdicas, Ariscé and Caulus and many other barons of the army with their men, and they advanced at once to confront the enemy with all their might. It was pitiless, and many were felled and killed in the clash, both sides being fighters of the highest calibre.

But in the end the Greeks played their parts so well that the Babylonians, whether they liked it or not, were driven from the camp and back into the open field. What a bloody mêlée then ensued, as they battered and hammered each other with almighty fury. The Greeks came charging out of camp, some in battalions, some in crowds, and attacked the Babylonians with all their force; they felled them in great numbers, for they were far more battle-hardened than the men of Babylon. And seeing how it was going and that they'd no chance of winning, the Babylonians started to fall back; like all good warriors they continued to defend themselves as they did so, but in retreating to their city they lost great numbers of their men, for many were taken captive as we'll explain.

Chapter LXXII

How many Babylonians were captured and others killed and put to death.

As the Babylonians withdrew in good order ever closer to their city, the emir and some of his most valiant knights such as Nabusardan, Pharés, Amillas, Cabamis and Rodoan stayed at the rear, superbly mounted and armed with stout lances which they frequently made the Greeks feel. There were numerous jousts and combats then; among them for certain, according to our source, was a joust between Nabusardan and Ptholomer in which the two of them laid each other flat on the ground. To the rescue rode Pharés from the Babylonian side and Danselin from the Greeks, and just as the two had fallen together, so together they regained their saddles. Many lost their lives in the mêlée that followed, as the two sides rained sword-blows on each other with all their might, sending sparks flying from their blades. Pharés was seized and taken prisoner in the fray, but Nabusardan with his might and prowess and the edge of his sword avoided capture and escaped with his men who gave him valiant support.

The attack may have been over, but moments later Emenidus of Arcadia was in hot pursuit of the Babylonians and challenging them to turn back and stop their unchivalrous retreat; and the emir, a valiant warrior indeed, suddenly and without a word lowered his lance and charged back at Emenidus in a blazing fury. They drove their lances at each other's shields with such ferocity that they flew into splinters; instantly they seized their swords and started striking and battering each other, every blow sending hooks and pieces flying from helmets, shields and armour. Other knights came charging into the fray to rescue them, among them from the Babylonian side Cabamis and Amillas. Amillas was killed there, and Cabamis had his hand cut off and was taken prisoner. The emir himself was sent crashing to the ground, and had it not been for a bastard son of his – named Nabugor after him – he'd have died or been taken captive; but thanks to his son's brave feats of arms, whether the Greeks liked it or not the emir was remounted and returned to his men, though they were so reduced in numbers that there were barely half as many as had ridden from the city. The emir of Babylon, seeing the loss and damage he'd suffered, forbade any further jousting and sounded a final retreat. The Babylonians fell back swiftly till they reached the city; and it was as well they did so, for Alexander, now alerted to the battle, was on his way with a huge company of knights. But when he saw the Babylonians had withdrawn inside their walls he returned to camp; and there, soon after, all the aforesaid captives were presented to him, much to his delight.

Chapter LXXIII
How the emir of Babylon sent an embassy to Alexander to recover his prisoners.

Back inside his city and out of his armour, the emir asked his men what losses he'd suffered. They told him he'd lost immeasurably more than he'd gained, and listed those taken captive by the Greeks. He was deeply dismayed, for he was sure he had no prisoners to offer in exchange, and there was no reason to suppose the Greeks would hand them back. Nonetheless, he selected seven knights of note and sent them to Alexander to negotiate the return of his men: according to the history, the emir offered for each prisoner one hundred bolts of silken cloth embroidered in fine gold, and one hundred packhorses, forty laden with gold and sixty with silver.

The seven knight-ambassadors came to Alexander's camp and delivered the emir's message and his proffered gifts. This was Alexander's answer:

'Your emir, my good Babylonian gentlemen, imagines he can soften and sweeten us with rich gifts and presents, and make us give way to greed and covetousness and lose the fine reputation we've always enjoyed for prowess and generosity. No! Never! You will tell him, if you please, and with absolute certainty, that sooner than return the prisoners in exchange for gold or silver or other treasure, we'd have them killed by the lowliest fellows in our army! You can go whenever you like. And tell your king that we'll be acting according to our will, not his – and we'll exercise our will indeed, so much so that it won't be long before we and our companions show him our worth.'

Chapter LXXIV
How Alexander returned the emir of Babylon's men.

With that the ambassadors departed and rode straight back to the emir and reported Alexander's reply. The emir was beside himself with rage, and swore he'd go on his own and do battle with Alexander man to man. Indeed, had an elderly knight at his court not intervened he'd have ridden to the Greek camp there and then.

Meanwhile Alexander, as soon as the ambassadors left, called all the prisoners before him and had them generously served with food and drink. Once they were thoroughly refreshed he presented them with rich and handsome gifts, each according to his quality and as befitted him, and then had fine, sleek palfreys brought for them to ride back to their emir. But before they mounted he said to them:

'We don't want your emir, my good Babylonians, to imagine we're returning you because we fear or dread him in any way. Understand this: such is our largesse that we want you to go back and give him all the help you can – because unless he surrenders his city to us we assure you he's going to need all the help he can find! Go as soon as you please: the palfreys are ready and we grant you safe conduct.'

They fell to their knees as one and gave thanks to Alexander and the attendant lords; then they mounted and set off and didn't stop riding till they reached the city. There's no need to ask if the emir was surprised to see them – all the more so when he heard how they'd been freed! He said:

'This Alexander acts in remarkable ways. I'd say he's more supernatural than human – or else so proud that he despises all men, no matter how mighty, because Fortune has lifted him so high that he thinks himself the ruler of all the world.'

CHAPTER LXXV
Of a reverse the Babylonians inflicted on the Greeks, according to the history.

Just as the emir was talking to his men about Alexander's spirit, some of his spies came before him in the hall and reported that a body of Greeks – about ten thousand, well mounted, equipped and armed – had ridden from Alexander's camp and gone foraging in the Vales of Daniel, to raid the land for livestock and supplies. As soon as he heard this the emir summoned a group of his captains and ordered them to prepare at once, for he wanted to go and attack these Greeks, now separated from the rest of their army, and keep them from the herds they meant to steal. The captains responded instantly, and according to the history more than fifty thousand horse and foot set out from the city.

They followed the trail of the Greeks with all speed, and kept going till they found them. Then they launched an attack so fierce that at the start the Greeks lost more than five hundred men before they could assemble and unite; their captains, seeing the huge number of Babylonians, had no time to do anything but rush into some gardens they chanced to find there, enclosed by thick hedges, and rally and deploy as best they could. Ptholomer, who was in command, told his companions they needed to alert Alexander and the army to their plight; but he could find no one willing to go – they all said there was no need yet! They seemed to think that if they sent the message they'd be accused of cowardice. It was to cost them dear, because while they were debating the point the Babylonians, who had seen them in the gardens, swarmed to the attack, smashing all the hedges to the ground. What a ferocious battle followed then, as the Greeks fought for their lives like fury with the blades of their swords. There was clearly little love lost: the two sides butchered each other mercilessly, leaving vast piles of dead. Our history says that Ptholomer was felled and left for dead among the slain.

At last Danselin, a fine knight indeed, escaped the battle and rode back to Alexander's camp to report the dire events. Alexander instantly bade the trumpets sound and mounted, fully armed and smartly followed by twenty thousand troops, and rode to find the foragers still fighting, holding firm, the Babylonians unable to drive them from the hedged enclosures. Into the fray charged Alexander, and the battle turned abruptly and cruelly against the men of Babylon: they were tiring while the Greek reinforcements were completely fresh. Seeing this, the emir sounded the retreat and began to fall back to his city. He took refuge there with his forces as soon as he could, but not without heavy losses of horses and knights. Indeed, his own horse was killed beneath him in the course of the retreat.

CHAPTER LXXVI

How Alexander had Ptholomer carried back to camp, gravely wounded.

With the pursuit now over and the Babylonians withdrawn inside their city, Alexander returned to the battlefield and ordered a search through all the wounded and the dead. Among them they found Ptholomer with terrible wounds all over his body. I don't think he would have risen again, as he lay there in agony among the dead; but the moment he saw Alexander he was so revivified that he seemed to be already half healed. The king had him lifted up and gently laid in a litter and carried straight back to camp and visited at once by his trusty surgeons; and when they'd seen and examined his wounds they assured the king he would recover well and swiftly. Alexander was overjoyed, and promised the surgeons they'd be well rewarded. Then he arranged for the knights who'd died to be collected from the field and buried with all honour, and for his surgeons to tend to those who'd survived.

Once this was done he summoned all the workmen in the army and ordered them to build wooden towers and siege engines, for he meant to advance now on the city. The workmen set about it, and it wasn't long before they'd built towers on wheels, and catapults and battering rams, springalds and arbalests in great numbers. When all these machines were ready for action Alexander ordered everyone to pack and load and head for the city. They did so; and the history says at this point that Alexander camped so close to the city that no man could leave it without being seized and held captive by his army. The emir and his barons and all the citizens were in a state of deep alarm, for Alexander had so many men, all well armed and equipped and ready, that they were beyond any man's counting: it seemed as if the whole world had come there to support him.

CHAPTER LXXVII

How the emir of Babylon was told by his god that Alexander was soon to die.

When Nabugor, emir of Babylon, saw Alexander's immense forces surrounding and blockading him, he called together all of the city's wisest men, both clerical and lay, to advise him what could be done for the best and how he should proceed – and indeed what would be the outcome of this war. Among the assembly was a learned man steeped in science, in geomancy, sorcery and divination by fire. He presented himself to the emir and said he felt it would be wise to refer to their god Apollo – Babylon's main temple was dedicated to him – and offer him a sacrifice and beg him in his mercy to give them a sign and indication of how the war would end. All the princes and barons agreed with his plan, and without delay the emir commanded that the temple of the god Apollo be opened and the people go and worship the idol as the learned man had advised.

They obeyed; and after due solemnities had been observed the emir had ten men, knights and squires all of noble stature, taken and led before the idol; and there, in the presence of all the people, they were sacrificed, burnt to ashes. And when the burning and the sacrifice were done, and everyone was kneeling before the idol, a voice was heard, saying:

'Alexander, king of Macedon, has now come to the place where he will meet his end. Soon his wheel will turn and bear him down to the nadir, and in this city he will not endure.'

Hearing this the people were beside themselves with joy, convinced that Alexander wouldn't enter Babylon and that his attack on the city would end as the voice had said.

But it didn't happen quite as they'd understood, for King Alexander by his prowess conquered the city of Babylon and sat in mighty, majestic state there, as you're about to hear. But after this worldly glory he did not live long, for he was wickedly betrayed and poisoned.

CHAPTER LXXVIII

How the noble King Alexander ordered the storming of the great city of Babylon.

With his army massed in incalculable numbers before the great city of Babylon, the noble King Alexander gave orders for his mighty array of siege engines to be drawn up and made ready, and for all his troops to prepare, men-at-arms and archers alike, for he meant to storm the city. Then you'd have seen all the engines – wheeled siege-towers, battering rams and catapults of every kind – rumbling towards the walls, boldly preceded by the men-at-arms clutching their lances, and the archers, crossbowmen and slingers proudly advancing, impressively shielded by their pavais.[1] Among them, too, were brave, tough and able fellows, some armed with picks and billhooks and others carrying ladders and the other gear needed for an assault. Right up to the walls they strode and began a furious, ferocious attack; but they met with a valiant response indeed: as brave as their attack was the Babylonians' defence. You'd have seen many a man-at-arms felled then, struck down by rocks and sling-stones flung in mighty volleys by the city's men; almost all were ranged along the walls and pitilessly dashing their attackers to the ground with axes, swords and lances. Women and men alike were pouring quicklime and boiling water down on Alexander's troops, inflicting dreadful damage. And then, when the siege towers were ready and wheeled up to the walls, the awesome feats of arms performed by both sides were wondrous to behold. And according to the history the men of the city hurled Greek fire at the towers, setting many of them ablaze with grievous loss to Alexander. But whatever damage he sustained, he pressed on with the assault with might and main, and the slaughter and the havoc raged till nightfall. By that time as many as six hundred of Alexander's knights lay dead and a good

---

[1]   The 'pavais' or 'pavache' was a shield, usually of wood and leather, big enough to protect a man from head to foot.

eight hundred foot; and in the city they'd lost, one way and another, around a thousand.

But with the coming of night, darkness forced the two sides to go their separate ways. Then Alexander, seeing the extent of the damage he'd suffered, swore by God omnipotent that he'd never leave till the city was at his mercy, or would die in the attempt. But if Alexander was upset about the men he'd lost, so was the emir, who'd lost almost all his finest knights.

CHAPTER LXXIX

How the emir sent another message to Alexander, demanding that he do battle or leave his land.

It wasn't long before the emir, who had countless forces to call on in the city, summoned all his chief barons for another council of war. When they were assembled he put it to them that they were suffering steady losses by the day, and that Alexander was now besieging the city and, despite the harm he'd suffered, was showing no sign of giving up – rather, seemed intent on conquering the city and all the land.

'That's why, dear friends and companions,' he said, 'I think it best to send an embassy to see if we can secure peace and persuade him to leave our land – with gifts or in some other way.'

But many protested that this would be deeply shameful, and said they'd never consent to sending Alexander anything other than a date for battle! 'There are enough of us in this city,' they said, 'to do battle with them – and even if you lose twenty thousand men you needn't worry: the gods' predictions will never fail us!'

So the decision was made to send two able, eloquent knights to make clear to Alexander that he had no claim to the land, as it had never belonged to any of his line, and that no one had done him any wrong to justify his waging war – especially without a formal challenge, which was unbecoming of a worthy man. And they were to defy him on behalf of the emir, telling him to leave the land or face certain battle. All agreed to this, and the knights were selected and given instructions at once, and set out with their commission and made their way to the besieging army with green branches in their hands, as was then the custom for all envoys. They delivered their message to Alexander with great care and precision, just as they'd been instructed.

Alexander replied that the emir ought to have considered himself challenged, in view of the noble, mighty conquests he'd made with the help of God and his companions. 'So you can inform your king,' he said, 'that we'll never leave this land till we have the city, land and people entirely in our power. As for battle, we're fully recovered! We're ready to meet him! And you can tell him we won't leave him a single foot of ground where he can rule or call himself king.'

Having heard Alexander's response the messengers departed; he gave them a most worthy escort, who let them go once they neared the city. Then the messengers rode in and came before the emir and reported Alexander's reply: that he wouldn't leave him a foot of ground and was fully recovered and ready for battle. The emir was aghast; he called his barons together and had Alexander's response relayed to them, so that they could reflect upon it and advise him what to do. After due consideration they all agreed that first thing next day, without further delay, they should go and attack him with banner unfurled and see then what transpired.

Present at the discussion was a young knight named Macabrin, the son of a king, who was desperate to perform some deed of chivalry and to test and prove his strength and courage. According to the history he'd come to Babylon with ten thousand troops to serve the emir, who I believe was a kinsman; and now this Macabrin, hearing of the impending battle with the Greeks, came to the emir and begged to be entrusted with the first battalion and the first charge when they met. The emir agreed, but reluctantly, for the youth seemed rash and fiery and he feared he'd take too many risks.

Chapter LXXX

How Macabrin challenged Ptholomer to joust, and how battalions were formed.

Having secured the emir's agreement Macabrin left court at once and went to his lodging. There he summoned one of his squires and bade him go straight to Alexander's camp and seek out a baron named Ptholomer, and tell him on his behalf that, if he dared, he should come next day and, for love of the ladies and especially of prowess, exchange a lance-blow with him – he would find him ready in front of the battle lines; for he'd heard such amazing reports of his deeds that he couldn't believe he'd achieved them all, and he challenged and summoned him now as the king's son that he was.

With that the squire set out and rode to the besiegers' camp and tracked down Ptholomer. After hearing Macabrin's summons, Ptholomer told the messenger to wait a moment till he'd spoken to the king; and he came to Alexander and asked him for honour's sake to give him leave to accept the challenge. The king, ever eager for his men to enhance their honour, freely agreed; so Ptholomer returned to the messenger and had him presented with a fine and handsome gift – a courser[1] – and told him to tell his master that he thanked him for honouring him with the challenge, and to assure him he'd find him ready next day as he'd requested.

Then the squire set off with his courser and returned to his master and told him how things had gone, just as you've heard. Macabrin was delighted, especially to hear his squire had been treated with such honour; and he instructed his marshal to ensure that all his men-at-arms were ready in the morning without fail, and to see whether his armour, horse or harness needed attention. Then he went to rest till morning, when he rose very early to fulfil his stated promise. As soon as he was up he had himself superbly armed; then he mounted along with his whole battalion.

---

[1]   See note 1, above, p.199.

Chapter LXXXI
How the battalions were drawn up on both sides, the emir's and Alexander's.

You've heard how the emir, with the backing of all his council, had summoned King Alexander to leave the land or face imminent battle, and had already granted Macabrin the honour of leading the first attack and squadron. As soon as Macabrin left, the emir ordered his other battalions as he saw fit. He immediately called for Nabusardan and appointed him captain of the second phalanx (that is to say, squadron), so that he would be close enough to help Macabrin if the need arose – which it did. The third battalion he gave to an elderly baron named Salligor, a man full of craft and courage; the fourth he entrusted to Pharés, whom we've mentioned before; the fifth to one named Rodoan and the sixth to a most worthy baron by the name of Samson. The emir would ride from squadron to squadron as he chose, with a company of twenty knights armed exactly like himself so that those who didn't know him would be unable to pick him out. In each of these squadrons were six thousand men-at-arms, good and strong, all braced and ready for the toughest of contests. He also formed a battalion of infantry, consisting of fifteen thousand men armed with axes or with gisarmes[1] which had hooks on the shafts to catch and haul down men-at-arms and knights if need be.

And so, with all prepared as I've described, first thing next morning the emir was ready for action. Before leaving the city he entrusted its defence to two valiant barons; then he called for the gate to be opened and rode out to battle.

Meanwhile Alexander, still in camp but well aware that the Babylonians were about to ride out, speedily prepared his own squadrons. Ptholomer was to command the first, so he gave him ten thousand of the finest men-at-arms in all the army, and bade Danselin share the captaincy with him, 'for,' he said, 'I know you've long been companions in arms, and I want you to be at each other's side to give mutual support and aid if need be.' Perdicas led the second battalion, Philotas the third, Ariscé the fourth, Antigonus the fifth, and Alexander took command of the sixth himself. He placed ten thousand men-at-arms in each battalion. When all was done he exhorted them all to fight well, as they always did.

Now, then, all the squadrons had been drawn up on both sides, and they began to make their way to the field where the deeds of arms would be done. And first we must tell of Macabrin and Ptholomer, who were due to joust with each other.

Chapter LXXXII
How Ptholomer jousted with Macabrin and unhorsed him in the field.

So, as you've heard, a great array of squadrons formed. First to ride from the city and into the field was Macabrin, superbly armed and equipped in every

---

[1]   See note 1, above, p.87.

detail, along with his whole battalion. As soon as he reached the battleground he told a knight of his named Crahes, captain of his cavalry, to stay with the squadron and keep the men in readiness to fall upon the foe with all their might when the moment came. He, meanwhile, rode a bowshot ahead of his squadron.

No sooner had he done so than Ptholomer arrived with his battalion, and like-wise bade Danselin hold their men in check and wait for him, for he could see his challenger was already there. Danselin did so, and Ptholomer, without fur-ther ado, rode to meet his man. As he drew near they both thrust in their spurs, and their horses bore them towards each other full tilt. The speed of their mounts and the might of their thrusts combined to make their clash a wonder to behold: Macabrin's blow to Ptholomer's shield sent his lance flying into splinters; but Ptholomer's lance was stout and strong, and he met Macabrin's shield with such mighty force that he sent him flying from his saddle and over his horse's rump and crashing to the ground so hard that it nearly killed him. His horse's speed bore him close to Macabrin's squadron before he could turn back; but turn he did, and throwing his lance to the ground and drawing his sword he rode at Macabrin, who was back on his feet with sword in hand, beside himself with shame and rage. He came to meet Ptholomer, and Ptholomer attacked him likewise and grabbed the nose-guard of his helm and would have hauled him away a prisoner had it not been for Crahes, captain of Macabrin's cavalry, who cried:

'Ah! Defend yourself, sir knight! You're taking him no further!'

If Ptholomer hadn't turned to face him he'd have struck him from behind, but he let Macabrin go and confronted Crahes; and as they locked swords, all the men-at-arms from both sides charged to join them in an immense, tremendous collision of blades and lances. Our history suggests that in this first charge more than six thousand men from both sides died.

CHAPTER LXXXIII

How the phalanxes – that is to say squadrons – of both sides joined in battle.

While these two – Macabrin and Ptholomer, that is – and all their men were fighting with might and main, and the other squadrons from both sides were advancing, bent on destroying one another, from the Babylonian side came Nabusardan at the head of his battalion, finely arrayed in serried ranks like the able men they were. Seeing the first squadrons now engaged as we've described, they promptly charged to join the fray. So the squadron led by Perdicas advanced to meet them, attacking with such fury that many were felled and killed amid mayhem so intense that they could barely recognise each other. And according to the history, both Macabrin and his companion – Crahes, that is, the captain of his cavalry – were slain there, along with many more whose names we don't know.

The Babylonians were driven back some fifty yards,[1] and Nabusardan, see-

---

[1]   Literally 'more than half an arpent': see note 2, above, p.87.

ing disaster looming, charged into the Greeks with such ferocity that he felled four of the finest knights in Ptholomer's and Perdicas's company. But before his charge was done his horse was killed beneath him in a hail of darts and lances and he was pitched to the ground; but he landed upright on his feet, and with the battle-axe he was clutching he made such a stand, holding all at bay, that no one could deny his valour. He battled bravely on till he was rescued and re-mounted, for the third Babylonian squadron, led by the elderly Salligor, charged into the fray with such vigour that they made the Greeks give ground and scatter. In the course of their charge Nabusardan was remounted, and he attacked the Greeks in a blaze of fury – especially Ptholomer, whom he'd come to hate; but Ptholomer was undaunted by him and rode to meet him, sword in hand, and they began to strike each other with awesome might: each blow made them buckle and slump over their saddle-bows, and sent shards of helm and armour flying to the ground – they looked like carpenters chopping wood.

Now all the squadrons from both sides were attacking and contesting ground, and as they met there was an appalling slaughter of men-at-arms and horses. It was now that the infantry we mentioned strode into the thickest part of the fray with their gisarmes and their espadons[1] and, whether the Greeks liked it or not, drove them back and forced them to give ground. Then Alexander, seeing these infantry performing tremendous feats of arms, started crying to his men:

'Oh, my beloved companions, what are you doing? Have you forgotten how you've vanquished all the nations on the earth and won so many famous victories? Now you recoil before men who are nothing by comparison! I pray you follow me, and take me as your example!'

Then without more ado Alexander, sword in hand and finely mounted on a handsome rouncey, charged into these men-at-arms on foot and sent them tumbling one upon another. With his knights behind him he drove them into a wild retreat, trampling each other down as they fled till they were piled in mountainous heaps: according to our history more than six thousand died without receiving a cut or blow. Truly, the wailing was so great, so terrible, that it sounded like the end of the world. And now Nabusardan, locked in combat with Ptholomer as you've heard, was met by such an awesome blow that his head was sent flying from his shoulders. His Babylonians at this were quite undone, and abandoned the fight and fled from Ptholomer and his knights.

CHAPTER LXXXIV
How, according to the history, the emir was slain and all his forces routed.

On hearing of his marshal's death the emir was beside himself with rage, ablaze with fury, his heart so gripped by wrath indeed that he began to curse himself and all his men; and to avenge his terrible loss he seized a stout spear from one of his knights, charged into the mass of his foes like a man deranged

---

[1]   See note 1, above, p.126.

and performed feats of arms appalling to behold. His knights rode after him, plunging into the Greeks with such ferocity that it seemed Alexander's forces would be utterly destroyed. You'd have seen brains scattered, hands and limbs and heads severed and many a man disembowelled, transfixed; there were herds of riderless horses everywhere. So great were the piles of dead that it seemed, truly, as if the world was about to end amid the deafening, monstrous, piteous wails. Then Alexander, seeing the emir's dreadful slaughter of his men, slung his shield from his neck again, gripped his lance and charged to meet him with such fury, felling everything in his path, that he sent him crashing to the ground with his legs in the air. He was too stunned by the fall to know if it was night or day; but his knights came rushing to rescue him and hoisted him up and put him back in the saddle – but not without great loss of life, for the Greeks, swords in hands, assailed them with all their might, determined to crush the Babylonians. Rescuing the emir cost them many of their captains, including Salligor, Pharés and Rodoan: such was the Babylonians' dismay at losing them that they almost lost control. The emir, now remounted and recovered, seeing his men being slain on every side, started crying:

'Alexander! Alexander! Come and fight me if you dare, man to man, foul murderer and plunderer that you are!'

Alexander heard him clearly, and charged at him full tilt and the emir at him. They rained hammering blows upon each other with their swords as if each was a smith and the other was an anvil; but in the end, after many a blow had been given and received, Alexander sent the emir's head flying across the field – according to some accounts, that is; the history we're following says he ran him through with a spear. But whatever the manner of the death-blow, it was dealt by Alexander's own hand. And when the emir fell the Babylonians started to break and flee in all directions: in no time at all they'd deserted the field and returned to their city – at least, those who could: others scuttled away into the wilds, where they thought they'd be safer. Alexander was left on the field victorious, and issued orders at once forbidding any pursuit: he was satisfied with what had been done.

CHAPTER LXXXV

How the people of Babylon brought the keys to Alexander, and how he entered the city.

With victory secured, Alexander and his barons retired to their tents where they were disarmed so that they could rest and recover as they urgently needed – and many were wounded and needed the surgeons.

It wasn't very long before the citizens of Babylon arrived at Alexander's camp, barefoot and stripped to their shifts, carrying the keys of the city; and they came before the king and surrendered the city, themselves and all their possessions to him. King Alexander, whose custom was always to show mercy to the humble, immediately made peace with them and assured them he would forgive them all his wrath, and that they could return to their city in confidence and tell their fellow citizens that, if they were willing to be good subjects, he would be a good lord, and that no man in the city would lose anything he owned, be it land or home or any other property. To ensure that all went safely to plan he sent Ptholomer with them to take possession of the city in his name.

Shortly afterwards he had the emir's body carried from the field and splendidly embalmed and prepared for burial. He did likewise with the other kings, princes, counts and barons, each as befitted his status. Some he had buried at once, along with the lesser men, but the bodies of the emir and other kings he had carried to the city; he rode there with them in great triumph and pomp until they reached the temple of their god Jupiter where he saw them buried with all possible honour.

According to our history the emir's sepulchre was made with amazing artistry: it had four handsomely carved pillars of marble and limestone which soared from their plinths to a height beyond any man's reach or throw; they supported a ribbed vault, superbly sculpted, on which the emir's body was laid in a lead tomb skilfully overlaid with tabernacles of gold and silver from which grew trees whose spreading branches covered the whole structure and protected it from rain or shower. The entire edifice was pinned and buttressed with lead and iron, and lamps burned upon it night and day. It had many other features, too, which I'll pass over for the sake of brevity.[1]

When all was done Alexander made his way to the principal palace in the city, where he was received with all pomp and honour. And in his admirable magnanimity he proclaimed peace and forbade any men-at-arms from either side, on pain of death, to molest or injure any man, for all people without exception were to be left to enjoy their possessions in freedom and safety as they had done before. And if any, by the fortunes of war, had ended up in foreign parts, Alexander bade that their friends inform them they could safely return: any deception in this matter would be punishable by death.

CHAPTER LXXXVI

How tribute was brought to Alexander from all parts of the world.

You heard earlier how Alexander had sent demands to many parts of the world that they send him tribute and acknowledge their subjugation. It wasn't long after his conquest of Babylon that, in response to his bidding, a stream of dukes, counts, princes and barons from all the kingdoms of the world began to flow in, bearing tribute and acknowledgement that he alone was their lord, their king, their emperor. These princes came from Rome, France, Spain and Germany, from England, Sicily, Sardinia and many other isles of the sea.

---

[1] Wauquelin greatly reduces the extravagant description of the tomb given in the verse *Roman d'Alexandre*, and interestingly shuns magical elements: with regard to the lamps, for example, according to his source 'four lamps hung [around the tomb] suspended in midair by magic...and burned brightly night and day without any oil being added' (Branch III stanza 421).

The Romans sent him a train of mules and horses laden with enormous sums of gold. This gift earned them a most honourable reception from Alexander, who said to them:

'It's clear that the people who sent me this present love me most cordially! In return we shall hold them in special affection.'

These words revealed his nature to be covetous and grasping, despite his long-standing reputation for largesse. It wasn't his true nature; but he was becoming so inclined, and could clearly see that his past generosity was now earning him greater gifts in return. In the words of the wise proverb: Date et dabitur vobis, which translated means: 'Give and it will be given to you.'

Among the other gifts and tributes brought to Alexander, the French gave him a magnificent shield, richly emblazoned with his arms. He accepted it with great delight, and said to the messengers who'd brought it, in the hearing of everyone:

'By nature and custom the people of France are the strongest and most valiant in all the world, so the gift they have sent is most appropriate for me, the shield's bearer, and for them, its senders.'

What he meant was that the shield was an apt gift for him to receive because he'd conquered the whole world by his chivalry, and an apt gift for them to send because to his knowledge the French were the finest warriors in the world in terms of skill and strength and strategy.

Of the other presents and gifts and letters and acknowledgements the histories make no mention, so we'll leave it at that.

Chapter LXXXVII

How Alexander sent letters to his mother and to his good master Aristotle.

With all the peoples of the world now obeying him without demur as their sovereign king and emperor, Alexander promptly dictated letters and sent them to his mother and his master Aristotle, telling them of the battles and trials he'd faced in conquering all the world's kingdoms, and of the strange peoples and creatures he'd found in many distant parts of India and elsewhere. To prove his words he sent his mother gifts of some of his most amazing discoveries: men with no head or one foot or one eye and other extraordinary things. And he told her, too, how he'd finally descended on Babylon and triumphantly conquered the city and was waiting for her there, for his intention was to be crowned there as emperor of the whole world. So he begged her most affectionately to be at this great occasion without fail, for it was his dearest wish that she should share in the celebration and rejoice in his glory.

When the lady Olympias received the message and call from her beloved son Alexander she was joyful beyond measure, and immediately summoned the noble philosopher Aristotle, Alexander's master and teacher, to share the news with him and to seek his help in making the journey possible. But the history says she never made it, as will become clear in due course. But it does say that master Aristotle wrote Alexander a letter which read something like this:

Chapter LXXXVIII

The contents of the letter sent by master Aristotle to Alexander.

'To Alexander of Macedon, emperor and king of all earthly kings, the philosopher Aristotle wishes health and joy. Mighty emperor, I have seen the missives you sent to my lady Olympias your mother and to me, which have made plain the phenomenal trials you've suffered in your conquest of the world. In the course of it your men have shown obedience to you that has earned them a reputation for all worthy qualities.

'It seems to us therefore that you have achieved your goal – lordship of the whole world, that is – by the will of God omnipotent and the valour of your men. So we give thanks to the God of nature for giving you the heart to learn and retain the knowledge and wisdom that have enabled you to accomplish this, but at the same time we give thanks to your men for their staunch determination to achieve what has never been seen before and will never be seen again. We pray you, be ever mindful of the blood they've shed in order to place you in your high and exalted position, and be sure to repay and reward their service and devotion: it will show the world that their service to you was effort well spent, and will earn you the approval of the great power divine that has no beginning and no end (and may it guide your steps forever).

'I say all this because in this world it seems there is nothing more contrary to nature than the retention of servants and the rewarding of their service! It's a sin that cries to the high God for vengeance, especially when the shedding of their blood goes unpaid.

'May almighty God grant you, wherever you may be, continued honour, joy, happiness and health.'

This letter once written was taken to Alexander at the city of Babylon, and he received it with delight; and he resolved to follow his good teacher's exhortations, for no advice Aristotle had given him in his life had ever proved to be other than sound. He decided to summon kings, princes, dukes, counts and barons to a sumptuous feast in his city of Babylon, and in their presence he would make his servants kings, dukes, counts, princes and great barons of the lands and mighty kingdoms he had conquered.

Chapter LXXXIX

Of a half-dead child born at this time in the city of Babylon.

Our history[1] records that at this time Queen Roxane, wife of the noble King Alexander, arrived in Babylon and there became pregnant with a child sired by Alexander and later to be named Hercules. But I have yet to find any histories that make much mention of him, only that he and his mother were imprisoned

---

[1]   Wauquelin has now returned to the Prose *Alexander* as his main source.

by Cassander in the city of Amphipolis[1] – though they don't specify whether or not he died there.

It wasn't long after Roxane's arrival that a lady in the city, whom Alexander had earlier known carnally, gave birth to a child. As soon as he was born she had him wrapped in sheets and taken to Alexander, bidding him look at what he'd sired. The reason she sent him was that the top half of the body, from the head to the navel, was in human shape, but devoid of life; and from the navel down the body took the form of a throng of beasts fighting and biting each other monstrously, apparently bent on devouring and destroying one another. Alexander was shocked by the sight of this deformity, and began to wonder what it could portend.

He suddenly remembered an astrologer in his entourage and sent for him at once. As soon as he arrived Alexander led him to a chamber – in private, just the two of them – and showed him the outlandish child and asked for his opinion. After looking at the deformed creature the astrologer pondered a little, and then sighed deeply and dissolved into tears, weeping bitterly. Alexander demanded that he say what he was thinking and not hold back through fear; and the astrologer, with much trepidation, began to say:

'Ah, mighty, glorious emperor! The days are near at hand when Fortune will deprive you of all those things with which She has ennobled and enriched you!'

Hearing this, Alexander asked him: 'What is it that tells you that, master?'

'I will make it plain, sir, truly,' he replied. 'It is thus: the half of this creature that takes the form of a dead man, separate from the beasts, signifies that, just as man is a nobler being than an animal, so you are finer and more noble than any other king now living and any king yet to come; but its being dead is a sign that your death approaches and the end of your days is near. And the beasts below, biting and clawing at each other, symbolise your barons, dukes and counts, who compared to you are as good as beasts and after your death will jealously vie for dominion. Indeed, they're already at odds with one another, but have never dared show it while you are lord of all the world; but once you're gone and the world is without a lord they'll all do battle with each other to win the biggest share as dogs do over a carcass. That's the meaning of the fighting beasts.'

Alexander was downcast and dismayed at hearing this; and after ordering the burial of the loathsome creature he retired to his chamber where he thought about nothing but his death. Weeping, he said:

'Dear Lord God, almighty Father, since I am about to end my days as several have now informed me, I pray you look upon me with pity, mortal that I am, and bestow such wisdom upon me in my final days that for the rest of time all mention of my name shall be to the praise of your infinite majesty.'

[1]   'Philopame'.

How Alexander summoned all the greatest princes in the world to a feast where he intended to be crowned king of all the earth.

As you've heard, Alexander was deeply disturbed and troubled in his heart, feeling sure now that it wouldn't be long till the predictions he'd been given by the trees in the Indian deserts – and King Calammus's prediction, too[1] – were fulfilled. As he pondered on this it struck him that man's only riches after his death are the good name and renown that remain when he's gone, gained by the works he achieved in his life. With this in mind he proclaimed a most noble feast in the city of Babylon, where he would hold open court amid great splendour and celebration. To it he would summon all his vassal kings, princes, dukes, counts and barons, bidding them attend in person to make the feast all the finer and more illustrious; and there before the whole assembly he would have them crown him king and lord of all the earth enclosed within the Ocean's bounds.

And so it was that he dictated letters and sent them at once to all the great princes known to him in the world, commanding them on receipt of the letters, and without any excuse, to come to the city of Babylon to attend a glorious feast he wished to celebrate in their presence. Once the messengers were dispatched and news of the feast spread, so many people started arriving from far and wide that, according to the histories, never before or since had such numbers assembled for a feast as then.

It should be added that among the messages sent by Alexander throughout the kingdoms of the world he sent word to Greece, to his mother the lady Olympias, informing her of the noble feast that he, her only hope, her beloved son, had proclaimed. His mother was beside herself with joy, seeing her son in a position never witnessed in the world before, and feeling certain in her heart that it would never be seen again – it remains, indeed, unequalled to this day. But she was certain, too, that among so many people there were bound to be some who didn't love her son but harboured some resentment of his honour and magnificence: she knew of some who particularly hated him, such as Antipater, lord of Tyre, and his children Cassander and Jobas. So she wrote to Alexander warning him to beware of treachery, especially from these three, telling him that she knew for sure that Antipater felt no true love for him, whatever he might pretend.

How Alexander sent messengers inviting Antipater to the feast.

Antipater was lord of Tyre, a city of which we've spoken earlier and which King Alexander had entrusted to him. According to our history he was also the guardian of Defur, a city and territory won by Alexander from Duke

---

[1] p.239.

Melcis.[1] Our history refers to this victory as taking place after the conquest of Babylon; with all respect this strikes me as improbable: it should surely rather be placed before the accomplishing of the Vows of the Peacock.[2] But since we've found it so in our source, we shall give a brief account of it in the following chapters, so that the details of the conquest are at least known. But we'll return for a moment to the matter in hand and tell how Alexander summoned Antipater to the feast.

There's no doubt that Alexander was shocked by his mother's letter, but he gave no sign of this to anyone. Our history suggests he didn't quite believe it, mainly because Antipater was a native of Macedon and, as I've said, he had given him the city of Tyre. All the same, to make certain, he dictated a letter requiring Antipater, as soon as he received it and setting all excuses aside, to come to the feast, for he greatly desired to have him in his company at the coronation he meant to stage in the presence of all the kings and princes of the world. Antipater was alarmed and dismayed by this summons, fearing that Alexander meant to strip him of his authority and bestow it elsewhere; and suddenly the Enemy of all goodness entered his body and inspired him to plot the death of Alexander, as you'll hear in due course. But first we'll explain what prompted him to this.

CHAPTER XCII

How the land of Defur was conquered and Duke Melcis killed at the prompting of Gracien, a knight of Tyre.

Our history[3] says that one day, as he was riding on one of his missions, King Alexander met a knight named Gracien of Tyre. When he came before the king he was questioned about what had brought him there, and he said he was from the land of Chaldea, from the city of Tyre or the country thereabouts, and had come in search of support because the lord of the land, whom he'd served for a long time, was wicked and craven; his retinue was filled with liars and flatterers and he paid heed to no one else. Gracien was so persuasive that Alexander mobilised all his forces and followed him to his land where there stood a mighty city. Here there was a rich duke of great age by the name of Asper[4] who had two valiant sons, one aged twenty and the other eighteen. We've frequently spoken of the twenty-year-old in the course of our story, for his name was Floridas – that's what makes us feel that this conquest of Defur is better placed before the Vows of the Peacock than here.[5] The other son was named Dauris.

---

1   See above, p.73.
2   Wauquelin is referring to the fact that *La Prise de Defur*, an anonymous thirteenth-century work of some 1,650 lines, is interpolated in some manuscripts of the verse *Roman d'Alexandre* (including, evidently, the manuscript from which he was working) towards the end of Branch III, after Alexander's conquest of Babylon.
3   i.e. the *Prise de Defur* section of the verse *Roman d'Alexandre*.
4   'Jaspar' in *La Prise de Defur*. In his edition of *La Prise* (p.91), Lawton P. G. Peckham notes that the names Jaspar and Melcis may have been inspired by two of the three Biblical magi.
5   i.e. because it's here, as we're about to see, that Alexander supposedly first meets Floridas, who featured prominently in the Vows of the Peacock.

As soon as Alexander reached the land – its overlord was the powerful duke named Melcis – he began to wage mighty war and seize towns and strongholds, until he arrived outside the city of which Asper was lord. Because of his age, however, he had now placed his two sons in charge, and when they saw Alexander and the Greeks descending on Chaldea they assembled all the men they could and launched many a sally and engaged in many a bloody combat and clash with Alexander. And on one such occasion Floridas's bold valour led to him being captured, and he was taken to Alexander and became his prisoner. He came to admire King Alexander greatly, just as Alexander admired Floridas's manner and courage.

CHAPTER XCIII

How Duke Melcis was killed, Dauris married and Floridas captured again.

When Floridas was taken captive his brother Dauris, seeing how Fortune was raising Alexander to the very top of Her wheel, swiftly informed his liege lord – Duke Melcis, that is – of the disaster that had befallen him. Melcis mustered all his forces as soon as he could, and while they were assembling he sent an embassy to Alexander to tell him that, unless he left his land and returned his liegeman to him, he would attack him in such numbers that he would repent too late. Alexander was unimpressed.

Then shortly after Floridas's capture, Dauris, in the city and raging at his brother's imprisonment, launched a sortie against the Greeks, so effectively that he captured Danselin, brother of Ptholomer (even if he wasn't his actual brother, we've always found him to have been his brother in arms), and thereby was able to win back his brother Floridas in exchange.

And it wasn't long after the exchange that Duke Melcis arrived outside the city with all his forces; a day was agreed for battle and the two armies advanced to confront each other. There was terrible slaughter on both sides, in the course of which Duke Melcis was killed and his whole army routed. And in this battle both the aforesaid brothers, Floridas and Dauris, were captured, and it's said that when they were taken to Alexander he said they were a prize worth more to him than twelve times the number of lands he'd conquered.[1] He was then informed that Duke Melcis had a most beautiful daughter; he bade that she be brought to him there at the city of Defur and gave her in marriage to the young knight Dauris, much to his joy, for he had long loved her and she him.

The conquest complete Alexander moved on; but to ensure the land remained safely under his lordship and dominion he appointed Antipater, of whom we've been speaking, to be its governor on his behalf.

---

[1]   In *La Prise de Defur* Alexander 'was overjoyed to have them in good shape, with neither of them harmed; he relished winning them more than any of the lands he'd conquered… and he said to his men: "I have the rose and the lily – I've never seen two braver men of their age!"' (vv.1003-9); and he notes that Floridas is well named, because "you are *'floris'* [embellished] with a noble heart!" (v.1025).

CHAPTER XCIV

How Antipater plotted to poison his good master King Alexander.

Back at his city of Babylon, Alexander, having received his mother's warning about Antipater, summoned him to the feast as you've heard, and Antipater, suspecting that Alexander meant to strip him of his office, decided to resolve the problem once and for all. To see to it, he made his way to a doctor-surgeon and wickedly persuaded him to supply him with a toxic potion designed to make people die after a certain time – as some foul murderers still do: would that they could be found and dealt with! Then Antipater took the potion and hurriedly passed it to one of his sons, Cassander, telling him to go straight to the city of Babylon and wait for him there, and in the meantime to take good care of what he'd given him, which he did.

Antipater soon arrived in the city, and Alexander greeted him warmly, giving no sign of heeding his mother's warning – and indeed, he was always reluctant to believe ill reports of men. He welcomed him in fact with the utmost respect, going so far – to fête and honour him all the more – as to take his son Cassander into his privy council and household! Ah, you wicked murderer, you foul rogue, Antipater! Couldn't you see how your lord was honouring you? How could you bring yourself to commit such a crime? You're like any wretched malcontent – the more they're indulged, the more they bite back.

Then one day, not long after, Alexander was asleep in bed, and as he slept he had a vision of Antipater's son Cassander trying to kill him with a sword – indeed he'd already run him through. The shock of it woke the king in alarm; and as he came to, he pondered long upon his dream and then rose and dressed. Then he summoned his astrologer to speak with him, and recounted his dream and asked him what he made of it. The astrologer replied:

'Mighty emperor, you may be sure that Cassander is ill disposed towards you, and has conceived some deep-seated grudge.'

And according to our history,[1] on the very day of Alexander's dream Cassander, on his father's orders, tried to pass the potion on to his brother – Jobas by name, a fine young man who often waited on Alexander at table, cutting his meat; but Jobas refused to take it, for he loved Alexander dearly for the honour he paid him, and Alexander was truly fond of him.

CHAPTER XCV

How Jobas took the potion from the hand of his brother Cassander in order to poison Alexander.

The king set little store by the astrologer's words: he couldn't believe that Cassander could conceive such hatred towards him as to seek his death when

---

[1]   Wauquelin returned to the Prose *Alexander* at the beginning of this chapter.

he'd treated him and his father and brother with such honour – for it seemed to him, and rightly, that it would lead to their own destruction as surely as his own, if not more so.

But Alexander was forgetting the fickleness of Fortune. Having taken him to the very top of Her wheel, She, ever turning just as She pleases, chose not to keep him in his state of majesty; perverse and inconstant, never to be trusted, she was bent on dragging him to the depths just as She'd raised him to the heights.

She somehow arranged it so that one day, so the histories say, Alexander, for no good reason, in a fit of temper struck Jobas on the head with a stick. Young Jobas was upset and humiliated, for it happened in public, and what angered him all the more was that it was quite unjustified; and as a consequence of this he sought out his brother and made his peace with him, to the point where he consented to the killing of his lord. Indeed, he took the potion from his brother into his own hand, and undertook to carry out the poisoning himself as soon as he saw the chance.

This wasn't as soon as he thought, because it was some time before he dared properly show his face to the king again. But he returned to performing his duties as soon as he could; and if he'd been a good and humble servant before he was even more so now – but it was all a sham, as you're about to hear in detail.

Chapter XCVI

How the noble King Alexander was poisoned, from which poison he passed from life to death.

You've already heard how Alexander sent letters to every kingdom in the world calling lords to his coronation. When the appointed day came, immense numbers gathered in Babylon, greater than any that had ever assembled for the honouring of a single man: the histories say they were beyond all counting. It was the fourteenth day of September, referred to as the eighteenth of the Calends of October – the day on which we Christians celebrate the Feast of the Exaltation of the Holy Cross – and it's reckoned to have been the year 4,900 after the creation of Adam.

When all the kings, princes, dukes, counts, barons and other lords of their various degrees had arrived and assembled, the noble King Alexander appeared before them and acknowledged them with a most respectful greeting which they returned in full measure. These honourable salutations duly exchanged, the highest, most noble of them all took King Alexander and crowned him with a golden crown, most precious and magnificent, and seated him on high, on a lofty royal throne; and they crowned him not as one might any other king, but as king, emperor and conquering lord of all the world from furthest East to furthest West, from furthest North to furthest South. Then they led him in great pomp and triumph to the Temple of Jupiter where they made sacrifices according to their custom. From there they returned to the royal palace, which had been so sumptuously adorned and bedecked that no mortal man could describe even half the abundant riches on display. The tables were set and laid most lavishly, and the king sat at the very highest in full view of the whole assembly; and truly, anyone who beheld him there would surely have rejoiced at his radiant mien.

Ah! Foul murderer Jobas! You're like the toad that's choked by the scent of the flowering vine! In the glorious presence of all earthly might, you somehow brought yourself to do what you did. Just because of a single blow dealt by your master, your lord, your king – a blow that caused no wound or hurt and was struck merely to exorcise his rage – did your own rage need to be so great that you, his subject, delivered him up to death? He asked you for a drink, and you gave him the last he ever drank as a healthy man. Here's how it happened:

The king, sitting in glorious state with all the kings, princes and barons in joyous spirits, wished to join in their revelry and called for the cup from which he always drank – the cup in which Jobas had slipped the poison. Jobas proffered it; the king took it. Cup in hand, he said:

'All you noble men here present, I thank you for the honour you have shown me. It is an honour deriving not from myself but from you, and so I drink to you all to wish you ever greater joy and good cheer!'

So saying, he raised the cup to his lips and drank. And truly, the moment he drank he slumped across the right side of his seat, feeling just as if a sword had been thrust through his heart; but for the sake of all his assembled guests, to avoid dampening their spirits, he gave no sign of this till the tables had been cleared.

CHAPTER XCVII

How King Alexander tried to vomit up the poison, but couldn't.

When the tables were cleared and Alexander rose, music and merry-making began in the hall. Then Alexander came to his barons and said:

'Dear friends and companions! Celebrate and make merry, I pray you, but excuse me if I don't stay: I need to go and rest a little.'

And he withdrew at once to a fine chamber, followed by the wicked murderer Jobas, ready to complete his work. As soon as he was inside Alexander bade Jobas give him a feather to put in his mouth so that he could vomit up something he'd eaten or drunk which he said was giving him dreadful pain around the heart; and Jobas promptly handed him a feather or plume which was also poisoned, and with a more evil venom than the one he'd drunk: the moment the king placed it in his mouth he started writhing in greater agony than ever. He was suddenly so hot that he felt his whole body was burning – he didn't know what to do. Then he called for a door to be opened: it overlooked the garden, at the foot of which flowed the Euphrates river; and as soon as the door was opened and the cool air struck him, he was overcome by the heaviest stupor and threw himself on a couch and was asleep in an instant. His wife Roxane and a party of ladies and damsels came to see how he was, and when they found him asleep they thought he was taking a rest as he often did for his health's sake. But far from being at rest, it seemed as he slept that he was racked by dreams: he kept making strange signs as a dreaming man will.

Alexander stayed like this till midnight, much to the surprise of the kings and princes who had never known him sleep like this before.

Chapter XCVIII

How the king tried to drown himself in the River Euphrates but was stopped by his wife Roxane.

The lady Roxane had never seen her husband sleeping so and was very worried, but didn't want to wake him for fear it might unnerve him; so she sat beside him with some of her ladies, waiting for him to wake and to see how he was.

About midnight he woke and rose from his bed, but with great difficulty, for he couldn't stand upright at all and had to go on all fours like an animal, so acute were the pains besetting his heart. He was in such agony that he crawled from the chamber and started struggling down to the river that flowed nearby, where, it's thought, in his despair he meant to throw himself in and drown – though it might have been just to drink, or to let the water's chill quench the poison that was burning his whole body. If he did intend to be swept away, it may have been that he didn't want his body to be found after his death – I can't think of any other reason, but that's what the histories suggest. His wife Queen Roxane, seeing him head for the river and realising he meant to kill himself, caught him and stopped him; and heavily pregnant as she was, she took him in her arms and, with some of her ladies, wept bitterly and said:

'Ah, most noble emperor! What despair makes you want to kill yourself so wretchedly without anyone knowing of your end?'

'Truly, lady,' Alexander replied, 'throughout my life I've done all I can to fill the lives of the good and worthy with joy and glory. So I wanted to end it in secret, so that when my body wasn't found they'd be less anguished and distressed.'

'Ah, noble emperor!' said the queen. 'You've always toiled and striven to win acclaim and reputation; now, it seems, the end of your labour is near. You know that a well-finished work earns praise; so I pray you, mighty emperor, order your affairs before your end so that the glorious renown you've won at the cost of so much effort, as everyone knows, may live in eternal memory after your death among future generations, and all worthy men may learn from your example and win honour and commendation.'

Then Alexander, knowing the queen was right, agreed to do as she asked. He returned to his chamber and lay down in bed; and as soon as he'd done so he called for Jobas, his chamberlain, the one who'd waited on him at table and cut his meat, the one he'd loved so dearly that he would never have guessed it was he who'd put him in this perilous state, and bade him send for his notary, which he duly did.

CHAPTER XCIX

How King Alexander made his testament, according to our history.

A s soon as Alexander saw his notary Simeon arrive, he bade him sit beside
him and write down his testament as he dictated. This he did; and the testament was drawn up as follows:

'I, Alexander, son of the god Ammon[1] and Queen Olympias, king of kings
and lord of the Earth, wish all who read or hear these words to know that by
the will of almighty God – without which nothing is done in this world – and
through the efforts of our men, we have won dominion over all the earth and
been crowned its lord in the great city of Babylon with all due solemnity and
splendour. But Fortune, who until the day of our coronation had placed us at the
very pinnacle of Her wheel in greater glory and honour than any man before by
making us supreme lord of all, wished to show all who come after us that no one
should trust in earthly glory, for it is often the case that a man imagines himself
to have hit the heights and the very next moment he hits rock bottom. So it was
that on the very day of our coronation, when I thought my work was done and I
could begin to enjoy the rewards of rest, we were fed a poison which we are sure
will be our death – and by the very people we had nurtured at our side with all
the love we would have shown our own children! But we don't want Fortune
boasting that She has brought us down; so we wish all to know that, though
nothing in life is more certain than death and nothing less certain than the hour
when it will come, Fortune cannot rob us of the fame won through our deeds, the
extent of which shall be all the plainer as we now make our testament, bequeathing all the lands and the possessions we have won.

'Firstly, we wish to be buried in the city of Alexandria which we founded.
And we wish our master Aristotle to send the Egyptian priests who serve in the
temple where our body shall rest a thousand gold bezants[2] – that is to say, one
hundred and twenty thousand pounds.[3] And because we have often in our life
considered who might rule Egypt after our death and found no one in our view
fitter for this than Ptholomer, we wish him to be their lord and governor – and
guardian of our body, too, that he may better keep our testament in mind.

CHAPTER C

*How Alexander in his testament made all his servants
kings and lords of various lands.*

'I t is our further wish and command that if our wife, the empress Roxane,
gives birth to a male child, he be emperor of all the world and the Macedo-

---

[1]   This is taken directly from the Prose *Alexander*, and is of course at odds with Wauquelin's ear-
       lier rejection of the idea that the god Ammon was Alexander's father. See above, pp.139, 150.
[2]   See note 2, above, p.138.
[3]   This is the figure given in the Prose *Alexander*; Wauquelin's text has the confused '*mil livres
       ou .X.c m'*.

nians give him a name of their choosing. If it be a daughter, we give the Macedonians full freedom and liberty to appoint a king as they see most fit, and for her part, let my wife keep all our chattels, without hindrance (and in the event that she bear a son, let her keep half of Macedon for her own).

'We wish the aforesaid Ptholomer to be prince of Egypt, Africa and Arabia and all territories to the east as far as Bactra,[1] and along with this lordship we give him for his wife the fair Cleopatras, whose marriage to our father Philip we long ago opposed.' (This is recorded above.)[2] 'Phiton is to be prince of Greater Syria, and Mileternus prince of Syria Minor; let Rotas be prince of the kingdom of Sicily, and Philotas prince of Media and Persia; Sino shall be prince of Sabienne, and Antigonus, Philip's son, shall be prince of Greater Phrygia; our notary Simeon shall be prince of Cappadocia and Paphlagonia; Nartus prince of Lycia and Pamphylia; Cassander, brother of Philotas, shall be prince of Phrygia Minor, and Meneador prince of the isle of Ponto; Philip the Affridian[3] shall rule the Peloponnese, and Seulencus whom we call Licanor, brother of Philotas, shall be lord of all the castles that belonged to King Anthiocus; Cassander and Jobas, Antipater's sons, in return for their fine services to us, shall be overlords and governors of all the princes we appointed in distant India; Cassitis shall be prince of the Seres[4] who dwell between the rivers Tigris and Euphrates; Phintonagre is to rule Escaloingne;[5] Osias shall be prince of Perapomenos as far as the Caucasus Mountains,[6] and Certamus shall be prince of the Persians; Siteus is to be prince of Ircanie, Ytacornos of the Persian desert and his brother Philip of the Ycarnians; Ptholomer's brother Clichons, whom we call Danselin, shall be lord of Babylon, and Antheo prince of Pelouse; the Ethiopians[7] are to be free, and let them appoint a lord of their own choosing, so long as he be worthy; the Gauls likewise shall be free and make their own king; and let Gracien be lord of Tyre and Defur.

'We further wish and decree that all men now in exile be recalled and all in captivity be set free. And we wish all people of every degree to know this: we are less concerned about having to leave our worldly glory and die a bitter, unworthy death than we are that our lands may be left in the hands of men who'll

---

[1] The Prose *Alexander* reads '*Bactrane*', while Wauquelin's text reads '*Britane*'. This is the first of a number of proper names in the passage which evidently caused Wauquelin (and the translator of the *Historia de Preliis*) some difficulty. I have rendered them differently when the meaning is clear or probable; otherwise I have retained the spellings as they appear in the text.

[2] See pp. 50–1.

[3] '*Phelippe li Affridiens*'. This name is probably a corruption of Arrhidaeus, Alexander's half-brother who became Alexander III. See also below, p.286 and footnote 1.

[4] Wauquelin has followed the Prose *Alexander*'s misreading of the Latin '*Seres*' as '*senes*' and written '*viellars*' ('old men'); the Seres were an Indian people who, says the Latin text of the *Historia de Preliis*, lived between the two rivers '*Ydaspem et Indum*'.

[5] Following the Prose *Alexander*, this is a misreading of '*Phiton Agenoris filius sit princeps in colonias…*' in the *Historia de Preliis*.

[6] '*au mont de Cassassy*'. 'Several of the Alexander historians attached the name of Caucasus to the Hindu Kush, in antiquity called Paropamisus.' Richard Stoneman, *op. cit.*, p.78.

[7] '*Ydiopien*'.

be unwilling to devote their resources to advancing and enhancing the honour of the worthy.'

*How the Macedonians came to the palace in great agitation
to ask Alexander to make Perdicas their king.*

While Alexander was dictating his testament a thunderous storm erupted, so fierce and awesome that it seemed the world was about to end: the whole sky was ablaze with lightning bolts, it seemed the earth would crumble under the force of its monstrous quaking, and men and women were pitching and tumbling over each other in panic. The history says the chaos lasted for the best part of two hours, in which time many towers, castles, forts and houses came crashing down. People started saying it was a sign of King Alexander's death; which is why, as soon as the storm had passed, the Macedonians and Greeks came rushing to the palace, fully armed, in a state of great agitation, and to the attendant lords they cried aloud:

'Sirs! Sirs! If you don't let us see our prince, our emperor and king Alexander, we'll slaughter you all right here and now!'

Alexander, in bed and dictating his testament as we've said, heard the yelling of the Greeks and Macedonians and asked what was going on.

'Mighty emperor,' came the reply, 'the princes and people from Greece and Macedon are threatening to kill us unless we show them their emperor!'

When Alexander heard this he bade them take him to the palace. He was bodily carried there on a couch as he commanded; and when he arrived and saw his people thronging there in such a state he began to weep most bitterly; and through his tears he called upon them in his eloquent and persuasive way to nurture peace and harmony between each other. Many words were then exchanged, until finally the Macedonians appealed to him as one, saying:

'Great and mighty emperor, since there's no remedy for your sickness and it seems that you must die, we pray you decide who will rule us when you're gone.'

Then Alexander answered: 'Great and valiant Macedonians, my beloved companions and friends, your king after my death shall be the one you decide yourselves according to your own best judgement.'

Then they all cried with one voice: 'Mighty emperor, if it please you we would have none but Perdicas. We pray you appoint him our king and governor before you die, as you've appointed many others among us here.'

At this, Alexander summoned Perdicas and said to him: 'My dear friend and companion, before all here present I bequeath to you the kingdom of Macedon and appoint you its lord and king, and commend to your care and protection my lady Roxane, my beloved wife and spouse.'

Hearing this, the Macedonian princes came to the king one after another, thanking him and tearfully kissing his hand as if taking their leave. And Perdicas, weeping and sighing deeply, came to him and said:

'Ah, great and awesome emperor! The Macedonians, Greeks and all other nations will find governors a-plenty; but truly, none to match your goodness and largesse will be found under heaven when you're gone.'

Chapter CII
How Alexander sat up in bed and gave them words of comfort, and then died.

While Perdicas was speaking, Alexander, seeing all his barons in floods of tears, had his attendants sit him up in bed so that he could see them properly. Then he summoned his notary who'd written down his testament and promptly bade him read it aloud in the presence of them all. When it had been read his barons came to him, one after the other, to kiss his hands, weeping so bitterly that no one who saw them could have failed to feel pity.

The common folk were grieving and wailing more than any, which makes me think that if Alexander had been ruthless, proud and cruel as some histories claim, he would surely have been no more spoken of or lamented than his father King Philip of Macedon, who was harsh and cruel indeed. What is beyond all doubt, I think, is that he was beloved of God Omnipotent, when He chose in His glorious might to endow him with so many qualities. So why would his men not weep at his death? And weep they did, that's certain – and so did the animals – and we read in the histories that at the death of the mighty emperor Alexander the sun withdrew its light from the world as if in an eclipse.

Then Alexander, sitting in his bed, seeing the desperate grieving of his barons and the constant bouts of thunder and darkness, and feeling death with its bitter pangs pressing him to leave this world, spoke in the Macedonian tongue to say:

'I feel more grief that so many good men are left in anguish at my death than I do that I must die!'

Then some of the Macedonians replied through their tears: 'Ah, gracious emperor! We'd rather die with you than live on after your death! We know the kingdom of Macedon will be unable to resist its enemies once you're gone, but we grieve more for the loss of your valiant heart than for the danger we'll now face.'

Chapter CIII
The year and time when Alexander passed from life to death,
and how he was buried.

Amid the terrible grieving and weeping and groaning of all the people of every degree, the noble King Alexander's death throes began. He suffered them for six hours; then he delivered up his soul to his creator God – so say some accounts: we may at least say his soul was placed at the mercy of the Great Judge. Alexander's death occurred in the thirty-second year after his birth, on the seventeenth[1]

---

[1]   The text reads 'XVIII'.

of the Calends of October – the fifteenth day of September, that is – in the year 4,900 after the Creation.

When he was dead and passed away, his men had his body embalmed and prepared for burial with all the splendour befitting his person, dressing him in royal robes and placing his crown upon his head. Then they laid him on a stately carriage and took him to the city of Alexandria as he had earlier commanded. When they arrived they sought out all the best, most skilful craftsmen, who made a tomb of such splendour and magnificence that a description would be accounted fanciful, so I'll say no more; but the histories tell us that it stands to this day, and is known by Greeks and Egyptians as a pyramid.[1] When the tomb was finished and ready they laid King Alexander's body inside amid bitter weeping and lamentation, and through his tears Ptholomer said:

'Alas! Most noble emperor, dubbed knight at the age of fifteen, king of Macedon at twenty, and in just twelve years the conqueror of all the world, crowned sovereign king of all the earth, what a disaster is your death! Alas! Now the world may rightly say it has been orphaned, left without a lord! It seems to me, truly, that the world should end forthwith, for it will never have such a lord again, and no man of such stature will ever be found who could match your achievements, even less your largesse and courtesy. Alas! Death, how did you dare take such a man, especially at the height of his powers, in his prime of life and at his pinnacle of wealth? Couldn't you have let him rest awhile in this present world rather than strike him down so cruelly at the age of only thirty-two?'

Such were the anguished words of lament uttered by Ptholomer and the other barons likewise, all beside themselves with grief. And they had an inscription carved upon his tomb that read:

'Here lies Alexander, king of Macedon. Iron could never vanquish him but he was put to death by poison, in the year 4,900 from the world's beginning, on the seventeenth[2] of the Calends of October.'

CHAPTER CIV
How after Alexander's death his barons started warring with each other.

When the burial of the noble King Alexander was complete, the barons began to leave the city of Alexandria and set out to take possession of the lands allotted and bequeathed to them by their master Alexander.

But once they'd been welcomed and installed, and worthily served and honoured by their men, then, despite Alexander's gracious deathbed plea and entreaty that they should always strive to live together in peace and harmony – and despite the clear and true examples he'd given of the dangers of doing otherwise

---

[1]   The long and elaborate description of the tomb in the verse *Roman d'Alexandre* includes the comment that 'the king's pyramid was very tall and broad, raised so high indeed that no crossbow shot could have reached the top; in Greek it was called a pyramid [*piramide*] because it was entirely faced in one and the same stone [*pierre*].' (Branch IV stanza 65).
[2]   This time the text reads 'XIIII'.

– they paid little heed and spurned his warnings, and were soon at each other's throats. They might rightly be compared to a lion's whelps, whose nature is such that, when the lion takes its prey and has eaten its fill and tosses the remainder to its young, they rise up and attack one another, each of them wanting all for itself and not wanting its companions to have any. So it was with Alexander: having taken his prey by conquering the whole world, he had to leave it all behind when he died; but the good king, knowing his great deeds were done and not wanting his barons whom he loved so dearly to start fighting like the lion's whelps, decided to give to each his share. But when he died they weren't satisfied: each of them wanted the whole lot for himself. It led to such cruel and deadly conflict, so bitter and so vicious, that in less than fourteen years all the princes, dukes, counts and lords of every degree who'd been companions of the good King Alexander were dead and slain, either in battle or by subterfuge.

CHAPTER CV

What sparked the war between Alexander's barons.

It's often said that what's of no use is soon forgotten, and that could be applied to King Alexander; for as soon as his body was laid in its exalted tomb and his barons considered it was now mere ash and that they'd be receiving none of their former rewards of gold and silver and horses and trinkets and gowns and jewels and all manner of other gifts, they started to show their true colours. Suddenly they were filled with envy and hatred, and it soon led them all to their own destruction. Let me tell you how it happened – and first what caused the deadly rift and disastrous hostility that could never be resolved.

You've already heard how before his death King Alexander had decreed in his testament that all held in captivity should be released and their rights and liberties restored. The chief men of the cities, the governors and protectors and the judges, called many an assembly and council to discuss the implementation of this decree; for they knew that if they freed these men as Alexander had bidden they'd seek revenge for all they'd suffered in imprisonment or exile, with no regard for the spirit of justice that had prompted their release: there were some, they felt sure, who'd show no respect for such decency. Nonetheless, in Athens and a number of other cities, after much debate and deliberation, to fulfil the last will of Alexander whom they'd loved more than any man in the world, they released all their prisoners and invited all those in exile to return to their cities in peace and love, if they were willing to respond in like spirit. But no: exiles from Athens and neighbouring cities assembled one day and found they numbered more than thirty thousand, with a fleet of two hundred ships; and they hired mercenaries from Argos and Corinth and many other cities who came to their support, and put to sea and terrorised all parts, till no one could travel anywhere by sea or land.

CHAPTER CVI

How these men killed King Leonis, and how
Perdicas attacked the city of Cappadocia.

Antipater, that wicked, faithless traitor, was in one part of Greece and plot-
ting how to gain mastery over his neighbours. In pursuit of his goal Antipater forged an alliance and exchanged certain promises with a king of a nearby
land named Leonis. These promises involved the conquest of the kingdom of
Macedon, now held by the good King Alexander's mother as decreed in his testament. To achieve this all the better and sooner, this Leonis went to the king of
Phrygia Minor and persuaded him to lend him more than fifty thousand troops
to go to Antipater's aid. This army set sail and put to sea and headed for the land
of Greece to join Antipater, who was ready and waiting with the mighty force
he'd mustered in his own land.

But they ran into the pirates and brigands from Athens, Argos and Corinth
– and it proved disastrous: as soon as they spotted them these pirates attacked
with such force and might that not a single Phrygian escaped: all were thrown in
the sea and drowned; and to the dismay of the false traitor Antipater they seized
King Leonis and promptly parted his head from his shoulders. Thus began the
avenging of King Alexander. And the Athenians and Argives and Corinthians
won an immense amount of booty, especially armour which they badly needed.

No man could describe Antipater's dismay at this disaster; but, being clever as
well as wicked, he was soon able to remedy the situation, and forged an alliance
with Ptholomer which caused no end of trouble. But later, according to some accounts, Ptholomer turned his back on him, as we'll explain in a short while.

CHAPTER CVII

How the Cappadocians burned themselves to death in their city when Perdicas had
them at his mercy.

While all this was happening Perdicas, not satisfied with the realm and cities
given to him by Alexander, was encouraged by members of his council to
raise a huge force of men-at-arms, numbering forty thousand; and assembled
under his banner and command they advanced upon the city of Cappadocia
and surrounded it, besieging it so tightly that no man could escape to seek help.
At the time their king, Medus by name, was in the kingdom called Passaglome[1]
with Antigonus and a great army, and had left the city in the hands of a valiant
captain named Leons who did all he could to hold and defend it, mounting a
series of sorties and skirmishes against the besieging foe. Perdicas suffered fre-
quent heavy losses, but finally launched such a fierce assault that the city was
taken by storm. Not that he gained much from its capture and conquest, and the

---

[1]   'Passagloines' in the Prose *Alexander*. This may be a transcription of Paphlagonia, which is
mentioned in the same phrase as Cappadocia above, p.277.

honour wasn't his (indeed, he himself was severely wounded, and for a while it was said he was close to death); for the people of the city hated him beyond all measure, and seeing there was no escape and the city was about to be at his mercy, and not wanting Perdicas to be able to brag that he'd conquered them, they set the whole town ablaze and burned themselves and all their possessions in the fire: Perdicas and his men didn't gain a single penny, and he didn't have the pleasure of forcing them into subjection.

This debacle sparked a ferocious, terrible, deadly war between Antigonus and Perdicas, both of whom were kings together in Macedon: they started attacking each other, seizing towns and destroying forts and castles, and engaged in many a clash and ambush, too lengthy to record. Each of them forged alliances in Asia as well as Macedon; but finally, after long and ruinous destruction that devastated many isles of the sea, King Perdicas was so hard pressed that he had to flee to Egypt where he met his death, as you'll hear in due course.

CHAPTER CVIII

How Emenidus and Neoptalemus began a war in which Neoptalemus was killed along with King Polipeton, whom Antipater had sent to his aid.

Neoptalemus, ruler of parts of the East and intent on conquering his neighbours, one day assembled a vast army and advanced against Emenidus, king of Arcadia. When Emenidus, a valiant, bold and daring man, as has often been apparent in our history, learned that Neoptalemeus was attacking him and had already burned and overrun part of his land, he straightway mustered forces from his kingdom and his other lands and marched with all speed to confront Neoptalemus. Battle was joined; Neoptalemus fought mightily, and the combat raged so long that both sides lost almost all their men, but Neoptalemus lost immeasurably more than Emenidus, whose troops were more battle-hardened than his own, and his losses were finally so great that he was vanquished and forced to flee the field in shame.

The history says he fled to the kingdom of Greece where Antipater was boldly holding sway, and he begged him for his support and aid; by way of persuasion, he told Antipater that Emenidus had been so battered that he'd scarcely any knights left.

'So, my dear lord,' he said, 'if you're willing to help me we'll easily win!'

Antipater, who hated Emenidus bitterly out of pure malice and envy (of which he was brimful), agreed very readily and gave him most of his men-at-arms under the captaincy of a valiant knight named Polipeton. With Antipater's support secured, Neoptalemus mustered all the troops he could and returned to the field to seek a way to kill Emenidus.

But Emenidus was undaunted; one of the wiliest warriors of the age, he'd learned from the example of his good master Alexander and sent spies everywhere, and they'd promptly informed him of the plans forged by Antipater and Neoptalemus. So he assembled all the knights he could and rode to one of the passes into his land through which he knew his enemies would have to enter.

There he lay in ambush, and as the unsuspecting Neoptalemus began to march through, Emenidus sprang the trap, striking and hewing and killing and felling the foe in a thunderous onslaught. Unable to deploy or hold their lines some fled in panic, imagining Emenidus had far greater numbers than he did. In the mayhem Polipeton, who tried repeatedly to hold his men in order, was killed. And Emenidus charged to meet Neoptalemus, who came to meet him likewise, with such ferocity that they brought each other crashing to the ground; Emenidus was gravely injured and confined to his bed for a long while, but Neoptalemus was killed in the clash. And so it was that Neoptalemus met his death, through mischance and through his pride. And according to the history, all the forces sent by Antipater were left dead on the field, their courage and their valour such that they wouldn't deign to flee. Antipater was beside himself with rage at this disaster; but nonetheless he later gave aid to Emenidus against Antigonus in return for like support, as you'll hear.

CHAPTER CIX

How Perdicas was killed by King Ptholomer.

W hen Ptholomer, now king of Egypt, learned that Perdicas had arrived in his land as we mentioned earlier, he sent word to him to leave or he'd make him regret it. Perdicas was enraged by this: he and Ptholomer had often been companions together in the service of the good King Alexander, and he was shocked that he should refuse him help. It sparked a deep hatred and a deadly war between them which lasted a long while, for Perdicas responded to the offence by raising support from a host of scoundrels, plunderers and pillagers, and plagued and harassed Ptholomer and inflicted endless damage, burning his land, wrecking his forts and slaughtering his people. Ptholomer waged mighty war against him, and in the turmoil many were slain on both sides, for both men had vast numbers and resources. They finally met in pitched battle; both armies suffered appalling slaughter, but Perdicas lost more than Ptholomer: he lost his life. And King Ptholomer, who won a great hoard of booty, returned to his towns and cities in triumph.

But some notable barons escaped the carnage: Perdicas's brother Altera, for instance, and Phiton, Yllirus and a good number of other knights and squires; and hearing that Emenidus was in need of troops they made their way to him and offered him their service if required. Emenidus was overjoyed; and, strongly urged by Perdicas's brother, he decided to make war on King Antigonus.

But Antigonus, in Macedon, always had his eye on the game – he was sharp, and had learned well from his master Alexander – and knew at once that King Emenidus of Arcadia and the aforesaid knights were joining forces and planning to move against him. So he swiftly assembled the Macedonians and Greeks, who had all returned to him and their homeland after hearing that Perdicas was slain, and advanced against that mightily wealthy king Emenidus and his army and met them in the open field. Many were wounded and killed on both sides, but Emenidus's losses were especially heavy; and as his army was routed he was

forced to flee in shame to avoid a miserable death. He took refuge in a strong castle nearby, but Antigonus soon learned where he was and advanced to lay siege
with all speed, surrounding the place with huge numbers of troops and engines.

Emenidus, seeing Antigonus besieging him, knew he wouldn't leave till he'd
destroyed him; so he decided to send word to Antipater, who wielded great
power in those parts, beseeching him to send him aid on the understanding that
in return he would always be his true friend and supporter against any and all.
When he heard this Antipater, eager to secure an alliance with Emenidus, one
of the most able warriors in the world, raised an immense army and advanced
against Antigonus. But Antigonus didn't wait to meet him: as soon as he heard
Antipater was coming he feared things would go amiss – he didn't feel strong
enough to resist two forces. So he and his army departed swiftly, leaving Emenidus be for the moment.

CHAPTER CX

How Emenidus was wretchedly killed through base treachery.

When Emenidus saw he was rid of his besiegers he went to present himself
to Antipater and thanked him for his timely intervention, and promised to
be always his true friend and ally. But then, fearing that Antipater might indulge
in the double-dealing of which he was eminently capable, Emenidus left as soon
as he decently could and made his way to the Argiraspidiens[1] and sought their
support in all matters, offering to aid them in return with all his might. These
Argiraspidiens had often earned renown as the most valiant warriors in Alexander's army, and their strength had won him many a fierce battle, but now they
were nomads, having no fixed abode when Emenidus found them, but staying
together in a fellowship with their wives and children and all their possessions,
which they took with them whenever they went into battle. They were called
Argiraspidiens because their armour, shields and everything were argent, being
silver or silver-plated.[2]

Emenidus, then, came to them and sought their aid, and finally led them
against Antigonus: they followed him very willingly. And Antigonus, seeing
Emenidus returning to confront him, mustered his forces again and advanced
to meet his enemies with fierce determination. He engaged them in a series of
fearsome battles, for the Argiraspidiens were formidable fighters; but they were
finally defeated and lost all their possessions, their wives and their children, and
Emenidus had to flee once more with just a handful of men.

The Argiraspidiens had lost all they'd won in serving Alexander; and in their
boundless anguish they conceived a terrible act of treachery. Meeting in secret

---

[1]   '*Agripidiens*'. I have used the spelling that appears in the Prose *Alexander* and makes sense
      of the derivation that is about to be given.
[2]   Historically, Alexander did indeed have in his army 'Silver Shields (*argyraspides*), the ma-
      jority of whom were accompanied by barbarian womenfolk and half-breed children': Wal-
      demar Heckel, *The Conquests of Alexander the Great* (Cambridge, 2008), p.140.

council, unbeknown to the good and valiant Emenidus, they sent a message to Antigonus begging him to return their wives and children and possessions; in return they would do all in their power to help him if he wished. Antigonus returned word that if they delivered Emenidus to him he would do as they asked, otherwise he would kill their wives and children. The Argiraspidiens told him to prepare to keep his promise and they would fulfil his demand. They promptly seized Emenidus – the good and valiant knight whom they'd made their prince and to whom they'd paid homage and sworn fealty – and bound him like a thief or murderer and delivered him into the hands of Antigonus, who hated him more than any man on earth. As soon as he had him in his clutches he killed him with his own hand – and with Emenidus's own sword. Antigonus should be praised indeed – if treachery is thought praiseworthy.

CHAPTER CXI

How Queen Olympias fled from Persia and returned to Macedon, where she had King Aridien and his wife Eurydice killed.

While all this treachery, murder and destruction was taking place the other lords were by no means quiet: there was hardly a kingdom in the world free of war, with conflict and devastation everywhere. Scarcely a day went by without news of fresh slaughter, either in pitched battles or in skirmishes.

In Greece at this time, in a region bordering Macedon, there was a king named Aridien[1] who had a wife by the name of Eurydice.[2] She felt little love for him; she was in love instead with King Cassander, Antipater's son, a young knight of great strength and vigour. She loved him so much indeed that she plied him with generous gifts and yearned for nothing so much as to be rid of her husband and to enhance Cassander's prestige and dominion. This foolish love led to the ruin and destruction of many cities and the death of many a knight, and I'll tell you how.

At the same time that Eurydice was carrying on with Cassander, the lady Queen Olympias, the good King Alexander's mother, had gone to Epirus[3] in pursuit of some matter, and was planning to stay there awhile in lands she possessed thereabouts. But the king of Morolen plotted a series of schemes bent on capturing or killing her, and would have succeeded but for a powerful lady of those parts who alerted Olympias to the danger and urged her to return to Macedon, which she did. But the moment she arrived Eurydice incited her lord Aridien to wage war upon her; and one day, to rouse her anger even more, Eurydice sent her a warning that she should leave the land or she'd make her regret it. But Queen Olympias, wise and valiant lady that she was, mustered all her Macedonian forces – a good many from Aridien's own lands, for they despised

[1]   The name derives from Arrhidaeus, Alexander's half-brother who became Philip III. See above, p.277 and footnote 3.
[2]   'Crudissen'.
[3]   'Perse'; the Prose *Alexander* reads '*Piree*'.

Aridien because of his wife's disloyalty – and met him in battle, in the course of which she captured him and put him to death at the prompting of the very people of whom he was supposedly lord. Soon afterwards Queen Eurydice was caught and burnt at the stake on the advice of Queen Olympias's barons – but she paid dearly for it later, as you're about to hear.

CHAPTER CXII

How Cassander had Queen Olympias killed to avenge his beloved.

It wasn't long before Cassander, enraged by the news, resolved to take such terrible revenge that it would awe any who heard of it. He swiftly raised a mighty army and advanced into Macedon, where Queen Olympias now held sway. He mounted mighty attacks and sieges upon her towns and forts and castles. The queen fought back manfully, which led to many tough and fearsome clashes and bloody skirmishes. But in the end Queen Olympias couldn't trust the Macedonians; she saw them bending to Cassander's appeals and urgings, and fled to a mighty city known by the people of the land as Pydna.[1] She took with her Roxane, her son Alexander's wife, who had given birth not long before to a handsome son named Hercules – sired by Alexander himself, Alexander having left her with child. This Hercules by now was about three years old.

Cassander, hearing that Olympias had gone to Pydna, felt free to do as he wished in the land, and took possession of towns and castles and strongholds, some by force and others willingly. With part of his aim fulfilled, he and his brother Jobas advanced upon the city where Olympias had taken refuge with Roxane and Hercules. He laid siege to it, surrounding it on all sides, and mounted a series of assaults. The lady Olympias defended it as best she could, but Cassander finally took the city by storm and slaughtered almost everything that breathed. As for Queen Olympias, who'd been more honoured, feared and respected throughout her life than any other lady had been for a single day, he had her killed and cut to pieces and thrown to the dogs and birds so that she would have no sepulchre. And as for Alexander's wife the fair Roxane and her son Hercules, Cassander had them imprisoned in the great tower of Amphipolis.[2] What befell them in the end – whether they ever escaped or died in prison – I haven't discovered: I can tell you no more about Queen Roxane and her child Hercules, son of the noble King Alexander, so I'll leave it at that.

Thus it was that the faithless Queen Eurydice was avenged at the tragic and unjust expense of the valiant Queen Olympias, mother of the good King Alexander.[3]

---

[1]   'Piduam'.

[2]   'Philopame'.

[3]   At this point the Prose *Alexander* ends. The verse *Roman d'Alexandre* effectively ends even sooner, with Alexander's death and burial.

CHAPTER CXIII

How Alior, Queen Candace's son, avenged the death of Alexander; and first how he assembled his army, according to my source.

A previous part of our history – which we've woven together from a number of sources, but principally from one whose author's name we don't know, as we've mentioned at several points – told how the noble King Alexander once visited the lady Candace, queen of Meroe.[1] But we haven't mentioned that he fathered a son upon the lady, though the aforesaid source refers to the matter at some length.[2]

Now, however, since we need to explain how Alexander's poisoners were put to death, we should certainly relay what one source suggests, whose author gives his name as Jehan le Nevelon.[3] He says he composed his work at the request of a count named Henry – count of where he doesn't specify, saying only that he was a lord of great generosity, piety, courtesy and graciousness, sincere, compassionate towards the poor and pitiless towards the wicked: an exceptional man, which may explain why he chose to omit this Count Henry's surname, implying that he was the worthiest Henry in the world! Just as in referring to Charlemagne, greatest of all French kings, or to Julius Caesar or Judas Maccabeus or Hercules there's no need to give their title because as soon as they're mentioned everyone knows who is meant, so I think Jehan le Nevelon intended his reference to 'Count Henry' to be understood.[4]

In any event, our author says that Queen Candace had a handsome son by Alexander; his name was Alior.[5] And when she heard of the tragic death of the good King Alexander, whose intimate company she had often enjoyed in secret places, she was as distraught as could be. Determined that the dreadful deed should not remain unpunished, she kept probing till she discovered exactly how he'd met his death: how Antipater and his sons had murdered him through foul

---

[1]   Above, pp.230–4.

[2]   Curiously, Wauquelin has become confused about his sources here: the verse *Roman d'Alexandre* does not in fact mention the birth of the son at all; the son, Alior, is introduced in the source he is about to cite, *La Venjance Alixandre*.

[3]   'Jehan Nevelaux'; Jehan le Nevelon was the author of *La Venjance Alixandre*, a poem of just under 2,000 lines written c.1180 and very widely read.

[4]   The Henry in question was Henry 1st, count of Champagne from 1152-81. He was indeed much respected, and under his very able rule not only did Champagne flourish economically but his court at Troyes became a literary centre of some note, featuring no less a figure than Chrétien de Troyes.

[5]   Jehan le Nevelon succinctly describes the process: after rescuing the wife of Candace's son Candaculus (as above, p.229), Alexander 'came to the queen in her hall of stone where she was lying beneath her blanket. Her skin was as white as may blossom; Alexander embraced her, took possession of her, made love to her under the ermine cover. The lady was left pregnant beneath her purple robe, and God gave her a son destined for greatness: he was handsome, gracious, worthy, being of most noble blood, and fierce and proud as a lion in the wild; he resembled Alexander in frame and build, in face and voice and hair and expression. His name was Alior.' (*La Venjance Alixandre*, ed. E. Billings Ham, Princeton 1931, vv.76-87).

and wicked treachery. She summoned her son at once, very young though he still was, and told him he was the son of the noblest king the world had ever seen – as the good King Alexander was indeed – and that he must avenge his father's death and show he was of his blood. The child replied that he was ready to do whatever she commanded.[1]

Then the lady Candace, seeing the late King Alexander's barons all fighting and destroying one another, decided to try to pacify some with gifts and promises. This she did, first making peace between Ptholomer and Ariscé who were locked in a bitter war, and they came to her aid with thirty thousand troops. She did likewise to gain the support of King Danselin and Antiocus, who each brought twenty thousand men. She won over kings Licanor and Philotas, too, who together provided fifty thousand.

CHAPTER CXIV

How the armies of Alexander's son Alior set out from Meroe and headed for Greece to attack Antipater and his children and avenge Alexander's death.

When Queen Candace Cleophis saw the multitudes brought by these noble kings to support her in her mission she was overjoyed, and not without cause. She mustered such forces of her own as she could, and had them superbly armed and equipped and entrusted them to her son Alior.[2] She then placed Alior in the care of the six aforesaid lords; they welcomed him most joyfully, for he was a fine young knight indeed, well built and strong despite his short stature: he was the very image of his father Alexander, which made the lords rejoice all the more.

When all the troops and gear were ready and in order, Queen Candace, accompanied by her other three sons, came to the six lords and stressed how it behove a king to avenge the death of another.

'And you, my knights, lords and friends,' she said, 'are all crowned kings thanks to the trials and labours you endured in the company of your good lord and king by whom, with God's help, you attained your high and illustrious stations. It seems to me that it would be a deep disgrace and an eternal stain upon you and your line if such a shameful deed as his death, perpetrated in your presence, went unavenged. So I pray you, dear sirs, help to avenge that base, foul murder and you'll be acting as worthy men should.'

After these words of exhortation they all declared they were ready and had come for that very reason, and that their forces would march as soon as she gave the word. So the customary orders and commands were issued and the army set

---

[1]   In *La Venjance Alixandre*, Alior needs no persuading: he is burning to avenge his father, but Candace isn't sure he's old enough: '"You'll only be fifteen at Easter – don't be rash – be patient a little longer: when you're twenty you can start doing great deeds!" At this her son cried: "Don't say that, mother, for God's sake! God bless me, I'd rather be a monk shut up in an abbey than fail to be celebrating with my great army at Pentecost!"' (vv.143-9).

[2]   It is interesting that Wauquelin, unlike Jehan le Nevelon, has the woman Candace rather than her son Alior take responsibility for raising the army.

out, and didn't stop till they reached Antipater's lands, where they promptly started to loot and burn towns and seize and sack castles and forts on such a scale that it seemed they were bent on total destruction.

CHAPTER CXV

How Antipater mustered his forces, and Alior besieged the city of Rochefleur and Antipater within.

W hen Antipater learned of the invasion he was shocked and enraged – above all with King Ptholomer with whom he thought he'd forged a special bond. He quickly summoned all his allies, in particular his sons in whom he had great faith. One of them, Florent by name, was a bold and valiant knight indeed, and Antipater had higher hopes of him than any other. He then had his capital city, Rochefleur, repaired and strengthened with mighty towers, ramparts and barbicans,[1] and stocked with all manner of weapons – Turkish bows, springalds and catapults and arbalests of every kind – along with hauberks, helmets, cuirasses and all other necessary armour and equipment so that his men couldn't use any shortage as an excuse for failing to fight well. He then stocked the city with abundant wine and victuals – indeed he left no supplies anywhere within ten leagues: everything was transported to the city.

Next he formed a strong body of men-at-arms under the captaincy of his son Florent, and ordered them to ride from the city to guard and scour the surrounding land and see which way the invaders were heading. But they'd hardly ventured forth before they ran into the foe and engaged in fierce and vigorous clashes; knights and men-at-arms were felled and killed, so many indeed that they had to withdraw and retreat to the city, for according to our source Alior had an army of at least one hundred thousand men. They chased Antipater's scouting party all the way to the city, which they then besieged, surrounding it on every side and setting up their tents and shelters as they always did.

It wasn't long before they'd built and deployed a countless number of strange and elaborate engines: wooden towers on wheels, and battering rams, and mangonels and couillards[2] with which they battered and pounded the city on every side in a bombardment that never relented, night or day.

CHAPTER CXVI

How the men of the city mounted a sortie against their enemies, and one named Cassadran was captured.

T he men of the city, seeing these invaders bombarding and tormenting them, decided one day to take action. They all armed, and as soon as they were in

---

[1]   In *La Venjance Alixandre* it is also forbiddingly sited on a rocky crag: "A mighty city indeed, my lord!" says Ptholomer to Alior. "Never was such a lofty height inhabited by men!" (vv.849-50).

[2]   One of many kinds of medieval catapult.

good order they came before Antipater at his principal palace and declared it shameful that they'd not yet gone to confront the enemy, and that they'd rather die in the field than like dumb beasts slaughtered in a stable.

'So give us a commander, sire,' they said. 'We want to go and show our enemies who we are!'

Then Antipater sent for his sons, in particular Florent, for the men of the city had most faith in him, and: 'Dear son,' he said, 'these good men have a powerful urge to sally forth and pay the enemy a visit! I pray you lead and command them, be their protector and captain, and do all you can to defend them and keep them safe.'

Florent replied that he was only too ready; he promptly armed and issued orders for all men to prepare, and soon they were marching forth with Florent at their head.

They launched their attack on the enemy, but with little profit: they were soundly beaten, wounded, maimed; before they could retreat to the city a vast number were left there on the field, and in this first sortie Florent himself was badly hurt and wounded. Now, before marching from the city he had appointed as his gonfalonnier – his standard-bearer, that is – a great baron by the name of Cassadran who had offered his aid; this Cassadran was enraged beyond measure to see the destruction and slaughter of the city's men, and being a man of the utmost courage and daring, he resolved to rescue them and reverse their fortunes by his prowess. He abandoned his guard of the banner and charged into the thick of the fray, plunging into the battalion led by Danselin and performing all possible feats of arms, bringing knights and horses crashing down. It seemed he would defeat them all, and Danselin, seeing this, grabbed a strong, stout spear and thrust in his spurs; his horse carried him swift and straight at Cassadran, and Danselin delivered such a blow to his shield that he bore him out of his saddle and over his rouncey's rump and smashing to the ground with his legs in the air. So heavy was his fall that the spike on his helm, which had lost its crest, plunged into the earth and left him planted like a pear tree. He was instantly seized and taken captive by Danselin's men – though not without cost, for Cassadran's men tried to rescue him and inflicted heavy losses on the Greeks; but Cassadran remained a prisoner and was led away to Danselin's tent.

Chapter CXVII
How Cassadran died a hideous death, roasted on a spit.

Once Cassadran was taken it wasn't long before the men of the city began to crumble; in any case, they weren't strong enough to withstand such a huge and battle-hardened force as their enemy, who'd spent their lives doing nothing else. So they were well advised to surrender the field to the foe and return with all speed to the city. But they were hard pressed to say the least: their besiegers were so hot on their heels that they hadn't time to wait for each other, and the history says they shut the gates before they were all inside; there's little doubt that great numbers were captured and killed.

After the rout the Greeks made their way back to camp, and the army's commanders gathered to decide what to do with their prisoners. They all agreed to return them to the enemy – but it wasn't to be a happy experience for the prisoners or for the citizens, as I'll explain. First it was discovered that Cassadran, who'd been captured as you've heard, was a member of Antipater's council and the very man who'd supplied the poison used to kill Alexander. So they vowed to roast him like a chicken on the fire. They promptly had a huge fire lit, and hauled Cassadran forward and stripped him instantly; then they bound him with iron chains to a wooden rod prepared as a spit and roasted him over the flames. He died a hideous, agonising death. And as soon as he was dead they took his body and dumped it in a catapult[1] along with other knights they'd captured in the battle, and hurled them over the city walls. That's how they returned their prisoners to the foe! And the people in the city, seeing their enemies' cruelty, were aghast: they surely faced disaster now, for it seemed the Greeks would show no mercy no matter what they offered them – they knew that if the Greeks had wanted, they could have had a massive ransom for Cassadran.

Chapter CXVIII
How the king of Hungary was boiled in a cauldron
along with one of Antipater's nephews.

To the city of Rochefleur, to aid Antipater, had come the king of Hungary – though my source doesn't record his name – with a company of more than fifty-six thousand Hungarians. With him too was a mighty lord named Tesson, a nephew of Florent by one of his sisters, Antipater's daughter. Tesson and this king of Hungary, himself related to Antipater, agreed one day to make a sortie against the enemy with all their forces. To make this possible they included Florent in their discussions, for he was in overall command of operations and no fighting took place without his approval, and no one, on pain of death, would dare to open a gate or postern without his leave. When Florent saw their bold resolve he agreed they should mount a sortie – with a mere thirty-one thousand men! They were jubilant! But they could be likened to the swan that sings before its death, for they were both to die most wretchedly as you're about to hear.

According to my source they made ready as soon as they had Florent's approval. They marched from the city in magnificent array, in perfectly ordered squadrons and battalions, and with the utmost zeal they fell upon their enemies and inflicted heavy damage. But it was all to no avail, for their foes struck back so effectively that both Tesson and the king of Hungary were seized and captured – though not without grave loss, for at the battle's height Florent and his brothers rode from the city with a mighty brigade of well-armed knights and charged into the fray with such fury that the very earth seemed to quake. The Greeks were

---

[1]   *'perriere'*: one of many kinds of catapult designed for slinging stones.

driven back, forced to give ground; but a well-judged counter-attack by Alexander's son Alior drove their assailants back once more and made them retreat, whether they liked it or not, right back into their city. They were hotly pursued with swords and lances, and vast mounds of dead were left behind.

Among those taken captive were the king of Hungary and Florent's nephew Tesson. They were promptly taken back to camp, and as soon as the battle was over and the barons returned, they declared that the king of Hungary should be boiled in a cauldron like a counterfeiter, and Tesson would be tied to four horses and pulled apart, each horse taking a limb. These sentences were duly carried out. And the other prisoners, regardless of status, were hanged right outside the city walls; their people were beside themselves with grief and anguish.

Chapter CXIX

How hunger forced the men of the city to come out and do battle,
in which they suffered dreadful losses.

For a good while after this reverse, some three months or so, no one from the city appeared in the fields to attack or assail the enemy. They'd all agreed to make no further sorties because of the terrible losses they'd already suffered – and because the Greeks showed no pity or mercy, only the utmost cruelty. They were confident they could afford to stay put because of the great river that flowed through the city: supplies could reach them down this river despite the enemy siege; they could go up and down it to the sea at will.

So their besiegers' leaders, finding themselves stuck outside this mighty city so long, and sensing that thanks to the river they'd be stuck there even longer unless something was done, met together to discuss how they could block the city's access to the river. All manner of workmen were summoned, and some of them suggested the building of a bridge. No sooner was it proposed than done: it was built of fine, strong oak, with great iron chains slung across it to stop any boat getting further than the bridge.

Thanks to this bridge the city was now blockaded on every side rather than just one; now it was filled with wails and cries as the people realised their end was near: the city was already severely depopulated, and now, to make matters worse, its supplies were dwindling by the day. How dismayed and aghast they were to see enemy tents on the side where before there'd been none! How distressed was Antipater, realising his foes were tightening their grip!

Chapter CXX

How Ariscé was caught and taken to the city as a prisoner,
and Florent taken prisoner to the camp.

Florent, seeing his father and the good people of the city in intolerable anguish, began to hearten them and quell their alarm with many a well-chosen word, like the man of spirit he was. He told them they'd no need to fear while he was alive, for if it pleased God he was determined to protect them well as long as he lived, and he was still confident that the enemy would repent too late of the havoc they were wreaking.

In an attempt to make this happen he promptly ordered his strongest, ablest men to arm, and rode from the city and launched a surprise attack on the enemy camp. Ariscé was in charge of the watch just then, and it cost him dear, for as he bravely tried to repulse the foe he was seized and bound and taken straight back to the city and placed in the hands of Antipater, who was overjoyed. It was Florent who'd captured him; and buoyed by having taken one notable prisoner, he charged even deeper into the enemy camp, aiming to do still better. It wasn't long before the enemy were all up in arms, and Ptholomer came to meet him and they joined in ferocious combat. Our source says King Ptholomer was badly wounded and rescued only with great difficulty and carried back to his tent. But Danselin finally joined the fighting, and charged into the fray with such fierce vigour that before he'd finished he felled four of the finest knights of Florent's company and rode right up to Florent himself crying:

'Ah! False rogue! Now that I have you in my reach you'll never escape! I'll deliver you to Alior, who'll deal with you as a murderer like you deserves!'

Then Florent, hearing Danselin's abuse, charged at him with sword in hand and they started exchanging awesome blows, smashing gems and flowers from their crests. Finally Danselin came right up to Florent and seized him in his arms, whether he liked it or not, and heaved him from his saddle and hauled him back to his men-at-arms who promptly took charge of him and tied him up, a prisoner. None of Florent's men could rescue him, though many risked their lives in desperate attempts.

CHAPTER CXXI

How Ariscé and Florent, Antipater's son, were returned in exchange for each other.

When Florent's men-at-arms realised they'd lost their master and there was no more to be done, they started fleeing to the city with all speed: those who could get back in time were mightily relieved to take refuge there.

It wasn't long before Antipater was told of his son's misfortune, and he was beside himself with rage and anguish. Ariscé was there in the palace, guarded by four men-at-arms; all day he'd been showered with abuse and threats that he'd suffer the same treatment as his fellows had dealt their captives, and now, seeing the distress of the citizens and especially King Antipater, he stood up and said:

'Don't upset yourself, lord king! You'll soon have your son back if you wish: send someone to our camp to negotiate with Alior, son of Alexander; offer to release me from captivity if he'll return your son. But do it quickly: for truly, if you didn't have me to bargain with it would be too late to get him back!'

Hearing this Antipater ordered four of his barons to go straight to the enemy camp, without delay, and negotiate the return of his son Florent in exchange for

Ariscé. This was duly done: Florent was led back to the barriers[1] outside the city and Ariscé was taken back to camp, much to the joy of both parties.

A short time later Antipater sued for peace. But no agreement could be reached, for Alior and his council refused to consider any conditions short of Antipater placing himself, his children and all he possessed entirely at Alior's mercy. Antipater replied that he and his followers would rather die resisting than agree to such a peace, and that he would never surrender on such terms to the bastard son of a bastard; but if Alior cared to accept a sum of money or other riches he was willing to make peace.

When Alior heard this he vowed by the faith he owed his gods that there would never be peace until he'd slaughtered Antipater and all his followers who'd been complicit in the killing of his father. As a greater incentive for his men, Alior, in the envoys' presence, gave Antipater's city to one of his brothers and all the city's riches to his barons.

Chapter CXXII
How the city was taken by storm, according to our source.

King Antipater's envoys, realising there was no way of striking a deal with Alior, returned to the city confounded and perturbed, very fearful of what would befall them now. They came to Antipater and made it plain that there would never be peace with Alior while both of them were alive, 'for,' they said, 'because of your antagonistic words he's sworn he'll make no treaty or accord! If you're not convinced, he's given your city to a brother of his and all its riches to his men-at-arms! And so, esteemed lord, you'd better seek counsel and consider your next move.'

Antipater was deeply shaken by their words; but he ordered all his men to arm, for 'before they have our city,' he said, 'most of them are going to lose their lives!'

Then you'd have seen all his men of every degree roused to a frenzy, swearing that, since there was nothing else for it, they would sell their lives dear.

Meanwhile Alior, as soon as the envoys had gone, summoned his whole council to discuss how they should act on his decision, for it was clear that the enemy were now so reduced in numbers and provisions that they wouldn't attempt another sortie, so they needed to decide how to attack and take the city. It was agreed that the first move should be to fill in the ditches so that they could reach the walls more readily. No sooner was this decision made than they ordered an assault; and all those commissioned to fill the ditches went about their business with such a will that, in less than half a day, they'd filled a stretch of ditch with earth and faggots long enough for ten thousand men to cross at once. Then up came the men-at-arms, along with stout lads with hefty picks and hammers and other gear to undermine and smash the walls. Others carried pavais[2] to shield

---

[1]   The 'barrieres' were outlying barricades, beyond a castle's walls, to impede besieging forces.
[2]   See note 1, above, p.258.

the archers who, as soon as they were in range, launched such a hail of arrows that no defender dared show his head above the battlements.

If I were to describe the assault in every detail it would be wordy to the point of wearisome, I fear, for countless numbers were felled and killed and wounded, and my source suggests they didn't take the city the first time or the second – indeed they mounted many attacks before it was theirs. But take it they finally did, breaking in and slaughtering all in their path or who tried to resist – men, women and children alike – until the city was completely in their hands.

CHAPTER CXXIII

How all of Antipater's barons were put to death and killed.

The lords in the city, including Antipater and his sons, carried on fighting as long as they could, but when they saw disaster looming they took refuge in one of the city's temples. They were trapped and seized there and taken straight to King Alior. But he wouldn't speak to them – he didn't want to see them plead for mercy; instead he ordered that they be imprisoned while it was decided what manner of death they should suffer.

Antipater was sentenced to being shut up in a brass ox[1] filled with iron spikes, dagger-sharp, which tore his flesh to pieces. It was made with impressive ingenuity, and to make his death even crueller a fire was lit beneath this ox to torture him and burn him: he died an agonising death indeed. Some of the other lords were flayed alive and covered in honey, and then placed on lofty scaffolds and exposed to a swarm of that variety of insect known as the bee; and the bee-swarm stung them to death.[2] Others were hanged, others slaughtered; and in the end, in less than two years, so many had been slain that all the traitors involved in the death of the good King Alexander had been wiped out: not a single one was to be found.

The annihilation complete, King Alior rewarded all the lords and princes as richly as they could wish, and promised to make himself and his resources available to them at all times. Then they departed, each returning to his own land. But according to the histories, in less than fourteen years[3] all King Alexander's barons were dead, killed in battles, wars and revolts. It would take a long time, I think, to record it all, and what later became of Alior, Queen Candace's son, I haven't yet discovered.

So if there is anything in my treatment of this present work that listeners find

---

[1]   In *La Venjance Alixandre* this is simply 'a brass barrel'. It is possible that Wauquelin misread 'tonnel' (barrel) as 'torel' (bullock, steer).

[2]   In different MSS of *La Venjance* the flayed and honeyed victims are exposed to either goats or dogs rather than bees: 'Let them be skinned with sharp razors and anointed with honey before and behind; then bring two goats [or dogs] to lick them – then you'll see them howl and wail with pain: they'll never have a moment's rest as long as they live: you couldn't condemn them to a more agonising torture.' (vv.1882-7).

[3]   Wauquelin takes this figure (already cited above, p.281) not from Jehan le Nevelon but from the Prose *Alexander* – hence the phrase 'according to the histories'.

other than commendable, I, its author, would ask them to forgive my incompetence and kindly emend it. And if they care to know my name, let them take the capital letters at the start of the second part of the book, beginning with a 'J' and continuing down to the eighteenth which is an 'N', and they'll discover it – and realise I'm not as clever as I might be![1] Whatever is lacking may God make good, and I pray He may grant us all in the end His blessed glory. Amen.

Explicit the history of the good King Alexander.

---

[1]   I haven't tried to contrive a way of reproducing the acrostic in the translation. In the French, the first words of each of the first eighteen chapters of Book Two are: Je, Or, Hardiment, Aprés, Ne, Nous, En, Sachans, Vous, Venus, A, Veans, Quant, Vous, En, La, Incontinent, Ne; hence JOHANNES VVAVQVELIN.

Appendix 1

How Nectanebus fathered Alexander
From the Prose Alexander[1]

Egypt is under threat from an alliance led by Artaxerxes, king of Persia, and…

Nectanebus, king of Egypt, who was Alexander's father, was at that time the most adept of all men in astronomy and astrology and the science of enchantments… He took his astrolabe and quadrant and began to examine the stars, and saw that the planet then ascendant was hostile to the Egyptians and smiling on the Persians. As soon as he realised this he went to another room and called for a barber and had his head and his beard shaved; then he took as much gold and silver as he thought he'd need and all the things required for the arts of magic and mathematics, and changed his clothes and left the land so secretly that no one knew what had become of him…

Leaving Egypt he went to a land called Pelusium[2] and from there to Ethiopia where he dressed in white samite in the manner of Egyptian prophets; and thus clad he made his way to the kingdom of Macedon, where he lived for a long while without anyone knowing who he was; and to all who came to him for counsel he would give guidance and divination of things to come…

At the time when Nectanebus arrived in the land, King Philip had gone on campaign against a neighbouring king… [and while he was away] Nectanebus came to a city where Philip's wife was residing; her name was Olympias. Hearing of the queen's presence there, he went straight to her palace and came before her and hailed her, saying: 'Salutations, queen of Macedon,' but he didn't deign to call her lady.

The queen replied: 'It appears you are an Egyptian master and sage; come forward and be seated – you are welcome…'

[He told her he could] 'interpret dreams and birdsong and animals' cries… and divine from the time of a person's birth what the future has in store…'

[So she asked him to] 'tell me the year, the month, the week, the day and the hour of the birth of the king.'

Nectanebus promptly began to calculate by the art of arithmetic the year, the month, the week, the day and the hour of the king's birth. Then he asked the queen if she wanted to hear anything else.

'I want you to tell me,' she said, 'if my husband King Philip, when he returns from campaign, will cast me aside and wed another.'

[1]   Translated from Hilka's edition of the Prose Alexander, pp.8-9, 11-12, 19-27.
[2]   'Peluse'; Pelusium was a major city on the Nile Delta.

'What you have said,' he replied, 'will not happen just yet but in a few years' time – and a few days later he will take you back as his wife.'

'I pray you, master, tell me more: tell me the whole truth.'

And Nectanebus answered: 'A mighty god will lie with you and will answer your every need.'[1]

'Who is this god,' said the queen, 'who will lie with me?'

'The god Ammon, who has the power to bestow all riches upon you.'

'I pray you, master,' said the queen, 'tell me what form this god has.'

'He is neither old nor young,' said Nectanebus, 'but in between; and he has rams' horns on his forehead and a beard of flowing curls.[2] You will see him in your dreaming, and in that dream he will lie with you.'

'If I could see the things you say,' the queen said then, 'I wouldn't esteem you as a prophet or seer: I would revere you as a very god!'

Then Nectanebus commended the queen to God and left the palace and went to a place in the wilds. There he gathered all manner of herbs, and used his demonic arts[3] to conjure a spell which, that very night, would make the queen see in a dream the god Ammon lying with her and saying: 'Woman, you have conceived your protector.'

When morning came and Queen Olympias rose from her sleep, she summoned Nectanebus and told him of the dream she'd seen.

'I know what you're telling me,' he replied, 'but if you give me a place in your palace I shall *really* show you the god – for dream is one thing and reality another! The god will come to you in the form of a dragon, and afterwards change to human shape.'

'Master,' said the queen, 'I shall have your bed made in my palace, and if I truly experience what you say, I shall worship you as the child's father!'

She immediately bade that a bed be prepared in her palace for Nectanebus. And when the first hour of the night was past Nectanebus used magic spells to turn himself into a dragon, and went hissing around the queen's bed before sliding in and kissing her; they took pleasure in each other's company for a long while. And when he finally rose from bed he embraced the queen and said: 'The one conceived here will be victorious and will never be overcome by any man.'

Thus it was that Queen Olympias was deceived into thinking she was with child by a god when she'd been made pregnant by a man.

In the morning the queen told Nectanebus what had happened to her, and he said he knew all about it. Then he left the palace and went and took lodging in the town.

The queen remained with child; and when she realised it was becoming plain she summoned Nectanebus and said: 'Master, I want to know what King Philip will do to me when he returns to this land.'

'Have no fear,' he replied. 'Through me the god Ammon will help you.'

---

1   Literally 'will aid you in all your doings'.
2   Literally 'a beard adorned with chains'.
3   Literally 'the art of the Enemy'.

And so saying, he left the palace and went out to a desert place and gathered herbs and crushed them; and he took the juice and with it anointed a sea bird and cast a spell upon it: he was using demonic sorcery[1] to delude King Philip with a dream. And he succeeded, for that very night King Philip dreamed that the god Ammon lay with Queen Olympias, and after lying with her said: 'Woman, you have conceived your protector, and the protector of your husband Philip.'

… Not long after, King Philip met his enemy in battle, and a dragon appeared before him; it flew ahead and slaughtered his foes, and with the dragon's aid he was victorious that day.

Having defeated his enemies he led his army straight back to Macedon, and as he dismounted outside his palace the queen came to meet him with a kiss. When he saw that she was pregnant he said:

'You have sinned, queen, giving yourself to someone other than me.' She began to flush, and when the king saw her colour change he said: 'But truly, you shouldn't be reproached, for you were overcome by the power of a god: I saw all that happened in a dream. So you shouldn't be condemned by me or anyone else.'

---

[1]   Literally 'enchantment of the Enemy'.

Appendix 2

Aristotle's Advice to Alexander[1]

How Alexander withdrew to his chamber to consider how to conduct the war he'd declared against King Nicolas of Armenia, and met his teacher Aristotle; and of the advice he received from him.

Aristotle, thin, wan and dishevelled, appeared from the chamber where he'd just completed his books of Logic. It was clear from his face that he'd been deep in study: burning the midnight oil had left his complexion pale; his face was nothing but skin and bone – no one spending long hours in study grows fat! As soon as he saw Alexander, whose flaming cheeks made his anger plain, he asked him what was wrong and what had upset him. The youth was unmanned by the sight of his teacher; he looked at the floor and dropped to his knees and began to weep and lament that his father was now too old to defend his land and that it was doomed to be enslaved by the king of Armenia.[2] When the teacher heard his pupil's words he said:

'Alexander, dear boy, be a man and learn to bear arms! It's timely that you've just been knighted, for you've enemies now to test your strength! And if you'll listen to me, I'll tell you how to succeed.

'Be advised only by worthy men and shun two-faced wretches and self-seeking rogues. Never give advancement to men of poor breeding: you've doubtless observed that a rain-swollen stream bursts proud from its banks, while the flow from a natural spring stays steady; likewise the lowborn promoted are more arrogant and cruel, unresponsive to prayers and lacking respect for true goodness. That's not to say that I'd forbid you to elevate a lowly man if you see he speaks and acts worthily, for men of good character, regardless of their wealth or their origins or lineage, have something worth more than gold or silver: wealth doesn't bestow good character – it's more likely to strip it away! Nothing corrupts the heart more than money! A man poor in wealth but rich in fine qualities can truly claim to have something of

---

[1]   In MS 456 of the Collection Dutuit, Bibliothèque du Petit Palais, Paris (and in Sandrine Hériché's edition of Wauquelin's text), this section appears between chapters XVII and XVIII of Book One (note 1, above, p.40). It sits reasonably well there, but was almost certainly not part of Wauquelin's work. Apart from its uncharacteristic prolixity, and the telltale repetition that results at the beginning of Chapter XVIII, the fact is that it appears in only that one manuscript, which was produced for Philip the Good in the late 1450s, several years after Wauquelin's death in 1452. It is closely based on a passage in Book I of the Latin *Alexandreis* of Walter of Châtillon (c.1180).

[2]   The text reads 'Persia', an inconsistency perhaps explained simply by the fact that this passage is an interpolation, not part of Wauquelin's work.

more value than silver or gold, something which can overcome defects and engender a noble line. Never judge goodness by outward appearance: a man filled with virtues does not display them; and in the end, nobility exists only in a man with an honest heart and good character.

'If you come to be the judge of any lawsuit, be sure to make sound judgement, and don't be swayed by personal feelings – or reward! Anyone taking payment to make false judgement should be censured indeed: bribery turns a judge's mind from the path of truth and plunges his heart into darkness, blinding him completely. As soon as greed, the mother of all vices, takes hold of a man's heart, he loses all integrity and commits all manner of unworthy deeds, heedless of law and decency. Show mercy to the meek and listen patiently to pleas. But crush the arrogant!

'And inspire your knights, give them true leadership and confront your foes: if you have the will to achieve great things, you have the power! And if when you come to battle you're too young and lack the strength to fight, let your knights at least see you armed and full of confidence: contribute to the fighting with your prayers and exhortations – and threats if need be – for sometimes a commander needs to play his part by steeling his knights when they're daunted and their hearts and limbs are shaking! If the army's commander exhorts them to fight well, he gives them all courage and they go boldly into battle.

'If your foes take to flight, be sure you're at the forefront in pursuit; but if by chance your own men flee, make sure you're at the rear: when they see you behind them they'll be ashamed to leave the battle without you. Then take good note of how many knights your enemies have, and how many foot soldiers, but don't be daunted by the number: if you see them pursuing with little conviction, turn your horse about and face them! Then you'll be able to show your worth – and you'll see how much your army loves you! Attack the foe so remorselessly that they'll hardly have the chance to admit defeat!

'On entering a city that you've taken by storm or forced to surrender, delve into your treasury and give generously to your knights when they're weary or wounded from fighting. Ease their pains with liberal gifts: they're a potent medicine for covetous man! That's how the rich relieve the poor (and the generous the grasping!). And if by chance your funds are running low and you have less than you'd wish, make sure you're no less rich in love and your heart is not impoverished: give pledges at least, and then deliver what you've promised as soon as time and place permit. For giving earns a man a worthy reputation; it binds the covetous to him, obscures the giver's vices and enhances his image. And it helps subdue his foes! A man who gives generously, especially when he's waging war, has no need of castles: if he's worried about his enemies, a prince can equip himself no better than by generous giving! But no walls or ramparts can protect a tight-fisted prince!

'What other advice should I give you? Ensure that licentiousness, which wastes the body and destroys cities, never corrupts you. If you give way to drunkenness and lust, then however all-conquering you may have been you'll be defeated yourself, for you'll have lost control of your own being: when the heat of lust takes hold the mind is corrupted, and drunkenness, which destroys all reason, provokes quarrels and discord and degrades a man's character. Those responsible for governing the people and upholding the laws should have no thought for the delights and pleasures of the flesh.

'Let Justice be your companion in all you do: call Her back from the heavens, where She has fled from the wickedness of the world! And ensure that mercy, compassion and love of righteousness never fail you. Study sacred scriptures. Respond kindly to petitions. And study the laws. Punish criminals according to established rule. And if anyone wrongs you, resist exacting vengeance until your anger has passed. And if you can be reconciled, forget the cause of discord once and for all.

'If you lead your life according to these precepts, you'll win renown that will endure till the world's end.'

Appendix 3

Jacques de Longuyon's excursus on the Nine Worthies
From Les Voeux du Paon ('The Vows of the Peacock')[1]

In striving to fulfil the vow he'd made before the peacock, Porus is performing such exceptional feats in the battle against Alexander (above, p.125) that…

…since God chose to make Adam, no knight was ever born who endured so much fighting in a single day.

It's true that **Hector** was immeasurably worthy; as the poets record, when King Menelaus came with all his forces to besiege the noble King Priam at Troy to win back his beloved wife Helen who'd been abducted by Paris, Hector took charge of the city, and in the sorties launched at his instigation he slew nineteen kings in hand-to-hand combat – and, I believe, more than a hundred emirs and counts – before he was treacherously killed by Achilles.

Most worthy, too, was **Alexander**, of whom I'm telling in this story; he vanquished Nicolas and Darius the Persian and slaughtered all the vermin in the deserts of the East, and captured Babylon, that great and mighty city where he later died by poison; in twelve years with his awesome vigour he conquered everything to be found beneath the heavens – and still he wasn't satisfied: he told his barons in council one day that he was ruler of very little land!

A long while ago **Caesar** conquered England, commonly known as Britain, and brought King Cassivelaunus[2] under Rome's dominion; waging war on his brother-in-law Pompey he defeated him in Greece along with greater numbers than any man alive had ever seen; then he captured Alexandria, that magnificent city of mighty wealth, and Africa, Arabia, Egypt and Syria likewise, and the isles of the sea to the furthest West.

These three were pagans, and I can say of them that finer men were never born, either before or since.

And I find written in the Bible, in the Old Testament, the names of three Jews who achieved such deeds in ancient times that they've won universal praise, praise which will live, I believe, till the world's end.

Joshua we shall name first: through his devout prayer and his courage alike he parted the waters of the Jordan so that the Jews he led could cross quite dry and unhindered; this worthy man fought long in the South, where he utterly

---

[1]   This passage is translated from the text of *Les Voeux du Paon* in *The Buik of Alexander*, Vol. IV, ed. R. L. Graeme Ritchie (Edinburgh, 1929), vv. 7481-7579.
[2]   'Cassibilant'.

vanquished forty-one kings, crushing and humbling them all, leaving them no land or city or refuge but bringing all under his subjection.

David slew the giant Goliath – who was at least seven cubits[1] tall, I believe – and destroyed many a wicked heathen, and was so fortunate in his many fearsome battles that he never had to admit defeat. We all must surely, boldly agree that he was a holy sinner!

Judas Maccabeus was likewise of such spirit that if he'd faced the whole world armed for awful, mortal battle, even if he'd been left outnumbered ten to one you wouldn't have seen him flee; this Judas whose virtues I'm extolling killed Apollonius in combat, and Antiochus when he waged war on him, and Nicanor, too, and many another tyrant.

I know of three Christians, too, such that no finer men were ever seen to wear a burnished helm.

The resounding tale of **Arthur**, king of Britain, tells how he vanquished Retho[2] in open field, a giant so fierce and strong and cocksure that he'd made a cloak from the beards of kings he'd forced into subjection: he wanted Arthur's, too, but he was out of luck! On Mont Saint-Michel Arthur slew this colossus, to the amazement of all in the land. And if history tells true, King Arthur won crushing victories over many princes in other countries far and wide.

Charlemagne, who had all France at his command, trampled Spain underfoot, leaving Agoulant[3] dead, and won all the lands of [King] Desier of Pavia, and beat the Saxons so decisively in many a fearsome assault and contest that they were forced into total submission; and he instituted baptism and the holy sacrament, remembering God's death for our salvation.

And worthy of high and ringing praise is **Godfrey of Bouillon**, who by his courage defeated Solimant on the plains of Romanie, and the emir Corbarant[4] before the walls of Antioch on the day when the sultan's son was slain; he was then crowned king of Jerusalem, though he held the title for only one year.[5]

Now I've set forth in clear order the nine worthiest men who have lived since God created the heavens and the earth and the winds. They all excelled for a fair while; but never in their lives – at least, not on any one day – did they endure such toil and trouble as did Porus on the day that I'm describing.

---

[1]   See footnote 1, above, p.197.
[2]   'Ruiston'.
[3]   One of Charlemagne's principal Saracen foes.
[4]   Solimant and King Corbarant of Oliferne are epic characters in the Crusade cycle; the latter is based on the historical Kerbogha, atabeg of Mosul, defeated at Antioch in 1098.
[5]   Godfrey did indeed die (in 1100) almost exactly a year after being made king of Jerusalem.

Milton Keynes UK
Ingram Content Group UK Ltd.
UKHW022147190924
448478UK00006BA/109